Advance Praise for
The Fifth Vital Sign

"I am so thankful to Lisa for writing The Fifth Vital Sign *— a book that contributes immeasurably to the field of fertility awareness. Using impeccable research standards, she has made her book easily accessible while being scientifically sound — a goldmine of practical advice for women wanting answers to the myriad of questions that usually arise around fertility and the menstrual cycle."*

— Toni Weschler, MPH, author of *Taking Charge of Your Fertility* and *Cycle Savvy*

"With The Fifth Vital Sign, *Lisa dives deep into the menstrual cycle and fertility and provides valuable new insights gleaned from more than 150 interviews with women's health experts! It's a reference that I will undoubtedly refer to again and again."*

— Lara Briden, ND, author of *Period Repair Manual*

"So many women struggle with reproductive health issues these days, often not knowing where to turn for accurate advice. Now they have a place to turn. The Fifth Vital Sign *provides easy-to-understand explanations for the menstrual cycle and how to approach key problem areas — from hormonal imbalances to thyroid function. The nutritional advice is especially good for not only restoring fertility but achieving overall health. Highly recommended!"*

— Sally Fallon Morell, president, The Weston A. Price Foundation

*"*The Fifth Vital Sign *is an essential book for every woman's library. Lisa blends science, tradition, and intuition in her writing — the result is a beautiful and practical guide to all things fertility!"*

— Dr. Fiona McCulloch, ND, author of *8 Steps to Reverse Your PCOS*

"At last, a book celebrating the menstrual cycle as the vital sign it is, an indicator of our overall health. Packed with useful information written in a warm, engaging style, *The Fifth Vital Sign* shows you how to take charge of your hormonal health and contraceptive needs in a way that nourishes and empowers. A must-have for all women in their menstruating years."

— Alexandra Pope and Sjanie Hugo Wurlitzer,
co-authors of *Wild Power* and co-directors of Red School

"If you menstruate, if you want to get pregnant, or if you don't want to get pregnant — run, don't walk, to buy this book! Lisa has produced a truly admirable, well-researched, highly readable resource for women, one that is sorely needed. Mainstream medicine has only recently begun to acknowledge the broader value of the ovulatory cycle and to seriously tackle issues such as endometriosis and dysmenorrhea, and it continues to be limited by two main factors: its complex relationship with the pharmaceutical industry and the institutionalized sexism that has allowed medicine to minimize female-only symptoms. In this impressive book, Lisa works at the intersection of these two worlds, bringing together cutting-edge medical science with the experiential knowledge of fertility awareness/menstrual cycle practitioners to create a vital resource of information and wisdom."

— Lara Owen, author of *Her Blood Is Gold*, researcher and consultant
on menstruation and menopause in the workplace

"In *The Fifth Vital Sign*, Lisa absolutely nails the case for fertility awareness as an essential and empowering healthcare practice for women. She elucidates key concepts with great finesse, like informed choice and the life-enhancing/life-saving power of understanding the menstrual cycle as a vital sign. Her incredible passion for fertility awareness and sharing this life-changing knowledge with women shines through. I will be recommending *The Fifth Vital Sign* widely and vigorously!"

— Jane Bennett, author and menstrual educator

"*The Fifth Vital Sign* is a must-have for your polycystic ovary syndrome (PCOS) library. Hormone imbalances play a central role in PCOS. The body literacy, fertility awareness, and menstrual cycle optimization tools offered in Lisa's book will be a game-changer in your healing process. *The Fifth Vital Sign* educates and empowers women to take control of their cycles and reach beyond to take charge of their total health. I could not recommend it more highly."

— Amy Medling, founder of PCOS Diva and author of *Healing PCOS*

"Lisa's *The Fifth Vital Sign* is highly informative, invaluable, and easy to read. It's a compendium on everything you want and need to know to take charge of your menstrual health and the plethora of factors that impact it from hormonal contraceptives to lifestyle factors. Thoughtfully written, this is a must read for anyone who is looking for guidance to avoid or to get pregnant."

— Mary Wong, author of *Pathways to Pregnancy*

"Lisa provides an accessible lay meta-analysis of literature pointing to the importance of understanding that menstrual cycle health is the fifth vital sign of health. She impresses upon readers the necessity of taking cycle health seriously and caring for it from menarche to menopause in order to preserve lifelong health. The anecdotal accounts are helpful and inspiring. Her fearless approach to the topic inspires and removes cultural, financial, and political obfuscation of the truth regarding menstrual cycle health."

— Geraldine Matus, PhD, founder of the Justisse Method and academic director and dean of Justisse College International

"Lisa uses a blend of personal experience, expert opinion, and published data to provide this easy to digest, comprehensive guide to the menstrual cycle and fertility. It is approachable, engaging, and thoroughly informative. I believe this book should be given to every pre-teen girl when entering puberty to provide her the knowledge and resources to make healthy choices for her body for the rest of her life."

— Miranda Naylor, DO and functional medicine doctor

"*The Fifth Vital Sign is THE book we should all have been given in preparation for puberty and beyond. From the very first page Lisa provides clear explanations for some of the most commonly asked questions about women's periods and hormones. In each chapter she walks you step by step through important concepts like what a healthy menstrual cycle should look like, how to expertly chart your cycle, different types of natural birth control options, and so much more! Lisa's book truly is a how-to guide for your menstrual cycle and I highly recommend it!*"

— Nicole Jardim, certified women's health coach

"*The Fifth Vital Sign is a must-have resource for women and healthcare providers. Packed with research and evidence-based facts, Lisa unfolds her message with a sincere and candid narrative. This book shares invaluable information regarding women's menstrual cycle health, eloquently challenging the status quo. This book offers a platform to further the understanding of, and discussion for, menstrual cycle health, fertility management, and women's health.*"

— Katelin Parkinson, ND and Justisse fertility awareness method educator

"*The Fifth Vital Sign is an incredibly detailed resource for the fertility awareness community. If you're determined to improve your menstrual cycle and your fertility, Lisa has put together a wealth of evidence-based research to help you do just that.*"

— Rose Yewchuk, fertility awareness educator and holistic reproductive health practitioner

"*You can't talk about fertility awareness without talking about The Fertility Friday Podcast. For years, Lisa has been sharing reliable and relatable information through her podcast. Now, she's compiled well-researched, empowering information into this comprehensive guide for anyone who wants to delve deeper into the power of the menstrual cycle. The Fifth Vital Sign is a tool to improve your health, transform your life, and become the best version of yourself. I'm recommending it to all of my clients.*"

— Chloe Skerlak, Justisse holistic reproductive health practitioner

the Fifth Vital Sign

LISA HENDRICKSON-JACK

the Fifth Vital Sign

MASTER YOUR CYCLES AND
OPTIMIZE YOUR FERTILITY

Published by Fertility Friday Publishing Inc.

Copyright © 2019 Fertility Friday Publishing Inc.

For ordering information or special discounts for bulk purchases please contact: info@fertilityfriday.com.

Cover design: Simon Avery
Copy editing: Mary Ann Blair
Proofreading: Dana Nichols

Print ISBN: 978-1-9994280-0-6
Digital ISBN: 978-1-9994280-1-3

First edition, January 2019

Contents

Foreword

I first met Lisa four years ago when she invited me to join her on her podcast, *Fertility Friday*. Together, she and I celebrated the value of women's natural hormones and spoke some hard truths about hormonal birth control. Since then, I've been an avid listener of *Fertility Friday* and have learned from Lisa's insightful conversations with expert guests such as endocrinology professor Jerilynn Prior and Toni Weschler, author of *Taking Charge of Your Fertility*.

I regularly refer my patients and readers to Lisa's site for information on fertility awareness, and I've returned as a guest on the show two more times. I also had the opportunity to meet Lisa in person when we teamed up for the New York grassroots women's health event Hack Your Cycles to Change Your Life.

Lisa is a leading voice in the women's health revolution, so you can imagine my delight when I learned that she was compiling her wisdom into a book! I knew she would draw on her nearly 20 years of experience teaching fertility awareness as well as her hundreds of interviews with the world's leading period experts.

The Fifth Vital Sign is everything I hoped it would be. It's a deep dive into how to have a healthy menstrual cycle and why that's important. Specifically, the book looks at why having healthy *ovulatory* menstrual cycles is an expression of health and a valuable *vital sign* that all is well with the body. An ovulatory cycle is a cycle in which ovulation occurs, and as Lisa explains, it is really the only type of cycle that can be considered a true menstrual cycle. The fake "cycles" that occur on hormonal birth control have created a false narrative that has led women to believe ovulation is not necessary for health — that they don't need ovulation until it's time to make a baby. However, *The Fifth Vital Sign* explains why we *do* need ovulation.

This book will teach you to track and understand your cycle, and it provides easy-to-implement nutritional and lifestyle recommendations to improve the health of your cycle. It also builds a solid case against hormonal birth control, citing fascinating research that I had not ever seen — and I've been working in this field for 20 years!

Whether your goal is avoiding pregnancy, achieving pregnancy, transitioning off birth control, general health, or simply better understanding your body, *The Fifth Vital Sign* will help you to get there.

— Lara Briden
Naturopathic doctor, period revolutionary,
and author of *Period Repair Manual*

Introduction

When I was a teenager, I loved sports; I played basketball and volleyball, I was a ballet dancer, and I did track and field, but my periods were extremely painful and heavy, making it difficult for me to participate. I didn't know how to control it, so I went to my doctor's office, at 15 years old, and asked for a prescription for the pill. I had barely uttered the words, "My periods are painful and heavy," before my doctor started writing out the prescription.

And voilà! My pill "periods" were light and painless. I took the pill for almost three years, but on some level, I knew it wasn't fixing anything. I came off the pill for a few months here and there to see if my real periods were still heavy and painful, and every time I did, they were worse than before. It was clear to me that the pill wasn't solving any of my problems, and I worried that staying on the pill long-term would mess up my fertility.

I grew up thinking I might have a hard time getting or staying pregnant because a number of my relatives struggled with uterine fibroids and other fertility challenges. My mother's periods, for instance, grew harder for her to manage as she got older. Her bleeding was so excessive that, at times, the blood would run down her legs when she stood up. She struggled with low iron and fatigue because of the heavy bleeding, and eventually had a hysterectomy. After the surgery one of my aunts came to stay with us, and I discovered that she had also had a hysterectomy several years prior for the same reason. I didn't know much back then, but I knew I wanted a family someday, and I also knew the pill wasn't going to fix whatever genetic predisposition for fertility problems I'd likely inherited; although I didn't know what the solution was at the time, I was sure there had to be another way.

When I needed birth control at age 19, I realized there was no way I could trust the pill to prevent pregnancy. Although I had been on the pill for a few years, I had never used it for birth control.

And since I was taking the pill for medical reasons, I would often forget to take it at the same time every day (when I remembered to take it at all). I knew I would always be wondering if it was working, so I decided to use condoms as my primary method of birth control. It was around this time I discovered fertility awareness.

The Women's Centre on my university campus held regular workshops and lectures on all kinds of feminist topics. I heard that Inga Muscio, author of the book *Cunt: A Declaration of Independence*, was coming for a book signing, so I decided to go check it out. She read several excerpts from her book, and from her I learned about a way to prevent pregnancy without relying on hormonal birth control. She described the two commonly accepted models of birth control: chemical manipulation of the hormones and barriers placed between the *os* (opening of the cervix) and sperm — and then she proposed a third option[1]:

> What I am about to discuss is not "the rhythm method." The objective here is not to understand the rhythm of your ovulatory cycle. The objective is to tap into the rhythm of your ovulatory cycle as a means of perceiving a broader rhythm inside yourself that shows you how powerful you are every day of your life.[2]

She went on to describe the way both your cervical mucus and cervical position change around ovulation — and that was all I needed to hear. It was the very first time anyone had told me that I couldn't get pregnant on every single day of my cycle. Fortunately, the Women's Centre had the resources I needed to figure out how I could really do this. I ran to the bookstore and bought Toni Weschler's *Taking Charge of Your Fertility*, and I also discovered a local organization on campus that taught fertility awareness (the Fertility Awareness Charting Circle). I started attending their monthly meetings and I was hooked. You won't be surprised to learn that I eventually joined the group, completed a fertility awareness education training program, and started teaching other women to chart their cycles.

I was so excited to learn that I could confidently prevent pregnancy without suppressing my natural cycles. It's funny if you think about it; most women go on the pill when they start having sex, but I did the opposite.

Discovering fertility awareness was a life-changing experience for me; I finally understood exactly what was happening in my cycles! The most significant shift for me was realizing that there were only a few days of my cycle when I could get pregnant. I felt that this knowledge put the power directly into my hands and I was no longer afraid of my fertility. As a result, I was able to avoid pregnancy naturally by avoiding unprotected sex during my fertile window. Little did I know that natural birth control was only the tip of the iceberg.

I soon discovered that my menstrual cycle was not exclusively related to having babies. Learning to chart my cycles among a group of women trained in fertility awareness charting was when I first encountered the idea that my menstrual cycle is a vital sign that changes in response to the state of my overall health.

When I started charting my cycles, I noticed they were typically 40 to 45 days in length. I asked my doctor what I could do to shorten them, and he told me the only thing I could do to "regulate" my cycles was to go back on the pill. It wasn't until my charting instructor had a look at my charts and suggested that I have my thyroid levels tested that I realized how intimately my cycles were connected to my health. The testing revealed that I had a subclinical thyroid disorder, and I was able to improve my cycle parameters naturally by attending to it. It blew my mind that someone could look at my menstrual cycle charts and identify underlying health issues.

My periods are normal now. I no longer experience crippling pain or excessive bleeding. My cycles are consistent, ovulatory, and well within the normal range. As I write this book, I have two beautiful boys, and I often wonder how different my life would have been if I had stayed on the pill all those years instead of tracking my cycles. I know that the only reason my thyroid issue was identified early is because I was charting my cycles. I have no idea how many years it would have taken to identify it if I hadn't been charting.

After I had my first son, I realized that most women have no idea how their menstrual cycles work. Many are shocked to discover that when they come off the pill it can take several months, or even years, for their cycles to return to normal; and most have no idea how their fertility changes with age.

I once received a message from a woman whose doctor had told her, "As a young woman, you're so fertile you could get pregnant sitting on a warm bus seat." Though ridiculous, this statement accurately describes how most young women view their fertility. Considering that most of us were taught that we can get pregnant on every day of our cycles, we spend most of our reproductive years figuring out how *not* to get pregnant instead of focusing on how to preserve our fertility as we get older.

This book, therefore, is your shortcut. It's the book I wish I had when I started down this path nearly 20 years ago. In this book you'll gain the tools to not only understand your cycles but to start healing them. You'll discover the connection between the health of your cycles and your overall health and fertility. You'll discover why your menstrual cycle matters whether or not you plan to have children.

I wrote this book because you deserve better. And since I haven't yet figured out how to get this information included in the standard curriculum of every school across the world, I figured this book is the next best thing. By the time you finish reading this book, you'll wonder why every woman doesn't already know these things. Don't worry — when I first discovered fertility awareness I felt the same way.

Now it's your turn ... Are you ready?

Chapter 1
The Fifth Vital Sign

*"Ovulation has been recognized as an event linked with reproduction;
however, recent evidence supports the role of ovulation as a sign of health."*

— Pilar Vigil et al., *The Linacre Quarterly*

Has anyone ever told you that your menstrual cycle is a vital sign? Just like your heart rate, body temperature, respiratory rate, and blood pressure, your menstrual cycle is such a central part of who you are that if your body isn't functioning normally, neither will your cycle.

Both the American Academy of Pediatrics (AAP) and The American College of Obstetricians and Gynecologists (ACOG) report that menstruation should be monitored as a vital sign in adolescent girls.[1] According to the AAP,

> Once young females begin menstruating, evaluation of the menstrual cycle should be included with an assessment of other vital signs. By including this information with the other vital signs, clinicians emphasize the important role of menstrual patterns in reflecting overall health status.[2]

Your menstrual cycle begins with the first day of your period and ends the day before your next one. While your period gets way more press and media attention, it's not actually the main event. *Ovulation* is — and you can only experience a true menstrual period after ovulation.

Ovulation is well-recognized for its role in reproduction; however, since regular ovulation is only possible when your endocrine system and reproductive system are functioning normally, an irregular or abnormal cycle is an early warning sign of an underlying health problem.[3]

You know how your phone can get glitchy sometimes? Your cycle can also act up when you have an underlying health issue, which could, for example, present as delayed ovulation, mid-cycle spotting, abnormal cervical mucus patterns, irregular periods, or even amenorrhea (when your period stops coming completely). Therefore, your menstrual cycle (with regular ovulation) is *the fifth vital sign* of your health and fertility.

What Is a Vital Sign?

A *vital sign* is a bodily response you can monitor to measure how your body is functioning. The four most commonly accepted vital signs are heart rate, body temperature, respiratory rate (the number of breaths you take each minute), and blood pressure. When health professionals measure your vitals, they're comparing your readings to a well-established normal range for each sign. High blood pressure may indicate a cardiovascular issue, while an elevated temperature may indicate an underlying infection. When overcoming an illness, your vital signs can be used to monitor improvements in your condition. By measuring your vitals, your practitioner gains a window into your overall health and is privy to the subtle warning signs of an underlying health issue.

One of my colleagues, Marguerite Duane, MD, says it best: "In the same way medical doctors are trained to read electrocardiograms, health professionals who specialize in interpreting the menstrual cycle can read your menstrual cycle charts." An electrocardiogram (EKG) is a test that records your heart's electrical activity, detects the rate and rhythm of your heartbeat, and identifies possible heart problems. A doctor can tell if there's something wrong with your EKG, just as a trained fertility awareness practitioner can identify cycle abnormalities by reviewing your charts.[4]

Just like with the four vital signs listed above, a well-established set of parameters will help you identify if your cycles are healthy and fall within the normal range (see Chapter 4). As you track your cycles (on your menstrual cycle chart), you may notice subtle changes when you eat certain foods, drink alcohol, travel, or modify your sleep patterns. Conversely, when underlying health issues are present, you may experience significant cycle disruptions.

The Value in Learning Your Fifth Vital Sign

Many of us were taught that we could get pregnant on every single day of our cycles — that there are no "safe" days — but that's simply not true. Ovulation happens on only 1 day, and once the egg is released, it disintegrates within 12 to 24 hours if not fertilized.[5] However, your cervical mucus appears before ovulation and extends that 1-day window of fertility to approximately 6 days of your cycle.[6] This is because cervical mucus can keep sperm alive for up to 5 days.[7] Outside of this short window of fertility, pregnancy is not possible.

You produce cervical mucus on the days leading up to ovulation as your estrogen levels rise; otherwise you produce little to no mucus (your dry days). Observing the cyclical changes in your mucus patterns forms the basis of most fertility awareness-based methods, which are up to 99.4 percent effective in preventing pregnancy when used correctly (see Chapter 5).[8] In other words, synthetic hormones are *not* required to successfully prevent pregnancy. Understanding your mucus helps you understand your fertility, the importance of regular ovulation, and at the most basic level, lets you know when your period is coming. Many women (myself included) experience feelings of frustration and anger at having not learned this information at an early age.

Fertility awareness (FA) is a general term that refers to having an awareness of your menstrual cycle and knowing how to identify your fertile signs — but FA alone is not a method of birth control. Using FA for birth control involves developing a practice of observing and recording your fertile signs, and there are specific rules you must follow to correctly identify your fertile window (see Chapter 10). When you learn to understand and interpret your fertile signs, a whole new world opens up. You can avoid pregnancy naturally, optimize your chances of conceiving, monitor your overall health, and experience the health benefits associated with regular ovulation.

I ~~Hate~~ Love My Period...

I love and appreciate my period *now*, but it took some serious depro-gramming for me to get there. You may have grown up thinking your period was "dirty" or "bad." The idea that women are so "unclean" during their periods that they have the capacity to "soil" others is found

4 | **The Fifth Vital Sign**

in many religious teachings. To this day, there are a number of religious ceremonies and holy spaces you literally can't go to, or participate in, when you're bleeding. Similarly, various religious practices restrict you from carrying out everyday functions such as cooking meals, serving food, or having sex with your partner when you're on your period.

These messages run deep. A woman once told me that if she could wave a magic wand and fix something related to her health, fertility, or her menstrual cycle, she would "be freed of the ancestral burden of being a woman."

Many healthcare practitioners don't believe it's physically necessary for women to have regular periods; they assume that women in hunter-gatherer societies had fewer menstrual cycles (possibly due to more frequent pregnancies, shorter life expectancies, and/or more frequent illness/famine) and argue that it would be beneficial for modern women to have fewer periods as well.[9] However, since most modern women aren't opting for a semicontinuous state of pregnancy, these practitioners are advocating for menstrual suppression — a practice involving the suppression of the menstrual cycle (and monthly withdrawal bleeding) through the continuous use of hormonal contraceptives. As this practice becomes more common, I can't help but wonder why so many women are lining up to temporarily "cure" themselves of their fertility.

Hormonal contraceptives are so ubiquitous that most women don't even consider them a drug. I use the term hormonal contraceptives (HCs) throughout the book to refer to all methods of hormonal birth control (including the pill, the shot, the implant, the ring, the patch, and the hormonal IUD). While these methods have their differences, the common thread is the introduction of artificial hormones into your bloodstream. HCs are infused with synthetic versions of your sex hormones, which cause varying degrees of endocrine disruption. On a molecular level, the hormones in HCs are *completely different* from the estrogen and progesterone your body naturally produces (see Figures 1–1 and 1–2).

HCs were the first drugs ever developed to shut down a perfectly normal and healthy process in the body (see Chapter 7), essentially treating your fertility as an illness that required treatment. HCs allow you to schedule your periods, skip them when they fall at an inconvenient time, and in some cases, avoid them altogether. You never have to wonder when your period is coming because it's always on time. Rain or shine, stress or relaxation, eating disorder or endocrine dysfunction, your fake period keeps coming every 28 days. In contrast, your natural cycles vary from month to month, responding to stress, illness, and many other lifestyle factors.

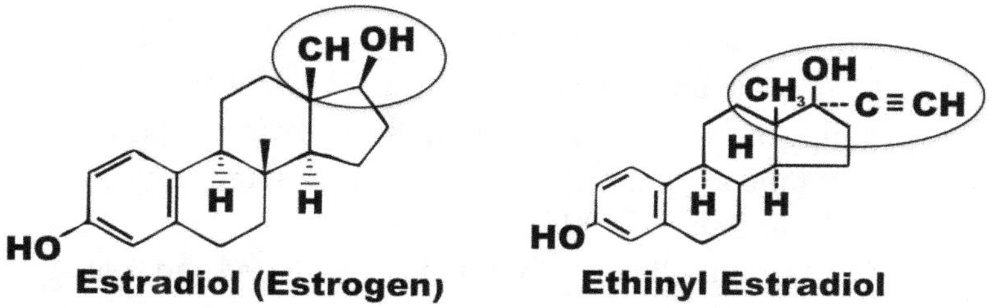

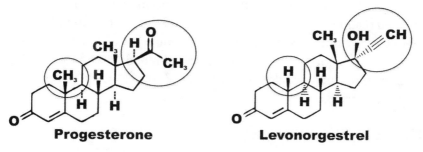

Figure 1-1: Synthetic versus natural estrogen. Estradiol is one of the natural estrogens your body produces. Compare this to ethinyl estradiol, a synthetic version of estrogen that is widely used in HCs. Note the difference in chemical structure (circled).

Progesterone   **Levonorgestrel**

Figure 1-2: Synthetic versus natural progesterone. Progesterone is the natural hormone your body produces, whereas levonorgestrel is one of the synthetic versions of progesterone used in HCs. Note the difference in chemical structure (circled).

True, managing monthly menstruation can be bothersome, but periods are a normal and healthy part of womanhood. The idea that your periods can be suppressed with hormones for years on end with no health consequences is not only false, it's dangerous. It's not always easy to embrace your cycles, especially when they're problematic, but I invite you to look at your menstrual cycle as a vital sign — an important sign of health.

In her essay, *If Men Could Menstruate*, Gloria Steinem paints a lovely picture of the many ways men would celebrate their periods if they had them. If you haven't read it, you should, and a simple online search will bring it up. Here is a small excerpt:

> So what would happen if suddenly, magically, men could menstruate and women could not?
> Clearly, menstruation would become an enviable, worthy, masculine event:
> Men would brag about how long and how much.
> Young boys would talk about it as the envied beginning of manhood. Gifts, religious ceremonies, family dinners, and stag parties would mark the day...
> Sanitary supplies would be federally funded and free...
> TV shows would treat the subject openly ... So would newspapers ... And so would movies.[10]

Wouldn't it be wonderful if our periods were celebrated in this way? Although you might not love your period today, once you've finished reading this book you might find it hard not to. After all, could there be anything more natural? Every human being on earth is here because of her (or his) mother's menstrual blood. If women stopped menstruating there would be no next generation. That's how important your period is.

The Fifth Vital Sign

You now know that healthy menstrual cycles are important for maintaining optimal health, and a healthy cycle is characterized by adequate production of your main ovarian hormones — estrogen[†] and progesterone. You only produce significant amounts of progesterone for about 12 to 14 days after ovulation, after which time you'll either have your period or a positive pregnancy test.

Estrogen stimulates cell growth, whereas progesterone mitigates the effects of estrogen by stimulating normal cell development,

---

[†] Estrogen is a general term that refers to a group of hormones including estradiol (E2), estrone (E1), estriol (E3), and others. Estradiol is responsible for most changes that occur throughout the menstrual cycle.

regulating cell differentiation, and promoting cell maturation.[11] Unopposed estrogen is associated with rapid cell proliferation, and is known to promote cell growth in certain types of cancer, including breast cancer and endometrial cancer.[12] Progesterone has been found to have a biphasic effect — initially stimulating cell growth, followed by a sustained antiproliferative effect on cancer cells over the course of two or more days of exposure.[13] In the case of endometrial cancer, progesterone protects the endometrium from the proliferative effects of estrogen.[14] Women with long, irregular cycles — as seen in women with polycystic ovary syndrome (PCOS) — are typically exposed to unopposed estrogen for several weeks or months prior to ovulation.[15] As a result, these women are nearly three times as likely to develop endometrial cancer compared to the general population.[16]

Like endometrial cancer, unopposed estrogen is also a risk factor for breast cancer. Although there are conflicting theories as to the effect of regular ovulation on the risk of breast cancer,[17] a number of researchers have suggested that regular ovulation plays a key role in reducing the risk of breast cancer by ensuring adequate progesterone production during the postovulatory phase of the menstrual cycle.[18] One study published in the *American Journal of Epidemiology* found that women who experienced irregular cycles (defined as cycles shorter or longer than 26 to 34 days) were nearly twice as likely to develop breast cancer in their lifetimes.[19]

Regular ovulation, followed by sufficient progesterone (and estrogen) production, is associated with building and maintaining optimal bone density in women.[20] By definition, women who either stop ovulating altogether, or experience ovulatory disturbances, are deficient in progesterone, putting them at an increased risk of developing osteoporosis.[21] This includes women who lose their periods as a result of stress, over-exercise, undereating, or ovulatory disorders.

Irregular ovulation is also associated with an increased risk of diabetes, cardiovascular disease, high blood pressure, and infertility (see Chapter 6).[22] Research suggests that regular ovulation (and thus, cyclical exposure to natural — endogenous — progesterone) mitigates certain cardiovascular risk factors and provides protection against the development of atherosclerosis, a disease characterized by the hardening and narrowing of the arteries due to plaque buildup.[23]

Whether or not you plan to have children, it's clear that maintaining healthy ovulatory menstrual cycles is important for preserving optimal health. Your menstrual cycle is a vital sign that constantly relays information back to you about your overall health. Variations in menstruation, overall cycle length, cervical mucus patterns, and other cycle parameters are often the first signs of an underlying health problem.

In the same way your home has a smoke detector, your body has a menstrual cycle. Your smoke detector remains silent most of the time, but if a grease fire starts raging in your kitchen, you'll hear it going off like crazy. Similarly, your menstrual cycle remains relatively silent when you're healthy, but when you have an underlying health issue, your menstrual cycle will typically start going haywire. The difference is that if your smoke detector were to go off, you'd never put a piece of tape over it, grab your headphones, and drown out the alarm bells with some super loud music. I'm thinking you'd grab your fire extinguisher and put out the fire.

Unfortunately, many health professionals take the "grab your headphones" approach to medical care by treating virtually all menstrual cycle abnormalities with HCs. You may have experienced this first-hand if you've ever found yourself in your doctor's office looking for support with painful periods, irregular cycles, or other cycle abnormalities. HCs are often presented as the panacea for all things menstrual: *Your period hasn't showed up in six months? No problem! Take this pill and you'll bleed every 28 days. Problem solved. You have debilitating cramps every period? No worries! Take this pill and poof! No more period pain. Again, problem solved.* Or is it?

While creating a predictable *withdrawal bleed*[†] each month might feel like a solution, it doesn't solve the underlying problem. Your house is essentially on fire, and instead of putting it out, you're sitting there with your headphones on pretending like it's not really burning down around you. What was that thing most of us did when we were kids and wanted to drown someone out? You'd plug your ears and say "la la la la la la la," right? That's essentially what's happening here.

[†] Withdrawal bleeding is caused by the sudden drop in synthetic hormone levels whenever you stop taking HCs (temporarily or permanently). It's not a true menstrual period, but many women mistake HC-related withdrawal bleeding for their period.

But we both know you deserve better. We all do. When I started my podcast, *Fertility Friday*, I knew how important this information is because of the profound impact it has had on my life, but I didn't know how many women I'd reach by simply sharing what I knew. Since releasing the very first episode back in 2014, I've interviewed over 150 experts in the field of women's health and fertility. I've also provided a space for women to share their stories as they take control of their menstrual cycles, their fertility, and their health. With more than one million downloads, and over 200 episodes released to date, I can't tell you how many times I've heard someone say, "Every woman needs to know this stuff!" and, "How come nobody taught me this in junior high school?"

In writing this book, my goal is to create a solid resource for women and health professionals alike. For that reason, I've spent countless hours dissecting thousands of research articles so that you don't have to take my word for it on any of the topics I cover. I've cited over 1000 research articles, which are available in the references section, to supplement what you read (which I know you'll appreciate, especially if you're a data nerd like I am).

It's time to take matters into your own hands. Fertility awareness is an essential part of the process, as it gives you the tools you need to understand your cycles. As I always say, regardless of whether you plan to use fertility awareness for birth control, conception, or to optimize your health, you have the right to know how both your body and your fertility work! We'll start by defining what a normal period looks like in the next chapter.

Summary

- Your menstrual cycle is a vital sign, just like your heart rate, body temperature, respiratory rate, and blood pressure.
- Ovulation is the main event to pay attention to in your cycle. If you don't ovulate, any bleeding you experience is not considered a true menstrual bleed.
- Regular ovulation is only possible when your endocrine and reproductive systems are functioning normally, so an irregular or abnormal cycle is an early warning sign of an underlying health problem.

- You are fertile for a maximum of 6 days per cycle — during your fertile window. This is because cervical mucus can keep sperm alive for up to 5 days as you approach ovulation.
- Progesterone is important because it mitigates the proliferative effects of estrogen, and it's only produced in significant quantities after ovulation.
- The value in learning your fifth vital sign is that it allows you to avoid pregnancy naturally, optimize your chances of conceiving, and monitor your overall health.
- Your menstrual cycle is a normal and healthy part of womanhood. Regular ovulation is a sign of health, and it is crucial for maintaining optimal health during your reproductive years.

Chapter 2
What Does a Normal Period Look Like?

"Something big is happening in period health. Periods are coming out in the open. They are no longer something to be endured, concealed, or regulated with hormonal birth control."

— Lara Briden, ND, *Period Repair Manual*

Considering that most biological women menstruate, you'd think we'd have a better idea of what a normal period is supposed to look like. Many women don't realize they're not experiencing a true menstruation unless they ovulate, and many more believe it's normal for their periods to be painful.

Let's set the record straight once and for all: severe pain of any kind is not normal, and is a clear indication that something is wrong. If you've experienced excessively heavy or painful periods, you know how deeply and negatively this experience can impact your life. Many women suffer in silence instead of reaching out for support, and those who seek support from their doctors already know how it plays out: painkillers and hormonal contraceptives (HCs). But neither HCs nor painkillers address the underlying cause — instead, they simply mask the pain.

This chapter will describe what a normal period really looks like, from how many days your period is supposed to last to how much you're supposed to bleed.

Is My Period Normal?

To determine this, you must first understand the difference between your true menstruation and other types of uterine bleeding.

During the first half of your cycle, your ovaries release estrogen, which causes your endometrial (uterine) lining† to thicken and grow. During the second half of your cycle, your ovaries produce progesterone, which causes your uterine lining to mature as it prepares for a fertilized egg to implant (see Figure 2–1). A true menstrual bleed can *only* happen *after* ovulation.

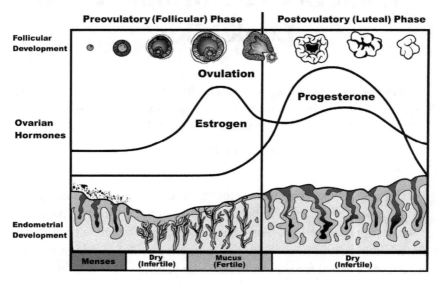

Figure 2-1: Endometrial development. The endometrial (uterine) lining grows and develops in response to rising estrogen and progesterone levels during the menstrual cycle.

Your menstrual cycle is a continuous process of proliferation, cell differentiation, and tissue degeneration.[1] Your period marks the beginning of your menstrual cycle and represents the tissue degeneration part of the process. Estrogen rebuilds your endometrial tissue and restores the base, or functional layer, of your endometrium. Progesterone takes that functional layer and makes it receptive to implantation. Progesterone causes your uterine lining to mature and to secrete fluids necessary to support the life of a developing embryo.

As I was writing this section, a number of Caribbean islands were hit by a series of powerful hurricanes. Two islands were completely

---

† The *endometrial lining* is the inner layer of the uterus that thickens during the menstrual cycle and is shed during menstruation. The terms *endometrium, endometrial lining*, and *uterine lining* are used interchangeably in this chapter.

wiped out. If you were to compare your monthly menstrual cycle to the process of rebuilding an entire island after a hurricane, estrogen would be responsible for the foundation (i.e., roads and infrastructure) and progesterone would be responsible for the houses and residential areas. Both hormones play equally important roles in your menstrual cycle because a normal and healthy menstrual cycle needs a healthy balance of both.[2]

Is This Actually My Period?

If you ovulate during your cycle, your period will arrive approximately 12 to 14 days later. That's how you identify a true menstrual period. You can confirm ovulation by tracking your three main fertile signs: *basal body temperature* (BBT), *cervical mucus* (CM), and *cervical position*. After ovulation, your BBT rises and stays high until your CM dries up, and your cervix shifts to a low position in the vagina and becomes firm to the touch (see Chapter 5).

Most HCs either partially or completely suppress ovulation. As such, the regular bleeding you have while taking them is not a true menstrual bleed. In terms of colour, your period should be a variation of red, from a bright red to a deep burgundy, like a rich red wine.[3] A normal period lasts about 4 to 5 days on average and follows a crescendo-decrescendo pattern, starting off heavy (particularly during the first 2 days) and then gradually getting lighter and tapering off.[4]

You may be wondering which day you should officially designate as day 1 of your period. Even if your period is preceded by several days of light spotting, the first day of your period is the first day of your true characteristic flow — the first day of bleeding that requires some sort of action on your part. Abnormal bleeding or premenstrual spotting is often very light, and most women can get away with using either a panty liner or nothing at all. However, when your period truly begins, you'll find that you actually have to use a pad, tampon, or menstrual cup.

If you've ever experienced bleeding that differed from your normal flow pattern, you'll know what I'm referring to here. You may notice that your bleeding is much lighter than usual, or that it doesn't follow the typical flow pattern you're used to. Spotting (for instance) is typically lighter than your period and is often pink or brownish in colour.

If you've recently come off HCs, it may take some time for you to rediscover what your real period looks and feels like. You may find that your bleeding pattern is noticeably heavier or lighter than what you experienced while on them. You may also notice symptoms you didn't have before, such as bloating, breast tenderness, or mild cramping. Once you've had a few true menstrual bleeds, you'll find it much easier to tell if your bleeding is really your period (as opposed to abnormal bleeding or premenstrual spotting).

How Many Days Should I Bleed?

On average, a normal menstrual period lasts about 4 to 5 days with an overall length of 3 to 7 days.[5] The first 2 to 3 days of your period will typically be the heaviest. You can expect that 90 percent of your total blood loss will take place within the first 3 days of your period, after having already lost over 70 percent by the end of the second day.[6] Some women experience as little as 2 days of bleeding, and others experience 9 or more, but these situations fall outside the normal range.[7]

How Much Should I Bleed?

Various studies that measure period volume show us that the total amount of bleeding women experience during their periods ranges from as little as 5 mL all the way up to 180 mL or more.[8] Although these numbers represent a fairly large range of bleeding, the research shows that the average total amount falls between 35 and 50 mL.[9] In an article published in *Human Reproduction,* the authors define normal bleeding as somewhere between 5 and 80 mL; but having only 5 mL (one teaspoon) of bleeding during your period is not healthy, nor is it normal.[10]

We often hear about the problems associated with excessive bleeding, but bleeding too little during your cycle can also indicate a problem. I find that there is much less emphasis on the issue of having excessively light periods, but this makes sense — given all the negative associations with menstruation that we grow up with, many women would consider it a blessing to have light periods, as opposed to recognizing that it could be a legitimate sign of a reproductive health issue.

I've worked with several women who've had extremely light periods (less than 25 mL of bleeding during their entire period), and none of them had completely normal menstrual cycles. When I work with women who consistently have less than 25 mL of bleeding cycle after cycle, they tend to have other abnormal cycle parameters that prompt further investigation, such as a short luteal phase length, premenstrual spotting, low progesterone levels, and scant cervical mucus observations. For this reason, I consider a normal and healthy range of menstrual bleeding to fall between 25 and 80 mL.

In order for you to develop a robust and healthy uterine lining capable of supporting and sustaining a pregnancy, your ovaries needs to produce enough estrogen and progesterone to build and maintain it. If you only have 5 to 10 mL (1 to 2 teaspoons) of bleeding over the course of your period, your uterine lining may not be thick enough to allow for normal implantation. It could also be a sign that your hormone levels are too low to stimulate normal endometrial growth and development.

Evidence supports the relationship between endometrial thickness and fertility.[11] In order for you to become pregnant and carry a pregnancy to term, your endometrial lining must be fully developed. The thickness of your endometrial lining can be measured with a transvaginal ultrasound, and the most useful measurement would be taken in the middle of your postovulatory (luteal) phase (about seven days after ovulation).

More specifically, if your endometrial lining is thinner than about 7 mm, your chances of conceiving are quite low.[12] If your lining measures somewhere between 6 and 8 mm, you're about twice as likely to miscarry than you would if your lining was at least 9 mm thick.[13] Generally speaking, if your uterine lining measures 10 mm or more during your luteal phase, you're more likely to conceive and carry a pregnancy to term.[14]

Although the thickness of your endometrial lining isn't the only factor that determines whether you'll be able to conceive, it's an important one to pay attention to. You can get a general sense of your endometrial thickness by monitoring your bleeding patterns from cycle to cycle. But I don't want you to panic if your period doesn't line up exactly with the normal parameters outlined in this chapter. There's no magical amount of bleeding you should have every cycle.

If you find that your bleeding pattern differs from the norm, take the opportunity to investigate if there could be an underlying problem.

Heavy bleeding, on the other hand, is much more readily identified as problematic. If you have 80 mL or more of bleeding during your period, or if your period lasts longer than seven days, you meet the definition of *menorrhagia,* which means excessively heavy and/or prolonged periods.[15] If you lose more than 80 mL of blood every time you have your period, you're more likely to develop iron-deficiency anemia.[16] Some practitioners have even suggested that 60 mL would be a more appropriate upper limit because women with heavier periods are more likely to become iron deficient.[17]

Heavy periods are often associated with disorders such as uterine fibroids,[18] endometrial polyps,[19] adenomyosis,[20] endometriosis,[21] and in some cases, cancer.[22] Heavy periods can also be related to endocrine dysfunction such as that seen in thyroid disorders.[23] Heavy menstrual bleeding is associated with an imbalance of estrogen and progesterone. Specifically, if you have too much estrogen in relation to progesterone, you're more likely to have heavier periods.[24] In addition, you are more likely to have heavy periods during your teenage years and in the years leading up to menopause, which both happen to be times in your reproductive life cycle when your estrogen levels tend to be higher relative to progesterone.[25]

Interestingly enough, the amount of bleeding you have during your period can be related to how tall you are, how big your uterus is, and whether or not you've had children.[26] With that in mind, you're never going to have the exact same amount of bleeding during your period as anyone else does. If your periods have always been on the lighter or heavier side, who's to say that's not normal for you? A cause for concern would be if your flow suddenly changed and became significantly heavier or lighter than it was before.[27]

I want to stress that there are times when abnormal uterine bleeding is a sign of a serious problem. As I was writing this section, I received a message from a woman who wanted information about the connection (if any) between menstrual cycle abnormalities and cancer. She writes:

> My best friend (36) has been diagnosed with uterine cancer.
> She has been bleeding since January and was waiting for a

laparoscopy [from the public healthcare system] until she couldn't take it anymore and went private. She didn't know how serious it was and neither did her doctors.

I received this message in June, meaning this woman experienced some degree of continuous bleeding for six months! This example highlights the link between your menstrual cycle and your health. While many women experience a day or two of spotting before or after their period, continuous or frequent bleeding is not normal. If you experience a pattern of abnormal bleeding that persists from cycle to cycle, seek support from a health professional who is willing to investigate further.

When you're trying to figure out if your menstrual cycle is normal and healthy, it's important to look at your cycle in its entirety, from the first day of your period to the last day before your next one starts, and consider how all the phases of your cycle fit together. As we talk more about the normal parameters of the menstrual cycle in Chapter 4, you'll notice that if one aspect of your cycle falls outside of the normal range on its own every now and then, it doesn't automatically mean your cycles aren't normal or healthy. To get an accurate picture of your cycles, take a step back, look at your menstrual cycle as a whole, and consider how all of the pieces fit together.

I always say that there's no such thing as a "perfect" period. Instead, there's an optimal range that gives us a sense of what's happening in your cycles. You won't fail the test if your period falls outside of these parameters, but the information you glean from paying attention can empower you to identify potential problems sooner and make the necessary changes to improve your period health.

Measuring how much you bleed

Measuring the amount of bleeding you have during your period is actually pretty easy. To put it into perspective, 80 mL of bleeding is roughly equivalent to going through 3 to 4 tampons each day for 4 to 5 days, depending on your flow pattern. A normal-sized tampon or pad holds 1 to 2 teaspoons, or about 5 to 12 mL when fully soaked.[28] It's harder to gauge the amount of bleeding when you use pads and tampons, but if you use a menstrual cup, you'll find that conceptualizing the amount of bleeding you have during your period is much easier.

A fun exercise that I do in my group classes is to fill a small measuring cup with water to demonstrate what 20, 40, 60, and 80 mL of bleeding looks like. I use a menstrual cup and fill it several times until I've used the entire amount to give a visual representation of normal bleeding patterns. To make it more realistic I dye the water red for effect (I don't know about you, but that blue dye they use in pad commercials has always freaked me out a little. It's blood, people, *not* blue liquid ... but I digress). As you can imagine, when I do this exercise in a group setting I get a range of reactions. Some women are floored to see how much bleeding is considered normal because it seems like so much to them, and others are thinking to themselves, "That's it? How could someone have so little bleeding throughout their entire period?"

Now that I have you wondering about your own experiences, where do you think you fit on the spectrum? If you've never given a second thought to the amount of bleeding you normally have, I have an exercise for you to try when your next period arrives. I want you to pay close attention to how many times you change your pads, tampons, and/or menstrual cup. If you're using pads and tampons, note how many you go through and if they're fully or partially soaked. You can use this legend as a guide:

- Light pads/tampons hold up to 3 mL when fully soaked
- Medium pads/tampons hold up to 4 mL when fully soaked
- Heavy pads/tampons hold up to 8 mL when fully soaked
- Super pads/tampons hold up to 12 mL when fully soaked[29]

If you're using a menstrual cup, keep in mind that most cups hold up to 30 mL (1 oz) of blood. Record how many times you empty it and about how full the cup is each time. By the end of your cycle, you'll have a much better idea of how much you're bleeding and where you fit along the spectrum.

Knowing whether the volume of your period bleeding is normal is important because it can alert you if there's something wrong. If, for instance, you find that you soak through your supersized pads or tampons every hour for the first 2 days of your cycle and you didn't realize that was outside of the normal range, you could be missing out on an extremely important clue about your health status.

Based on my example, soaking at least 6 pads or tampons per day on the first 2 days of your cycle would equal about 144 mL of bleeding, and in that scenario your period hasn't even finished yet.

Although the go-to solution for heavy periods tends to be HCs, they only offer temporary relief from the symptoms. That relief might be helpful and convenient in the short term, but if you don't address the underlying issue, you'll eventually be affected by it later on.

Is It Normal for My Periods to Be Painful?

Though common, moderate to severe pain with menstruation is not normal or healthy. Pain that requires the use of painkillers — or is so severe that you're unable to go about your normal daily activities — is a universal sign that something is wrong. Unfortunately, there's a long history in modern medicine that minimizes the experiences of women as a whole.

What occurred to me as I was writing this section was that, although you know that you bleed every month, you've likely never had a good explanation of what menstruation actually is. What is physically happening inside your uterus that causes your endometrial lining to shed and for you to bleed? After all, as women, we're the ones who bleed for several days each month as a normal part of our reproductive cycle, whereas outside of this context, bleeding is associated with injury or tissue damage.

It turns out that many of our normal reproductive processes, including ovulation, menstruation, implantation, and labour, are all inflammatory events.[30] What this means is that menstruation is the result of a normal inflammatory process that involves cyclical tissue injury and restoration as we move through our menstrual cycles. As described in an article published in *Reproduction,*

> The human endometrium undergoes extensive remodelling during every menstrual cycle. This process involves the disintegration of the functional layer of the endometrium and regeneration and differentiation of a new layer in preparation for an implanting embryo.[31]

A similar process happens inside your ovaries during ovulation. Here's how ovulation is described in the same article:

> The process of ovulation destroys the ovarian surface epithelium and vasculature at the site of oocyte expulsion ... Following rupture of the ovarian surface epithelium, repair and organization of the site is necessary to form a corpus luteum.[32]

When you think of menstruation as an inflammatory process that involves tissue degeneration and restoration, it makes sense that when this normal process is disrupted it could lead to excessive bleeding and/or pain during your period. Look no further than the average time it takes for a woman to receive a diagnosis of endometriosis for proof that painful periods don't rank very high on the priority scale as far as the medical establishment is concerned. A study published in *Human Reproduction* surveyed 218 women with surgically confirmed endometriosis to determine the length of time between the onset of their painful symptoms and their confirmed endometriosis diagnosis.[33] The average delay in diagnosis for women from the UK was just under 8 years, and for women from the US it was just under 12 years.[34]

In case you've never experienced severe menstrual pain, it feels like you're dying. A woman in one of my group classes described the feeling as being simultaneously stabbed in the abdomen while being set on fire. Another woman described it as if someone had reached inside her abdomen, grabbed her uterus, and started wrenching it back and forth (like it was wet laundry).[35] For me, personally, I didn't even realize I was in labour with my first son for several hours because I kept thinking, *I can't be in labour, my period cramps hurt more than this!* Why on earth would a woman be expected to suffer with such severe pain for nearly a decade before her medical provider starts taking it seriously?

Between 20 to 90 percent of women who suffer specifically with pelvic pain or infertility have endometriosis, so it's time we start recognizing that pain with menstruation is an important indication that something is wrong.[36] *Endometriosis* is a condition characterized by abnormal growth of endometrial tissue. Instead of growing inside the uterus, endometrial tissue may grow on the ovaries, fallopian tubes, and other organs in the pelvic cavity. As one researcher describes it: "Dysmenorrhea is associated with cyclical recurrent microbleeding within various entities of ectopic endometriotic implants and consequent inflammation. Endometriosis-related adhesions ... also cause painful symptoms."[37] Endometriosis is associated with unexplained infertility, and laparoscopic surgery is required for a formal diagnosis.[38]

The standard treatment for period pain of any kind is typically painkillers or HCs, but neither option addresses the underlying cause of the pain, leaving many of us with the impression that menstrual pain is just a normal and inescapable part of being a woman. Fortunately, there are a variety of effective ways to address period pain without having to rely on painkillers or HCs (see Chapter 14).

Now that we've hashed out periods, we get to move on to one of my favourite topics ... cervical mucus!

Summary

- You only experience a true menstrual period after ovulation.
- A normal period lasts from 3 to 7 days (4 to 5 days on average) and has a flow pattern that starts heavy and gradually tapers off.
- The total bleeding in a normal period ranges from 25 to 80 mL.
- A normal period colour is a variant of red — bright red to a deep burgundy.
- Painful periods are not normal. In a normal period, you should experience either no cramping or very mild cramping or discomfort.
- Extreme pain with periods may be associated with endometriosis.

Chapter 3
Cervical Mucus

"The cervix acts like a gate. The gate is open when cervical mucus is flowing and ... closed when mucus stops flowing."

— Geraldine Matus, PhD,
Justisse Method: Fertility Awareness and Body Literacy

Before we get any deeper into your menstrual cycle, it's time to introduce you to your cervical mucus. Cervical mucus (CM) is the key to understanding and using fertility awareness (FA), and by the end of this chapter you'll appreciate just how *amazing* it is.

What Is Cervical Mucus?

CM is a hydrogel comprised of mucus molecules, water, a variety of enzymes, protein chains, and other biochemical compounds including sodium, chloride, and potassium.[1] CM is critical for fertility because sperm depend on it for survival. Without CM, sperm would not survive long enough to get a shot at fertilizing your eggs!

As the name indicates, CM is produced by your cervix. Estrogen and progesterone are the two main hormones that affect your CM production. You produce estrogen as you approach ovulation, and estrogen stimulates your cervical crypts to produce E-type (estrogenic) mucus. When your cycle is healthy, you produce E-type mucus for an average of five days before ovulation.[2] This is your *fertile window* (see Figure 3–1); during these days it's possible for sperm to survive until ovulation, which means that pregnancy is possible when you have sex on any day you produce CM (prior to ovulation).

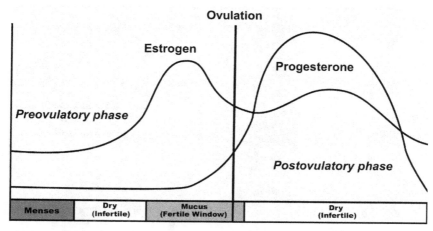

Figure 3-1: The reproductive hormone cycle

After ovulation, your progesterone production dramatically increases and stays high for the remainder of your cycle (and if you get pregnant, your progesterone will continue to rise throughout your pregnancy). Progesterone suppresses further CM production by directing your cervical cells to produce a thick, gelatinous mucus plug — these are your dry (*infertile*) days.

Your cervix (see Figure 3-2) is the narrow, neck-like structure at the base of your uterus. If you were to look inside of your cervix you would see your *endocervical canal*. Your endocervical canal is lined with specialized cells that produce mucus.[3] As you can see, the lining of your cervical canal has many folds and creases called *cervical crypts*. The cells that line your cervical crypts are highly receptive to the hormonal changes that happen throughout your menstrual cycle, and they produce increasing amounts of mucus as your estrogen levels rise.

There are about 100 cervical crypts in your endocervical canal, and together they produce an average of 20 to 60 mg of CM per day.[4] During your fertile window your mucus production rises dramatically to anywhere from 10 to 20 times that amount.[5] In practical terms, this amounts to about one-quarter to one-half of a teaspoon of CM *per day* during the fertile window. This may not seem like much, but when you start paying attention to your mucus, you'll notice an obvious difference in your observations on the days leading up to ovulation.

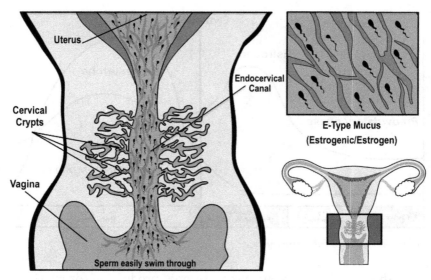

Figure 3-2: Your cervix during your fertile window

Your cervix controls whether sperm can pass through your endocervical canal and gain access to your uterus. For this reason, the cervix is often referred to as a *biological valve* that is either open or closed, depending on where you are in your cycle.[6] It's kind of like having a security guard on duty — your cervix decides who can come in, when they can enter, and when to close the doors.

Put simply, you are fertile on the days you observe CM (your mucus days) and infertile on the days you do not (your dry days). During your fertile window, your cervix is open and actively producing CM that you can readily observe (when you pay attention to it). Outside of your fertile window, your cervix is closed and blocked with a thick, gelatinous mucus plug that prevents sperm from getting through (see Figure 3-3).

This basic principle is at the heart of fertility awareness-based methods. If you plan to use FA as your primary method of birth control, you can read more about it in Chapter 10, but for now, remember this: *mucus days are fertile and dry days are infertile.*

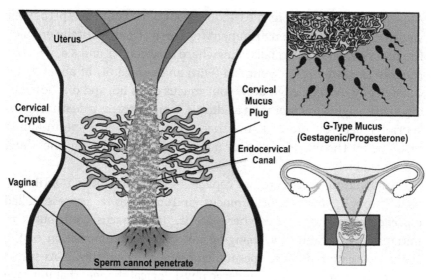

Figure 3-3: Your cervix on your dry (infertile) days

What Makes Cervical Mucus "Fertile"?

CM is considered fertile for three important reasons:

1. It is the perfect pH for sperm,
2. It keeps sperm alive for up to 5 days as you approach ovulation, and
3. It prepares the sperm to be able to fertilize an oocyte (egg).

In case you haven't heard, you have an incredible ecosystem of diverse microorganisms living inside of your vagina — this is referred to as your *vaginal microbiome*.[7] The most abundant of these microorganisms are a group of bacteria called *lactobacillus*.[8] These bacteria work very hard to keep the pH of your vagina acidic throughout your menstrual cycle, and this offers you protection against bacterial vaginosis, yeast infections, sexually transmitted infections (STIs), urinary tract infections (UTIs), and any other foreign invaders that could wreak havoc inside your vagina and uterus.[9] Lactobacillus bacteria produce lactic acid, and that helps to maintain an acidic vaginal pH between 3.5 and 4.9.[10] Consequently, your vagina is quite acidic. So acidic, in fact, that sperm can't survive inside of your vagina for more than a couple of hours because they need a much higher (more alkaline) pH to thrive.

Amazingly, during your fertile window, your CM changes the pH of your vagina into the perfect environment for sperm. Coincidentally enough, the pH of a man's semen falls somewhere between 7.2 and 8.4, which is roughly the same pH as your CM (with an average pH of about 7.0).[11] Outside of your fertile window, your mucus dries up, and on these dry days your vagina maintains an acidic pH, which creates a death trap for sperm! I bet you didn't know that your vagina is a sperm-killing machine for the majority of your menstrual cycle, but I, for one, think it's incredible!

In addition, sperm are not capable of fertilizing an egg until they pass through your cervical mucus and undergo a process called *capacitation*.[12] As one researcher puts it, "The mucus contributes to initiating capacitation by changing not only the composition of the sperm population but also sperm membrane biochemistry."[13] As sperm swim through your CM, they undergo physiological changes that improve their motility and make it possible for them to penetrate an egg.[14]

Peak Mucus Versus Non-Peak Mucus

During your fertile window, you produce two main types of CM: *peak mucus* and *non-peak mucus* (see Figure 3–4).[15]

- *Peak mucus* is clear, stretchy, and/or lubricative/slippery, has the quality of raw egg whites, and typically forms a thin thread when you stretch it between your fingers. When you have peak mucus, you'll notice that it feels lubricative when you wipe yourself after using the bathroom, and you may experience an obvious feeling of wetness throughout the day.
- *Non-peak mucus* is cloudy or white in colour and doesn't stretch very much between your fingers. It's similar to the quality of creamy white hand lotion, and many FA resources will refer to non-peak mucus as having a creamy or sticky texture. *Spinnbarkeit* is a German word for the thread that forms between your fingers when you stretch peak-quality mucus. Non-peak mucus doesn't have this thread-like quality and doesn't stretch very much between your fingers at all.

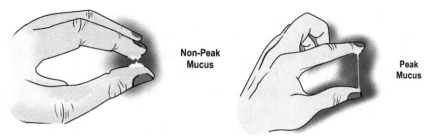

Figure 3–4: Peak and non-peak mucus

Whether you're trying to get pregnant or not, remember that both peak and non-peak mucus are considered fertile because they keep sperm alive for up to 5 days. As I'll expand on below, don't think of your mucus in terms of more or less fertile. On each day of your cycle you're either *fertile* or *not fertile*. After all, you can't be more or less pregnant!

Why Distinguish Between "Peak" and "Non-Peak" Mucus if Both Are Fertile?

There are four important reasons to make the distinction between peak and non-peak mucus:

1. Achieving the high efficacy of fertility awareness-based methods of birth control,
2. Optimizing your chances of conception,
3. Confirming ovulation, and
4. Monitoring your menstrual cycle health.

Achieving the high efficacy of fertility awareness-based methods of birth control

Your menstrual cycle has two main phases: the preovulatory (follicular) phase and the postovulatory (luteal) phase. Your fertile days occur in your preovulatory phase on the days leading up to ovulation. Once you've confirmed ovulation, you're actually infertile during the remainder of your cycle. In order to use FA successfully to avoid pregnancy, you must learn how to tell the difference between your fertile and infertile days.

FA is a legitimate (and highly effective) method of birth control, with an effectiveness rate of up to 99.4 percent.[16] However, this high level of effectiveness is contingent upon having a clear and accurate understanding of CM. Knowing the difference between peak and non-peak mucus is of particular importance for women who wish to gain the full effectiveness of FA as their primary method of birth control.

When you can make the distinction between peak and non-peak CM, it allows you to clearly identify your fertile window. It also minimizes the chance of an unplanned pregnancy. Many women who are new to FA charting make the mistake of thinking non-peak mucus is *not* fertile and experience the difficult lesson of an unplanned pregnancy to illustrate that it *is*. When you know that peak and non-peak mucus are both fertile, you won't be tempted to have unprotected sex on a day of non-peak mucus in your preovulatory phase. You'll know that you're never more or less fertile. Whenever you see mucus, either peak or non-peak, you'll know it's a fertile day.

Optimizing your chances of conception

Peak CM is optimal for conception. While it's possible to conceive when you have sex on your days of non-peak mucus, having unprotected sex on your days of peak mucus optimizes the chance of conception for two main reasons:

1. Peak mucus is produced closer to ovulation, and
2. Peak mucus has specific sperm-friendly qualities in greater amounts.

As you track your cycles, you'll notice that you produce increasing amounts of peak mucus on the days leading up to ovulation (mirroring your estrogen production). Your CM (both peak and non-peak) has incredible qualities that facilitate rapid sperm transport into the uterine cavity, prepare sperm to fertilize an oocyte, and filter out defective sperm. However, peak mucus contains these sperm-friendly qualities in greater amounts.

High levels of estrogen around ovulation stimulate the production of your peak mucus — mucus that is clear, stretchy, and/or lubricative — and it's these qualities that play key roles in rapid sperm transport and sperm filtration.[17] In addition, your days of peak mucus occur shortly before, and during, ovulation, making them particularly useful to pay attention to when timing sex for conception. For these reasons, your days of peak mucus are your prime baby-making days!

Mother Nature has designed an incredible system that ensures that the highest-quality sperm are available (and ready) at the perfect time. Understanding the role of CM (particularly the ability of mucus to keep sperm alive for several days prior to ovulation) shows you that paying attention to your mucus is the most effective way to time sex to optimize your chance of conceiving (see Chapter 10).

Confirming ovulation

Knowing the difference between peak and non-peak mucus helps you confirm ovulation — especially when you can identify what's called your *peak day*. A common misconception about peak day is that it's when you see the most CM, but that's not the case at all. Peak day is simply the *last* day of your cycle that you observe any peak mucus. Peak day (see Figure 3–5) is important because it's highly correlated with ovulation. Some sources indicate that ovulation happens on your peak day up to 80 percent of the time.[18]

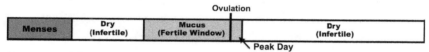

Figure 3–5: Peak day

Your progesterone production surges after ovulation, and this causes your mucus to dry up. You would expect to have dry days (no CM) until your period arrives about 12 to 14 days later. This shift from mucus days to dry days can be used to confirm that you've ovulated. For instance, if you observe a few days of non-peak mucus followed by several days of peak mucus, and then you notice an abrupt shift back to dry days, you can be fairly certain you've ovulated (provided that your other fertile signs match up).

Monitoring your menstrual cycle health

Making the distinction between peak mucus and non-peak mucus can also help you monitor your menstrual cycle health and your cervical health. Paying attention to your mucus patterns can be the first line of defence for identifying yeast infections, cervical infections, or even the presence of abnormal cervical cells. When you understand the normal parameters of CM production, you can act quickly if you notice that something is wrong.

Approximately 20 to 30 percent of the women I work with have one or more of the following abnormal CM observations:

- CM that appears yellowish in colour,
- CM that appears gummy (like the goo on the back of a new credit card) or gluey (like sticky white glue),
- Non-peak CM observations on nearly every day of the menstrual cycle, with no dry days before or after ovulation, and
- Watery discharge during both the preovulatory and postovulatory infertile phases (wet discharge, and/or periodic "gushes" throughout the cycle that are *not* lubricative and *not* related to ovulation).

These observations have led to a number of discoveries that would otherwise have gone unnoticed if my clients hadn't been charting. In many cases, these abnormal observations gave them the opportunity to identify existing yeast or bacterial infections that were flying under the radar. In some cases these observations were the early signs of something more serious, leading to the identification of cervical dysplasia (abnormal cells of the cervix) or cervical ectropion (when inner cervical cells spread to the outer surface of the cervix).[19]

All this is to say that paying attention to your mucus patterns, and having the ability to differentiate between peak and non-peak mucus, is helpful for a number of different reasons — from timing sex for conception to identifying potential health issues. As you become more comfortable observing and recording your mucus patterns, it will begin to feel more like second nature.

Doesn't Vaginal Discharge Mean I Have an Infection?

Not necessarily! CM is a normal and healthy fluid with so many amazing properties that your head will be spinning by the time you get to the end of this chapter. My colleague Nora Pope, ND, refers to CM as *white flow* — the flow that signifies fertility because it coincides with ovulation.[20] We're all taught about our *red flow*, but this exclusive focus on periods overshadows any discussion of our CM. Even if you've never paid attention to your CM, you've probably experienced it before and just had no idea what it was.

Have you ever felt certain that your period had started, only to run to the bathroom and discover that you have no bleeding whatsoever? Perhaps you've found yourself running to the doctor convinced you had a vaginal infection. Maybe you were repeatedly tested for STIs, bacterial vaginosis, or other infections, only to have them all come back negative. Or maybe you've noticed that on some days you feel super wet down there and have no idea why. If any of these statements sound familiar, you've probably noticed your mucus before, but no one told you what it was. Instead of knowing that it's a normal and healthy part of being a woman, you were left thinking there was something wrong with you — but there's nothing wrong with you at all!

Many women have found themselves going back to their doctor month after month thinking they have some sort of infection, only to discover that the discharge they're seeing is actually their CM. You'd think your doctor would know, but sadly most doctors are just as uneducated about mucus as we are; no one taught them about white flow either.

Here are the five types of vaginal discharge you should be aware of (see Figure 3–6):

- *Cervical mucus* is a type of discharge related specifically to fertility because it allows sperm to make its way to your fallopian tubes where it can go on to fertilize an egg. You produce CM as you approach ovulation, and once you've ovulated you'll notice a shift to dry days until your period comes and your cycle starts again.
- *Vaginal cell slough* refers to the normal shedding of your vaginal cells each day. Your vagina is constantly cleaning and rejuvenating itself, shedding and replacing dead cells, just like your skin does. If you've ever wondered about that crumbly white or yellow discharge in your underwear most days, that's your vaginal cell slough. It may also appear as a shiny film on your toilet paper when you wipe yourself — and for the record, it's completely normal and healthy.

Normal		
Cervical mucus	*Vaginal cell slough*	*Arousal fluid*
Creamy and white (like hand lotion), or clear and stretchy (like raw egg whites)	Crumbly white/yellow discharge seen on underwear	Clear and stretchy
Can stretch it between your fingers up to an inch or more; may stretch multiple times Causes a smooth or lubricative sensation when you wipe yourself	Cannot be stretched between your fingers Causes a dry or smooth sensation when you wipe yourself; the toilet paper may appear shiny	Forms a thin thread between your fingers, but unlike cervical mucus, it quickly dissipates as you stretch it Causes a lubricative sensation when you wipe yourself
Present in your fertile window as you approach ovulation; dries up after ovulation Some women observe non-peak mucus outside their fertile window	Present on any day of the menstrual cycle; does not dry up after ovulation	Present following sexual stimulation and/or sexual arousal on any day of the menstrual cycle; does not dry up after ovulation Women may observe arousal fluid when breastfeeding due to increased oxytocin production
Very little or no scent	Very little or no scent	Very little or no scent
No irritation	No irritation	No irritation

Abnormal	
Infections/bacterial or yeast overgrowth	*Abnormal cervical cells/cervical dysplasia*
White, yellow, or greenish discharge	Non-lubricative, watery discharge
May appear thick and gummy (like glue), chunky like cottage cheese, or creamy and white with a yellowish tinge	Causes a damp or wet spot on your underwear and/or the toilet paper when you wipe yourself. You may also experience occasional gushes of what feels like water Causes a dry or smooth sensation when you wipe yourself but is *not* lubricative
Present on any day of the menstrual cycle; does not dry up after ovulation	Present on any day of the menstrual cycle; does not dry up after ovulation
May smell yeasty or fishy	Very little or no scent
May experience itchiness and irritation in your vaginal/vulvar region	No irritation

Figure 3-6: Vaginal discharge. Is what I'm seeing normal or abnormal?

- *Arousal fluid* is a type of vaginal secretion released during periods of sexual arousal and/or sexual activity. Unlike CM, arousal fluid is *not* produced by the cervix, and it may be produced on any day of your cycle.[21] When you're sexually aroused, the veins and capillaries inside of your vaginal tissues dilate and fill with blood (similar to an erection).[22] When this happens, the additional pressure forces arousal fluid through your vaginal tissues, causing your vagina to become moist and slippery. Arousal fluid is clear and stretchy (much like peak CM) but has a lighter and thinner texture. It rapidly dissipates when you touch and stretch it between your fingers, whereas CM does not. Breastfeeding women often produce arousal fluid in response to the release of hormones that are triggered when the baby nurses.

- *Discharge related to infections* such as STIs (or an overgrowth of yeast or bacteria) is a different type that you'll want to be on the lookout for. Infections can cause a continuous pattern of vaginal discharge that does not stop after ovulation. You may notice discharge that appears white, yellow, or green, and you may notice that it has a yeasty or fishy smell (though this is not always the case). Infections may cause irritation, itchiness, and discomfort, whereas CM and vaginal cell slough do not. If you notice any of these signs, it's time to head to your doctor.

- *Abnormal cervical cells and/or cervical dysplasia* cause an additional type of discharge you should be aware of. Cervical dysplasia is characterized by abnormal cell growth on the surface of the cervix, and approximately 15 to 20 percent of the women I've worked with show signs of it. Cervical dysplasia causes a non-lubricative, watery discharge that occurs consistently throughout the menstrual cycle. Women describe having occasional gushes of what feels like water, and they rarely experience dry days — instead they consistently observe a wet, watery discharge when they wipe. To be clear, this is not CM. Cervical dysplasia is characterized by the rapid development of abnormal cervical cells, and this abnormal cell growth causes a type of watery discharge that often goes unnoticed unless a woman is charting her cycles. If you notice an observation like this, you'll want to make an appointment with your doctor and request a pap smear (see Chapter 11 for details).

Estrogen, Progesterone, and Your Cervical Mucus

Now it's time for a little biology lesson. To understand what's happening in your cervix, you must first understand your hormone cycle. Your cervix produces CM in response to the varying levels of estrogen and progesterone that your ovaries produce during your menstrual cycle.

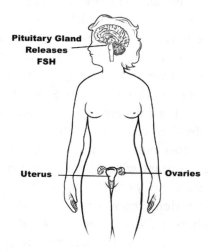

Figure 3-7: The release of FSH from your pituitary gland

I'll break down the process so you can get a sense of what's going on:

1. As your period comes to an end, your pituitary gland sends a message to your ovaries telling them it's time to start preparing for ovulation. A *follicle* is a small cyst-like structure inside your ovary that contains an egg (oocyte); it starts as a *primordial follicle*, or a follicle that contains an immature oocyte, and your ovaries contain several hundred thousand of these *primordial follicles*.[23] At the beginning of your menstrual cycle, several of these *primordial follicles* begin to develop. One follicle, the *dominant follicle*, is chosen to reach maturity and will go on to release an egg during ovulation.[24] To initiate this process your pituitary gland releases

follicle-stimulating hormone (FSH), and FSH stimulates the follicles to develop and grow (see Figure 3–7).

2. As the follicles grow and develop they produce increasing amounts of estrogen as you approach ovulation. Your estrogen production continues to rise until it peaks just before ovulation, which is what causes you to ovulate. Peak estrogen levels trigger your pituitary gland to release luteinizing hormone (LH; also known as the *LH surge*).[25] The LH surge triggers ovulation by causing the follicle to rupture and release the egg (see Figure 3–8). Ovulation predictor kits (OPKs) are designed to detect your LH surge, and therefore predict that ovulation will typically occur approximately 24 to 36 hours later (see Chapter 6).

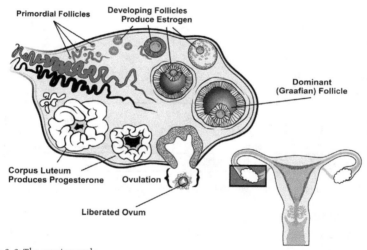

Figure 3–8: The ovarian cycle

3. Your cervical crypts are sensitive to both estrogen and progesterone. As your ovaries produce estrogen, estrogen stimulates your cervical crypts to produce E-type (*estrogenic*) mucus as you approach ovulation. Your CM production is directly related to your hormone production — as your ovaries produce estrogen your cervical crypts respond by producing E-type CM (refer back to Figure 3–2).[26]

4. After ovulation, the same follicle that was producing all that estrogen (the dominant follicle) turns into a yellowish structure called the *corpus luteum* and promptly starts producing progesterone (the term comes from the Latin *corpus luteus,* which

translates to "yellow body").[27] As you can see, progesterone production rises dramatically after ovulation (see Figure 3–9).

5. Progesterone suppresses further ovulation and dries up your E-type CM. Progesterone also increases your metabolism and causes a noticeable increase in your basal body temperature after you ovulate (see Chapter 5). Your cervical crypts produce G-type (*gestagenic*) mucus under the influence of progesterone, but more on both G- and E-type mucus in a moment.

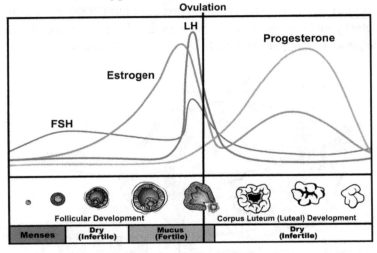

Figure 3–9: The reproductive hormone cycle with follicular development

6. Following ovulation, your progesterone levels remain high for the next 12 to 14 days until one of two things happen: either you get your period or you become pregnant. In the event that one lucky sperm was successfully able to fertilize an egg during ovulation and you are now pregnant, your corpus luteum will continue producing progesterone throughout your pregnancy (although the placenta will take over the bulk of the hormone production at about 12 weeks gestation).[28] If you're not pregnant, your corpus luteum will break down about 12 to 14 days after ovulation, your progesterone levels will drop, and you'll get your period.[29]

G-Type Mucus: Your Infertile (Dry) Days

You may be surprised by how many dry days you actually have throughout your menstrual cycle. Once you get into the habit of checking for mucus every day, you may notice that you're actually dry most of the time. If you refer back to Figure 3–5, you'll see that dry days typically make up about two-thirds of your cycle.

On your dry days, your cervix produces a type of mucus you don't actually get to see: *G-type mucus*. The "G" stands for *gestagenic* (affected by progesterone — see Figure 3–10).[30] G-type mucus forms a thick mucus plug inside your cervical canal, acting as a barrier between your vagina and your uterus (refer back to Figure 3–3).[31] These are your infertile days because sperm can't penetrate your G-type mucus plug. When your plug is in place, your biological valve is closed. Imagine trying to walk through a giant volleyball net that is immersed in several feet of wet cement. There's no way you'll make it through no matter how hard you try.

Infertile Dry Days	Fertile Mucus Days
G-Type (gestagenic) mucus	*E-Type (estrogenic) mucus*
Progesterone stimulates G-type mucus production, which forms a thick mucus plug inside your cervix.	**Estrogen** stimulates E-type mucus production, producing both peak and non-peak cervical mucus.
This serves as a barrier to sperm, preventing them from passing through the cervix.	Sperm easily penetrate E-type mucus and freely pass through the cervix.
You may feel a dry or smooth sensation due to vaginal cell slough, but there is no observable cervical mucus.	E-type mucus causes a smooth or lubricative sensation when wiping with observable cervical mucus.

Figure 3–10: Infertile days versus fertile days

If you use FA as a method of birth control, know that your dry days are infertile for four important reasons:

1. Sperm can't penetrate G-type mucus, so they can't swim through your cervix,
2. G-type mucus is naturally acidic and creates an environment that sperm can't survive in,
3. Your estrogen levels are too low to trigger ovulation on your preovulatory dry days, and
4. Your progesterone suppresses E-type mucus production on your postovulatory dry days (and once you ovulate you're not fertile again until your next cycle!).[32]

Since your CM is produced in response to rising estrogen levels (and your estrogen levels rise as you approach ovulation), the presence or absence of CM indicates how close you are to ovulation. Dry days mean that you have no mucus you can observe, and when you have no mucus it either means that you haven't started to approach ovulation yet or you've ovulated already (depending on where you are in your menstrual cycle). Now let's talk about what happens on your fertile days.

E-Type Mucus: Your Fertile (Mucus) Days

During your preovulatory phase, you're considered fertile on *all* the days you produce CM (whether you observe peak or non-peak mucus). You produce CM under the influence of estrogen as you approach ovulation. If you track your cycles, you'll typically observe a combination of both peak and non-peak mucus during this phase. You already know that one of the ways your mucus keeps sperm alive is by having the perfect pH level for them to thrive in — but that's just the tip of the iceberg. As we'll explore later in this chapter, E-type mucus can be further broken down into three subcategories: S (*sperm-transmission*), L (*locking-in*), and P (*peak*) mucus. Together these three types of mucus play a key role in ensuring that only the best sperm make it through.[33]

Non-peak mucus

When you check for CM each day, you'll want to pay attention to what's called *the point of change*. For many women this happens when they first begin to observe non-peak mucus in their menstrual cycle. The point of change is another way of referring to the first day you see something different than what you saw before. You may notice that you have several dry days after your period, and then, all of a sudden, you notice a shift and start to observe CM (refer back to Figure 3–4). Perhaps you went from having no mucus to seeing mucus on the toilet paper when you wipe yourself. As you move into your fertile window, it's common to see non-peak mucus before you start to see peak mucus (though many women go straight from dry days to peak mucus). The point of change represents a shift from the infertile phase of your cycle to your fertile phase.

When you start to see CM, you know your body is gearing up toward ovulation. This change is triggered by the rise in your estrogen levels as you approach ovulation. As your estrogen levels rise, your cervix starts producing E-type CM, which promptly loosens and dissolves your G-type mucus plug, marking the beginning of your fertile window.[34] As your mucus plug dissolves, you may start to see CM that looks white and creamy; or you may start observing peak mucus right off the bat.

The most important thing to remember about non-peak mucus is that it's fertile. Sperm can survive for several days in non-peak mucus and go on to fertilize an egg when you ovulate — just like they would in peak mucus.[35] When you start to see non-peak mucus, know that your cervix is officially open for business and you are fertile.

Peak mucus

As your estrogen levels continue to rise, you'll notice that your creamy, white non-peak mucus changes to clear, stretchy, and/or lubricative peak mucus (refer back to Figure 3–4). As you approach ovulation, the consistency of your CM changes from thick and viscous to thin and watery. Your CM is comprised of over 90 percent water, and during your fertile window the water content of your mucus can rise as high as 99 percent.[36] Since peak mucus is produced in response to rising estrogen levels, you typically begin to observe it as you get closer to ovulation.

Keep in mind that not every woman will experience an abundance of clear mucus that she can pick up and stretch between her fingers. Many women don't produce a significant amount of peak mucus when they ovulate, but most women will experience a lubricative sensation (and possibly a sensation of wetness) as they approach ovulation.

How Does Cervical Mucus Help Make a Baby?

If you're interested in nerding out on CM for a minute, this section is for you! CM is nothing short of magical, and you should know about all of the ways that your mucus helps you make babies! (If you're not going for babies now, though, this section is still relevant.) Not only does your CM keep sperm alive for up to 5 days, but it carefully filters out defective sperm, prepares them for fertilization, and rapidly transports the best sperm directly into your fallopian tubes when the time is right.

E-type mucus can be broken down into three subcategories:

1. S ("*sperm-transmission*" or "*string*") mucus,
2. L ("*locking-in*" or "*loaf*") mucus, and
3. P ("*peak*" or "*push*") mucus.

Keep in mind that you'll never observe any of these mucus types separately. Whenever you observe CM it's made from a combination of these three main subtypes (and possibly some G-type mucus and vaginal cell slough mixed in for good measure — particularly on the days you observe non-peak mucus).

Erik Odeblad, PhD, was the first to identify and categorize the different types of CM covered in this chapter. His extensive research into CM forms the basis of fertility awareness-based methods as we know them today. He identified that there are different crypts within the cervical canal that produce different types of mucus under the influence of both estrogen and progesterone.[37]

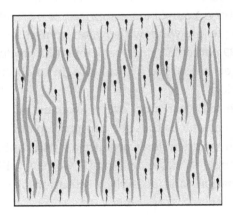

Figure 3–11: S mucus. The pathway for sperm

Sperm-transmission or string (S) mucus gets its name for two reasons: the first is the ability of S mucus to rapidly transport sperm into your cervical crypts; the second is the string-like structures in S mucus that facilitate sperm transport.[38] S mucus has a thin, watery consistency that makes it easy for sperm to swim through, and if you were to look at S mucus under a microscope you'd notice that it forms a network of parallel fibres or channels (see Figure 3–11).[39] These channels create a pathway for sperm to quickly travel through your mucus to your cervical crypts and then onward into your uterus and fallopian tubes. Studies have demonstrated that sperm can make their way into the uterus and fallopian tubes within as little as one minute after ejaculation (or insemination).[40] S mucus (in combination with L mucus) is what gives peak mucus its ability to form a thread between your fingers, and an increase in S mucus production is what first causes you to start feeling a lubricative sensation when you wipe yourself.

Peak or push (P) mucus gets its name because it works together with L mucus to dissolve your mucus plug and initiate your CM production at the beginning of your fertile window. In addition to initiating the flow of CM, your P mucus production rises just before ovulation and changes the quality of your mucus. P mucus contributes to the extremely lubricative sensation you feel on your days of peak mucus when wiping after using the bathroom.[41] P mucus also plays a role in pushing sperm out of the cervical crypts and into the uterine cavity shortly before ovulation (see Figure 3–12).

As I've mentioned, one of the roles of S mucus is to rapidly shuttle the sperm into your cervical crypts, where they can remain for several days before ovulation. As Hanna Klaus, MD, states in a publication released by the Natural Family Planning Center of Washington, DC, "[P mucus] serves to open the barriers at the mouths of the S crypts to release the sperm at the time of ovulation."[42]

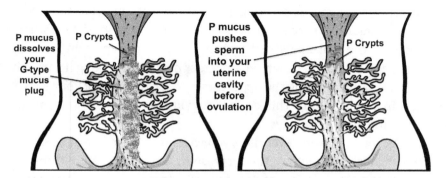

Figure 3-12: P mucus. This image depicts the actions of P mucus dissolving the G-type mucus plug and pushing sperm into the uterine cavity before ovulation.

Your cervix is basically a bed and breakfast for sperm! Not only do your cervical crypts produce different types of CM, they also act as a reservoir for sperm, holding them inside for several days before ovulation.[43] With the help of your P mucus, your cervical crypts gradually release sperm into your uterus and fallopian tubes shortly before ovulation to ensure they are ready and waiting for their chance to fertilize the egg when it arrives on the scene.

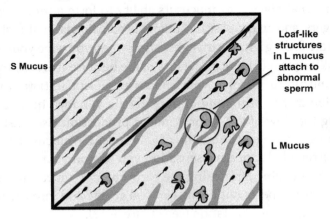

Figure 3–13: L mucus. This image shows the action of L mucus. The loaf-like structures in L mucus attach to abnormal sperm and prevent them from having an opportunity to fertilize an egg (not to scale).

Locking-in or loaf (L) mucus, on the other hand, is not as thin and watery as S and P. L mucus gets its name from the loaf-like structures that prevent abnormal sperm from getting through (see Figure 3–13).[44] L mucus serves as a barrier to abnormal sperm on two important fronts: firstly, L mucus has a thicker consistency compared to S and P mucus, making it harder for abnormal sperm to swim through, and secondly, the loaf-like structures in L mucus attach to malformed sperm and lock them in, which prevents them from making it through your mucus and getting the opportunity to fertilize one of your eggs.[45] Amazing, right? I often think of it like a video game, and your L mucus is fighting off the bad guys.

As your estrogen level rises, your mucus becomes clear, stretchy, and/or lubricative due to the increase in E-type (S, L, and P) mucus production. On your days of peak mucus, estrogen triggers your cervix to produce *more* S and P.[46] As you approach ovulation, your CM is comprised of 95 to 99 percent E-type mucus with only 2 to 5 percent

G-type mucus, giving your mucus its peak mucus qualities.[47] This means that non-peak mucus contains a higher percentage of G-type mucus (and vaginal cell slough), and that's what gives non-peak mucus its creamy quality. As you can see, cervical mucus is amazing! It's essential for optimal fertility and plays a key role in conception. This is why understanding your mucus is central to using FA. Now that we've established how important your CM is, let's explore some of the factors that can have a negative impact on your mucus production.

How Does My Cervical Mucus Change with Age?

The fewer days of CM you have each cycle, the fewer days you have to work with when you're trying to conceive. What if you only produced CM on 1 or 2 days of your cycle? Theoretically, you'd have to time sex on one of those days to conceive. Even if you had sex 5 days per week for an entire month, if you didn't hit one of those days of mucus, you would dramatically reduce your chances of conception.

What does this have to do with your age? Ever wonder why 18-year-olds get pregnant so easily when they're not even trying? One of the reasons is that at puberty you start out with a large number of S cervical crypts. S mucus is responsible for much of the clear, stretchy, and/or lubricative qualities of peak mucus. Since you have so many S crypts in your early teenage years, you produce significantly more peak-quality mucus in your late teens and early twenties.[48] As you age, your S crypts are gradually replaced by L, L are replaced by G, and over time you'll produce less mucus during your cycle.[49]

If you could observe your mucus patterns from your late teens through your twenties, thirties, and forties, you would notice a steady and gradual decline in the amount of peak mucus you produce as well as a reduction in the number of days that you notice it. Up until about age 22, you can expect to have about 7.5 days of mucus (on average) during your cycle, compared to 6 days from about age 23 to 37, and 3.5 days from about age 38 to 47.[50] In my client work this holds true. It's not uncommon for women in their late thirties and early forties to see only 1 to 3 days of mucus leading up to ovulation.

The implications of this are far beyond anything you or I were ever taught about our bodies in school. Knowing how to identify your fertile days is especially important as you get older. For information about improving CM production and restoring cervical health, see Chapter 11.

In the next chapter we'll put it all together and talk about the parameters of a healthy cycle from start to finish.

Summary

- CM is the key to understanding your fertility as it relates to your menstrual cycle.
- CM can keep sperm alive for up to 5 days as you approach ovulation.
- On average, women produce CM on about 2 to 7 days of their cycle — this is called the fertile window.
- Peak mucus is clear, stretchy, and/or lubricative, similar to the quality of raw egg whites, and non-peak mucus looks like creamy hand lotion. Your peak mucus is optimal for conception, although both peak and non-peak mucus are considered fertile.
- Monitoring your mucus patterns is helpful when using FA for conception, birth control, confirming ovulation, and monitoring your menstrual cycle health.
- There are five main types of vaginal discharge you should be aware of: CM, vaginal cell slough, arousal fluid, discharge related to infections, and discharge related to abnormal cervical cells.
- You produce CM in response to changing levels of estrogen and progesterone throughout your cycle.
- You produce both peak and non-peak CM on your fertile days as you approach ovulation (E-type mucus).
- Your cervix is filled with a mucus plug on your dry, infertile days (G-type mucus).
- Your CM contains channels for sperm to swim through that also filter out abnormal sperm, prepare them for fertilization, and guide them to your fallopian tubes just in time for ovulation.
- Your CM production gradually declines with age.

Chapter 4
What Does a Healthy Menstrual Cycle Look Like?

"How often have you heard that a menstrual cycle should be 28 days and that ovulation usually occurs on Day 14? This is a myth, pure and simple."

— Toni Weschler, *Taking Charge of Your Fertility*

Most women learn that a normal menstrual cycle is *always* 28 days long and ovulation *always* happens on day 14; however, there are exactly *zero* women on planet earth who have 28-day cycles throughout their entire reproductive lives.[1] Virtually all women *regularly* experience minor fluctuations in the length of their cycles — but there's much more to your menstrual cycle than its length. In fact, your cycle length is only one of several indicators that tell us if your cycle is healthy and normal.

In a 1995 paper published in *Epidemiologic Reviews*, the authors state:

The medical textbook image of the 28-day menstrual cycle is an idealized model of the hormonal changes that occur during an ovulatory menstrual cycle. The majority of women, however, neither consistently experience 28-day cycles nor ovulate on day 14. Most women experience numerous changes in their menstrual cycle patterns during their reproductive life.[2]

One of the largest studies conducted on the menstrual cycle was published in 1967 in the *International Journal of Fertility* by Alan Treloar and his colleagues.[3] This study examined the menstrual cycles of over 2700 women who, when added together, provided data for over a quarter of a million menstrual cycles over a 30-year period. They found that the length of the menstrual cycle varied the most during the first 5 to 7 years after *menarche* (a woman's first period) and the 10 years before *menopause* (a woman's last period). This led the authors of the study to identify three distinct phases of a woman's reproductive life: postmenarche, middle life, and premenopause (see Figure 4–1).

	Postmenarche	Middle life	Premenopause
Average Cycle Length	32 days	29 days	33 days
Range	23–90 days	23–38 days	22–148 days

Figure 4–1: Variation in menstrual cycle length

A distinct phase of cycle maturation follows a woman's first period. The menstrual cycle takes several years to mature and fall into a normal cyclical pattern. Once this maturation occurs, women typically experience fewer menstrual cycle fluctuations during their middle life phase. There's also a distinct phase leading up to menopause in which the menstrual cycle begins to wind down (commonly referred to as perimenopause or premenopause); this phase is characterized by significant fluctuations in the menstrual cycle.

Put into more practical terms, girls are more likely to have longer and more varied cycles during the first few years of menstruation. The data collected from this study demonstrates that it may take up to seven years before the menstrual cycle shifts into a regular and robust pattern. During the 10-year phase leading up to menopause, it's not uncommon for women to ovulate earlier, resulting in shorter menstrual cycles, especially during the beginning of this phase. However, as menopause approaches, it's not uncommon for this trend to shift. Many women find that their cycles begin to lengthen, resulting in fewer and fewer menstrual periods each year — especially during the last 1 to 2 years before their cycles stop altogether.[4] That explains why the cycle lengths observed in this study ranged from 22 to 148 days for women during the 10 years before menopause.

It's worth noting that the data for this study was collected between 1934 and 1961; the study ended just as the first birth control pill was put on the market in 1960. The results of this study therefore show the typical menstrual cycle variability of women with "virgin cycles" — a phrase I use to describe menstrual cycles that have never been altered with artificial hormones. As we'll cover more in Chapters 7 and 8, hormonal contraceptive (HC) use creates an additional phase of menstrual cycle irregularity during the one to two years after you stop taking them.

Even though Treloar and his colleagues demonstrated that menstrual cycle variation is normal, the study also found that the menstrual cycle stays relatively constant for the majority of a woman's reproductive life. Outside of the normal variation we would expect toward the beginning and end of a woman's reproductive years (and the variation women experience related to HC use), the menstrual cycle tends to hover somewhere around 29 days.

The "Perfect" Cycle?

Believe me, there's no such thing as a perfect period or a perfect menstrual cycle. Every woman's cycle is unique and reflects her health, fertility, and life situation. I've worked with women who have unhealthy 28-day cycles and women who have healthy 33-day cycles.

When you think of your menstrual cycle as the fifth vital sign of your health and fertility, you can appreciate that your cycle will respond in times of stress, illness, and a number of other situations we'll cover throughout the book — a certain degree of fluctuation is normal from cycle to cycle. I invite you to look at your menstrual cycle patterns as information, and I encourage you to take the role of journalist or objective observer when you start monitoring your cycles. Record what you see without jumping to conclusions or making judgments. Your menstrual cycle is simply responding to its environment.

For instance, your cycles will look very different if you've recently come off HCs. Since your body can't speak to you using words, it must find other ways to communicate. Your menstrual cycle is a vital sign — one that responds to what's happening in your life. If you give up caffeine for a while, or quit a high-stress job, you'll see how these changes affect your cycle. The hard part is to remember that when your cycles fall outside the normal range, your body isn't "broken" — your cycle is simply giving you information about your fertility and your overall health. It's your very own personalized early warning system. It's your fifth vital sign in action.

Does My Cycle Have to Be 28 Days to Be Normal?

By now you know the answer to this question. Even if you didn't know much about your menstrual cycle before picking up this book, the one thing you've probably heard is that your cycles are supposed to be 28 days long. From that perspective, any deviation from 28 days would mean your cycles are irregular. However, as we just covered, the one thing you can count on is some degree of variation in the length of your menstrual cycle over the course of your reproductive life. HCs have distorted our view of the menstrual cycle. Our natural and variable menstrual cycle pattern has been both literally and figuratively replaced by an artificial (and largely mechanistic) 28-day cycle. But since you're a real person (and not a computer program), such a restrictive model does not accurately reflect the normal pattern and flow of your menstrual cycle throughout your reproductive life (not to mention that the length of your cycle is not the only factor that helps determine if your cycles are normal and healthy).

A normal menstrual cycle ranges in length from 24 to 35 days with an average length of 29 days.[5] Some degree of variation from cycle to cycle, and from woman to woman, is normal, as is a greater degree of variation postmenarche and premenopause. The concept of a regular 28-day cycle doesn't consider the way your body responds to external factors like stress, illness, travel, and other important life events.

A normal cycle length can vary by up to 8 days over the course of a year, which means that a cycle that fluctuates between 27 and 34 days in length is not irregular.[6] What's problematic are cycles that regularly fall outside the 24- to 35-day range or vary in length by more than 8 days from cycle to cycle. I want to stress the word *regularly* in that statement because everyone has an outlier every now and then. If your cycles are fairly consistent, but one month your cycle is way off, I wouldn't assume there's a huge problem. One key indicator that we look for is a pattern. If there's something to be worried about, it will regularly show up in your cycles.

How Do I Know If My Cycle Is Irregular?

Many women mistakenly think their cycles are irregular when they're not, so let's define what an irregular cycle really is. If your cycle, for example, is 24 days one month, 42 days the next, and then you don't have another period for 60 days, that's irregular. If you have fewer than 9 periods per year, that's also irregular. Your cycle is not irregular unless you experience fluctuations of more than 8 days from cycle to cycle. Significant variations in cycle length occur when ovulation is delayed. Consistently irregular cycles should be monitored closely, as this is often an early sign of a deeper issue (see Chapter 6).

What Does a Normal Cycle Look Like?

Several aspects of the menstrual cycle will help to determine if your cycle is normal and healthy including your period, the total length of your cycle, your cervical mucus (CM) patterns, ovulation, and the length of your luteal phase. The parameters of a normal menstrual cycle are defined below. I've derived these values from a number of different studies conducted on the menstrual cycle; the common thread among these studies is some degree of variation between women and their menstrual cycles (see Figure 4–2).

Your menstrual cycle has two main phases:

1. The *preovulatory (follicular)* phase, and
2. The *postovulatory (luteal)* phase.

Event	Normal Range	Average
Menstrual Cycle	24–35 days	29 days
Period	3–7 days	5 days
Preovulatory Phase	10–23 days	15 days
Preovulatory Dry Days	2–10 days	6 days
Fertile Window	2–7 days	5 days
Ovulation	Days 10–23	Days 15–16
Postovulatory Phase	10–16 days	13 days

Figure 4-2: Parameters of a normal menstrual cycle[7]

The preovulatory (follicular) phase

Your preovulatory phase begins with your period and ends when you ovulate. The normal length of the preovulatory phase ranges from 10 to 23 days with an average length of 15 days.[8] You'll remember from the two previous chapters that estrogen stimulates your CM production and the growth of your endometrial lining as you approach ovulation (refer back to Figure 3–8 on page 35).

The first day of your period is day 1 of your menstrual cycle. A normal period lasts 3 to 7 days (the average is 5 days); after your period stops, expect to see, on average, 6 dry days before you move into your fertile window and start to see CM.[9] Expect 2 to 7 days of CM with at least 1 day of peak mucus leading up to ovulation (see Figure 4–3).[10]

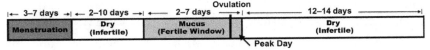

Figure 4–3: Normal parameters of the menstrual cycle

When menstrual cycles are on the shorter end of normal, it's not uncommon to have *zero* dry days leading up to ovulation. Some women may start observing CM immediately after their period stops, and others will even notice mucus during the last days of their period. The key to using fertility awareness (FA) effectively is to start observing your mucus patterns on a daily basis. Then you'll always know where you are in your cycle regardless of how early or late your CM shows up.

Ovulation is an essential part of a healthy menstrual cycle, and a healthy cycle will display clear signs of ovulation between days 10 and 23.[11] One study measured 1060 menstrual cycles in 141 women and found that only 25 percent of the participants experienced their fertile window between days 10 and 17 of their cycles.[12] The idea that every woman regularly ovulates on day 14 can be harmful, especially for women who are trying to conceive and attempt to time sex on day 14 to optimize their chances. If you happen to ovulate early or late in your cycle, timing sex based on a specific date can unintentionally prevent conception.

Since the date of ovulation isn't constant from cycle to cycle, it's the length of your preovulatory phase that determines if your cycle will be long or short. As you can see in Figure 4–4, the preovulatory phase is variable, but the postovulatory phase remains fairly constant. It's the date of ovulation that shifts from cycle to cycle, and any variability in the length of your cycle is based on how late in your cycle you ovulated. What this means for you is that if you start tracking your menstrual cycles and you notice that your luteal phase is about 12 days long, you'll find that it's always about 12 days long regardless of any fluctuations in the total length of your cycle.

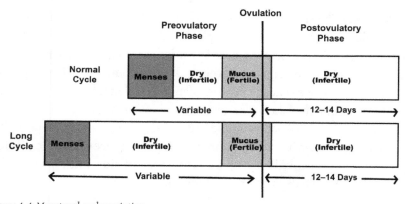

Figure 4-4: Menstrual cycle variation

The postovulatory (luteal) phase

The postovulatory phase begins the day after ovulation and ends the day before your next period starts. As we discussed above, the luteal phase is much more consistent than the follicular phase — whether your cycle is 26, 32, or 45 days, your luteal phase will always be about the same length.

The luteal phase normally lasts 12 to 14 days, with an average length of 13 days (but it can range from 10 to 16 days in length — refer back to Figure 4-2).[13] Its length is determined by the life cycle of your corpus luteum and its ability to produce adequate amounts of progesterone. Progesterone transforms the uterine lining and makes it receptive to a fertilized egg when it's time for implantation (refer back to Chapter 2). In addition to the role progesterone plays in preparing the endometrium for implantation, you need progesterone to maintain your endometrial lining throughout your luteal phase.

Imagine a plastic bag full of heavy groceries bulging at the seams. All of a sudden, the bag bursts open, spilling your precious items. That's what it's like to have low progesterone, since progesterone is what gives the bag its strength. Progesterone holds up your uterine lining and prevents it from shedding long enough to allow for implantation. When your progesterone is low, you're more likely to experience premenstrual spotting and/or have a short luteal phase.[14] This is one of the reasons we want to pay close attention to the length of your luteal phase.

Progesterone levels peak in the middle of the luteal phase; you'll also notice estrogen has a second peak at around the same time (see Figure 4–5). These peaks coincide with the relatively small window when a fertilized egg is able to implant into your endometrial lining. Implantation is a tightly regulated process that begins 7 to 10 days after ovulation and takes approximately 7 days to complete.[15] If you do the math, you'll notice that the process of implantation takes approximately the same number of days you'd expect to have in a normal luteal phase. What this means for women who are actively trying to conceive is that the length of their luteal phase matters. If you've recently come off HCs, your luteal phase is likely to be on the short side until your cycles normalize.[16] We'll expand on this more in Chapter 8.

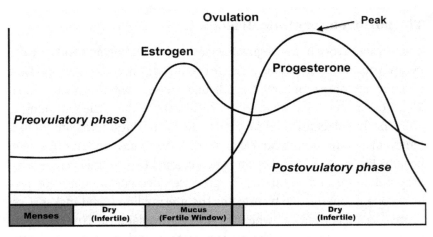

Figure 4–5: Hormonal peaks in the reproductive cycle

It's also possible, however, for your luteal phase to be too long. If it's often longer than 16 days (and you're definitely not pregnant), you should consider having an ultrasound (or a series of ultrasounds) to determine if ovulation is happening normally. For instance, with luteinized unruptured follicle (LUF) syndrome, a follicle develops during the preovulatory phase but does not actually release an egg. Even though the ovary does not release an egg, the unruptured follicle begins producing progesterone, which creates a fairly normal-looking cycle. LUF has been investigated as one of the possible causes of unexplained infertility.[17]

The Menstrual Cycle, Light Exposure, and the Moon

One of the factors that affects menstrual cycle length is light exposure, and light exposure also has an impact on circadian rhythms. Before the advent of artificial light, it was common for women to cycle with the moon. Ovulation would occur more frequently around the full moon, and menstruation would follow two weeks later during the new moon. This relationship between the moon and the menstrual cycle is still present in modern culture — menstruation is often referred to as a woman's "moon time." It's also worth noting that the average length of the menstrual cycle is 29 days, which corresponds to the length of the lunar cycle.[18]

Although every woman's cycle is unique, one study of 826 women aged 16 to 25 showed that 28.3 percent of the women menstruated around the new moon — a coincidence worth noting.[19] The possible connection between the length of the menstrual cycle and the lunar cycle has led to the theory that ovulation is related to light exposure.

A number of studies have been conducted to determine if mid-cycle light exposure could shorten the menstrual cycle length of women with long and irregular cycles.[20] The women in these studies were instructed to sleep with a light on during days 13 to 17 of their menstrual cycles as a way of simulating natural moonlight around the presumed time of ovulation. What two of these studies found is that mid-cycle light exposure decreased the average menstrual cycle length of the study participants from about 45 to 33 days.[21] These results demonstrate that light exposure has a direct impact on the menstrual cycle — something we'll cover in more detail in Chapter 13.

Stress and Your Menstrual Cycle

When you begin to track your cycles, you'll notice that a number of factors can delay ovulation, most noticeably stress, illness, and travel. Even though you may find it incredibly inconvenient when you don't ovulate "on time," it's helpful to consider that your ovaries are incredibly intelligent and will protect you from the added stress of a potential pregnancy during an already stressful time. In a research study of 166 female college students, stress was found to significantly increase the likelihood of having a long menstrual cycle (defined as 43 days or more).[22] Women who experienced higher levels of perceived stress due to major life events (e.g., starting a new job or getting married) and had multiple demands on their time (e.g., family responsibilities, final exams, work deadlines) were up to twice as likely to have long cycles compared to women who did not report significant stressors during their cycles.

Just like any of your other vital signs, your menstrual cycle will respond to stress in real time, whether it's chronic, acute, or situational. I've supported women who've experienced stressful events that you may not automatically think of as stressful (e.g., a vacation, a wedding, or a promotion at work) as well as events we more commonly recognize as stressful (e.g., death in the family or termination of employment). For instance, many women notice that they ovulate later than normal in their cycles when they travel during their preovulatory phase. These women have also noticed that their luteal phase is a day or two shorter than normal, or they have a few days of spotting leading up to their period, when they experience stressful events *after* ovulation.

I'd like to share Joy's story with you to illustrate the most common way I've found that stress affects the cycle. In Joy's menstrual cycle chart (Figure 4-6), you'll see that she had her period on days 1 through 7, and her period was followed by several dry days on days 8 through 14.

On day 15, she began seeing CM, and it looked as though she was approaching ovulation. On day 18, her mucus went away, and she had several more dry days. On day 22, her mucus returned, and she ovulated around day 23, which is confirmed by a sustained increase in her basal body temperature (BBT) — see Chapter 5. Her luteal phase was 11 days, and she started her period on what would have been day 35.

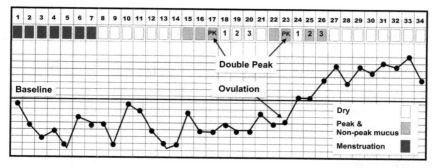

Figure 4-6: Joy's menstrual cycle chart

The pattern you see in Joy's chart — several days of CM followed by dry days and then a second patch of mucus showing up again — is called a *double peak*. What this pattern shows us is that Joy's body started gearing up to ovulate during the first mucus patch, but then backed off on day 18. In Joy's case, her mucus pattern was stress-related.

Joy brought up this double peak in our session because she wanted to gain some insight into why this might have happened. I asked her to think back to that week and consider if anything out of the ordinary had happened. When she thought back, she realized that she had been in the midst of several days of work-related stress. I asked her if she could tell me more about the situation at work and she remembered that there had been a round of layoffs, which had created tension in the office, and she had found the whole situation extremely stressful.

As you can see from Joy's experience, the impact of stress on the menstrual cycle shows one of the many ways your cycle can be used to monitor your overall health. Delayed ovulation in times of stress is your body's way of protecting you. Most women are genuinely surprised by how responsive their menstrual cycle is to the stressful events in their lives. Whenever I host group classes, there are always plenty of examples of the way stress affects the menstrual cycle among the women in the group. When you think of your menstrual cycle as a vital sign, it makes perfect sense; it also makes it much easier to track and interpret any fluctuations you see. In Joy's case it took a little digging, but she was able to connect a stressful work situation with a very timely delay in her ovulation. When you have this level of understanding about your cycle you're able to move from, "Why is my period so late this month? Am I pregnant?" to, "I ovulated a little later this cycle, so even though my cycle is a bit longer this month I know exactly when my period is coming."

Now that you know what a healthy cycle looks like, we'll move on to FA in the next chapter. There we'll cover how to monitor your cycles by paying attention to the three main fertile signs: CM, BBT, and cervical position.

Summary

- A normal and healthy menstrual cycle ranges in length from 24 to 35 days, with an average length of 29 days.
- Women normally experience a higher degree of menstrual cycle variation during the 5 to 7 years post-menarche and the 10 years before menopause.
- The length of the menstrual cycle is most stable during the middle life phase after the menstrual cycle has matured.
- HCs are associated with a third period of menstrual cycle variation during the 1 to 2 years after discontinuing use.
- Your menstrual cycle is not considered irregular unless its length consistently varies by more than 8 days from cycle to cycle.
- Ovulation does not consistently occur on day 14 of the cycle. Ovulation typically occurs between days 10 and 23 of the cycle, with day 15 being the average.
- Variations in the preovulatory phase determine whether your cycle will be long or short.
- The length of the postovulatory phase normally lasts 12 to 14 days, with an average length of 13 days.
- Light exposure has a known impact on the menstrual cycle, and a small percentage of women regularly cycle with the moon.
- Stress has a direct impact on the menstrual cycle by delaying ovulation in the preovulatory phase or shortening the luteal phase.

Chapter 5
What Is Fertility Awareness?

"In order to reclaim our full selves, to integrate each of these aspects through which we pass over the course of our lives, we must first learn to embrace them through our cycles."

— Lucy H. Pearce, *Moon Time*

Fertility awareness (FA) allows you to determine which days of your cycle are fertile and infertile. FA involves tracking your three main fertile signs: cervical mucus (CM), basal body temperature (BBT), and cervical position, and together, these signs help you identify your fertile window. One side benefit of FA is that it has no impact on your fertility. There's no transition period when you're ready to start a family; you simply start having unprotected sex on your fertile days. In that way, FA *preserves* your fertility.

After nearly 20 years of teaching fertility awareness, there are two responses I hear from pretty much every woman I work with:

1. "Why didn't anyone ever tell me about this before?" and
2. "Every woman needs to know this!"

If you're anything like me, the initial excitement you felt when you first discovered FA quickly transformed into a deep sense of anger and frustration. After all, it's not rocket science. Yes, there are complexities, but most women learn to chart within two to three cycles of tracking. The simple concept that CM signifies fertility during the menstrual cycle could easily be taught as a standard part of every sex ed curriculum. As far as I'm concerned, the blatant omission of specific and accurate education about the menstrual cycle, CM, and female fertility is a systematic tool of disempowerment.

We could easily compare the practice of preventing women from developing a complete understanding of their fertility to the historical practice of preventing women from learning to read and write. Even though literacy rates have dramatically increased over the years, two-thirds of the estimated 750 million adults who remain illiterate throughout the world are women.[1]

The global market for oral contraceptives alone is estimated at over $13 billion, and it's expected to rise to over $22.9 billion by the year 2023.[2] In other words, there's a multi*billion*-dollar industry that depends on you *not* fully understanding how your body works.

There's no right birth control option for every woman, but *body literacy is every woman's right*. Body literacy refers to your ability to monitor and understand your signs of fertility.[3] Beyond natural birth control, FA allows you to maintain your natural menstrual cycles over the course of your entire reproductive life and enjoy the health benefits associated with regular ovulation. When you go off track with diet and lifestyle choices (as we all do from time to time), or experience health challenges, you'll see how your cycles respond in real time.

Tracking the Three Main Fertile Signs

There's no one universal fertility awareness-based method. Instead, there are a variety of charting systems and methods of FA tracking that use one or a combination of the main fertile signs: CM, BBT, and cervical position. I teach women to monitor all three fertile signs — often referred to as the *symptothermal method*.

The "sympto" in symptothermal refers to mucus and cervical position, and the "thermal" refers to the thermal shift that occurs after ovulation. One study of 900 women who contributed 17 638 menstrual cycles worth of data found the symptothermal method to be 99.4 percent effective in preventing pregnancy when used correctly.[4] The rate of unintended pregnancy was 0.43 percent for women who abstained from sex during their fertile window and 0.59 percent for women who used barrier methods during their fertile window. In other words, with perfect use, FA results in less than one pregnancy per 100 women per year (though typical use varies widely, from 66.4 percent to 98 percent effectiveness, depending on the user and their chosen method).[5] All of the women in the above study were taught the symptothermal method by qualified instructors.

If you're serious about using FA for birth control, seek support from a qualified instructor. It's possible to learn the basics of charting on your own, but like learning to drive, there are many nuances to learn and a variety of unexpected situations that can arise. Working with a qualified instructor will teach you how to confidently chart your cycles throughout your reproductive life, including times when your cycles aren't regular or predictable.

Cervical Mucus (CM) Charting

CM is the primary sign to watch for, as the presence or absence of mucus helps you identify your fertile window. After all, sperm can't survive without it! Most women find that understanding their CM patterns is the most challenging part of learning FA. Most FA resources contain relatively vague instructions for both observing and recording CM. For instance, many of the available resources don't fully explain how to determine *sensation*. Although most FA resources talk about the significance of dry days, they don't typically describe how to tell the difference between dry, smooth, and lubricative sensations.

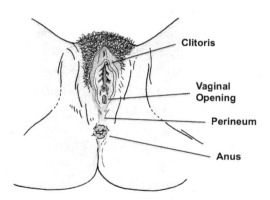

Figure 5-1: The vulva

Sensation is one of the most misunderstood aspects of fertility awareness-based methods. Many women believe that sensation refers to an elusive "feeling" you get as you walk around throughout the day. However, the sensation I'm referring to is much more literal. Sensation refers to the way it feels when you wipe your vulva with toilet paper (see Figure 5–1).[6] The next time you go to the bathroom, I want you to take a piece of toilet paper, fold it flat, and wipe your vulva from front to back. Pay close attention to how it *feels* as you wipe the toilet paper across your perineum (the smooth patch of skin between your vaginal opening and your anus). You'll notice a dry, smooth, or lubricative sensation. Understanding sensation makes it much easier to identify the difference between dry days and mucus days. On your dry days you'll notice that it feels dry or smooth when you wipe, and when you look at the toilet paper there isn't any mucus you can pick up and stretch between your fingers. On your mucus days you'll actually see mucus on the toilet paper that you can stretch between your fingers. Your mucus will fall into one of two categories: peak or non-peak mucus (and *both* peak and non-peak mucus are considered fertile because sperm are able to survive in both types — refer back to Chapter 3).

The key to understanding your mucus observations involves the following three steps:

1. Know the difference between a dry day and a mucus day,
2. Check for mucus regularly throughout the day, and
3. Record what you see.

Know the difference between a dry day and a mucus day

Since the "dry" in dry days refers to the sensation you feel when you wipe yourself, if you're not wiping yourself when you check for mucus, by definition, you will never feel a dry sensation (or have a dry day). Many women check for mucus by inserting their finger into their vagina and running it along their cervix. This is referred to as internal checking. The problem with this way of checking is that your vagina is *never* dry. Whenever you insert your finger into your vagina you'll *always* find moisture, leaving most women at a loss for what it really means to have a dry day. To set the record straight, a dry day is a day when you feel either a dry (or smooth) sensation when you wipe yourself *and* there's nothing on the toilet paper that you can pick up and stretch between your fingers. A mucus day, on the other hand, is a day where you have mucus (either peak or non-peak) on your toilet paper that you can pick up and stretch between your fingers — *or* you may feel a lubricative sensation when you wipe but have no mucus you can stretch between your fingers. Not all women observe a large amount of clear and stretchy mucus on their mucus days, but a lubricative sensation (alone) lets you know it's a fertile (mucus) day.

Check for mucus frequently throughout the day

When you establish the habit of checking for mucus frequently throughout the day, it quickly becomes second nature. In his book *The Power of Habit*, Charles Duhigg writes about how habits form and what makes them stick. One of the quickest ways to establish a new habit is to add it to an already established habit. With that in mind, I want you to start wiping yourself — on purpose — both before *and* after you go to the bathroom. You already wipe yourself when you go to the bathroom; you're simply adding the new habit of checking for mucus to what you already do.

Record what you see

FA only works when you make your daily observations — and then record them. Simply observing your mucus patterns won't help you! You need a system to record your data. To illustrate this point, I have a question for you: Do you remember what you had for dinner last Tuesday? Even if by some miracle you remember what you ate, you probably had to do some serious mental gymnastics to figure it out. However, if you had a system for keeping track of your meals, you'd be able to pull it up instantly. This is what we're going for with your charting records.

Lots of different charting apps are available nowadays. Most use algorithms that estimate your fertile window based on your previous cycles. When you rely on an app to tell you when you're in your fertile window, you're using a modern-day version of the rhythm method (explained later in this chapter). A number of apps give you the ability to turn off the prediction settings, and those are the ones to look for. If apps aren't your thing, use paper charts instead (see the *Fertility Awareness Mastery Charting Workbook* in the resources section at the end of the book). Personally, I'm a paper-charting girl at heart. I keep my charting book on my nightstand as a reminder to record my fertile signs every night.

When you use paper charts, or apps that don't pre-fill any information automatically, you can learn to chart without any outside influences, which prevents unnecessary confusion. You have to decide what you saw, know how to classify it, and figure out where to put it on your chart. The moment an app starts filling in information for you, you'll start second guessing yourself. If you're more of a visual person, head over to thefifthvitalsignbook.com/bonuses to access a free training video I've put together that demonstrates how to check and chart your cervical mucus.

How do I confirm ovulation with my cervical mucus?

You produce CM as you approach ovulation, but after ovulation your progesterone levels rise and suppress further mucus production. To confirm ovulation, you must first identify your peak day (the last day of your cycle that you observe mucus that is clear, stretchy, and/or lubricative — see Chapter 3). You can't identify your peak day until the day afterwards. You'll notice a clear and obvious change from peak mucus to either non-peak or dry. To confirm ovulation, wait three full days after your peak day to ensure your mucus has dried up. The clear and sustained shift from mucus days to dry days confirms ovulation. With that said, you'll benefit from cross-checking your mucus changes with your BBT.

Basal Body Temperature (BBT) Charting

Not every method of FA recommends BBT charting, but it's an extremely helpful way to confirm ovulation. BBT is especially valuable when you're new to charting and haven't yet learned to understand your CM patterns.

BBT is a measure of your resting (or baseline) metabolism. Think of your metabolism as a measure of how efficiently your body transforms raw materials (protein, fat, and carbohydrates) into the vital energy you need to thrive, i.e., your rate of energy expenditure.[7] When you measure your BBT each morning (and plot it on a graph), you'll notice a clear difference between your preovulatory and postovulatory temperatures (see Figure 5–2). Progesterone has a thermogenic effect on the body (meaning it increases body temperature). Your progesterone level rises after ovulation, and this causes your BBT to rise and remain high for the rest of your cycle. This is called a *sustained thermal shift*.

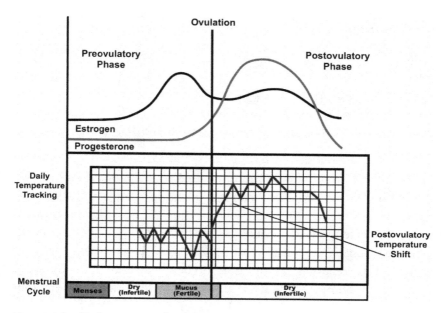

Figure 5-2: Basal body temperature (BBT) charting

This shift in temperature is one of the ways your body prepares for pregnancy. Similar to the way a mother hen sits on her eggs to keep them warm, your body temperature increases to keep *your* eggs warm during the second half of your cycle. This effect continues through pregnancy due to the sustained increase in progesterone. By the time you reach full gestation at 40 weeks, your progesterone levels are more than 10 times the amount you produce during a normal cycle.[8] For this reason, 18 high temperatures after ovulation is an early sign of pregnancy. If you're not pregnant, your temperatures will drop back down 12 to 14 days after your thermal shift, and your period will start.

The simplest way to measure your BBT is to take your temperature each morning before you get out of bed. Tracking CM and BBT together increase the effectiveness of FA. You can only confirm ovulation when these signs line up (see Chapter 10). You'll appreciate BBT for its two main functions: confirming ovulation and helping you predict when your period is coming. Since your sustained thermal shift happens *after* ovulation, BBT can only help you confirm ovulation, *not* predict it. BBT helps you predict when your period is coming, because the number of days between ovulation and your period stays fairly constant. Once you know how long your luteal phase is, you can predict your period within a day or so every time. Keep in mind that although BBT helps you confirm ovulation, it doesn't confirm if ovulation is happening *normally*. This can only be done via ultrasound — see the section about luteinized unruptured follicle syndrome (LUF) in Chapter 4.

How do I get an accurate temperature reading?

You'll need a basal body thermometer that measures to two decimal places (e.g., 97.62 °F). Basic thermometers start at about $20 and full-on fertility recording devices can cost upwards of $400. It really comes down to preference. You may want a thermometer that saves your most recent temperature readings, one that switches between Celsius and Fahrenheit, one that has a backlight so you can see your temperature readings in the dark, or one that automatically syncs with your phone so you don't have to manually enter your temperature readings each day. However, none of these features are absolutely necessary. The most important part of charting your temperatures is simply getting started. Go online (or go to your local drugstore), find a basic thermometer, and get on with it. You can always buy a fancy thermometer later on if you decide you need one.

Take your temperature from one of three locations: orally, vaginally, or axillary (under your arm). Most women measure their temperature orally, so if you're unsure, start there, and follow these three steps to get an accurate reading:

1. Take your temperature first thing in the morning *before* you get out of bed each day, after a minimum of five hours of consecutive sleep   For an accurate measure of your resting metabolism, you need to allow enough time for your body to "reset" itself. The best time to take your BBT is right after you wake up in the morning after you've slept for at least five consecutive hours.[9] If you jump out of bed and walk around before you take your temperature, you won't get an accurate reading. Try to leave your thermometer on your nightstand, or place it on top of your alarm clock (or phone!) to remind you to take your temperature before you get out of bed.

2. Leave your thermometer in place for 10 minutes before pushing the button   Most of my clients want to skip this step when I first introduce it! Unfortunately, it makes a big difference. When you leave your thermometer in place for 10 minutes before taking your temperature, you're allowing sufficient time for the thermometer to warm up and for the temperature reading to stabilize. When you use a digital thermometer it typically beeps within 10 seconds. However, if you were to take your temperature three times in a row, you'd likely get three different readings. After a full cycle of taking their temperature this way (commonly called temping), my clients consistently (albeit reluctantly) admit that their temperatures are more stable, with far fewer abnormal spikes and dips in their charts.

3. Take your temperature around the same time every morning
Your BBT increases with every additional 30 minutes you sleep. If you wake up at 6 a.m. one morning and 10 a.m. the next, you'll notice a difference in your temperature. However, most people don't wake up at exactly the same time each day. From a practical standpoint, it's more important to get a good night's sleep than it is to wake up extra early just to take your temperature (see Chapter 13). For that reason, my approach in this area is relaxed and realistic. Aim to take your temperature at about the same time each day. When you wake up earlier or later, or have a rough night's sleep, simply add a note to your chart with the time you woke up and a short explanation.

Many women have asked me if I think it's worth it to take their temperature when they know it will be disrupted or questionable, and my answer is always *yes*. By taking and recording your temperature when it's not "perfect," you'll learn how your temperature is affected by life's disruptions. That's where the notes come in. By making accurate notes, you'll find it easier to interpret your temperatures when you review your chart, even when some of them are questionable. For the record, there's no such thing as a perfect chart. You'll *always* have one or more questionable temperatures in every cycle you chart. Your job is understanding how to work *with* the anomalies, instead of pretending they're not there, or trying to avoid having them in the first place.

What factors affect my temperature readings?

Knowing what can affect your temperatures makes interpreting your charts much easier. Below is a list of the factors that may affect your BBT:

- Stress
- Illness or fever
- Shift work, night wakings, or restless sleep
- Alcohol consumption the previous day
- Travel, flights, time zone changes, and daylight savings time changes
- Food allergies, seasonal allergies, and food sensitivities
- Taking your temperature after you've gotten out of bed
- Drinking water or tea in the morning before you take your temperature (orally)
- Switching how you take your temperatures (i.e., from oral to underarm or vaginally)
- Switching thermometers mid-cycle

Every woman is different. Some of these factors can dramatically affect one woman's BBT, whereas another woman won't notice much of a change. Your job is to figure out what factors impact *your* temperature so you can accurately interpret your charts.

How do I confirm ovulation with my BBT?

You're looking for a clear and obvious shift between your preovulatory and postovulatory temperatures. Anyone should be able to look at your chart and see the temperature shift from low to high. To confirm ovulation with your BBT you need 3 consecutive (normal) temperatures that are higher than the previous 6 (normal) preovulatory temperatures. *Normal* means temperatures that are not abnormally high due to illness, sleep disturbances, or any of the other factors above. The baseline (also referred to as the coverline) refers to the line that divides the low and high temperatures. You draw the baseline *after* your temperature shift. In Figure 5–3, the preovulatory temperatures are below the baseline, and the postovulatory temperatures are above the baseline. You'll also want to do a *cross check* between your BBT and CM. You can confirm ovulation once you observe 3 normal high temperatures that are higher than the previous 6 — *and* you've observed a clear and obvious shift from mucus days to dry days (see Chapters 3 and 10).

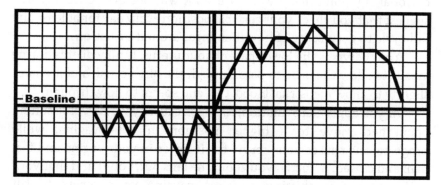

Figure 5–3: BBT chart

What if I can't make sense of my temperatures?

If you're sick for several days and your temperatures are all over the place, you're still looking for three normal temperatures that are higher than your previous six normal preovulatory temps. If your temperatures are questionable (due to the factors listed earlier in this chapter), wait until they stabilize.

Remember these two important steps:

1. When in doubt, wait three days until your observations start to make sense again, and
2. Rely on your cervical mucus observations in the meantime.

If you can't see a clear pattern between your low preovulatory temperatures and your high postovulatory temperatures, assume you haven't ovulated until your temperature pattern becomes clear and consistent. If you're ever unsure of your observations, consider yourself fertile until it all makes sense again (even if it takes several days!). Head over to thefifthvitalsignbook.com/bonuses to access a free training video where I address a variety of common questions about BBT charting.

Cervical Position Charting

Now that you know how to monitor your CM and BBT, it's time to introduce you to your cervix. The position and texture of your cervix both change during your fertile window, and these changes give you another way to identify it. Your cervical position is considered an optional sign, and many women use FA without ever checking it. I suggest that you check your cervical position every day for at least one full cycle to get a sense of how it changes around ovulation.

Your cervix is the lower part of your uterus. It fully dilates during labour to allow the baby to pass through the birth canal, and it dilates slightly to allow menstrual blood, CM, and sperm to flow through.

As you approach ovulation, estrogen causes your cervix to soften, open, and move to a higher position in your vagina, while progesterone causes your cervix to sit lower in your vagina and feel firm and closed. In fact, if you zoom the lens out, you'll find that your entire uterus is shifting position, causing your cervix to tilt backwards or forwards depending on where you are in your cycle. The challenging part about monitoring your cervical position is that not every woman experiences the same level of softness during her fertile window, and it's not always easy to differentiate between "high," "medium," and "low." Fortunately, with a little persistence, you can learn to identify how *your* cervix changes throughout your cycle.

How do I check my cervix?

If you've never checked your cervix before, or if you've always found interpreting your cervical changes confusing, I highly recommend that you commit to checking it every day for one full cycle. Think of it as your own personal *cervical position challenge.* Choose a time of day that makes sense for you and try to stay consistent. Insert your middle finger into your vagina, touch your cervix, and see what it feels like. A good time to check your cervix is when you're in the shower — I mean, you're already naked and your hands are clean, so it makes perfect sense! If you're having a hard time finding your cervix, try squatting while you check, which can make it easier to reach.

The disclaimer is that not a whole lot changes until you approach ovulation. The most common complaint I hear is that it always feels the same! Most women only check their cervix for a few days before giving up because they feel frustrated when they don't notice any changes. This is why you're going to commit to checking your cervix every day for one full cycle.

If your cervix were a newspaper, most days would be pretty boring, with nothing to report. But as soon as you start approaching ovulation, you'd notice a buzz of news. The "breaking news" in your cervical newspaper is the shift that happens after ovulation. After you ovulate, you'll notice a dramatic shift from high, soft, and open to low, firm, and closed. You'll also notice an abrupt change in the tilt of your cervix. You may find that it's tilted backwards, whereas before it was facing down. That's it! That's the big event. After the dramatic shift you'll go back to not really feeling any changes from one day to the next for the remainder of your cycle.

Once you feel the shift, you'll have an additional fertile sign to help you identify your fertile window and confirm ovulation. Trust me, if you stick with it and keep checking, you'll feel the shift!

How do I confirm ovulation with my cervical position?

Cervical position is more of a secondary sign that works best in conjunction with CM and BBT observations. Tracking changes in your cervical position allows you to feel even more confident in your observations by giving you an additional data point. Cervical position is particularly helpful when you can't rely on your temperatures or when you have little to no mucus (but are still ovulating). Knowing all three signs gives you the versatility to use FA through virtually any charting scenario you can think of.

You can confirm ovulation by observing the dramatic and obvious shift that occurs afterwards. After ovulation, your cervix will not revert back to the position it was in during your fertile window. Your cervix will remain low, firm, closed, and tilted for the rest of your cycle. The change in your cervical position will line up with your sustained thermal shift and your clear and obvious shift from mucus days to dry days.

Letting Go of the Rhythm Method

The *rhythm method* involves estimating when ovulation will take place based on the average length of your past cycles. It's based on the assumption that your cycles will always follow the same pattern, and it is therefore restricted to women with exceptionally regular cycles. As defined in a 1996 issue of *Advances in Contraception*,

In the calendar rhythm method, a woman makes an estimate of the days she is fertile based on past menstrual cycle length. She does this with the expectation that the current length of her cycle, and thus the timing of her fertile phase, will not vary greatly from previous menstrual cycles.[10]

However, menstrual cycle variability is the one thing all women have in common. In one study of 2316 women (contributing a total of 30 655 cycles), only 30 percent of the study participants had cycles regular enough to use the rhythm method.[11] As the saying goes, *What do you call couples who use the rhythm method? ... Parents!* This saying exists because, as you already know, the rhythm method is not effective or reliable for the vast majority of women.

Most women who opt for FA vehemently express how different it is from the rhythm method, but it's easy to fall into what I often refer to as "rhythm method thinking." Even though, in theory, you know your cycle may fluctuate from month to month, you're still likely to start anticipating what your cycle will be like based on what you've seen before. I encourage you to become familiar with your patterns — like how long your period typically lasts, what your mucus pattern typically looks like, and the length of your luteal phase — but I strongly discourage you from trying to predict ovulation.

As soon as you start thinking, "I usually ovulate around day 17 so I know I won't be fertile right after my period..." or, "I can't be fertile today because I always ovulate on day 13 or 14..." or, "This can't be CM because I never get it this early..." you've jumped right into rhythm method territory. After a solid 18 years of charting my own cycles and observing thousands of cycle charts from hundreds of women, I can tell you that no matter how regular your cycles are, you can (and will!) experience an early or late ovulation at some point in your reproductive life. This doesn't mean FA won't work for you; it just means you have to let go of the idea that your cycles will always be regular and predictable.

FA charting is similar to mindfulness meditation. With meditation, the whole point is to continue bringing your attention back to the present moment. When you notice that your mind starts wandering to the future (*What am I going to cook for dinner tonight?*)

or the past (*I can't believe I forgot to hand in that report on time at work*), your job is to keep bringing your attention back to your breathing to return to the present moment. In the same way, FA charting is about paying attention to the fertile signs your body is showing to you *today* — not yesterday, not last month, and not tomorrow. Your job is to pay attention to what you see and to record it, even when you're convinced that you shouldn't be seeing it. So even if you see CM on day 6 of your cycle and you've never ovulated before day 15, or if you "always" ovulate on day 14, but you're on day 21 of your cycle and your temperatures haven't shifted yet, your job is to make your observations objectively and record them accurately — *especially* when they don't follow the normal pattern. In order to do this, you have to stay in the present moment and record your observations one day at a time, regardless of what happened last cycle or what you think should be happening this cycle. Only then can you determine whether you're fertile or not each day and truly use this method effectively.

My mentor, Rose Yewchuk, has a great analogy for it; she compares trying to predict ovulation to relying on a long-range weather forecast. You can either look at the forecast for the week and try to figure out if it's going to rain, or you can step outside and see if it's raining. FA allows you to step outside and see if it's actually raining *right now*, instead of relying on last week's weather forecast. See Chapter 10 for more on using FA for birth control and/or conception.

Summary

- When used for birth control, FA allows you to preserve your fertility while enjoying an effectiveness rate of up to 99.4 percent.
- The symptothermal method of FA charting involves observing CM, BBT, and cervical position.
- To successfully chart your CM, you must know the difference between a mucus day and a dry day, check for mucus regularly, and record what you see.
- To get an accurate BBT reading, you must take your temperature first thing in the morning (after getting enough rest) and note the factors that can affect it.

- Your BBT doesn't help you predict ovulation; instead, it helps you confirm ovulation after the fact.
- Together, your cervical position, CM, and BBT allow you to confidently identify your fertile window and confirm ovulation.
- FA is not the rhythm method. It involves observing and recording your fertile signs each day instead of trying to predict your fertile window based on past cycles.

Chapter 6
Your Menstrual Cycle as a Diagnostic Tool

"The menstrual cycle is a window into the general health and well-being of women, and not just a reproductive event ... It can indicate the status of bone health, heart disease, and ovarian failure, as well as long-term fertility. Therefore, if a woman is not having her period, it is the first sign that something else could be going on."

— Paula Hillard, MD, Professor of Obstetrics and Gynecology, Stanford University School of Medicine

When you first start charting your cycles, your main focus is on mastering the basics. You're learning to interpret your cervical mucus (CM) patterns, take your basal body temperature (BBT), and find your cervix. The learning curve is steep, but with the right instruction, you can become a proficient charter within two to three cycles. For many women, that's when the real challenges begin. Once you've wrapped your head around how to track your cycles, you may find that your cycle doesn't fall within normal parameters.

The underlying health issues that cause menstrual cycle irregularities are extremely complex. It's tempting to think that you can take a few supplements, make a few lifestyle changes, and your cycles will magically return to normal overnight, but that's not often the case. Each of the health challenges I cover in this chapter will require the support of a qualified team of health professionals to fully address. (See Chapter 18 for more on assembling your healthcare team.)

The health challenges we'll cover in this chapter are as follows:

- Thyroid disorders
- Polycystic ovary syndrome (PCOS)
- Hypothalamic amenorrhea (HA)
- Additional health issues that can interfere with your menstrual cycle

Thyroid Disorders

Think of your thyroid as your body's master thermostat: every cell in your body has thyroid receptors, making thyroid hormone crucial for the optimal function of every muscle, organ, and cell in your body. Your thyroid regulates your metabolic rate, and as such, your BBT is highly responsive to changes in thyroid function.[1] When your thyroid is underfunctioning (as is the case in *hypothyroidism*), your BBT will consistently fall below the normal range. Conversely, when your thyroid is overfunctioning (as in *hyperthyroidism*), your temperatures will consistently fall above the normal range.

Thyroid disorders are extremely common — especially in women. Women are anywhere from 5 to 10 times more likely than men to be diagnosed with a thyroid disorder.[2] Hypothyroidism is much more common than hyperthyroidism, and many women with hypothyroidism develop a condition called *Hashimoto's Thyroiditis*.[3] Hashimoto's Thyroiditis is an autoimmune condition characterized by a dysregulation of the immune system, and it is the most common type of thyroid disorder observed in Western nations. When you have Hashimoto's, the immune system launches an attack against your thyroid, resulting in localized inflammation and tissue damage. If your thyroid isn't functioning properly, you may experience a combination of the following symptoms:

- Cold hands and feet
- Cold intolerance
- Dry skin
- Hair loss
- Menstrual cycle irregularities
- Weight gain
- Poor memory

- Poor concentration
- Elevated cholesterol
- Swelling of the thyroid gland (goitre)
- Constipation
- Heart palpitations

Diagnosis

The standard way to diagnose a thyroid disorder involves testing your *thyroid-stimulating hormone* (TSH) level. Unfortunately, practitioners widely disagree on what constitutes a normal result. Although the standard range for TSH levels is 0.4 to 4.5 mIU/L, a growing number of practitioners believe the upper range is too high and should be lowered to 2.5 mIU/L.[4] This is especially important for women of reproductive age, because the top of the normal range *immediately* changes to 2.5 mIU/L when they become pregnant.[5] This would indicate that the standard range is not suitable for identifying *optimal* thyroid function in women. If you suspect you have a thyroid disorder, you may want to request a full thyroid panel, including:

- TSH
- FT_4 (free T_4 - thyroxine)
- FT_3 (free T_3 - triiodothyronine)
- RT_3 (reverse T_3)
- Anti-TPOAb (thyroid peroxidase antibodies)
- Anti-TgAb (thyroglobulin antibodies)

In addition to lab testing, your menstrual cycle provides helpful information about how well your thyroid is functioning. For many women, charting their cycle is what first alerts them to a possible issue with their thyroid. Thyroid dysfunction throws off the menstrual cycle in a number of different ways, and when you know what to look for, it's easier to identify and address earlier in the game.

How do thyroid disorders show up in my menstrual cycle?

Thyroid disorders are often at the root of menstrual cycle irregularities because the menstrual cycle is extremely sensitive to subtle fluctuations in thyroid function. It's safe to say that if your thyroid is off, your menstrual cycle will also be off.

The most common signs of low thyroid function include:

- Preovulatory BBT consistently below 97.5 °F/36.4 °C
- *Oligomenorrhea* — delayed ovulation with cycles longer than 35 days, and/or fewer than nine periods per year[6]
- *Polymenorrhea* — extremely short cycles (approximately 21 days or less)[7]
- *Hypomenorrhea* — extremely short and/or light periods[8]
- *Menorrhagia* — abnormally heavy or prolonged menstrual bleeding[9]
- Abnormal CM patterns (either scant or prolonged)
- Short luteal phase (10 days or less), premenstrual spotting, and/or other signs of low progesterone in the luteal phase[10]

The signs vary from woman to woman, but when you start to see abnormal patterns that persist from cycle to cycle, it should prompt you to investigate further. When you monitor your charts for thyroid health, you get a real-time measure of how effectively your treatment is working. With each new cycle you'll clearly see whether or not there have been any improvements. See Figure 6-1 for an example of how thyroid dysfunction (low metabolism) can show up on a chart.

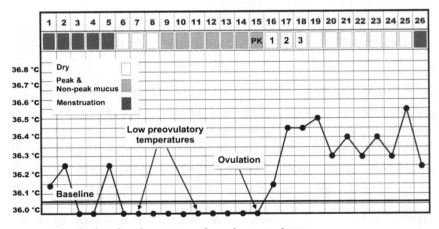

Figure 6-1: Sarah's first chart demonstrates a lower than optimal BBT

Sarah had already been officially diagnosed with hypothyroidism (and she had been taking thyroid medication for some time).

However, as you can see from her charts, her preovulatory temperatures were all extremely low, well below the normal cut-off point of 36.4 °C. Ovulation took place either on day 15 or 16 (confirmed by her sustained thermal shift, and the change in her CM pattern from day 16 onward). Even though her practitioner was satisfied with her lab results, her temperatures demonstrated that her metabolism was considerably lower than optimal.

What causes thyroid disorders?

There are many factors that contribute to thyroid dysfunction. This list is not meant to be exhaustive, but to give you a sense of the variety of factors that can directly and indirectly affect your thyroid health.

- Nutrient deficiencies (including iodine, selenium, zinc, iron, B vitamins, and others)[11]
- Overexposure to toxic halides (specifically fluoride, chloride, and bromide)[12]
- Exposure to environmental toxins (including environmental pollutants, pesticides, xenoestrogens, and radioactive iodine)[13]
- Heavy metal toxicity (lead and mercury)[14]
- Intestinal permeability (leaky gut) and autoimmune disorders
- Consumption of foods you are sensitive or allergic to (the most common food sensitivities include gluten, dairy, eggs, corn, and soy)[15]
- Infections (such as Epstein-Barr, herpes simplex, and rubella)[16]
- Long-term use of hormonal birth control
- Overconsumption of foods that suppress thyroid function (i.e., goitrogens such as soy products and raw cruciferous vegetables such as broccoli and kale)[17]

How does my thyroid work?

Your thyroid gland produces two main thyroid hormones that are responsible for regulating your cell metabolism: *thyroxine* (T_4) and *triiodothyronine* (T_3). Your thyroid produces significantly more T_4 than T_3 (a ratio of about 11:1), but T_3 is the *biologically active* hormone that actually gets into your cells and raises your metabolism.[18] T_4 is considered a *prohormone* because it acts as a precursor to T_3.[19] T_4 exerts very little (if any) direct action on your cell metabolism and must be converted into the active thyroid hormone (T_3) before it can be used.[20] T_3 is several times more potent than T_4 (given that your thyroid hormone receptors are up to 10 times more receptive to it), but only a small percentage of T_3 is secreted directly from your thyroid gland.[21] The vast majority of your T_3 (about 80 to 90 percent) is converted peripherally by different tissues in your body (including your liver, heart, brain, and kidneys) by a group of enzymes called *deiodinases*.[22] These enzymes convert T_4 to T_3 by removing an iodine atom (thus the name de-*iodin*-ase). When you consider that up to 90 percent of your active thyroid hormones are produced by this conversion process, it makes sense that your ability to convert thyroid hormones is crucial for normal cell metabolism. When you are not able to effectively convert T_4 to T_3, your metabolism will be low, and you'll see that reflected in low BBTs on your chart.

Many women with thyroid disorders find that they continue to have symptoms even after their practitioners tell them their lab results are normal. But when you chart your cycles and your BBT is still too low, it's a sign of low metabolism that must be addressed. After all, you're a human being, not a lab test, and it's possible to have poor thyroid function in the face of "normal" lab results.

The standard treatment for hypothyroidism is replacement thyroid hormone in the form of thyroxine (T_4).[23] However, many patients report better results with desiccated thyroid preparations (thyroid replacement hormone that is derived from the thyroid gland of a pig or cow) or treatment with T_3 only.[24] Desiccated thyroid naturally contains a combination of thyroxine (T_4) and triiodothyronine (T_3), and this may be why many patients report feeling better when they take it. However, regardless of which type of hormone replacement therapy you choose, hormone replacement therapy alone does not address any of the underlying nutrient deficiencies or related health conditions that may also impair normal thyroid function.

Thyroid disorders are complex, but it's possible to restore normal thyroid function (and normal menstrual cycle parameters) with a combination of medical care (thyroid hormone replacement when necessary), dietary and lifestyle changes, and supplementation (see Chapter 16).

Polycystic Ovary Syndrome (PCOS)

Polycystic ovary syndrome (PCOS) is a common disorder that causes menstrual cycle disruptions including abnormal patterns of ovulation and irregular cycles. PCOS affects anywhere from 6 to 15 percent of women in developed countries, and over 100 million women worldwide, making it the single most common endocrine disorder in women of reproductive age.[25] Although there's some disagreement as to how PCOS should be diagnosed, PCOS is characterized by a combination of these three symptoms:

1. *Oligomenorrhea or anovulation* — delayed ovulation with cycles longer than 35 days, and/or fewer than nine periods per year;
2. *Hyperandrogenism* — excess androgen[†] production; and
3. *Polycystic ovaries on an ultrasound* — presence of 12 or more follicles on each ovary and/or an increased ovarian volume.[26]

PCOS is considered a syndrome because it presents differently in different women. There's no single diagnostic criterion that all women with PCOS have 100 percent of the time. The Rotterdam Criteria are the most widely used diagnostic criteria to identify and diagnose PCOS. According to these criteria, a woman receives a formal PCOS diagnosis when she has two of the three criteria listed above.[27] However, the Androgen Excess Society has called for PCOS to be identified as a disorder of excess androgen production and has suggested that women *must* show signs of hyperandrogenism along with either of the other two criteria to receive a formal diagnosis.[28]

According to the Androgen Excess Society, 75 percent of women with a clinical diagnosis of PCOS have polycystic ovaries, 60 to 80 percent of PCOS patients have elevated androgen levels, and 75 percent of women diagnosed with PCOS experience ovulatory disturbances.[29] In addition to the three main diagnostic criteria, there are a variety of other symptoms associated with PCOS, including:

- Weight gain/obesity
- Difficulty losing weight

[†] The term *androgen* refers to these "male" hormones: testosterone, androstenedione, and dehydroepiandrosterone (DHEA). Excess androgen production can lead to hirsutism (male-pattern hair growth), acne, and/or androgenic alopecia (male-pattern hair loss).

- Insulin resistance/elevated insulin levels
- Abnormal/unwanted facial/body hair
- Hirsutism (male-pattern hair growth: coarse hair on the face (chin, upper lip), around the nipples, on the chest or stomach, upper arm, thighs, and other areas of the body)
- Thinning hair on the head
- Androgenic alopecia (male-pattern hair loss)
- Acne (particularly on the jaw line or on the back; moderate to severe)
- Irregular menstruation and/or no menstruation
- Long and/or irregular menstrual cycles
- Heavy bleeding/long periods
- Pelvic pain (painful periods)
- Chronic inflammation
- Type 2 diabetes
- Cardiovascular disease
- High blood pressure
- High triglyceride levels
- Abnormal HDL/LDL cholesterol levels
- Headaches
- Fatigue/low energy
- Poor sleep/sleep disturbances
- Mood changes (depression, anxiety)
- Poor body image
- Anorexia/bulimia
- Infertility
- High luteinizing hormone (LH) levels
- Elevated LH-to-follicle-stimulating hormone (FSH) ratio
- High prolactin levels
- Elevated anti-Müllerian hormone (AMH) levels
- Low sex hormone-binding globulin (SHBG) levels

Given that women don't even need to have polycystic ovaries for a formal diagnosis, it's clear that PCOS is a health issue that extends well beyond your menstrual cycle. In my interview with Fiona McCulloch, ND, author of *8 Steps to Reverse Your PCOS*, she described PCOS as a complex condition that affects a woman's entire hormonal and metabolic systems.[30] Women with PCOS have an increased risk of developing cardiovascular disease, high blood pressure, type 2 diabetes, and cancer (endometrial and ovarian cancer in particular).[31] The concept of your menstrual cycle as a vital sign could not be more clear in the example of PCOS, because the menstrual cycle abnormalities you experience clearly indicate an underlying health issue. Put another way, the disruption that you see in your menstrual cycle is the *result* of the disease process that's happening in the background (not the disease itself!). It's your body's inner alarm system going off.

How does PCOS show up in my menstrual cycle?

Women with PCOS typically experience delayed (or missing) ovulation leading to long, irregular cycles. This can be extremely frustrating for you as you track your cycles because your menstrual cycle remains in somewhat of a holding pattern until your ovaries decide it's time to release an egg.

The most common signs of PCOS include:

- *Oligomenorrhea* — delayed ovulation with cycles longer than 35 days, and/or fewer than nine periods per year
- *Amenorrhea* — temporary cessation of ovulation (and menstruation)
- Extended phase of CM production — seven or more days of CM prior to ovulation
- Multiple patches of CM as you approach ovulation — this often happens in long cycles when your body attempts to ovulate, but estrogen levels don't rise high enough to trigger ovulation
- *Menorrhagia* — abnormally heavy or prolonged menstrual bleeding [32]

Here's an example of how PCOS can show up in the menstrual cycle (see Figure 6-2). Tara received a diagnosis of PCOS from her doctor prior to our work together. As you can see, her cycle extended well past the normal range of 24 to 35 days. Her chart indicates that ovulation happened on about day 41. What you see throughout her preovulatory phase is typical of a PCOS chart. There are several patches of CM before she actually ovulated, which tells us that her ovaries were gearing up for ovulation. You can almost hear her ovaries saying, "OK, I think we're ready to ovulate ... never mind. Alright, *now* we're ready to ovulate ... never mind, maybe later," until ovulation finally happens on day 41, making her cycle 52 days in total.

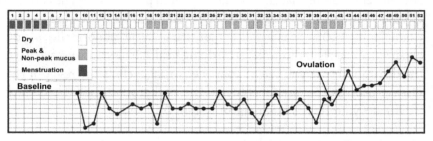

Figure 6–2: Tara's chart. An example of how PCOS can show up in the menstrual cycle.

A note on ovulation predictor kits and PCOS

Ovulation predictor kits (OPKs) test for the LH surge that happens about 24 to 36 hours before ovulation (see Chapter 3). If you have PCOS, you're more likely to have elevated LH levels throughout your cycle, leading to frequent false positive results. This can be extremely frustrating when you rely on OPKs to identify ovulation.

OPKs should *always* come second to your mucus observations. When you chart your cycles, you can identify your fertile window by paying attention to your CM patterns regardless of what shows up on your OPK (see Chapter 10).

Clinical features of PCOS

Given that PCOS shows up differently in different women, many women have a hard time obtaining an official diagnosis — especially when their symptoms don't match their practitioner's expectations. A great example of this is body size.[33] Many practitioners are unlikely to consider a PCOS diagnosis unless the patient is somewhat overweight. PCOS is associated with weight gain and obesity, and many practitioners are less likely to diagnose lean women with PCOS — *even when they meet the diagnostic criteria.* Knowing the common signs and symptoms of PCOS will help you advocate for the testing and support you need in order to receive a formal diagnosis.

Menstrual cycle disturbances   Up to 85 percent of women with PCOS experience menstrual cycle disturbances including delayed ovulation (cycles longer than 35 days), irregular cycles, and/or amenorrhea.[34] Having irregular periods doesn't automatically mean you have PCOS, but if you regularly have infrequent (or absent) periods, along with other common PCOS-related symptoms, you'll want to consider testing just in case.

Polycystic ovaries　　Not all women with PCOS have polycystic ovaries, but approximately 75 percent of women with PCOS show signs of polycystic ovaries when examined.[35] Polycystic ovaries are identified via ultrasound and are defined as having one (or both) of the following criteria:

- The ovary contains 12 or more follicles measuring 2 to 9 mm in diameter, or
- The ovary has an increased volume of 10 mm or more.[36]

Polycystic ovaries contain several small follicles and are typically enlarged compared to normal ovaries. However, *20 to 30 percent of all women have polycystic ovaries*, so having ovarian cysts and/or an increased ovarian volume is not enough to warrant a PCOS diagnosis.[37]

Hyperandrogenism　　Up to 80 percent of women with PCOS have elevated androgen levels, specifically testosterone, androstenedione, and DHEA.[38] Much of the excess androgen production happens in your ovaries because your ovaries produce both testosterone and androstenedione. In a normal menstrual cycle, your ovaries produce increasing amounts of estrogen in the preovulatory phase as your body prepares for ovulation. Once your estrogen levels rise high enough, your pituitary gland releases LH, which triggers ovulation. In women with PCOS, however, the pituitary gland releases significantly more LH throughout the menstrual cycle via rapid LH pulse secretions (approximately once per hour in the preovulatory phase).[39]

In addition (as I'll expand on in the next section), as many as 70 percent of women with PCOS are insulin resistant.[40] This means that women with PCOS tend to have higher circulating levels of insulin in their bloodstream. Together, the elevated levels of LH and insulin in women with PCOS stimulate the ovarian theca cells to produce excess testosterone and androstenedione.[41] Excess androgen production leads to a number of related issues, including:

- *Hirsutism* — male-pattern hair growth: coarse hair on the face (chin, upper lip), around the nipples, on the chest or stomach, upper arm, thighs, and other areas of the body
- *Acne* — adult acne that appears on the chin, jawline, and/or other areas of the body
- *Androgenic alopecia* — male-pattern hair loss

Hirsutism is strongly correlated with PCOS. Studies have shown that anywhere from 50 to 78 percent of women with textbook hirsutism wind up with a PCOS diagnosis.[42] Acne and alopecia are also correlated with PCOS but to a lesser extent. These symptoms are early indicators that your androgen levels may be too high, and can alert you to the possibility that your symptoms may be related to PCOS.

Insulin resistance   Insulin is responsible for regulating your blood sugar. When you eat, your blood sugar rises, and your pancreas secretes insulin to move the excess sugar out of your bloodstream and into your cells. However, the vast majority of women with PCOS don't respond normally to insulin. Anywhere from 50 to 70 percent of women with PCOS are insulin resistant.[43] When a woman is resistant to insulin, her cells don't respond normally when her pancreas secretes it. Instead of moving the excess sugar out of her bloodstream after a meal (or snack), her blood sugar levels remain high, which causes her pancreas to secrete even more insulin in order to get the job done, leading to *hyperinsulinemia*. Hyperinsulinemia simply means that your insulin levels are higher than they're supposed to be because you have a problem regulating your blood sugar. You don't respond well to carbohydrates (sugar) because when you consume them, your body has a hard time bringing your blood sugar levels back to normal. To put it into perspective, the insulin sensitivity in women with PCOS is similar to that found in people with *type 2 diabetes mellitus*.[44]

Imagine trying to put out a fire that keeps burning no matter how much water you pour on it. Eventually you put out the fire, but you end up using nearly three times as much water as you should have. Not to mention that it takes twice as long to put it out, meaning the fire has caused significantly more damage. This is what it's like to be insulin resistant.

Excess insulin interferes with ovulation, contributes to chronic inflammation, and is associated with diabetes and high blood pressure.[45] For this reason, balancing your blood sugar is a crucial part of managing PCOS. The less your blood sugar spikes, the less your pancreas has to pump out excessive amounts of insulin to control it (see Chapter 16).

Inflammation Inflammation is an important part of your body's natural immune response to injury, infection, and tissue damage. If you were to get a cut on your finger, you would experience redness, swelling, and pain — all signs of localized inflammation. Similarly, when you have the flu, your body typically responds by causing fever, which raises your core body temperature high enough to kill the virus. These short-term inflammatory responses allow your body to protect itself from external threats (such as viruses and bacteria) and facilitate the healing of damaged tissues in your body.[46] One of the hallmarks of PCOS is low-grade, chronic inflammation; but unlike short-term inflammatory responses that occur in response to specific events, chronic inflammation is ongoing and is associated with a number of serious chronic health conditions such as diabetes and cardiovascular disease.[47]

Metabolic disturbances The term *metabolic syndrome* refers to a collection of specific risk factors that together raise a person's risk of developing cardiovascular (heart) disease, type 2 diabetes, gestational diabetes, and other related metabolic issues.[48] These factors include elevated blood sugar, insulin resistance, glucose intolerance, central obesity (excess weight primarily in your abdomen/stomach area), chronic inflammation, high cholesterol, and high blood pressure. This applies to PCOS because women with PCOS typically have a number of these risk factors.

A growing number of health professionals feel the name PCOS doesn't accurately reflect the underlying condition.[49] The name implies that PCOS is only related to ovarian dysfunction and does not accurately capture the significant health consequences associated with it. Names such as *chronic hyperandrogenic anovulation* or *metabolic reproductive syndrome* have been proposed to capture the metabolic issues that characterize this condition. I'm not entirely convinced that a name change will solve the real issue, which (in my opinion) is related to the way we view the reproductive system in women as somehow separate from our health.

The standard treatment for PCOS offered by many healthcare practitioners is hormonal contraceptives (HCs), but HCs simply cover up the early warning signs and have even been shown to *increase* certain metabolic risk factors (such as insulin resistance, glucose intolerance, and deep-vein thrombosis — read: blood clots and stroke).[50] Like thyroid disorders, PCOS is extremely complex, but when you understand the factors that contribute to this condition, it's possible to restore normal, ovulatory menstrual cycles. Many women successfully reverse their PCOS through a combination of dietary and lifestyle changes as well as supplementation (with the support of a qualified healthcare practitioner). See Chapter 16 for details.

Hypothalamic Amenorrhea (HA)

Hypothalamic amenorrhea (HA) (also known as *functional hypothalamic amenorrhea*) is a condition characterized by the absence of menstruation due to the suppression of the hypothalamic-pituitary-ovarian (HPO) axis.[51] HA is the result of chronic undernutrition, over-exercise, and/or stress, which can each cause a disruption in the communication between the hypothalamus, pituitary gland, and ovaries.[52] Once this communication is disrupted, you stop ovulating, which causes you to stop having your period.

If you experience HA, your hypothalamus is not releasing the hormones that trigger ovulation. At first glance it may seem as though your hypothalamus is malfunctioning, but as we'll learn further in this section, your hypothalamus is simply responding to a combination of several specific (and significant) stressors. When you have HA, your hypothalamus is actually protecting you from additional stress by taking pregnancy off the table for a while; your hypothalamus (and ovaries) have declared that now is *not* a good time to reproduce.

To receive a diagnosis of HA, you would typically have to go six months or more without a period (and other conditions that could cause amenorrhea, such as PCOS, thyroid disorders, and autoimmune issues, would have to be ruled out). On the surface, HA may seem similar to

PCOS, but the two conditions are very different. Women with PCOS typically experience delayed or irregular ovulation, whereas women with HA stop ovulating altogether for several months (or even years) at a time. In PCOS, the disruption in regular ovulation is related to metabolic disturbances such as insulin resistance, inflammation, and elevated androgen levels; but in HA, ovulation stops due to the suppression of the HPO axis as a result of specific behavioural factors (undereating, over-exercising, and/or stress).

How does HA show up in my menstrual cycle?

HA is characterized by the complete lack of a menstrual cycle. You stop ovulating, and therefore you also stop menstruating for months or years at a time. Your hypothalamus and your ovaries have reached a stalemate.

The most common signs of HA include:

- *Anovulation* — your ovaries aren't releasing any eggs
- *Amenorrhea* — temporary cessation of ovulation (and menstruation) for a period of six months or more
- The absence of CM

The three main types of HA

HA is a clear sign that something is wrong. When you stop ovulating for months or years at a time, your inner alarm system is *screaming* at you. Since reproduction is not a vital bodily function, when you are under extreme stress, and/or extremely underweight, your body actively protects you from the additional stress of pregnancy by suppressing ovulation.

HA can be divided into three main types:

1. Weight loss-related
2. Exercise-related
3. Stress-related

Most women with HA have some combination of these three types, and you'll notice some overlap as we go through them.

Weight loss-related   Regular menstruation is dependent on a minimum level of body fat. Although the exact number isn't important (and varies from woman to woman), research shows that a total body fat percentage of about 22 percent is required to maintain regular ovulation (and menstruation).[53] Women who adopt strict eating practices that limit their overall caloric intake are at an increased risk of losing their periods. This can be related to a full-blown eating disorder such as anorexia, bulimia, or orthorexia; chronic undereating; and/or adopting an extremely restrictive diet.

- *Anorexia* (*anorexia nervosa*) is an eating disorder characterized by food restriction and an intense desire to be thin. Women with anorexia typically view themselves as overweight even if they are dangerously underweight.
- *Bulimia* (*bulimia nervosa*) is an eating disorder characterized by binge eating, followed by purging (through induced vomiting, diarrhea, fasting, over-exercise, or other means).
- *Orthorexia* (*orthorexia nervosa*) is characterized by an excessive preoccupation with eating "healthy food," resulting in a severely restricted diet. Orthorexia is not officially recognized as an eating disorder but can cause significant health problems nonetheless.

One study measured the body fat composition of a group of 113 women with a history of anorexia.[54] All of the study participants were in complete remission at the time of the study (and no longer met the diagnostic criteria for anorexia), but not all of them had started menstruating again. The women who had not regained their periods had significantly less body fat compared to the women who were menstruating regularly, with average fat percentages of 23.1 and 26.8 percent, respectively. This study shows us that your body fat composition plays an important role in maintaining regular menstrual cycles. The women who regained their periods had to gain weight in order to restore normal ovulatory function and start menstruating again.

Exercise-related   It's well known that female athletes are at a greater risk of losing their periods from excessive exercise. One study found that 70 percent of female athletes reported having irregular cycles, 21 percent reported amenorrhea, and 44 percent reported using HCs to regulate their cycles.[55] The rate of menstrual cycle disruption among athletes is significantly higher than the general population, where amenorrhea only occurs at a rate of about 2 to 5 percent.[56]

Many women think that losing their period is a normal side effect of intense athleticism, but it's not normal or healthy. There are serious health consequences associated with amenorrhea that go far beyond your ability to procreate. This is evident in a condition referred to as the *female athlete triad,* which is a combination of:

1. Disordered eating,
2. Amenorrhea, and
3. Osteoporosis.

Yes, you read that correctly — *osteoporosis.* Although the triad is seen across various sports, it's most prevalent in sports with an emphasis on thinness, such as ballet, gymnastics, and figure skating. The triad is characterized by a desire to excel in a sport and maintain a specific (thin) body type. As one researcher puts it,

> The female athlete, seeking an improved body image to enhance athletic prowess, begins to restrict caloric intake. This restrictive dieting behavior then progresses, eventually predisposing the athlete to menstrual irregularity and decreased [bone mineral density].[57]

Another researcher describes it as "the dietary inadequacy of female athletes in relation to their high energy expenditure."[58] Put simply, more energy is going out than coming in. These women are doing intense exercise nearly every day and not eating enough to support such a high level of activity. It's like expecting your car to drive twice as far with half as much fuel.

For the record, you can experience HA whether or not you consider yourself an athlete. Working out several times per week or several hours per day without providing your body with sufficient fuel is equivalent to intense athletic training. Your body responds to this chronic state of energetic deficiency by stopping your menstrual cycle. Since women with exercise-related HA don't provide their bodies with enough fuel to match their activity level, it stands to reason that increasing their daily caloric intake would have a positive impact on their menstrual cycle.

One study tested this theory by providing a group of 8 endurance-trained amenorrheic women (who had not had their menses for the past 3 to 12 months or more) with a daily, high-calorie nutritional supplement (containing 54 g carbohydrate, 20 g protein, and 8 g fat), for a 6-month period.[59] This nutritional supplement was provided in addition to their regular dietary practices in order to increase their total caloric intake over the 6-month study period. The study participants exercised 6 to 7 days per week and consumed their high-calorie nutritional beverage shortly after their daily exercise routine, as well as on their days off. The researchers compared the study group to a control group of 10 endurance-trained women with regular menstrual cycles.

The addition of the high-calorie supplement increased the overall body fat, BMI, and weight in the women who had not recovered their periods. It also brought their periods back within 1 to 7 months. The women who hadn't had their periods for over a year took the longest to start menstruating again (6 to 7 months versus 1 to 2 months for the women with amenorrhea for less than 1 year). Interestingly, the 6-month period of increased caloric intake brought the amenorrheic women to about the same body fat percentage as the control group of athletic women who were already menstruating regularly. The amenorrheic women increased their average body fat from 22.9 to 24.1 percent over the course of the study, compared to the control group who had an average body fat of 23.2 percent when the study began.

Once the amenorrheic women gave their bodies sufficient fuel, their periods came back within a matter of months. In many ways, exercise-related HA is fairly straightforward. If you don't eat enough food to cover your energy expenditures, you force your body to compensate in other ways (namely, the loss of your period to conserve vital energy). By no means does this make it easy to treat, but it does illuminate why it happens and provides a clear picture of what must happen if you wish to recover.

Stress-related   Stress has a significant impact on the menstrual cycle. It can shorten your luteal phase, delay ovulation, and in some cases, suppress ovulation altogether. Women with HA rarely have just one of the three main factors; it's usually a combination of undernutrition, over-exercise, and stress.

Studies have shown that women with HA have elevated cortisol levels compared to women who have regular cycles. In one study, the HA patients had baseline cortisol levels that were more than twice the levels found in the control group.[60] Perhaps women with HA are more sensitive to stressful situations, or maybe they're more prone to HPO axis dysregulation. On the other hand, women with HA might just be under an enormous amount of stress. After all, undereating and over-exercising are both legitimate stressors (as far as your body is concerned). As challenging as stress is to deal with, developing solid self-care practices are key to managing it (more on managing stress in Chapter 13).

HA and bone loss

HA is associated with a decrease in overall bone and mineral density that worsens over time, contributing to an increased risk of bone fracture and osteoporosis later in life.[61] One study compared the bone mineral density of a group of women with HA to a control group of women who were menstruating normally.[62] Compared to the control group, the spinal bone mass was 22 to 29 percent lower in the amenorrheic women. Based on the results of the study, the researchers estimated that women with HA lose approximately 4.5 percent of their bone and mineral density annually.

As women recover from HA, their bone mineral density improves, but doesn't completely reverse. The longer the amenorrhea lasts, the less likely full bone mineral density will be restored.[63] This is particularly important for young women who have not yet reached their *peak bone mass*. Peak bone mass refers to the maximum amount of bone density you reach in your lifetime (which happens between age 19 and 40 in women).[64] Since women accumulate the majority of their bone mineral density during the first 20 years of life, young women with HA are at an even greater risk of permanent bone loss.

HCs have been shown to slow the loss of bone mineral density in amenorrheic women, and as such, are commonly prescribed as treatment.[65] However, studies have shown that HCs do not slow bone loss in all areas of the body.[66] Women who take HCs for HA still experience some degree of bone loss. In a recent meta-analysis, a group of researchers evaluated nine separate studies on the use of hormonal therapies (including HCs) as treatment for HA.[67] While hormonal treatment increased bone density in the lumbar spine (lower back) area, it did not improve bone density in other areas of the body (in the hip area, specifically).

Given that HA involves HPO axis dysregulation, the primary approach to treatment should involve changing caloric consumption (eating more), exercise habits (exercising less), and managing stress — not covering up the issue with synthetic hormones. Like PCOS, HA demonstrates the importance of regular ovulation for health in a way that's not directly related to your ability to reproduce. We should consider HA an emergency! In women with HA, restoring normal ovulatory patterns (and regular menstrual cycles) is a crucial part of maintaining optimal health — but it may take time. For more on recovering from HA, see Chapter 16.

Additional Health Issues that Can Interfere with Your Menstrual Cycle

In addition to the three main health issues we've discussed, several other conditions can affect your menstrual cycle. A variety of health issues can delay ovulation, cause irregular cervical mucus patterns, shorten your luteal phase, and/or cause irregular bleeding patterns. When your menstrual cycles consistently fall outside normal parameters, you'll want to consider whether any underlying health issues could be responsible. Below is a list of several of the most common health issues that contribute to menstrual cycle irregularities:

- *Irritable bowel syndrome (IBS)/Crohn's disease/ulcerative colitis* — These three conditions are characterized by chronic bowel inflammation. The most common symptoms include excessive diarrhea, constipation, and abdominal pain. These reactions are typically exacerbated by the consumption of certain foods (such as gluten and commercially processed dairy) that trigger these reactions. Women with IBS may experience changes in their cycles when they consume certain foods. These changes can include delayed ovulation, abnormal CM production, and abnormal bleeding patterns.

- *Small intestinal bacterial overgrowth (SIBO)* — SIBO is a gut infection characterized by the overgrowth of bacteria in the small intestine. SIBO is associated with a variety of symptoms including constipation, diarrhea, gas, abdominal pain/discomfort, and often closely resembles IBS. Similar to women with IBS, women with SIBO may experience delayed ovulation, abnormal CM production, and abnormal bleeding patterns.
- *Chronic underlying infections (including Lyme disease and Epstein-Barr)* — Chronic infections are fairly common but will often go undetected (until your practitioner has you tested). I've worked with a number of women who describe feeling excessively fatigued most of the time regardless of how much they sleep. Women with chronic underlying infections may experience erratic BBTs, abnormal CM patterns (in some cases limited or no mucus at ovulation), a short luteal phase, and/or abnormal bleeding patterns.

For women who monitor their cycles, abnormal cycle parameters are often the very first sign of an underlying problem. Your cycle is what prompts you to investigate further, and as you track your cycle, you can monitor your progress. As your health improves, your cycles will improve as well.

Whether you plan to have children or not, your menstrual cycles are connected to your health. It's time to acknowledge that the menstrual cycle is an accurate and legitimate biomarker of a woman's health. We must recognize the menstrual cycle as a vital sign and monitor it accordingly, because menstrual cycle abnormalities affect much more than our ability to procreate.

Summary

- Menstrual cycle disruptions are often the first sign of an underlying health issue.
- Thyroid disorders are one of the most common causes of menstrual cycle disruptions; they can be identified through a combination of

symptoms including low BBTs, cycles that are longer (or shorter) than normal, abnormal bleeding patterns, and abnormal CM patterns.

- PCOS disrupts the normal pattern of ovulation and typically causes long, irregular menstrual cycles.
- Women with PCOS are at a greater risk of developing cardio-vascular disease and type 2 diabetes.
- The three main types of hypothalamic amenorrhea (HA) are related to weight loss, exercise, and stress, and most women with HA are affected by a combination of all three.
- Women who experience HA for an extended period have a higher lifetime risk of developing osteoporosis.
- Many additional health issues can affect your menstrual cycle in both subtle and obvious ways.
- Your menstrual cycle is a vital sign you can monitor as a sign of overall health beyond your ability or desire to have children.

Chapter 7
The Pill and Your Fertility

"The truth will set you free, but first it will piss you off."

— Gloria Steinem

The pill is a complicated topic for many reasons. As a feminist, it may seem strange for me *not* to be an avid cheerleader of hormonal contraceptives (HCs), since HCs are credited for giving women control over their bodies by empowering them to choose if and when they wish to have children. From an advertising standpoint, HCs are perfectly positioned in the market. Given that most women believe they're fertile every day, the most logical solution is a birth control method that provides continuous protection from pregnancy. However, most women have no idea what HCs are really doing to their body.

You may have heard that the pill regulates your cycles and tricks your body into thinking you're pregnant, but neither statement is accurate. Most HCs (including the pill, the patch, the ring, the implant, the progestin-releasing IUD, and the shot) greatly suppress your body's natural production of estrogen, progesterone, and testosterone by interfering with the hypothalamic-pituitary-ovarian (HPO) axis (more on that in a moment). If you were to measure the natural hormone levels of a woman on HCs, they would more closely resemble the hormonal profile of a woman in menopause (as menopause is characterized by a significant drop in sex hormone production).[1]

HCs have fundamentally changed how we view our menstrual cycles. Before HCs came on the market, having a monthly bleed was, for the most part, inescapable. If you weren't pregnant, breastfeeding, menopausal, or experiencing a medical condition that caused you to stop menstruating, there was nothing you could do to stop having your period. HCs have made menstruation optional, and nowadays many women opt not to bleed at all.

Although originally designed to prevent pregnancy, HCs are regularly prescribed for a growing number of health concerns that have nothing to do with birth control, including:

- Acne
- Dysmenorrhea (period pain)
- Menorrhagia (abnormally heavy or prolonged menstrual bleeding)
- Irregular cycles
- Amenorrhea (temporary cessation of ovulation and menstruation)
- Polycystic ovary syndrome (PCOS)
- Hypothalamic amenorrhea (HA)
- Ovarian cysts
- Endometriosis
- Adenomyosis
- Uterine fibroids

And the list goes on...

But covering up menstrual cycle abnormalities with hormonal birth control is not the answer. Many physicians prescribe HCs to "regulate" their patients' menstrual cycles, and to this day, most women who take HCs believe they're still getting their period every 28 days. How could two entire generations of women have been misled? The answer lies in the original design of Enovid, the very first birth control pill.

A Brief History of the Pill

The first oral contraceptive pill, Enovid, was approved by the US Food and Drug Administration (FDA) in 1960 after several years of research and clinical testing.[2] When first brought to market, Enovid contained 3 to 7 times as much synthetic estrogen, and 3 to 98 times the synthetic progestins compared to today's formulations.[3] Chemist Carl Djerassi was the first to synthesize an orally active progestin (synthetic version of progesterone — see Chapter 1) for use in pill form; together obstetrician and gynecologist John Rock and biologist and researcher Gregory Pincus discovered that exposing women to synthetic estrogen and progestins had the effect of suppressing ovulation.[4]

At that time women had virtually no access to the contraceptive options we take for granted today. Imagine what it would have been like to have eight children before your 30th birthday and to know that a hysterectomy was the only option if you wanted to stop having kids. When Dr. Rock and Dr. Pincus developed Enovid, they were at least partially motivated by a desire to give women an effective, alternative contraceptive method that gave them greater control over their family size.

Enovid was the first drug ever developed to shut down a perfectly normal bodily function in healthy individuals. The women who participated in the first round of testing stopped getting their periods and quickly became convinced they were pregnant, as outlined in this excerpt:

> Rock told Pincus that he was encouraged by his work with progesterone, but that he had a big problem: patients receiving the hormone believed that they were pregnant, no matter how much he assured them they were not. And they were crushed when the truth finally became clear to them.[5]

The creators of the pill needed to answer two key questions: How could they convince women to take medication every day when they weren't sick? And how could they convince women to take a pill that stopped their menstrual cycles?

Presenting hormonal birth control in a way that mimicked a woman's natural menstrual cycle was the solution. From the very beginning, women were lied to about what hormonal birth control was doing to their bodies: the creators of the pill quite literally added in a fake menstrual bleed to the original design to get women to go along with it. Without that fake monthly bleed, the women of the '60s wouldn't have agreed to take the pill in the first place.

Dr. Rock and Dr. Pincus designed the pill to follow a 28-day pattern, though there's no medical reason to induce a fake bleed between pill packs. The number of days in a pill-induced cycle is arbitrary. They could have easily selected 100, 36, or 75 days, but the fake 28-day pill cycle allowed these women to think they were still getting their periods.

Why Are Hormonal Contraceptives (HCs) So Effective?

HCs are extremely effective in preventing pregnancy, no one's debating that; but have you considered what makes them work so well?

All HCs prevent pregnancy by combining the following three actions:

1. They interfere with ovulation,
2. They interfere with implantation, and
3. They prevent your cervix from producing fertile-quality mucus.

They interfere with ovulation

Your hypothalamus, pituitary gland, and ovaries must have an open line of communication for ovulation to happen normally; this threesome is referred to as your *HPO axis*. Your hypothalamus releases a hormone called gonadotropin-releasing hormone (GnRH), which causes your pituitary gland to release follicle-stimulating hormone (FSH), which then stimulates your ovaries to start preparing your eggs for ovulation.[6] It's like an incredibly detailed (and super-complicated) game of telephone.

Taking HCs causes a break in this communication system by interfering with the connection between your hypothalamus, pituitary gland, and ovaries. In many cases, HCs completely shut down your ovaries and stop you from ovulating altogether. If you were to take a closer look at your ovaries, you'd find that they appear inactive, similar to what you'd see if you were to observe the ovaries of a woman in menopause.[7]

With that said, not all HCs completely suppress ovulation.[8] A certain percentage of women who use progestin-releasing intrauterine devices (IUDs) and progestin-only pills continue to ovulate while using them — but it would be incorrect to say these women continue having normal menstrual cycles. By definition, all HCs expose women to varying doses of synthetic hormones (often continuously). All women on HCs experience some degree of HPO axis dysregulation and hormonal imbalance.[9]

You may wonder how HCs effectively prevent pregnancy if they don't always suppress ovulation. Not to worry — HCs work collectively on three fronts to prevent pregnancy. When ovulation is not entirely suppressed, there are two additional measures.

They interfere with implantation

Pregnancy can only occur when your endometrial lining has fully developed. Estrogen supports the proliferation of your endometrium prior to ovulation, and progesterone supports endometrial thickening and maturation after ovulation (refer back to Chapter 2). Since most HCs prevent ovulation, your endometrial lining never gets the chance to fully develop — the result is a very thin, flat endometrium.[10] For this reason, it's no surprise that many women have shorter and lighter bleeding on HCs compared to their real periods (although this isn't the case for every woman).[11]

Without a sufficiently thick and juicy endometrial lining you're much less likely to conceive.[12] In a study designed to measure how endometrial thickness impacts conception rates, the researchers found that women with an endometrial thickness of less than 7 mm were unable to conceive.[13] Other studies have shown that an endometrial lining of 10 mm or thicker is optimal for achieving pregnancy.[14] HCs (including the progestin-releasing IUD and progestin-only pill) cause your endometrial lining to be extremely thin (2 to 5 mm), making it theoretically impossible for a fertilized egg to successfully implant.[15] This is why HCs are equally effective in women who continue to ovulate while using them — because even if you were to ovulate, a fertilized egg would have nowhere to implant, making pregnancy extremely unlikely.[16]

They prevent your cervix from producing fertile-quality cervical mucus

The progestins in HCs stimulate the excessive development of your G cervical crypts. When you take HCs, your cervical canal fills with a thick, impenetrable G-type mucus plug that prevents sperm from reaching your uterine cavity.[17] The sperm have nowhere to go. They can't make it past your cervix because they can't swim through your mucus plug (refer back to Figure 3–3 on page 25). If the sperm can't make it anywhere near your uterus, fallopian tubes, or ovaries, pregnancy is impossible.

Together, these three actions give HCs an effectiveness rate of up to 99.7 percent with perfect use (in the case of the pill, typical use reduces the effectiveness to about 92 percent).[18] HCs suppress ovulation, they prevent your endometrial lining from fully developing, and they create an impenetrable death trap for sperm. In many ways this sounds like the perfect solution for preventing pregnancy; but the question isn't whether HCs are effective. The real question is, effectiveness *at what cost?*

Side Effects

Now that you know why HCs are so incredibly effective, let's talk about their many, many (*many!*) side effects. I highly encourage you to check out the website for any of the big HC brands (Yaz®, Ortho Tri-Cyclen®, Implanon®, Depo-Provera®, Seasonale®, etc.). Seriously, I want you to go to the website of the first HC brand that comes to mind. If you can't find a website for the brand you're looking for, search online for "prescribing information pdf" (and the brand name). Go ahead, I'll wait...

Regardless of what website you go to or which document you find, you'll notice the ominous black box warning right there at the top. In case you're not familiar with black box warnings, they're mandated by the government. In the US, black box warnings are the strongest warning that the FDA requires. Any drug with a black box warning carries a significant risk of serious or even life-threatening adverse effects. As far as HCs go, warnings are typically labelled "important safety information" or "prescribing information." Whichever site you choose, I encourage you to read the full page (or PDF boxed warning) in its entirety. It's pretty scary stuff.

Have you looked at a cigarette carton lately? Here in Canada, cigarettes are also sold with black box warnings on the package — often with graphic pictures of lung and mouth cancer. Let's just say it doesn't warm my heart to know that both HCs and cigarettes are known to cause such severe health risks that they require a black box warning.

Might I remind you that when you eat bananas and chicken you don't run the risk of developing:

> Persistent leg pain; sudden shortness of breath; sudden blindness, partial or complete; severe pain in your chest; sudden, severe headache unlike your usual headaches; weakness or numbness in an arm or leg, or trouble speaking; [or] yellowing of the skin or eyes.[19]

Just sayin'. A more accurate warning label for HCs would read like this (see Figure 7–1):

WARNING: HORMONAL CONTRACEPTIVES INCREASE YOUR MORTALITY RATE BY INCREASING YOUR RISK OF DEVELOPING DEEP VEIN THROMBOSIS, ISCHAEMIC STROKE, CERVICAL CANCER, BREAST CANCER, AND LIVER CANCER. THIS PRODUCT HAS BEEN SHOWN TO CAUSE CLITORAL SHRINKAGE, SHRINKAGE OF VULVAR TISSUES, VULVODYNIA (PAINFUL SEX), LOW LIBIDO, LOSS OF SEX DRIVE, DEPRESSION, ANXIETY, PANIC ATTACKS, MIGRAINE HEADACHES, IRRITABILITY, INTRUSIVE THOUGHTS, EMOTIONAL OUTBURSTS, MOOD DISORDERS, MULTIPLE NUTRIENT DEFICIENCIES, RECURRENT YEAST INFECTIONS, PERSISTENT HPV INFECTION, CERVICAL DYSPLASIA, WEIGHT GAIN, INSOMNIA, FATIGUE, FEELINGS OF DREAD AND HOPELESSNESS, UNCONTROLLABLE CRYING, SUICIDAL THOUGHTS, INCREASED TENDENCY TOWARDS ANGER AND/OR AGGRESSION.

*CONSULT YOUR PHYSICIAN IMMEDIATELY IF YOU EXPERIENCE ANY OF THESE SYMPTOMS

Figure 7-1: A more appropriate warning label for HCs

When you take HCs, your risk of *thrombosis* is anywhere from four to seven times your normal risk.[20] If you're not clear on exactly what thrombosis is, the official definition is the formation of a blood clot inside a blood vessel, obstructing the flow of blood through the circulatory system.[21] For years I thought the risk of stroke and blood clots was the primary issue with hormonal birth control — until I interviewed Lara Briden, ND, on my weekly radio show, *Fertility Friday*. In our first interview, I asked Dr. Briden about the most common side effects her patients experienced on HCs, and her reply was depression and low libido.[22]

Contrary to what we often see in the media, there are a number of lesser-known side effects you're much more likely to experience; however, most women aren't fully counselled about the side effects of HCs by their healthcare practitioners. Since HCs affect every woman who takes them, it's not a question of whether you'll have side effects — it's which ones.

Several population studies have found that as many as half of the women who use the pill stop taking it within the first year.[23] At the 3- to 4-year mark up to 69 percent of women have stopped taking it.[24] Injectable contraceptives have an even lower continuation rate, with only 23 percent of women still using it at the 1-year mark.[25]

The hormones your ovaries produce affect your entire body, both emotionally and physically. When you suppress normal ovarian function, it doesn't only affect your fertility. Recognizing the vital role your menstrual cycle plays in your overall health helps you appreciate how such a tiny little pill can negatively impact your sex drive, your mood, your gut flora, your risk of getting certain cancers, and even your choice of an intimate partner.

I believe in *informed consent* — full disclosure of the risks and benefits of any medication you take. Knowing the most common side effects allows you to identify and respond promptly when you have symptoms; however, many women experience related symptoms for months (or years) before they make the connection.

As we go deeper into the discussion of side effects, note that all HCs are not created equal. Most HCs contain a combination of synthetic estrogens and progestins (the pill, patch, and vaginal ring), but some contain only synthetic progestins (the progestin-only pill, the implant, and the shot). All HCs disrupt normal endocrine function to some degree, but not all HCs affect the body in the same way. This chapter is meant to highlight several of the most common side effects women experience, with a focus on those caused by combined HCs.

Does the Pill Mess with Your Libido?

In a word, *yes*. There are a few reasons why the pill (and other HCs) have a negative impact on libido; the main one being the way HCs affect your testosterone levels.

HCs lower your testosterone levels

Although women produce 90 percent less testosterone than men, we depend on the small amount we produce for healthy sexual and reproductive function.[26] Testosterone plays an important role in sexual desire, interest in sex, and sexual gratification (to name a few).[27] If you have low testosterone, you're more likely to experience low libido, vaginal dryness, and a lack of sexual desire.[28]

HCs have been shown to lower free testosterone by an average of 61 percent.[29] The pill and other combined HCs lower testosterone production by suppressing ovarian and adrenal testosterone production and increasing sex hormone-binding globulin (SHBG) levels.[30]

SHBG is a protein that binds primarily to circulating testosterone and estrogen in your bloodstream.[31] When testosterone is bound, it's not available for your body to use. Have you ever used a magnet to attract iron filings? Just picture SHBG as the magnet and your testosterone as the filings. SHBG travels around your bloodstream and attracts free testosterone in the same way a magnet attracts iron filings. The more SHBG you have, the lower your free testosterone will be.

Combined HCs are associated with a significant increase in how much SHBG you produce — an increase of 200 to 400 percent.[32] The scariest part is that your SHBG levels will remain high for a very long time, even after you've come off the pill.[33]

One study measured the SHBG levels of 124 women 106 days after they came off HCs, and their levels were more than double the participants who'd never used them.[34] The researchers tested several of the participants again, one full year after they had discontinued HCs, and found that their SHBG levels were still significantly higher than the women who had never used them.[35]

In a separate study of 1297 women with PCOS, the SHBG levels of HC users were elevated well beyond the 1-year mark, and remained elevated until at least 5 years after they stopped using it.[36] Although the statistical significance wears off around year 5, the results of the study indicate that women who have used HCs continue to have high SHBG levels for 10 or more years after discontinuing use (average SHGB levels at the 10-plus year mark were 36 nmol/L in past HC users, compared to 29 nmol/L in non-users).

Orgasms, vaginal lubrication, and painful sex

In case you didn't already know this, you deserve to have phenomenal sex. You deserve to experience pleasure, orgasms, and as many juicy, delectable sexual experiences as you want — completely free of any pain or discomfort. It's your birthright. If something is standing between you and amazing sex, your concerns about it need to be heard, respected, and addressed. Period.

Pain with sex is often dismissed as psychosomatic — as though it's all in your head. If you've had the unfortunate experience of painful intercourse, it could be related to your use of HCs.

If you've used HCs before, your risk of developing *vulvodynia* (pain in your vulvar area) is significantly higher compared to women who've never used them.[37] You're at an even greater risk of having painful sex if you started using HCs prior to age 16.[38] If that wasn't bad enough, HCs are associated with a decrease in the volume of your vulvar tissues. To put it bluntly, HCs shrink your clitoris and decrease the thickness of your labia minora and vaginal opening.[39]

Your *labia minora* (or your "inner lips," if you will) are the flaps on either side of your *vaginal introitus* (your vaginal opening). Many women with vulvodynia experience pain specifically at the vaginal opening, often causing painful intercourse (also known as *dyspareunia*).

One study measured the effects of combined oral contraceptives on the vulvar tissues of 21 female students over a three-month period. The study participants experienced a significant drop in their estrogen and testosterone levels, as well as a decrease in the thickness of their labia minora and a reduction in the diameter of their vaginal introitus.[40] The participants reported increased pain with intercourse, lower libido, and reduced frequency of sex and orgasm.

A separate study measured the effect of oral contraceptives and the vaginal ring over a six-month period.[41] HC use was associated with increased pain with sex and a decrease in the frequency of sex and orgasm. In addition, the researchers measured the clitoral volume of the study participants both before and after the administration of HCs. Scary results: *all* of the study participants experienced a decrease in their clitoral volume over the course of the study — the average decrease was about 20 percent. Find me a man who would willingly take a drug that shrinks his penis by 20 percent! (But I digress.)

You'll remember when I referenced my first podcast interview with Dr. Briden. Here's what she said when I asked her to describe what the pill does in the body:

> It shuts down the ovaries — temporarily, although I'm sure you know from women's experiences ... that sometimes that effect is less temporary than we'd like.
>
> The pill is a form of castration. It's a chemical castration ... it shuts down hormones, it shuts down libido, it affects mood, it affects hormonal vitality and health in the same way that castration would affect men ... and I don't understand how women have put up with it for so long.[42]

Castration refers to any action, surgical, chemical, or otherwise, by which a man loses use of his testicles and experiences a significant drop in his testosterone levels.[43] Without me having to say anything, you immediately understand that removing a man's testicles changes who he is, not just his ability to bear children. Most HCs suppress normal ovarian function and could arguably be considered a temporary form of female castration.

I'll draw your attention back to the definition of castration. If I replace "man" with "woman" and rework the sentence accordingly, it reads that castration is *any action, surgical, chemical, or otherwise by which a woman loses use of her ovaries and experiences a significant drop in her natural estrogen, progesterone, and testosterone levels.* Imagine if advertisements for the pill invited you to be *temporarily castrated* as an effective way of preventing you from getting pregnant. "Birth control" has a much better ring to it.

Many women experience sexual side effects while taking HCs but don't make the connection. That was certainly the case for Madeline. She writes:

> I had a pretty rough time with the pill. I started taking it when I was about 19 and I suffered with chronic yeast infections and eventually vulvodynia for years. What is amazing is for so long I never suspected the birth control pill. I went to doctor after doctor and received antibiotics that swung me back and forth between yeast and bacteria overgrowth.

The vulvodynia made sex very painful. It wasn't until I went to a naturopath who suggested I get off the pill that the yeast infections stopped, but unfortunately the vulvodynia did not.

I went to acupuncture and pelvic floor physical therapy. Finally, I was told about a doctor at OHSU Women's Clinic, who, for the first time in my life, identified my symptoms as vulvodynia, a word I had never heard before. I'm sure you can imagine dealing with a "mysterious" pain for years and finally being with a woman who could name it. It brought great relief. Finally, I opted for a vulvectomy. The surgery removed the part of my vulva where I felt the pain. I was so sure I had finally found the answer after so many years, but I still had the pain even after I had the surgery.

After the surgery, the physical therapist I was working with pointed me to an article she had read: "Do oral contraceptive pills cause vulvodynia?" This was the first I'd ever heard of any evidence or theory that what I was going through could be caused by birth control. I brought the article to my doctor, and the only solution proposed by the article was testosterone cream, so I asked her to prescribe it for me. She didn't believe the pill could have any connection, but she agreed to prescribe the cream. I applied the testosterone cream and that was when the pain finally went away.

Madeline's story represents so many women out there who haven't been adequately counselled on the potential side effects associated with HCs. If we all knew that HCs could interfere with our sex drive and cause painful sex, at least we'd have the opportunity to make the connection earlier in the game. Unfortunately, what typically happens is that, if sex is painful or your libido has gone away, you're likely to blame yourself and assume there's just something wrong with you.

The consequence for Madeline was having a piece of her vulva removed so she would no longer experience painful sex, and in her case that didn't even get rid of the pain. If having a piece of your vulva removed to treat painful sex isn't a serious side effect, then I don't know what is.

Does the Pill Mess with Your Mind?

HC use is associated with an increased risk of anxiety and depression; and adolescent girls, in particular, are more vulnerable.[44] One study found that adolescent girls aged 15 to 19 were 2 to 3 times more likely to be on antidepressants while on HCs compared to non-users.[45] But how do HCs increase your risk of depression and other mood disorders?

HCs impair your body's ability to metabolize tryptophan normally by rapidly depleting vitamin B_6.[46] This decreases your serotonin production, and consequently increases your risk of experiencing symptoms of depression.[47] Serotonin is a neuro-transmitter that contributes to feelings of well-being and happiness, and tryptophan is an essential amino acid.[48] Your body requires both tryptophan and vitamin B_6 to synthesize serotonin.

Vitamin B_6 supplementation has been shown to improve depressive symptoms in women on HCs, but in order to restore normal tryptophan metabolism, you would need to take anywhere from 25 to 50 mg.[49] To put those numbers into perspective, the recommended dietary allowance (RDA) for vitamin B_6 is about 1.3 to 2 mg for a woman of reproductive age. A dose of 25 to 50 mg (as would be required by a woman on HCs) is about 20 to 38 times the RDA (increasing the daily requirement by nearly 4000 percent!).

With such a specific link to depression, why aren't most women aware of the mood-related risks associated with HCs?

Do healthcare practitioners warn women about the risks?

While not all women on HCs suffer from depression, it's clear that HC use is associated with an increased risk.[50] Why, then, are most women on HCs unaware of the risks? I decided to search for the answer. I scoured numerous research studies that examined the relationship between HCs and mood disorders, and I wasn't impressed with what I found. Two things became clear to me:

1. There is a definite link in the research between HCs and mood disorders, and
2. The research being conducted is often aimed at helping doctors prescribe birth control pills to women despite that link.

When it comes to HCs, what's highlighted is their effectiveness. Their side effects therefore tend to be downplayed. When side effects are mentioned, they're often described as minor or mild. Even though all women are affected by HCs in one way or another, I get the distinct sense that the medical establishment is willing to sacrifice "the few" for the perceived benefit of "the many."[51]

In a study published in the *Journal of Obstetrics and Gynaecology Canada*, the objective is listed as follows: "To describe the characteristics of women who experience sexual and mood side effects associated with use of hormonal contraception, and to compare them with women who do not."[52] Instead of trying to determine *why* HCs cause women to experience these side effects in the first place, the researchers chose to examine the women who experienced these effects to figure out what's wrong with them.

The researchers state that "women who complained of mood or sexual side effects with use of hormonal contraception may have different physiological reactions to hormones."[53] If the researchers could figure out how to isolate the women who complained about side effects, they wouldn't have to look at the drug itself as the problem. They could simply shift the responsibility onto the women who experienced side effects, proclaiming that these women were just "too sensitive" to the hormones. It's similar to how a sexual assault survivor is grilled about what she was wearing when the assault took place. My question is always: *Why are they focusing on her when they should be looking at the perpetrator?*

The study found that 51 percent of women experienced at least one mood-related side effect (depression, anxiety, mood changes, etc.), and 38 percent experienced at least one sexual side effect (loss of libido, pain with sex, etc.).[54] Here's a sample of what the study uncovered:

> Our finding that women who were more educated and unmarried complained more of sexual side effects may be related to higher expectations related to sexual pleasure.[55]
>
> In our study, complaints of mood side effects were related to complaints of sexual side effects. We may assume that mood and sexual satisfaction are linked, but it is also likely that women with low mood would have more complaints in general.[56]

This final conclusion was drawn:

> Understanding more about which women report mood and sexual side effects with hormonal contraception may be useful when counselling women about contraception. It is likely that both physiological susceptibility and psychosocial and cultural issues affect which women complain of these side effects ... **It is a major challenge for clinicians to provide the information women need to make choices without unduly discouraging them from using the most effective methods.** More research is needed to determine the best way to inform women about potential risks and benefits of hormonal contraception.[57]

Although half of the women in the study experienced a change in their mood, and over one-third experienced sexual side effects, the conclusion drawn from this data is that *doctors must improve their ability to prescribe contraceptives more effectively,* not that perhaps there's something wrong with the pill. The fact that women are complaining about it falls on deaf ears.

The message is loud and clear: Yes, we know that it might leave you depressed, anxious, and cause issues for you sexually, *but you should take it anyways because it works.*

Briana experienced this first-hand. She writes:

> The first time I went on the pill was shortly after I became sexually active. My doctor gave me a prescription for Ortho Tri-Cyclen, but it caused severe anxiety, uncontrollable crying, and depression. I couldn't function after three days of taking it. When I went back to the clinic, they saw how unstable I was and made an appointment for me. In the meantime, I stopped taking the pills, and by the time the appointment rolled around I was back to my normal self.
>
> I went back on the pill about a year later after I had a pregnancy scare (now I know that I was most likely a stressed-out college student with delayed ovulation). This time I tried a different pill. I was on Yaz for 18 months, and while I didn't have the severe side effects that I had the first time, I ultimately went off of it due to low libido. There were

times when I would cry with my partner because of lack of interest or inability to orgasm. Within a month of stopping, my libido was healthy again and I noticed (in retrospect) that during that entire 18 months I had been angry, irritable, and judgmental.

After vowing not to go on the pill again, I began considering it because my husband and I wanted a way to avoid barrier methods now that we were married. I originally wanted an IUD, but my doctor suggested that I try something less invasive at first and gave me a new pill, Sronyx®. When I shared my hesitation about going back on the pill, she simply invited me back for a follow-up appointment if the side effects were too much.

I went back unsatisfied after a month and my doctor asked me to keep trying, as it had only been a few weeks. Over the next few "cycles," I was travelling for work, I went on vacation, and I didn't have time to go back to the doctor. During that time, I developed severe anxiety that caused me to cry in front of my boss at work, I had frequent blow-ups with my husband (my reactions to these situations were, in retrospect, psychotic), and I had a lack of energy to do anything.

I started going to a therapist and for the first three sessions I cried the entire way through. While my life had legitimate stressors, the synthetic hormones in the pill I was taking exacerbated the stress and caused me to have severe anxiety. While Yaz had previously caused low libido, I now had no libido and extremely painful intercourse. The depression/anxiety also caused me to cry during sex. While I did eventually change which pill I was taking (and it was a little better for a few months) after nine total months on three different pills I had to say no for good.

While researching side effects of hormonal birth control, I found that seemingly unrelated symptoms that I had while I was taking it, like blurry vision and bloating, were surely caused by it. I simply did not feel like myself. I felt so sluggish that at times I felt physically, mentally, and emotionally worthless.

Most of these side effects went away within days of getting off of the pill and luckily I started menstruating right away. However, my libido took a few months to get back to normal.

What if a similar drug caused *men* to experience anxiety and depression?

If a woman has an emotional outburst or experiences depressive episodes, we often consider it a normal part of being a woman. "It's her hormones," we say, or, "It's probably just that time of the month." But would we react differently if men were having the emotional outbursts instead? Would the exact same side effects be taken more seriously if men experienced them?

In December 2016, a study in the *Journal of Clinical Endocrinology & Metabolism* evaluated the efficacy and safety of an injectable contraceptive for men (containing synthetic versions of estrogen and testosterone) by studying a group of 320 male participants.[58] The drug was extremely effective in reducing sperm count, thus demonstrating its efficacy as a contraceptive method.[59] However, during the study a number of participants developed "mood changes, depression, pain at the injection site, and increased libido" among other related side effects.[60] According to the study,

> Twenty men discontinued the study due to product-related side effects. Of these 20, six men discontinued only for changes in mood, and six men discontinued for the following single reasons: acne, pain or panic at first injection, palpitations, hypertension, and erectile dysfunction. Eight men discontinued for more than one side effect, including multiple reasons related to changes in mood.[61]

In addition, the study reported that "there was one death by suicide in the efficacy phase. The participant received three injections and committed suicide one month after the last injection," but this death was "assessed as not related to the study regimen."[62]

As you read these side effects, I have a feeling that you're thinking what I'm thinking. This sounds familiar, doesn't it? Sexual dysfunction, depression, mood changes, and changes in libido? That sounds a lot like the ways HCs affect women. Go figure. Messing with men's hormone levels has effects that extend beyond spermatogenesis?[†] You don't say.

[†] Sperm production.

Guess what happened? The drug was brought to market and is now available for men everywhere? You see commercials of young, handsome men walking down the street in snazzy outfits, laughing with their friends because of the new-found freedom this amazing new contraceptive drug will give them?

In a word ... No. What happened was *the trial was discontinued early.* An independent committee (developed to monitor the safety of clinical studies) reviewed the data mid-study and determined that "for safety reasons, recruitment should be stopped and enrolled participants should discontinue receiving injections and be transitioned to the recovery phase."[63] The conclusion was drawn that "the risks to the study participants outweighed the potential benefits to the study participants."[64]

As I stare at my computer screen thinking of what to write next, I'm at a loss for words. As far as I'm concerned, women are going through this same "drug trial" whenever we take HCs. Women all over the world experience depression, loss of libido, sexual dysfunction, and mood changes (such as anxiety and loss of affect) when they take HCs. Many women go on to develop severe migraines, deep-vein thrombosis, and/or have fatal strokes. Why doesn't someone call off *that* study — the one that's happening every single day whenever a woman pops one of those little pills? Where's her safety committee? Where was yours? And why did a committee jump in to protect the health and safety of the men in the study who experienced the same side effects that women experience every single day? Why is it that when we have virtually identical symptoms it isn't considered to be as serious? And why are we putting up with it?

Will the Pill Cause You to Choose the Wrong Partner?

Your menstrual cycle plays a central role in partner attraction. As you approach ovulation, you're more likely to prefer certain individuals based on how they smell.[65] The technical term is the *major histocompatibility complex* (MHC).[66] Your MHC genes influence both the way you smell to others and the way you perceive scent. HCs alter your MHC response and affect your mate choice based on scent and attractiveness.[67]

When cycling naturally, you'll more likely select a more genetically diverse partner whose face is more symmetrical and whose features (i.e., face and voice) and behaviour are more masculine.[68] However, when you take HCs, you're more likely to select a partner whose genetic makeup is more like yours and whose features, behaviour, and characteristics are more feminine.[69]

On a more troubling front, research shows a possible link between mate choice and infertility. When fertile couples are compared to infertile couples, infertile couples are more likely to share more of the same genes.[70] Similarly, couples with similar genetic patterns have been shown to have a higher rate of recurrent miscarriage.[71]

They say truth is stranger than fiction, and seriously, you can't make this stuff up. Put simply, HCs interfere with your natural ability to select an optimal mate (from a genetic standpoint). Since HCs change your hormonal pattern and interrupt your natural menstrual cycle, the natural process that governs your "pickers" is interrupted by the pill — and it's not just on your end. When you're off HCs, men are likely to find you more sexually attractive, and they even prefer the sound of your voice more during your fertile window.[72] This gives naturally-cycling women an advantage over women on HCs because they're more effectively able to compete for a mate.[73]

If you're looking for some compelling evidence, a study released in 2007 found that naturally-cycling women working as professional lap dancers in nightclubs earned significantly more money during their fertile window compared to the rest of their menstrual cycle.[74] They earned an average of $354 per shift during their fertile window compared to $260 per shift during their luteal phase and $185 per shift during menstruation. This worked out to an overall average of $276 per shift. Women on HCs during the study showed little variation in their day-to-day earnings and made an average of $193 per shift. In case math isn't your thing, the naturally-cycling women earned an average of $83 more per shift than women on hormonal birth control. Looks like naturally-cycling women have a competitive advantage after all.

Many women worry that they won't be attracted to their partner anymore when they come off HCs, similar to Samantha's situation. She writes:

I was put on the pill when I was 15 to help control my painful cramps. My teen years were rough to say the least. I was uncontrollable at times. My mood and attitude were awful. I spent a lot of time crying. My parents thought it was normal. I stayed on the pill for three years before switching over to the Depo shot at 19 when I started a serious relationship. When that relationship ended nearly a year later I decided not to go in for my next shot.

After the breakup, I enrolled in college, turned 21 (a huge deal in Wisconsin), met new friends, visited new places, lost 15 pounds effortlessly, and had the absolute time of my life. When I think back to those days, I genuinely don't remember a time I had been happier, aside from maybe early childhood. Every day I woke with a smile and I had such a thirst for life. My breasts hurt terribly pre-menses and my cramps were back, but damn was I loving life!!! I hadn't attributed any of this to coming off of hormonal contraceptives ... yet.

At 22 I met someone. I decided to go back on the pill. This is the period in my life that I refer to as the dark period. I was having a lot of family issues, which I had attributed my poor mood and attitude to. I moved out on my own, I was alone, and for the first time I was responsible for my own living expenses on top of my schoolwork.

Slowly but surely I became increasingly more depressed. The anxiety that I had had throughout my teenage years (still hadn't made the connection) was back and through the roof. I literally walked out of work one day (retail/customer service) in complete flight mode, tears streaming down my face, drove home, and sobbed for hours straight because I was convinced I was very ill and dying.

It was at this time that I chose to stop taking all of my medication, including my birth control pill. I wanted a fresh start. Within weeks, I found that my significant other was less attractive to me. He had a smell I had never noticed, and a couple of months post-pill I was finding that he completely disgusted me. Don't get me wrong, great guy!! He's very sweet, hard-working, would never treat a woman badly, but I couldn't even bear to kiss him anymore, so I broke it off.

I still hadn't attributed any of this to ending the pill. Fast forward a few years and I found myself in a serious relationship with my current boyfriend. Naturally I jumped back into the world of hormonal contraceptives. In the year and a half that I spent on those pills, I graduated college, quit smoking three times, started my career, and considered committing suicide. It finally occurred to me that the pill could be related and I began researching "pill anxiety," "pill depression," "pill mood," anything that could validate what I was feeling. I finally made the connection and went off the pill for good. I've been using fertility awareness for over a year now and I couldn't be happier I discovered it.

Does the Pill Cause Nutrient Deficiencies?

HCs are associated with the depletion of a number of key nutrients. Not only do they disrupt your nutrient stores, but they also disrupt the delicate balance of minerals in your body. Some of the ways this can affect you are well documented; others we don't fully understand yet.

Folate (vitamin B₉)

Folate (folic acid) is an essential nutrient for fertility and pregnancy. A deficiency in folate puts you at a much greater risk of having a baby born with neural tube defects. Unfortunately, HCs reduce your serum folate levels by impairing your folate metabolism.[75] In a systematic review of 17 studies conducted on 2831 women, the effect of oral contraceptives (OCs) on plasma and red blood cell folate concentration was measured.[76] The serum folate concentrations of OC users were significantly lower than for non-users, and this effect was more pronounced with long-term use.[77]

A few recent studies suggest HCs don't have a significant impact on your serum folate levels.[78] You won't be surprised that I'm skeptical of the idea that suddenly there's no association between HCs and folic acid depletion in women after decades of research showing the opposite effect. However, there seems to be a loophole that skews how the results can be interpreted — dietary and supplemental intake of folate.

Although HCs lower your serum folate levels, folate supplementation can normalize your levels. When the researchers allow the study participants to take vitamins for the duration of the study, they can draw the conclusion that there's no link between HCs and folate deficiency.[79] Many of these studies take place over a relatively short period of time (three months or less), thus failing to consider the compound effect that occurs over time.[80]

The realization that folate supplementation covers up the link between HCs and folate deficiency has set the stage for a new line of oral contraceptives that contain folic acid.[81] Instead of the headline — *HCs deplete serum folate levels in women of childbearing age and increases their risk of having a baby with neural tube defects* — marketers can say — *the pill provides a reliable source of folic acid for women of childbearing age and reduces the risk of neural tube defects.* Bayer (the drug company that makes Yaz) recently came out with Beyaz®, a birth control pill that contains folic acid.[82] But if the pill doesn't cause you to be deficient in folic acid, why add it in the first place? I think it draws attention away from the inherent risks associated with HC use and puts the focus back on you (as in, it's your fault if you develop a nutrient deficiency on the pill because of your poor diet).

Pyridoxine (vitamin B$_6$)

The research is much less contentious in the vitamin B$_6$ department. As we covered previously, HCs dramatically increase your requirements for vitamin B$_6$ by just under 4000 percent.[83] Unlike folate, the researchers can't rely on supplementation to make the study results look better.

Other vitamin and nutrient deficiencies

HC use puts women at an increased risk for various nutrient deficiencies, most notably B vitamins and trace minerals.[84] HCs are associated with a reduction in your serum levels of zinc, selenium, phosphorus, magnesium, and coenzyme Q10.[85] As if that wasn't enough, your nutritional requirements for vitamin C, vitamin A, and vitamin E increase significantly when you take HCs because your body metabolizes these vitamins differently.[86] On the flip side, HCs raise your serum levels of copper, iron, calcium, and cadmium.[87]

The *unscientific* term for this is a hot mess. Imagine that you're holding a bucket with a pencil-sized hole in the bottom. What happens when you fill the bucket with water? Naturally the water will slowly start draining out of the bottom. Trying to supplement away the nutrient depletion caused by HCs is kind of like solving your bucket problem by adding more water when you should just fix the leak.

If you're currently taking HCs, first consider taking a quality multivitamin and a vitamin B complex to mitigate the steady stream of nutrient depletion.[88] Then consider coming off the pill at some point in the future to give you time to restore the normal balance of nutrients that was altered by HCs.

Does the Pill Cause Cancer?

Long-term HC use is associated with an increased risk of cervical cancer.[89] While you may assume that women who use HCs are more likely to have unprotected sex (therefore putting themselves at a higher risk), that's not what's going on.[90]

In many ways *human papillomavirus* (HPV) is like the flu. We're pretty much all exposed to it when we become sexually active; there are over 100 different strains, and over 80 percent of women will be infected with it by age 50.[91] However, HCs inhibit your body's natural ability to fight it off and make you up to 85 percent less likely to clear up an HPV infection.[92] Chronic HPV infections increase your chances of developing cervical cancer, as chronic cervical infections cause more extensive tissue damage.[93]

Part of the reason your body is less able to fight off HPV while on HCs is related to folate deficiency. The longer you use HCs, the more pronounced this deficiency becomes, and your folate levels are inextricably linked to the health of your cervix. Folate deficiency increases your risk of developing a persistent HPV infection, cervical dysplasia, and cervical cancer.[94]

HCs also increase your risk of breast cancer and liver cancer.[95] These risks are often minimized in the literature because HCs are associated with a decreased risk of endometrial, ovarian, and colorectal cancer.[96] The researchers stress that the "net effect" is positive because HCs increase the risk of certain cancers while reducing others.[97] For the record, the International Agency for Research on Cancer (IARC) has classified combined oral contraceptives as a *group one carcinogen* due to a clear link between HC use and cancers of the cervix, breasts, and liver.[98]

The researchers don't seem to mind that HCs increase the risk of certain cancers. They may as well be saying, *So what if you have an increased risk of developing cervical, breast, and liver cancer? That's not important because HCs reduce your risk of developing endometrial, ovarian, and colorectal cancer. Did I mention how effective they are at preventing pregnancy? Don't worry about that whole cervical cancer/breast cancer/liver cancer thing — it's not that serious ... or is it?*

Let's talk stats for a moment. The IARC released a report in 2005 that examined the factors associated with the risk of developing cervical cancer after having an HPV infection.[99] The study analyzed 10 058 women with cervical cancer and 4151 women with high-grade squamous intraepithelial lesions (HSIL) — a fancy way of saying precancerous cervical cells. The study uncovered that when you use OCs for less than 5 years, you're 10 percent more likely to develop cervical cancer.[100] If you use them for 5 to 9 years, you're 60 percent more likely to develop cervical cancer, and if you use them for 10 years or more, you're 120 percent more likely to develop cervical cancer.[101] After 10 or more years on OCs, you're 4 times as likely to die from cervical cancer and 3 times more likely to die from liver disease.[102]

Are You Saying We Shouldn't Ever Use The Pill?

I'm thankful I had the option to use the pill as a teenager. However, I wasn't fully informed about the risks. If every woman were fully counselled on the risks and benefits of HCs, some women would choose never to take them, some would take them for a shorter period of time, and others would take them for just as long. It's important for each woman to have the opportunity to decide what's best for her, given all the facts. It's unacceptable for physicians to continue prescribing HCs without providing complete details about the side effects.

Although the pill has been associated with women's liberation (and I don't want to completely ignore the significance of that), numerous issues associated with HCs need to be put out in the open. After all, the heart of the women's liberation movement is freedom. For me, freedom is the right to exist in this world exactly as I am — *as a woman*. I recognize that there's more to being a woman than simply having a uterus and being able to menstruate, but as a biological woman with a menstrual cycle, I don't want to be part of a feminist movement that doesn't allow me to cycle naturally.

HCs subject your body to a cascade of hormonal changes that have untold effects on every part of your experience as a woman. They affect your physical body (your clitoris and vulva), your emotional well-being (increasing your chances of experiencing depression and anxiety), your sex life (lowered libido and increased chance of painful sex), your choice of an intimate partner, and they disrupt how your body metabolizes and stores nutrients (B vitamins and others).

I can't tell you how many women I've spoken to who had no idea the pill was affecting them ... until they stopped taking it. They suddenly realized they'd been living in a haze — a haze that was only lifted when they stopped taking the hormones. They immediately began feeling like themselves again, their libido came back, they had more energy, and their depression and anxiety went away (see Chapter 9).

What if we instead called HCs synthetic hormone suppressants? Or exogenous endocrine disruptors? How about xenoestrogens? Or hormone disrupting chemicals? What if we called them a form of chemical castration? It's not so much of a stretch considering the research linking HCs to clitoral shrinkage and low libido.

Did you know that Depo-Provera (an injectable HC) is used to chemically castrate sex offenders? It has been shown to reduce the incidences of recidivism in convicted sex offenders (i.e., it has been shown to prevent convicted sex offenders from committing new sex crimes).[103] When you think of it that way, it sounds ludicrous to give a woman the same medication that has been used to chemically castrate men and think it won't have any adverse effects.

While researching and writing this chapter, I found myself feeling sad, angry, and frustrated, but in the end, I was more compelled than ever to share this information with you. Think of that cliché that says *the truth will set you free.* Once you discover what these artificial hormones are really doing to your body, take the opportunity to do something about it. In the next chapter, we'll focus on what happens when you come off HCs.

Summary

- A fake menstrual bleed was added to the original design of the pill to get women to go along with it, leading to the artificial 28-day pill cycle.
- HCs are effective because they interfere with ovulation and implantation, and they prevent your cervix from producing fertile-quality CM.
- Although HCs increase your risk of deep-vein thrombosis and stroke, there are several other, more common, side effects to watch out for.
- HCs have been shown to lower libido and dramatically decrease testosterone levels.
- HCs have been shown to shrink the clitoris and surrounding vulvar tissues (especially the vaginal opening), which increases the risk of painful sex.
- HCs are associated with an increased risk of anxiety and depression.
- HCs have been shown to alter your choice of an intimate partner by changing the way you perceive their "scent."
- HCs cause nutrient deficiencies by disrupting the normal balance of vitamins and minerals in the body.
- Long-term HC use is associated with higher rates of cervical, breast, and liver cancer (and reduced rates of ovarian, endometrial, and colorectal cancer).
- You have the right to make an informed choice about the medications you use.

Chapter 8
Coming Off the Pill

"When the pill was released women had to stand up to their doctors to get it, today they must fight to get off it."

— Holly Grigg-Spall, *Sweetening the Pill*

Now that you know what happens when you take HCs, let's focus on what happens when you stop taking them. Given the link between HCs and nutrient depletion, women who come off HCs to conceive will want to pay particular attention to replenishing their nutritional stores. However, the health benefits associated with restoring your natural menstrual cycle apply to all women. All HCs disrupt normal ovulation to some degree, whether ovulation is suppressed completely or your natural hormone levels are disrupted.[1] Coming off the pill or other HCs gives you the opportunity to benefit from your natural ovarian hormones, particularly progesterone (see Chapter 1).

Here are the two important questions we address in this chapter:

1. How do HCs affect fertility?
2. How long will it take for my menstrual cycles to return to normal once I stop taking them?

When Should I Come Off the Pill?

We all have an internal guidance system that tells us when we're on the right path. It's the feeling you get when you meet someone new and there's something off about your interaction — when something doesn't feel right, but you can't fully explain why. It's the inner voice that protests when you do things you know are bad for you (like bingeing on junk food or watching TV 'till 2 a.m. knowing you have to get up early). But unfortunately, many of us are disconnected from it. If you're not as connected to your intuition as you'd like to be, I encourage you to start paying closer attention.

I've spoken to many women who had a feeling they should come off HCs several months before they started trying for a baby, but their healthcare practitioners told them not to. Their intuition was trying to break through, but, as many of us often do, they ignored their inner voice. Though some women get pregnant immediately after coming off HCs (or even while taking them!), not every woman does.

Whether you plan ahead for it or not, your body goes through a transition period when you come off HCs. There is a well-documented, temporary period of menstrual cycle irregularity and subfertility that lasts anywhere from 6 to 18 months (or more) when you stop taking HCs (depending on which type you used). When deciding how soon to come off HCs, you must account for this period of transition in your calculations. If you are coming off HCs to get pregnant, a minimum of 18 months to 2 years is warranted to allow your cycles to return to normal (see Chapter 17).

Will My Period Come Back Right Away?

What if a team of scientists created a drug that could stop you from needing to urinate every few hours? By taking your pill every morning, you'd only have to urinate once every 3 to 5 days — so you decided to try it. Now after 7 years on the drug, your productivity has skyrocketed and you love the freedom you've gained, but you're wondering how long it will take your body to return to normal once you stop taking it...

How could a drug that suppresses urination affect your health in the long-term? Would you be at an increased risk for gallstones? Would it affect your ability to excrete toxins? Would you be more susceptible to bladder infections? Would it take time for urinary function to resume normally when you stop taking it?

Your period is an equally normal and natural bodily function, so perhaps we should be asking similar questions about HCs. Is it reasonable to assume that shutting down a normal bodily function for years at a time won't affect your health? Given the ridiculous notion of not urinating for several days at a time, why do we think suppressing our menstrual cycles won't have an impact? And why do we think our cycles will bounce back immediately after we come off of them?

Studies show that ovulation is typically delayed during a woman's first few cycles off HCs (as evidenced by longer post-HC cycles), and the luteal phase is shorter than normal.[2] One study compared the menstrual cycle parameters of 175 women immediately after coming off combined oral contraceptives (OCs) to 284 non-users (i.e., the control group).[3] Compared to non-users, OC users experienced major cycle disturbances for several months after coming off. OC users experienced shorter luteal phases during their first 12 months off OCs (most notably during the first 2 cycles). OC users had significantly longer menstrual cycles, and it took an average of 9 to 12 cycles before their cycle parameters normalized (see Chapter 4). Note that the study reported an average period of 9 to 12 *menstrual cycles* — not months — before cycle patterns normalized. Depending on the actual length of your cycles it could take anywhere from 9 to 18 months (or more) for your cycles to normalize, based on the results of this study.

Much of the research in the area of HCs excludes women with a history of irregular or abnormal cycles; however, women with a history of irregular cycles, ovulatory disturbances, or amenorrhea are much more likely to experience *post-pill amenorrhea* (when your period doesn't return for 6 months or more).[4] As much as I'd like to say this is a recent discovery, I found a mention of the link between irregular cycles and post-pill amenorrhea in a study published in 1969.[5] The study examined the cycles of 515 women immediately after they stopped taking OCs — 4 of whom did not get their period back for more than 180 days after coming off the hormones. The researchers made the following statement about the results:

> In the present study four out of 515 subjects developed amenorrhea lasting more than 180 days. It is noteworthy that three of these four women had had irregular menstrual periods before the therapy. The main conclusion of this investigation is therefore that combined oral contraceptive agents should be used with caution in women who have irregular menstruation, especially in those who have not completed their family.[6]

Fast forward 50 years and HCs are routinely prescribed to women with irregular cycles as treatment, even though these women are more likely to experience a delay in the return of their normal fertility when they come off. HCs aren't causing amenorrhea in these women, but instead masking the underlying problem while it remains unaddressed. HCs prevent women with legitimate ovulatory disorders from observing changes in their menstrual cycle patterns. It's often only when they come off HCs that the full extent of their condition is revealed, either through post-pill amenorrhea, menstrual abnormalities, or infertility.[7]

If you were put on HCs to regulate your cycles, you may experience a greater delay in the return of your normal periods. In a study of 63 women who developed amenorrhea after coming off OCs, 40 of them had suffered from amenorrhea or prolonged, irregular cycles before they started taking the pill.[8] These researchers came to the same conclusion as the researchers who published the 1969 study: "Combined oestrogen-progestogen oral contraceptives should be used with caution in women with irregular menstruation."[9]

If you had fairly normal cycles before you went on HCs, you have a much lower chance of developing post-pill amenorrhea; but even if your period comes back right away, it doesn't mean that everything has immediately gone back to normal.

HCs and Your Ovaries

In addition to shrinking your vulvar tissues (see Chapter 7), combined HCs shrink your ovaries by about 50 percent.[10] (Yes, you did read that correctly!) One study measured the ovarian volume of 887 women between the ages of 19 and 46.[11] The participants were divided into two groups: HC users and non-users. The ovarian volume of HC users was *49.6 percent lower* than the ovarian volume of non-users. A separate study of 70 women between the ages of 18 and 35 compared women who used HCs for 1 year or more to women who had not used HCs within the last year.[12] In this case, the ovarian volume of HC users was about *58 percent lower* compared to non-users — and volume is only one of the markers used to assess a woman's ovarian reserve parameters.

An ovarian reserve assessment is used to provide an estimate of your reproductive potential by estimating your remaining reproductive lifespan. The most common markers include *anti-Müllerian hormone* (AMH), *antral follicle count*, and *ovarian volume*. Serum AMH levels provide an indirect measure of how many antral follicles you have in your ovaries, and your antral follicle count gives you a measure of your current egg supply. For women undergoing in vitro fertilization (IVF), serum AMH levels have been shown to be a good predictor of how many eggs your doctor will be able to retrieve during the IVF process.[13]

Women who've recently come off HCs have significantly lower ovarian reserve parameters compared to non-users.[14] Not only are their ovaries smaller, but their AMH levels are lower, and they have fewer follicles.[15] This effect is thought to be temporary because a woman's ovarian reserve parameters return to normal several months after going off HCs. In a study of 743 women who had undergone *fertility preservation* — a procedure involving the use of cryopreservation techniques (i.e., egg freezing) to save a woman's eggs for future use — women who had taken a 6- to 7-month break after coming off HCs saw an improvement in their antral follicle count and had more eggs available to harvest.[16] The findings of this study prompted the researchers to suggest that women who wish to undergo egg freezing wait at least 6 to 7 months after coming off HCs before undergoing the procedure for better results. But why is the recommendation any different for women who wish to conceive naturally? If it takes at least 6 to 7 months for a woman's ovaries to normalize post HCs, why aren't all women advised to come off HCs ahead of time when planning for pregnancy?

Delayed Return of Fertility Post HCs

The research is clear — HCs are associated with a temporary delay in the return of your normal fertility, most notably in the first 6 months immediately after you stop taking them.[17] One study compared the time it took 2841 women to become pregnant after coming off a number of different contraceptive methods.[18] The results are staggering — on average, it took 4 months for women who had previously used condoms to conceive, 6 months for progestin-only pill users, 8 months for combined OC users, 10 months for implant users, and 15 months for injectable contraceptive (IC) users. Women using intrauterine devices (IUDs) conceived within an average of 8 months, though the researchers didn't clarify whether the IUDs were hormonal or non-hormonal.

The study results are in line with what I've seen in my work with women. Compared to women using non-hormonal methods of birth control, it often takes former HC users longer to conceive — usually twice as long — and nearly 4 times as long for IC users, especially with long-term use (long-term was defined as 2 or more years, and short-term was defined as less than 2 years).

In the case of OCs and ICs, the duration of use made a significant difference. Even though the average time it took women coming off OCs to conceive was about 8 months, the average length of time to conception for short-term users was 4.5 months, compared to 8.5 months for long-term users. Similarly with ICs, the average time to conception was 15 months, but for short-term users the average time to conception was 8.5 months compared to 18.8 months for long-term users.[19] In other words, both the type of HC, and the duration of use have a significant impact on the length of time it takes your fertility to normalize.

In a separate study, not only did it take about twice as long for past OC users to conceive compared to non-users (5.88 versus 3.64 cycles), OC users had a significantly lower chance of conceiving within the first 6 months after coming off.[20] This trend of reduced fertility continued for a full year after the participants had stopped taking OCs. According to the researchers,

> We believe that women who plan to become pregnant should be aware of the possible, even though temporary, delay in their ability to conceive after the cessation of pill use. Furthermore, it has been accepted generally that couples could be considered for an infertility evaluation if they had tried unsuccessfully to conceive for at least 12 months after stopping all birth control methods. In view of the findings of this study, at least 15 months before an infertility evaluation might be an acceptable interval for prior pill users.[21]

The researchers are calling for a special designation for women who've recently come off HCs. Instead of jumping to diagnose women with infertility before normal fertility is restored, they're suggesting we add a buffer period to the normal calculation.

Most physicians require that you try to conceive naturally for a year or more before referring you to a fertility specialist. If you're over 35, this time frame is truncated to 6 months. Although it's always a good idea to have a fertility assessment as early as possible when you have concerns about your fertility, you could be referred for expensive fertility treatments before your body has fully normalized post HCs.

As I was going through the research, I noticed a clear tendency to downplay the delay in the return of normal fertility post HCs. But most women aren't aware of this delay, and therefore don't take it into consideration when deciding how early to come off. Since we spend the majority of our adult lives preventing pregnancy, we assume that we'll get pregnant the first time we try. Most women become increasingly distressed when they're not pregnant after 2 months of trying — let alone 12!

As I was writing this section, I had a consultation with a woman named Carla (age 37). She had been trying to conceive for over a year when she reached out to me. She had been on the pill for 10 years before coming off when she got married. Before her wedding, Carla went to see her doctor to find out if she should consider coming off the pill ahead of time because she knew she wanted to start a family. Unfortunately, her physician told her there was no point in coming off early, leaving her with the impression that she would conceive right away. Based on the above studies, the average length of time to pregnancy for women coming off the pill is 8 months, and there is a trend towards decreased fertility for a full year post HCs (which would put her within the expected time frame). The doctor also failed to counsel her on the impact of age on fertility (see Chapter 17).

Don't get me wrong; I'm not saying that it's impossible to come off the pill and get pregnant right away. Many women get pregnant within the first few months off the pill, but you don't know how long it will take *you*. Coming off HCs early doesn't guarantee you'll conceive naturally, but it certainly increases your chances. By observing your natural cycles off the pill, you'll have the opportunity to address any issues that arise before you start feeling the time pressure kick in. You'll also give your body the time it needs to recover from years of HC use.

Coming Off HCs When You Don't Want to Get Pregnant

Though many women come off HCs to conceive, coming off HCs is equally important when you don't want to get pregnant. As a biological woman, your body functions optimally when you're healthy and when your menstrual cycle is normal and ovulatory. From a biological standpoint, we're all here to reproduce — as such, your natural cycles are inextricably linked to your physiology.

You can only produce optimal levels of estrogen, progesterone, and testosterone when you ovulate regularly. Women on HCs have an increased risk of developing breast cancer, cervical cancer, and liver cancer, not to mention a clear increase in cardiovascular risk factors (and the list goes on — see Chapter 7). HCs were never designed to improve your health; they were created to suppress a completely natural and healthy function in your body. Somehow, after 50 years of advertising, we've become convinced that our natural cycles aren't natural, and it's beneficial for us to chemically suppress the very function that makes us female — our ability to reproduce.

Given that one of the most common side effects associated with HCs is low libido, coming off them allows you to reconnect with your sexuality. As your testosterone (and other hormone) levels normalize, you may notice an obvious increase in libido (though this can take some time). You may find it easier to reach orgasm, and you may find that your orgasms are more intense! Even if you don't want to get pregnant, you shouldn't have to give up your right to experience sexual pleasure.

Recognizing that your natural cycles are an essential part of optimal health is the first step. The second step is figuring out how to manage your fertility without hormones. We'll focus more on using fertility awareness for birth control in Chapter 10.

Post-Pill Recovery

Given that the post-pill recovery phase lasts anywhere from 6 months to 2 years or more, aim to focus on 4 key areas to support your body during this transition:

1. Replenishing nutrients,
2. Supporting your natural hormone production,
3. Restoring gut health, and
4. Supporting your liver.

Replenishing nutrients

Since HC use is associated with nutrient depletion, identifying which nutrients are depleted and replenishing them is critical. The most effective way to replenish these key nutrients is to incorporate foods known to contain high levels, though supplementation is often required when deficiencies are identified. Key nutrients depleted by HCs include:

- Riboflavin (vitamin B_2)
- Pyridoxine (vitamin B_6)
- Folate (vitamin B_9)
- Cobalamin (vitamin B_{12})
- Ascorbic acid (vitamin C)
- *alpha*-Tocopherol (vitamin E)
- Retinol (vitamin A)
- Selenium
- Magnesium
- Zinc
- Coenzyme Q10

See Figure 8–1 for a breakdown of foods highest in five of these key nutrients. Also see Chapter 12 for a full discussion of foods that support menstrual cycle health and fertility.

Supporting your natural hormone production

All of your steroid hormones are synthesized from cholesterol (including estrogen, progesterone, testosterone, and cortisol).[22] As such, cholesterol is required for optimal hormone production, as are a variety of key nutrients that support hormone production including vitamin A, all the B vitamins including vitamin B_6 and folate, as well as vitamin C, vitamin D, iodine, selenium, and zinc (see Chapter 12).[23]

Vitamin B_9 (Folate)	Vitamin B_6 (Pyridoxine)	Vitamin B_{12} (Cobalamin)	Selenium	Zinc
Duck/goose liver (738 mcg)	Pistachios (1.3 mg)	Clams (98.9 mcg)	Brazil nuts (1917 mcg)	Oysters (90.8 mg)
Turkey liver (691 mcg)	Turkey liver (1.0 mg)	Lamb liver (85.7 mcg)	Pork kidney (312 mcg)	Beef (roasted) (10.3 mg)
Chicken liver (588 mcg)	Beef liver (1.0 mg)	Beef liver (70.6 mcg)	Lamb kidney (219 mcg)	Pumpkin seeds (10.3 mg)
Lamb liver (400 mcg)	Wild salmon (0.9 mg)	Turkey liver (58.2 mcg)	Beef kidney (168 mcg)	Lamb liver (7.9 mg)
Beef liver (253 mcg)	Duck/goose liver (0.8 mg)	Duck/goose liver (54.0 mcg)	Lamb liver (116.0 mcg)	Sesame seeds (7.2 mg)
Sunflower seeds (237 mcg)	Chicken liver (0.8 mg)	Chicken liver (16.8 mcg)	Chicken liver (82.4 mcg)	Beef liver (5.3 mg)
Raw spinach (194 mcg)	Sunflower seeds (0.8 mg)	Oysters (19.5 mcg)	Sunflower seeds (79.3 mcg)	Sunflower seeds (5.3 mg)
Cooked chickpeas (172 mcg)	Beef (roasted) (0.3 mg)	Fish roe (eggs) (11.5 mcg)	Oysters (63.7 mcg)	Lamb (roasted) (5.2 mg)
Fish roe (eggs) (92.0 mcg)	Chicken breast (0.3 mg)	Sardines (8.9 mcg)	Clams (64.0 mcg)	Chicken liver (4.0 mg)
Avocado (89.0 mcg)	Avocado (0.3 mg)	Lamb (roasted) (3.1 mg)	Fish roe (eggs) (51.7 mcg)	Duck/goose liver (3.1 mg)
Cooked lentils (67 mcg)	Fish roe (eggs) (0.2 mg)	Wild salmon (3.0 mcg)	Sardines (52.7 mcg)	Clams (2.7 mg)
Eggs (51.0 mcg)	Eggs (0.2 mg)	Beef (roasted) (2.0 mcg)	Wild salmon (46.8 mcg)	Turkey liver (2.6 mg)
Wild salmon (29.0 mcg)	Raw spinach (0.2 mg)	Eggs (1.4 mcg)	Beef liver (36.1 mcg)	Chicken breast (1.0 mg)
Clams (29.0 mcg)	Cooked chickpeas (0.1 mg)	Chicken breast (0.2 mcg)	Eggs (34.2 mcg)	Wild salmon (0.8 mg)
Oysters (18.0 mcg)	Sardines (0.1 mg)	Raw spinach (0.0 mcg)	Beef (roasted) (26.7 mcg)	Avocados (0.7 mg)
Cooked kale (13 mcg)	Oysters (0.1 mg)	Avocados (0.0 mcg)	Raw spinach (1.0 mcg)	Raw spinach (0.5 mg)
Chicken breast (4.0 mcg)	Cooked kale (0.1 mg)	Cooked kale (0.0 mcg)	Cooked kale (0.9 mcg)	Cooked kale (0.2 mg)

Figure 8-1: Food sources of key nutrients[24]

Thyroid disorders are the most common cause of menstrual cycle disturbances and HCs have been shown to alter normal thyroid function.[25] Iodine, zinc, and selenium are required for thyroid hormone synthesis, so aim to incorporate foods that contain these key nutrients (see Chapter 16 for more on supporting thyroid function).[26]

Lifestyle factors are equally important in optimizing your natural hormone production. From ensuring that you're getting adequate sleep to reducing your chemical exposure, a multitude of lifestyle factors can improve your reproductive hormone levels. See Chapter 13 for a full discussion.

Restoring gut health

Long-term use of HCs disrupts the balance of friendly bacteria in the digestive tract (gut), leaving HC users at an increased risk of developing irritable bowel syndrome (IBS).[27] The digestive tract contains estrogen receptors, and exposure to excess estrogen (as is the case when using estrogen containing HCs) has been shown to influence the integrity of the intestinal barrier — a risk factor for developing IBS.[28] HC use has also been shown to alter the vaginal microflora, making you more susceptible to contracting bacterial vaginosis (BV), *candida albicans* (yeast infections), and other infections, especially during the first few months of use.[29] I've worked with several women who developed recurrent yeast infections shortly after they began using HCs — an issue that typically resolves once they stop taking them.

Your cycles are an extremely helpful window into your digestive function. If your digestion is off you may notice abnormal cervical mucus patterns, or even abnormal bleeding patterns, throughout your cycle. As your health improves, you can track the changes in your cycle patterns. Digestive issues can interfere with nutrient intake, hormonal balance, menstrual cycle health, and immune function, not to mention the significant impact they can have on your quality of life. Focusing on gut-healing foods such as bone broth and fermented foods are a good place to start (see Chapter 12).[30]

You'll also want to identify any existing allergies or food sensitivities you may have. Imagine you have a cut on your finger, but whenever it starts healing you re-injure it. In the same way, consuming foods you are sensitive or allergic to can prevent your gut from healing and lead to chronic inflammation.

Supporting your liver

Your liver breaks down fat, produces energy, and plays a key role in maintaining your blood sugar balance.[31] Your liver also cleanses your blood, regulates your cholesterol levels, and (back to the topic of recovering from HC use) regulates the balance of sex hormones in your body.[32] Your liver is working continuously — day and night — to break down hormones, chemicals, and toxins to get them out of your bloodstream so you can go on functioning normally. Whether you're taking synthetic estrogen and progestins via hormonal birth control or using scented beauty products, your actions are putting more stress on your already-overburdened liver.

More strain on your liver makes it more likely that your hormones will be out of balance. Poor liver function can worsen premenstrual symptoms, acne, irregular menstrual cycles, and menstrual cramps. Although it may be tempting to assume that the best way to support your liver is by doing a liver detox or taking supplements, it's best to start by reducing your toxic load.

You may also wish to incorporate cruciferous vegetables into your diet, as they contain a compound called *indole-3-carbinol* (I3C) that helps your liver metabolize estrogen more efficiently and reduces the harmful effects associated with excess estrogen in the body (see Chapter 13).[33] I3C can also be found in supplement form along with *diindolylmethane* (DIM), an active compound that is derived from I3C.[34]

Know When to Seek Support

Knowing that long-term HC use is associated with a delay in the return of your normal fertility is helpful because you'll know what to expect when you stop. If your cycles don't immediately normalize within the first few months, you'll know not to panic.

With that said, if you're still waiting for your period to show up after 4 to 6 months, or if you're not having relatively regular periods 12 to 18 months post HCs, seek professional support sooner rather than later. See Chapter 18 for a full discussion of assembling your healthcare support team.

Summary

- When coming off HCs to start a family, allow for a transition period of at least 18 months to 2 years to allow your cycles to normalize, since this can take anywhere from 9 to 12 cycles.
- HCs shrink your ovaries and suppress your ovarian reserve parameters. Allow a minimum of 6 to 7 months post HCs for your ovarian reserve parameters to return to normal.

- HCs have been shown to cause a temporary delay in the return of your normal fertility — anywhere from 3 to 18 months or more, depending on what type of HC you were taking and for how long.
- Irregular menstrual cycles are associated with an increased risk of experiencing a delay in the return of your normal fertility post HCs.
- Coming off HCs is equally important even when you're not planning to have children.
- Focus on replenishing nutrients, supporting your natural hormone production, restoring gut health, and supporting your liver during the post-pill recovery phase.
- If your period hasn't returned within 4 to 6 months after coming off HCs, or your cycles haven't normalized within 12 to 18 months, seek professional support.

Chapter 9
The Wisdom of Your Menstrual Cycles

"We can reclaim the wisdom of the menstrual cycle by tuning in to our cyclic nature and celebrating it as a source of our female power."

— Christiane Northrup, MD, *Women's Bodies, Women's Wisdom*

My menstrual cycle has been one of the greatest teachers in my life. I spent most of my late teens and early twenties managing extremely painful periods. At times, the pain was so severe it felt like my insides were on fire. I could easily have decided that I hated being a woman or that my body was broken and useless, but deep down I knew my body was trying to send me an important message about my health.

Like a caterpillar's transformation into a butterfly, each menstrual cycle represents an opportunity to work through life's challenges; and like a butterfly, emerge transformed each time a new cycle begins. Experiencing this cyclical process each month over the past two decades has led me to leave unfulfilling relationships, change my career path, heal from some of the most painful losses I've experienced, and write this book.

When you think of your menstrual cycle as a vital sign (and monitor it accordingly), you can observe how your daily actions and lifestyle habits affect your cycles. I invite you to think of your menstrual cycle as a tool — a powerful ally and friend that's always on your side (even when it doesn't seem that way).

When the Connection Is Severed...

Part of tapping into the wisdom of your menstrual cycle is appreciating what happens when you're *not* connected to it. If your menstrual cycle can connect you with your inner guidance system and help you to feel more like yourself, does that mean HCs can disconnect you from your true self?

When I interviewed Lara Owen, author of *Her Blood is Gold*, she described her experience coming off the pill as follows:

> When I was about 22, I had been on the pill (on and off) for about four years, and I had started to become increasingly anxious. I thought, "Well ... I'll just see if it's got anything to do with the pill," but I didn't really know. So about two weeks after I stopped taking it, I had this thought that I felt like myself again — and I thought, goodness, that's an interesting thought — there [are] a lot of implications with that. Did somehow being on the pill stop me from feeling like myself? And [if so] ... what was that about?[1]

I've heard eerily similar stories time and time again in my interviews with women who've taken HCs. They use words like "the dark period," "the dark years," "anxiety," "depression," "fatigue," "uncontrollable crying," "numb," "fog," "crazy," and "paranoid." When describing how they felt after coming off HCs, they say things like, "It felt like the fog had lifted," "I actually have a sex drive now," and "I started feeling like myself again." One woman referred to her time off HCs as "the golden years" — because she couldn't remember a time when she had felt happier.

In my interview with Sjanie Hugo Wurlitzer, co-author of *Wild Power*, this is how she described it:

> My journey began in my early twenties when I thought I was being responsible and got onto contraception as a way to make sure that I wouldn't get pregnant. I had no fertility education growing up — truth be told, the only education I had was, "Don't get pregnant," and the best way to avoid that was to take contraception. I tried the pill and had a huge reaction and eventually I was offered the contraceptive injection

and went on that instead. At the time I was just delighted that it completely stopped my menstrual cycle — it seemed like an added bonus, and I was on that contraceptive injection for seven years. I now refer to that time in my life as the seven lean years or seven dark years.

After a period of time I started experiencing problems, and I just had a hunch that it was connected to the contraception, so I came off. When my cycles started coming back, I'll never forget it 'cause it was such a stark contrast from what I'd experienced before. Having had no menstrual cycle, and having been in this wasteland plateau emotionally, mentally — things had really become stagnant. My menstrual cycles came back, and it was like my inner lights were being turned back on.

My emotional landscape was being reignited, and with that my drive, my desire, my passion, my calling all just began to come alive again in me, and suddenly I had a renewed sense of purpose. I was connected back to my intuition — back to my inner compass. It was a crazy time, I won't lie, but in time I began to find my ground. As my cycle began to regulate I began to discover it as an amazing resource. I started to feel like a woman for the first time *ever* in my life. It woke the woman in me up. It was so beautiful — and of course my entire life changed at that point.[2]

She goes on to say:

It's like ... from the moment we're born, we all have within us a blueprint for our highest potential and possibility. What it is we're here to serve in our life — what it is we're here to do — and our menstrual cycle supports us to grow into that. Now, with me being on contraception, it was like that line between myself and that intelligence was severed.[3]

In Jennifer's case, HCs severed her connection to her creativity — an integral part of her identity. She writes:

The biggest difference I've noticed now that I've been off hormonal birth control for a while is that it robbed me of my creativity. I'm an artist, and while on hormonal birth control I lost my drive and passion to create. I had completely quit making art for two years while on it. I felt like my true identity and self was suppressed to the point where I found no fault in that, and this spilled into other areas of my life as well. Now that I'm off it I'm back to my creative self and making art again. It's terrifying that I couldn't even see what was happening until I got off it.

Both Sjanie and Jennifer's experiences highlight something that I have come to know about the menstrual cycle: *your menstrual cycle contains a great deal of wisdom and power.* Your cycles are part of a greater force that propels you toward a greater purpose in life — a force that wants you to become the most vibrant and authentic version of yourself, both mentally and physically. When you take HCs, you're severing your connection to a source of intelligence and wisdom that lies deep inside of you.

In my interview with Alexandra Pope, the other co-author of *Wild Power*, this is how she described it:

There is an extraordinary kind of presence or energy within us that gets unleashed when we start to engage with our menstrual cycle. When women start to really engage, in an intimate way, with their menstrual cycle — to trust it, to believe in it, and to move with that rhythm ... it's as though they unlock this whole new inner resource, and inner territory, which has a quality of holiness about it. A quality of ... wow ... wonder almost — a feeling of being home. A feeling that they are inside themselves and something feels right. It's like they're stepping onto hallowed ground — sacred ground within themselves. The cycle process (in general) invites in this energy — a lovely feeling of presence with oneself. A feeling of love and self-acceptance that grows over time. But most particularly ... women are able to really touch into their unique self — what we call their holy essence — and from that, what their calling is.[4]

Sexual energy, by its very nature, is creative energy. HCs prevent you from experiencing the full expression of your sexuality by suppressing your libido — but suppressing this energy affects far more than your desire to be sexual with someone. The sooner you embrace your cycles, the sooner you can get about the business of doing whatever it is you're supposed to be doing with your life.

A Time to Retreat...

Although menstruation has received a great deal of media attention in the past few years, periods are still taboo. One of the challenges of being a woman in a male-dominated workforce is that our worthiness is judged in comparison to our male counterparts. Since men don't share our experience of monthly cycling (and menstruation), we're expected to actively hide our periods from the world, both physically and emotionally. Beyond hiding any physical evidence of our monthly bleed with menstrual products, there's an added expectation that our productivity will remain unchanged.

The fast-paced, modern world doesn't make it easy to step back from our busy lives when our periods come around. For decades, women have been striving to prove they're just as capable as men, yet as of this writing, Canadian women earn an average of 87 cents for every dollar earned by a man.[5] The last thing we need to do is admit we need time to rest during our periods.

Advertisements for tampons and pads convey the message that your periods shouldn't hold you back. Somehow it's always a sunny day, the women are always wearing white, they appear to be overjoyed (for no apparent reason), and they're usually in the midst of some sort of strenuous athletic activity. They're determined to do the exact same activities they'd be doing if they weren't on their periods. *Except they are on their periods.*

I'm not saying you shouldn't do whatever you want to do when you have your period. If you want to climb a mountain or run a marathon, go for it! However, when I'm on *my* period I don't feel like climbing a mountain or running a marathon — and I think that's okay too. It's normal for your mood and energy level to shift when you have your period. If you feel like taking time to withdraw from the world, you're not showing weakness, you're simply tuning into the wisdom of your cycles and prioritizing your needs over everyone else's. After all, it's much easier to give *of* yourself than to take time *for* yourself. How long has it been since you took time away from your busy schedule to focus on you — *without feeling guilty about it*? If you feel less outgoing and energetic when you're menstruating, there's no reason to force yourself to pretend otherwise.

If your periods are unbearable, there's a reason for that. Your inner guidance system is trying to communicate with you, and the message will continue getting louder unless you start paying attention. In my interview with Clare Blake, founder of Fertility Massage Therapy™, this is how she described it:

> Physically, when we release our bleed, we're releasing that lining, but we are energetically releasing all that we've taken on for that whole month, and then we're letting it go. If we don't slow down and we don't listen to our bodies throughout the month, and we don't honour our menstrual cycle, then our bodies are going to give us painful periods, and problems with our periods — because it's our womb literally screaming out at us, *You're not listening to me!*[6]

What would happen if you embraced the natural ebb and flow of your menstrual cycle? What if you allowed yourself to go deeply into your feelings of frustration, unhappiness, or even anger during your premenstrual phase? What if you allowed yourself to experience these feelings as they arose, without judgment, and took the necessary time to discover what you could learn from them?

In case you need to hear this, *I give you permission to feel however you need to feel when you have your period.* If that means you withdraw from your social commitments and take some much-needed time for yourself, then so be it. If you feel a bit moody or bitchy on the days leading up to your period, or if you're not your usual shiny, happy self for a few days, that's alright too. You may need more sleep to feel rested, you may feel more emotional or react more abruptly in certain situations, and you may not feel like attending parties or social gatherings. Life becomes more manageable when you give yourself the permission and space to honour your natural inclination to withdraw from the world during your period — even if just for a few hours.

The Four Phases of Your Menstrual Cycle

With each period, you shed the energy from your past cycle and embark on a new journey. Passing through the phases of your menstrual cycle is like experiencing the changing seasons of the year.[7] In their book, *Wild Power*, Alexandra Pope and Sjanie Hugo Wurlitzer beautifully describe how the menstrual cycle aligns with the seasons of the year:

> Each month you move through an inner winter, spring, summer, and autumn and back to winter again. Each phase ushers in a set of very specific psychological challenges. In meeting these challenges, you rise to the initiatory task, grow your power, and build the inner container to hold your full magnificence.[8]

Your menstrual cycle has a natural ebb and flow, leaving you feeling more energized and vibrant at certain times and more introspective and withdrawn at others. It's time to embrace the cyclical nature of your menstrual cycle and acknowledge the physical and emotional changes that come along with it. In nature there's always a balance. Both sun and rain are needed to nurture crops. Alexandra Pope said it best during our interview: "That's why we're awake during the day and we sleep at night — it's part of the natural order of things."[9]

The follicular phase

Your follicular phase is the spring of your menstrual cycle. After your bleeding stops, a new cycle begins. There's a sense of hope and excitement in the air. In Canada, spring comes after a long stretch of snow, cold, and ice. The snow melts, the rain starts to fall, and there's a promise of new life. A powerful creative force brings everything back to life after being dormant all winter.

Your follicles are rapidly growing and producing ever-increasing amounts of estrogen, which triggers your uterine lining to start proliferating as your body prepares for ovulation. Your follicular phase is a wonderful time to tap into your creative energy, work on creative projects, visit friends, and, of course, contemplate your dreams.

Ovulation

Just as spring leads to summer, the follicular phase of your cycle leads to ovulation. Summer is bursting with life! The weather is hot and everything is in full bloom. Ovulation is a miraculous event. Your ovary literally bursts open in response to your luteinizing hormone (LH) surge and releases a tiny egg into your abdominal cavity. Your fallopian tubes catch the egg with their fimbriae, which (potentially) begins the process of creating a new human being. It's no wonder ovulation corresponds to a time of increased energy and creativity.

Estrogen reaches its peak just before ovulation and is linked to increased motor activity, improved sleep patterns, and increased creativity.[10] Many women have more physical, sexual, and creative energy as they approach ovulation and are therefore more outgoing, confident, and extroverted. You may feel a deeper sense of attraction to your partner (or other individuals), and men are more likely to find you sexually attractive.[11]

The luteal phase

The luteal phase is characterized by an energetic shift from creative and outgoing to somber and introspective. Fall has a certain calmness to it as the hustle and bustle of summer ends. The hot summer sun is gradually replaced by a significant drop in temperature as winter draws near.

Progesterone levels peak during this phase, suppressing any further ovulation and cervical mucus production. This can be a tumultuous time, especially if you're intent on fighting your natural inclination to retreat. Things that used to mildly irritate you might really grate on you, and you may find yourself reacting more ... (ahem) ... *emphatically* than usual.

It's easy to dismiss your emotions by assuming you're just too sensitive or hormonal, but you're neither of those things. Your luteal phase forces you to face the not-so-great stuff in your life. It's like having a tiny assistant inside of you who takes everything that isn't working in your life and throws it on your desk to deal with. When you pay attention, you'll notice that certain things keep coming up repeatedly — these are the areas of opportunity for growth you should be paying attention to.

As described in *Wild Power,*

> The premenstruum is the classic feedback moment in the cycle. You're being shown exactly what needs your attention, what needs to change, and what isn't working. You get feedback on your overall health and stress levels, how well you're caring for yourself, your relationships, creative projects, spiritual life, and more. Your task is to stay present and receive the feedback with as much self-kindness as you can muster.[12]

Embracing this part of your cycle and discovering what you can learn from it can truly transform your life. It's not easy to face your demons, but *not* facing them causes more pain in the long run. If you can harness the inherent wisdom and power that lies in your menstrual cycle, it can become a powerful gift; one that strives to keep pushing you towards becoming the woman you were meant to be.

Menstruation

You can think of your period as the end *or* the beginning. Like winter, menstruation is a time when you may feel like hibernating. When you bleed, you're shedding the lining that has developed during your cycle, but you're also releasing the emotional and spiritual energy that has built up.

I always feel an emotional shift when I start my period — a sense of relief whenever I start bleeding again. I honour the messages my body sends me while I bleed by relaxing at home and indulging more than I normally do. Over the course of my cycle, I've given of myself both emotionally and physically to family, friends, clients, and everyone I've come into contact with. Everyone has had a piece of me, and now it's my turn to take some much-needed time for myself. You'll likely find me sleeping in a little longer, watching a little more TV, catching up on some great movies, journalling more, or eating a little more chocolate (okay ... a lot more chocolate).

Do you take time for yourself during your period? Perhaps you like to read, colour, or paint. Maybe you like going for nature walks or spending quality time with your favourite people. Whatever you like, I give you permission to take time for yourself during your period —

and feel absolutely no guilt about it. You deserve to have a day or two for yourself each cycle. You don't have to peace out completely and leave your family behind, but you'll want to intentionally carve out some quality downtime for yourself. In my case, there will be no marathons or mountain climbing — not because I *can't* do it, but because *I don't want to.*

When Your Periods Are a Problem

I've read a few books that suggest period pain is tied to emotional issues. It was always frustrating to hear about women who would simply journal for an hour, have a good cry, and never have painful periods again (of course I'm exaggerating a little, but you see my point). If you've experienced severe PMS or intense period pain, you know how brutal it can be. The last thing you need is to have someone minimizing your experience by telling you it's all in your head. If your periods are extremely problematic, irregular, or have stopped coming altogether, take it as a sign of an underlying issue. This was true for my client Corrina.

When Corrina joined my group coaching program, she hadn't had her period in six months. Corrina works full-time in the school system and maintains a part-time counselling practice on the side. I asked her if anything happened around the time she stopped menstruating, and she mentioned that her period stopped in September, shortly after returning to her full-time position (after summer holidays). When I asked her how she felt about going back to her full-time job, she said, "The word that comes to mind is devastated, but that's being overly dramatic ... I think I was dreading going back and trying to talk myself into it."

We all downplay our true feelings from time to time. Corrina really was devastated at the thought of returning to work — and no wonder. Since her return, she had worked 12 hours a day, 6 to 7 days a week, *for 6 months straight!* She wasn't getting much sleep, she barely had time to prepare meals for her family, and she wasn't taking any time for herself. To add to this already-stressful situation, Corrina and her partner had been trying to conceive for several years with no success, and they had recently initiated the adoption process.

Although it wasn't obvious to Corrina because she was in the middle of it, it was obvious to all of the women in our group. Her body was now screaming at her. She hadn't had time to pay attention to the initial whispers, and her period had come to a screeching halt. Over the course of the program, Corrina started making more time for herself. She prioritized sleep and started making more meals at home. Her period returned by the end of the program — the first one she had had in over half a year. By no means were her cycles completely back to normal, but her experience shows us that our menstrual cycles are incredibly sensitive to our life experiences, stress levels, and overall health.

Corrina is still left to sort out the bigger questions in her life. How can she follow her dreams and build her counselling practice without compromising her health? How will she navigate the adoption process? How will she manage the stress of doing all these things while working two jobs and trying to conceive naturally? But even with a challenging path ahead, Corrina has been able to make amazing progress simply by listening to the wisdom of her cycles.

We all have access to the wisdom of our menstrual cycles when we pay attention. As women, we've been programmed with a monthly reset feature. It's as though there's a force within you that knew you would be such an amazing light for everyone else that you'd forget to shine it on yourself. Your period ensures that you pay attention to your own needs once in a while. Oh, and if you try to ignore it, it just keeps banging on your door until you start paying attention. As Lara Owen puts it in her book, *Her Blood is Gold*:

> Symptoms wake us up. They draw our attention to the part of the body where they occur. We can't escape our wombs if they are making pain, and we can't ignore the menstrual cycle if it makes us behave differently for a week every month.[13]

With each new menstrual cycle comes an opportunity to know yourself better, to connect with your inner wisdom, and to step into your power as a woman.

Summary

- Your body is an intelligent source of information, but since it can't communicate with you using words, you can tune into its wisdom by paying attention to (and understanding) your menstrual cycles.

- Your menstrual cycle connects you to a much deeper source of wisdom and power — a force that wants you to become the most vibrant and authentic version of yourself, both mentally and physically.
- HCs interfere with your ability to tap into your inner guidance system. When women come off HCs, it's not uncommon for them to say that they "feel like themselves again."
- Part of tapping into the wisdom of your menstrual cycle involves giving yourself permission to retreat for as long as you need to when you have your period.
- You can compare the phases of the menstrual cycle to the seasons of the year — each phase is characterized by changes in mood, energy, and creativity.
- The cyclical experience of your menstrual cycle provides the opportunity to examine any areas of your life that need your attention as you approach your period. When your period arrives, the tension is released and a new cycle begins.
- Each cycle gives you an opportunity to connect with your inner wisdom and step into your power as a woman.

Chapter 10
Charting Your Cycles

"I want young women to realize they have choices beyond hormonal birth control and menstrual cycle distress ... so that body literacy becomes the norm, not the exception, for girls and women."

— Laura Wershler, *Femme Fertile newsletter*

To benefit from the wisdom of your cycles, you must pay attention. Tracking your cycles is an essential part of developing body literacy. Not only does body literacy allow you to understand your signs of fertility as they happen, it allows you to track changes in your health and fertility as they unfold over time. The first step is tracking your three main fertile signs!

How to Chart Successfully

The following steps will help you successfully (and consistently) chart your menstrual cycles:

- Create a daily habit of checking and charting your fertile signs.
- Chart your observations for a minimum of three full cycles before you begin using fertility awareness (FA) for birth control (one full cycle when working with an instructor).
- If you're ever unsure of your observations (or forget to do them), *consider yourself fertile.*
- Find your tribe! Connect with other women who chart their cycles.
- Work with a qualified FA instructor (see thefifthvitalsignbook.com/bonuses).

It's tempting to think that FA gives you the ability to just *know* where you are in your cycle all the time, but that's not what happens. Successful charting involves making your observations each day, recording them, and knowing how to interpret them.

Like any new skill, it takes time and practice to gain full confidence using FA. Learning how to chart on your own through books and other solo resources takes anywhere from three to six full cycles of charting. You can speed up your learning curve by working with a qualified charting instructor. Consider seeking support if you plan to rely on FA as your primary birth control method, or if you have any difficulties interpreting your charts.

Using Fertility Awareness to Avoid Pregnancy

The key to using FA to avoid pregnancy is understanding your fertile window. The biggest challenge my clients face is accepting that they can't predict ovulation. It's easy to assume your next cycle will be just like your previous one, which can lead you to make decisions based on what *should* be happening in your cycle (as far as you're concerned) instead of what's really happening. If you want to be successful with FA, you must base your actions on today's observations. Also, if you forget to check your mucus one day (or you're unsure about what you're seeing) — you must *always* assume you're fertile as an added safety measure.

Your times of fertility

Identifying your fertile window is crucial for success when using FA to avoid pregnancy. Your fertile window begins when you first start observing cervical mucus (CM) and ends after you confirm ovulation (by cross-checking your CM, BBT, and cervical position — see Chapter 5). In addition, consider yourself fertile in the following situations:

- On each day you observe CM (both peak and non-peak) during your preovulatory phase.
- For three full days after your last day of clear, stretchy, and/or lubricative mucus (your peak day).
- On any day(s) of anovulatory bleeding or mid-cycle spotting (plus three full days afterwards).

- On the light and very light days of your period — *unless* you've checked for mucus throughout the day to confirm it's a dry day (no mucus).
- On any day(s) you fail to make (and record) your observations (plus three full days afterwards).

Pay close attention to your CM. When you notice a shift from dry days to mucus days, you're officially in your fertile window until your mucus dries up again — *and* you've confirmed ovulation with your temperature shift. Your last day of clear, stretchy (and/or lubricative) mucus is called your *peak day,* and your postovulatory infertile phase begins the latest of:

- The evening of the fourth day *after* your peak day, or
- The evening of your third high temperature above the baseline.

These two signs (your CM and BBT) must *always* match up before you consider it safe to have unprotected sex on your postovulatory dry days. In the event of any discrepancies, always go with the *latest of the two,* and use cervical position as an additional sign when in doubt (see Figure 10–1).

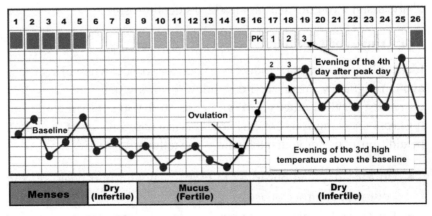

Figure 10–1: The postovulatory infertile phase. The fourth day after peak day is day 19, and the third (normal) high temperature above the baseline is on day 18. She would consider herself infertile the evening of day 19 of her cycle because it is the later of the two.

Your times of infertility

Identifying your infertile days is equally important. Consider yourself infertile in the following situations:

- On your postovulatory dry days — assuming you've confirmed ovulation by cross-checking CM, BBT, and cervical position.
- The evening of your preovulatory dry days — assuming you've checked for mucus all day to confirm it's a dry day and you haven't entered your fertile window.
- Your days of heavy or moderate bleeding during your true menstrual period — assuming you've confirmed ovulation 12 to 14 days before your period started and you're 100 percent confident you're having a real period as opposed to anovulatory bleeding or spotting.

Prior to using these rules, track a minimum of three full cycles when learning on your own or a minimum of one full cycle when working with an instructor. Begin by gaining confidence during your postovulatory infertile phase for several cycles until you feel confident enough to incorporate preovulatory dry days. I strongly recommend seeking support from a certified FA instructor prior to using the preovulatory rules, especially if you don't yet feel confident interpreting your mucus patterns and wish to benefit from the highest possible efficacy of the method.

Checking for mucus the day after sex

Checking for CM the day after sex is challenging because it's virtually impossible to tell the difference between mucus and semen. Unlike CM, semen tends to have a musty smell, it is typically an off-white cloudy colour, and it doesn't stretch between your fingers multiple times. However, there is no reliable way to differentiate between the two — meaning that when you check for mucus the day after sex you must simply call it as you see it. If it looks like mucus, you must mark it accordingly (and consider it a fertile day).

To minimize confusion the day after sex, consider this. The next time you have sex (and your partner ejaculates inside of your vagina) head to the bathroom 5 to 15 minutes afterwards and sit on the toilet. Engage your pelvic floor muscles (push as if you were about to urinate or have a bowel movement) and then wipe your vulva with toilet paper.[1] Continue pushing and wiping (alternating between the two) until all of the semen is gone. You can rinse yourself off to remove any remaining traces of semen once you've finished.

By removing the semen from your vagina after sex, you'll find it much easier to make your observations the following day. You may have noticed wetness or dampness in your underwear the day after sex (prior to doing this) because of the way semen interacts with your vaginal secretions. However, by doing this, you'll notice a clear difference between your dry and mucus observations. You won't find yourself trying to determine the difference between mucus and semen anymore (and feeling confused about it), and you'll be able to trust your observations the day after sex.

Managing your fertile window

To use FA effectively, you must decide how you're going to manage your fertile window. The high effectiveness rate of FA is based on abstaining from intercourse during your fertile window.[2] If you choose to have sex during your fertile window using a barrier method (or withdrawal), you're not technically using FA; instead, you're relying entirely on the effectiveness of your chosen method of birth control. This subtle distinction is important because non-hormonal methods of birth control can only fail during your fertile window — as, by definition, it's the only time you can get pregnant. Understanding this allows you to choose a method of birth control you're comfortable with and use it *perfectly* every time.

Your options for managing your fertile window include barrier methods, withdrawal, alternative sex, or abstaining from sex entirely:

- *Barrier methods* — condoms, diaphragm, and cervical cap;
- *Alternative sex* — sexual activity such as oral sex, manual stimulation (i.e., fingering), or anal sex, which does not involve penis-in-vagina intercourse;
- *Withdrawal* — penis-in-vagina intercourse with ejaculation occurring outside of the vagina; and
- *Abstaining from sex* — no genital contact whatsoever during your fertile window.

Although many women (even those who use it) don't really think of withdrawal as birth control, it's much more common than you think. Withdrawal is up to 96 percent effective in preventing pregnancy when used *perfectly*, though typical use is closer to 85 percent.[3] The main issue with withdrawal is that it can only be effective if there's no sperm present in your partner's pre-ejaculatory fluid. Pre-ejaculatory fluid is produced by the Cowper's gland, which (theoretically) doesn't contain any sperm.[4] Numerous studies have been unable to detect any sperm in pre-ejaculatory fluid;[5] however, one study found that out of 27 men, 11 men produced pre-ejaculatory samples that contained sperm, whereas the pre-ejaculatory samples of the other 16 men did not contain any sperm.[6] Each participant either had sperm in his pre-ejaculate or did not, suggesting that some men leak sperm into their pre-ejaculatory fluid. Given that the research doesn't provide a clear answer, it's possible that withdrawal may work effectively for some couples but not others. In the end, whether you're using condoms, withdrawal, or a cervical cap/diaphragm during your fertile window, you'll want to be clear on what perfect use looks like to maximize effectiveness.

What is perfect use?

Perfect use is another way of saying that you use your chosen method of birth control correctly every single time you have sex with your partner.

Condoms   Choose the appropriate size (length and width). We all wear different sizes of shoes, so it only makes sense that men wear different sizes of condoms. (A company called One Condom makes 60 different sizes of condoms of varying lengths and widths.) Check the expiry date, open the package carefully (so as not to damage it), pinch the tip of the condom to allow space for the ejaculate, and roll it all the way down the shaft, ensuring you've secured it properly so it's less likely to slip off during sex. Put the condom on first, before any sexual activity, and keep it on until after he ejaculates. If the condom breaks or slips off during intercourse, have him put on a new condom immediately. If you have sex a second time, have him wash his hands and penis, and use a new condom. Know what types of lubricants are safe to use with condoms. Oil-based lubricants (such as petroleum jelly, coconut oil, and olive oil) cause condoms to disintegrate, so stick with water-based or silicone-based lubricants. If you ever want to test this out, simply pull a condom over your hand, rub some oil on it, and see what happens (but I digress).

Cervical cap/diaphragm   Both diaphragms and cervical caps are designed to be used with spermicide, so apply the spermicide first, and insert it up to two hours before sex. Choose a spermicide that does not contain nonoxynol-9 or other harsh chemicals. Nonoxynol-9 is a proven sperm killer, but women who use it are at an increased risk of developing inflammation, irritation, disruption of their vaginal microflora, and other negative effects.[7] Choose a natural alternative (such as Contragel®) to get the full benefits of spermicide without the harmful side effects. Leave your cervical cap or diaphragm inserted for a minimum of 6 hours after sex before removing it. If you have sex again (before the 6 hours is up) leave your diaphragm in place and apply additional spermicide before you go for round 2 (or 3 for that matter). You may wish to use your cervical cap or diaphragm with condoms and/or withdrawal to improve overall effectiveness.

Withdrawal   Ensure that your partner urinates prior to any sexual activity to clear the urethra of any sperm. Withdrawal is largely dependent on your partner's ability to know his body and pull out in time (given that if he doesn't withdraw *you have no method*). Your partner must withdraw his penis from your vagina *prior* to ejaculation — that may mean 10 seconds, 30 seconds, or several minutes prior, depending on your comfort level — and he must not ejaculate anywhere near your vulva. If any of his semen comes into contact with your cervical mucus, pregnancy can occur. After he ejaculates, he must wash both his penis and his hands, and he must urinate (again) before you engage in any further sexual activity. Some couples combine withdrawal with condoms for greater efficacy (i.e. using condoms during sex and withdrawing — with the condom on — prior to ejaculation).

What is my risk tolerance?

A big part of being successful in using FA for birth control is knowing the level of risk you're willing to tolerate. Many women opt to completely avoid intercourse during their fertile window, some use withdrawal on their fertile days, and others occasionally have unprotected sex during their fertile window. I picture a continuum with women actively trying to conceive on one end and women who don't want to become pregnant under any circumstances on the other. All women fall somewhere on the spectrum, and it's important to know where you currently stand (as it may change over time). It's not uncommon for women on the *zero pregnancies* end of the spectrum to keep the morning after pill (Plan B®, ella®, etc.) on hand for emergencies (or take it with them when they travel). On the rare occasion that the condom breaks, or their partner fails to withdraw in time, they're prepared, thus reducing their stress.

FA is only as effective as you are. It's up to you to decide how vigilant you're going to be during your fertile window. Know that it's possible to use FA correctly to avoid pregnancy and achieve the 99.4 percent efficacy quoted in the study, provided you receive adequate support, and determine how to make it work for you.[8] Perfect use is possible with FA, provided you give yourself the opportunity to learn the method fully *before* you start using it for birth control!

Using Fertility Awareness to Get Pregnant

On the flip side, you must understand your fertile window to optimize your chances of conception. (Hint: the best days for sex are your days of peak CM!)

Optimizing sex for conception

Your fertile window is the only phase of your cycle when pregnancy is possible. It begins when you first start observing CM and ends after you confirm ovulation (by cross-checking your CM, BBT, and cervical position). Consider the following points to further optimize your chances of conception:

- Have sex when you observe CM, both peak and non-peak, particularly on your days of peak CM, as it is optimal for conception.
- CM is your primary sign of fertility, so don't wait for a positive ovulation predictor kit (OPK) result or time sex based on a particular day of your cycle — just have sex when you see mucus!

- Continue having sex until you're 100 percent certain you've ovulated (by cross-checking your CM, BBT, and cervical position).

Many women spend hundreds of dollars on OPKs to time ovulation. In case you're not familiar with these kits, they test for your luteinizing hormone (LH) surge. Your LH surge triggers ovulation but doesn't confirm that you've *actually* ovulated, just that you'll *likely* ovulate within the next 24 to 36 hours.[9] A number of situations can delay ovulation in your cycle, and I've seen women miss their fertile window because they paid more attention to the OPK than to their own bodies. Not to mention that OPKs don't work for everyone. For example, women with PCOS tend to have elevated LH levels, leading to false positive OPK results (see Chapter 6). Your mucus should *always* be the first thing you pay attention to when you're trying to time sex for pregnancy; OPKs should always come second to your mucus observations.

You'll notice I'm *not* advising you to have sex on day 14 of your cycle. One of the biggest myths about timing sex for conception is that you need to have sex on ovulation day. Of course, it doesn't hurt to have sex on ovulation day, but you don't want to miss several days of prime baby-making CM while you wait for it! Since CM keeps sperm alive for up to five days, and you produce it as you approach ovulation, the goal is to have sex on your mucus days. Not to mention that ovulation doesn't consistently occur on the same day from cycle to cycle, and you can't predict ovulation day ahead of time. Even if you typically ovulate around a certain day of your cycle, CM is your most reliable sign of fertility. Always time sex based on what you actually see. If you find yourself thinking, "I've never ovulated this early (or late) in my cycle, so I can't be fertile," *you would be wrong.* Cycle fluctuations can and do happen, and you don't want to accidentally miss your fertile window if it happens earlier or later than usual. Also, don't stop having sex until you've confirmed ovulation (by cross-checking your BBT, CM, and cervical position). Don't accidentally miss out on your best fertile days by quitting too early, which is more common than you think!

Addressing poor sperm count or quality

Over the past 60 to 70 years, the world population has witnessed an alarming decline in sperm count and quality.[10] One study found that over a 50-year period (from 1940 to 1990), average sperm concentrations fell from 113 million sperm per mL to 66 million sperm per mL (a 42 percent decrease).[11] A more recent analysis of data from 42 935 men found that from 1973 to 2011 both the average sperm concentration and total sperm count of men in Western countries declined by 52 percent and 60 percent respectively.[12] As of 2011, the average sperm concentration sits at 47 million sperm per mL — 58 percent lower than the average man in the 1940s.[13] Sperm quality, as evidenced by average motility and morphology values, has also steadily declined over the past 20 to 30 years.[14] *Motility* and *morphology* are two important measures of sperm quality. Motility refers to the ability of sperm to swim normally, and morphology refers to the percentage of sperm that are normal in shape and size. Normal sperm are sperm that are free from abnormalities and/or defects and are capable of successfully fertilizing an egg.

As more couples struggle with fertility challenges, and given that of all infertility cases, male factor infertility is responsible approximately 40 to 50 percent of the time, having your partner's sperm tested early on is imperative.[15]

If you know you have an issue with sperm count or quality, there are a few strategies you can use to optimize your chances of conception:

- Have your partner abstain from ejaculating several days before your fertile window begins (3 to 5 days before you start observing mucus, but no longer than 7).
- Have sex every other day during your fertile window.
- Consider a well-timed *home insemination* using a cervical cap (see Chapter 17).

Although men produce sperm every day, the amount of sperm in their ejaculate varies widely from day to day. Optimizing your chances of conception in the face of sperm quality issues is only possible when you can correctly identify your fertile window. However, for women who struggle with fertility challenges, timing is rarely the only issue. Fertility challenges are extremely complex, with a wide variety of factors contributing to your chances of successfully conceiving and carrying a pregnancy to term. Charting your cycles allows you to get the timing right and also provides you with a wealth of information about your overall health and fertility, making it a crucial step when trying to conceive (see Chapter 17 for more on preparing for pregnancy and improving sperm quality).

Now that you're ready to start charting your cycles, you'll need additional support and resources. I've listed my top resources, including my *Fertility Awareness Mastery Online Study Course*, and my podcast, *The Fertility Friday Podcast*, in the resource section at the end of this book.

Summary

- To chart successfully, establish the daily habit of checking your fertile signs, stay consistent with it, and ensure you have adequate support.
- The key to using FA to avoid pregnancy is knowing how to identify which phases of your cycle are fertile.
- When using FA for birth control, you must decide how to manage your fertile window.
- If you opt to have (protected) sex during your fertile window, you're not technically using FA — you're relying entirely on the effectiveness of your chosen birth control method.
- When relying on another method of birth control during your fertile window, familiarize yourself with how to use it *perfectly* and consider combining two methods to mitigate your risk of an unplanned pregnancy.
- When trying to conceive, the best days to have sex are your days of peak CM.
- When you know your partner has an issue with sperm count or quality, time sex in specific ways to optimize his sperm concentration and ensure accurate timing.

Chapter 11
Improving Cervical Mucus Production

"Since the beginning of the 20th century it has been known that the ovarian cycle causes variations in the secretions of the mucus membrane of the cervix."

— Erik Odeblad, PhD,
The Discovery of Different Types of Cervical Mucus

Cervical mucus (CM) plays a key role in fertility, from facilitating rapid sperm transport to filtering out defective sperm (see Chapter 3). You may assume your CM production is low if you don't observe several days of mucus before ovulation, but first consider whether it falls within the normal range. In a healthy cycle you would expect to observe CM for 2 to 7 days (5 is average), with at least 1 day of peak mucus. During your fertile window you would expect to produce one-quarter to one-half teaspoon of CM per day.[1]

Women who produce very little (or no) CM may find it more difficult to conceive, and it's helpful to know what factors contribute to low mucus production. If you don't observe any peak or non-peak mucus as you approach ovulation (also known as a *dry cycle*), or if you notice an abrupt shift in your mucus production, you'll want to investigate further.

Drugs that Interfere with Cervical Mucus Production

Very few women (nor their healthcare providers) understand how various drugs affect CM production. Several drugs — including hormonal contraceptives (HCs), antihistamines, and even fertility drugs such as Clomid® and Tamoxifen — reduce (or suppress) your CM production.

Hormonal contraceptives

HCs directly affect your CM production. One of the reasons HCs are such an effective method of birth control is because they stimulate your cervical crypts to produce G-type mucus. G-type mucus forms a thick mucus plug inside your cervical canal creating a barrier to sperm (see Chapter 3). Unfortunately, by overstimulating your G cervical crypts, HCs accelerate the natural aging process of your cervix over time.

As your cervix naturally ages, the number of S and L cervical crypts gradually declines. This causes you to experience fewer days of both peak and non-peak CM as you approach your mid-40s. But for every year you take HCs, your cervix ages an extra year or two — an effect that's more pronounced the longer you take them.[2] Conversely, pregnancy has the opposite effect on your cervical crypts. During pregnancy the number of S and L crypts you have increases in relation to your G crypts, reversing the aging process by about two to three years.[3]

Consider for a moment the compound effect of long-term HC use and aging. If you take HCs for 15 years, not only are they negatively affecting your cervical crypts and their ability to produce mucus, but you're also 15 years older than you were before. Even if you hadn't taken the HCs, you would still expect to observe less mucus over time.

Antihistamines

Some medications are known for reducing CM production, including antihistamines, cold remedies, antidepressants, and diuretics.[4] They reduce your CM production to the point that you may experience a cycle that's completely dry. I've had several clients experience dry cycles (no mucus even though they confirmed ovulation) after taking antihistamines.

Fertility drugs like Clomid and Tamoxifen

Clomid (also known as *clomiphene citrate*) is used to induce ovulation. Clomid works by preventing your brain from accurately perceiving how much estrogen is really circulating in your blood.[5] This causes your pituitary gland to release higher amounts of follicle-stimulating hormone (FSH) and luteinizing hormone (LH), which leads to ovulation. Clomid is used to trigger ovulation prior to Intrauterine Insemination (IUI), a procedure that involves placing sperm directly into your uterus (see Chapter 17). It's also used to force ovulation in women who aren't ovulating regularly, such as women with hypothalamic amenorrhea (HA) or polycystic ovary syndrome (PCOS).

Unfortunately, Clomid has been shown to reduce CM production.[6] Clomid significantly increases the viscosity (thickness) of your CM, making it difficult for sperm to penetrate and successfully fertilize an egg.[7] Clomid suppresses CM production by blocking the estrogen receptors in your cervix and preventing them from responding normally to estrogen.[8] Regardless of how much estrogen you have circulating in your bloodstream, you would either produce significantly less mucus or have dry days as you approach ovulation. Not to mention that Clomid has a relatively long half-life — it remains in your system longer, and the effects of the drug take longer to wear off.[9]

Tamoxifen has also been shown to significantly reduce CM production.[10] Tamoxifen works in much the same way as Clomid, causing the body to resist the effects of estrogen, often triggering ovulation in the process. If you take either of these drugs (or other drugs with similar effects), you may notice significantly less CM during your fertile window, and this effect becomes more pronounced with repeated use.[11]

On the extreme end of the spectrum, you may experience cycles that are entirely dry (no mucus). Your chances of conceiving are lower in a dry cycle because, as you know, sperm need mucus to survive long enough to fertilize an egg (although conception is possible in any cycle in which ovulation takes place).

Cervical Dysplasia, HPV, and Cervical Surgery

Cervical dysplasia, also referred to as *cervical intraepithelial neoplasia* (CIN), is characterized by abnormal cell growth on the surface of the cervix. Cervical dysplasia can progress into cervical cancer, but fortunately, early signs of dysplasia can be detected by paying close attention to changes in your CM.

A common sign of cervical dysplasia is a wet/watery discharge that is not lubricative and occurs consistently throughout your menstrual cycle (not related to ovulation — see Chapter 3). You may notice that you never feel dry when you wipe yourself. If you establish the habit of checking for mucus before and after you use the bathroom, you'll notice that the toilet paper is frequently damp or wet. This subtle but consistent sign may be your only alert.

Research suggests that cervical dysplasia is associated with a deficiency in folate and other B vitamins.[12] Since HCs are known to deplete these nutrients, there's a well-established link between long-term HC use, *human papillomavirus* (HPV), and cervical cancer.[13] There are over 100 different varieties of HPV, and over 80 percent of women will be infected with it by the age of 50.[14] HPV is similar to the common cold in that it easily spreads from one person to another. If you've ever had sexual contact with another human being, you've likely contracted it. The difference is that you're less able to fight off HPV when you're on HCs. When you're on HCs long-term, you're more likely to develop abnormal cervical cells.[15] As such, a growing number of women are undergoing surgical procedures to have these abnormal cells removed.

Surgical options include cryosurgery, laser surgery, conization, loop electrosurgical excision procedure (LEEP), and trachelectomy. These procedures have their differences, but they all involve the physical or surgical removal of abnormal cervical cells. The amount of cervical tissue removed depends on the extent of the abnormal cell growth that has developed on the cervix.

Any physical damage done to the cervix during surgery can result in a temporary or permanent loss of cervical function — including a noticeable reduction in CM production. I've worked with women who've had cervical surgeries to remove abnormal cells, and the reduction in CM production is often striking. They typically have fewer days of mucus overall, and produce significantly less peak mucus.

Can I reverse abnormal cervical cells without surgery?

The short answer is *yes*. Women who develop abnormal cervical cells have lower serum levels of folate, B_{12}, and vitamin A (retinol); correcting these underlying deficiencies has been shown to reverse the condition.[16]

In one study, 47 women with mild or moderate cervical dysplasia received either a daily 10 mg supplement of folic acid or a placebo for 3 months.[17] These women had all used oral contraceptives for at least 6 months and continued using them throughout the study. The women who were treated with folate saw significant improvements in their dysplasia compared to the placebo group (whose results either remained the same or worsened). The researchers concluded that cervical dysplasia "may be arrested or in some cases reversed by oral folic acid supplementation."[18]

In a separate study, 58 women were given either 5 mg of folate per day or a daily placebo over a 6-month period.[19] Folate supplementation caused the regression of cervical dysplasia — a result they did not observe in the placebo group. Taken together, these studies demonstrate that folate supplementation reverses the progression and development of abnormal cervical cells.

In addition to folate, vitamin A (β-all-trans-retinoic acid) has been shown to reverse the progression of cervical dysplasia.[20] In a study published in the *Western Journal of Medicine,* 20 patients with mild, moderate, or severe cervical dysplasia applied vitamin A (β-all-trans-retinoic acid) topically to the cervix daily over a period of 3 to 9 months.[21] At the end of the study, the abnormal cells had completely disappeared in 50 percent of the participants.

Indole-3-carbinol (I3C), a compound found in cruciferous vegetables (broccoli, cauliflower, kale, and brussels sprouts), has also been shown to reverse precancerous cervical cells in women. In a study published in *Gynecologic Oncology,* 30 women were randomized to receive either a placebo, 200 mg of I3C, or 400 mg of I3C per day over a 12-week period. Just under *half* of the women in the I3C groups experienced a *complete regression* of their precancerous lesions, while none of the women in the placebo group experienced a complete regression.[22] These approaches are much less invasive compared to surgery, and do not have any lasting negative effects on your future fertility.

Many of the women I've worked with who've had abnormal cervical cells have a history of long-term HC use. If you've been diagnosed with cervical dysplasia or abnormal cervical cells, talk to your practitioner about using a combination of folate, topical vitamin A (applied directly to the cervix), and I3C prior to opting for a surgical procedure. I've seen women adopt the above treatment protocols (under the supervision of their healthcare practitioners) and reverse their abnormal cervical cells within three to six months. Once the dysplasia clears up, they no longer experience damp or wet sensations throughout their cycles and instead experience dry days outside of their fertile window. As the cervix heals, it's not uncommon to see an increase in both the quantity and quality of CM.

Additional Factors that Negatively Impact Your Cervical Mucus Production

Your CM production is tied both to your cervical health and your reproductive hormone production. Monitoring your CM helps inform you if either factor is out of balance. Several factors can affect your CM production:

- *The natural aging process* — It's normal to observe fewer days of mucus as you get older. By the time you reach your early 40s, expect to observe mucus for an average of 1 to 3 days of your cycle (as opposed to 5 or 6).[23]
- *Nutrient deficiencies* (including folate, vitamin A, and zinc) — Cervical health is central to normal CM production. You may find your CM production improves once you address any underlying nutrient deficiencies.
- *Medical procedures that affect the cervix* (including abortion, dilation and curettage (D&C), and intrauterine device (IUD) insertion/removal) — D&C is a surgical procedure in which the cervix is dilated and an instrument is inserted to scrape the uterine lining. This procedure may be done if you've had a miscarriage or an abortion, and it can temporarily affect your CM production. Other procedures include IUD insertion/ removal and procedures done to address abnormal cervical cells.
- *Endocrine dysfunction* (including thyroid disorders, PCOS, and adrenal fatigue) — Since CM is produced in response to your rising estrogen levels, anything that causes changes to your hormone levels may have an impact.
- *Stress* — Similar to endocrine dysfunction, stress can affect your reproductive hormone levels and, in turn, your CM production.
- *Allergies/food sensitivities* — Allergies and food sensitivities can increase the number of days you observe CM. Consuming foods

that trigger an immune response often causes an increase in CM that results in very few dry days. Not all women respond in the same way, but if you notice a pattern of chronic or continuous mucus (i.e., you see CM pretty much every day), you'll want to consider the possibility.

- *Infections* — Common vaginal infections such as bacterial vaginosis, yeast infections, or sexually transmitted infections (STIs) can also affect your mucus production. You may notice an increase or decrease in your CM production, or you may notice that your mucus looks yellow or has a gummy texture.

Charting your CM gives you an opportunity to establish a baseline. Over time you get a sense of what's normal for you. Pay close attention to any abrupt shifts in the number of days of mucus you observe, or its quality. If your CM is often yellow or gummy, consult your healthcare practitioner to investigate further. If you regularly experience a wet sensation (or gushes of water) outside of your fertile window, request a pap smear. Above all, know that abnormal CM observations are an indication of the health of your cervix.

How to improve your mucus production:

- Ensure you're getting enough of the key nutrients that promote cervical health, including folate, vitamin A (retinol), beta-carotene, zinc, vitamin C, vitamin B_6, and vitamin B_{12}.
- Many women report that evening primrose oil improves CM production; however, more research is needed to confirm this link.
- Optimize your sleep environment to support natural hormone production.
- Minimize your xenoestrogen and chemical exposure (see Chapter 13).
- Identify and address any allergies or food sensitivities.
- Rule out any endocrine disorders and/or hormonal issues (thyroid conditions, PCOS, HA, and adrenal issues).
- Seek professional support if you have abnormal patterns of CM production.

Summary

- Some drugs interfere with CM production, including HCs, antihistamines, and certain fertility drugs.
- If you've had cervical surgery, you may experience limited mucus production, depending on the extent of the damage done to your cervical crypts.
- There is a relationship between long-term HC use, HPV, and cervical cancer. Long-term HC use is associated with an increased risk of having abnormal cervical cells and developing cervical cancer.
- Clinical trials have shown that certain nutrients reverse abnormal cervical cell growth in women.
- Your CM production is tied to both your cervical health and your reproductive hormone production.

Chapter 12
Nutrition for Healthy Cycles

"The doctor of the future will no longer treat the human frame with drugs, but rather will cure and prevent disease with nutrition."

— Thomas Edison

Your diet plays an essential role in the health of your cycles. Whether you're looking to improve your cycles, or simply maintain them, you must first consider that food is more than just fuel for your body. Food is both nutrition *and* information.

The whole concept of "calorie counting" has warped the way most of us think about food — that if all calories are made equal, it doesn't really matter what we eat as long as we get enough, right? You can eat 100 calories of gummy candies or 100 calories of grass-fed beef liver and think they're the same — but they're not!

Health Canada's official dietary recommendation is to eat more grains, replace saturated fat with vegetable oil, and limit your meat consumption.[1] This approach to eating is very different than that of our ancestors in the recent (and distant) past. Traditional cultures had a clear sense of the importance of food, especially as it related to fertility and pregnancy.[2] It's well documented that many traditional cultures followed specific dietary practices both prior to and during pregnancy and lactation to ensure the health of the next generation (see Chapter 17).[3] Fortunately, we can draw from the wisdom of ancestral diets, and the wonders of modern science, to identify the foods best suited to support healthy cycles, fertility, and overall health.

Real Food

When you think of the way our distant ancestors ate, what should immediately come to mind is real, *unprocessed* food. Think vegetables, fruit, meat, fish, eggs, dairy, legumes, nuts, and seeds — foods that eventually rot when you leave them out for too long. Prior to the adoption of modern food-processing practices, our ancestors thrived primarily on foods that underwent little (if any) processing. If you can prepare it in your kitchen without using industrial machinery, then it's probably real food.

Processed foods can be broken down into three main categories: *minimally processed, processed, and ultra-processed.*[4]

- *Minimally processed foods* are foods you still recognize, but they have been altered in some way, usually to extend their shelf life. This includes foods that have undergone refrigeration, freezing, pasteurization, fermentation, canning, bottling, and packaging.
- *Processed foods* are the isolated ingredients that we extract from real foods, including flour, sugar, oil, and cornstarch. We know they came from food, but a significant amount of processing has taken place to extract these ingredients from their real food sources.
- *Ultra-processed foods* are the food-like products that we create from these ingredients, such as bread, cupcakes, cookies, cake, candy, hot dogs, chips, dry breakfast cereal, and chocolate bars.

The thought of eliminating (or even reducing) processed food is daunting. It's everywhere and often hard to avoid. Not to mention that *billions* of advertising dollars are spent each year to convince you to buy it. One way to determine if a food is processed or not is to ask yourself if it has a commercial. I'm fairly certain you've never seen a commercial for zucchini or kale. As the saying goes, *if it has a commercial, you probably shouldn't eat it.*

Nutrient-Dense Fertility Foods

Part of eating for healthy cycles means recognizing that the nutritional value of food varies immensely.

Everything you eat falls into three macronutrient categories:

- Protein
- Carbohydrates
- Fat

Sources of protein include meat, poultry, fish, and eggs; sources of carbohydrates include vegetables, fruit, and legumes (as well as bread, pasta, pastries, and other processed foods); and sources of fat include coconut oil, olive oil, avocados, butter, eggs, full-fat dairy products, and the naturally-occurring fats found in meat, poultry, and fish. Each macronutrient category contains both nutritious, *real food* options and less-nutritious, *highly processed* options.

In addition to *macronutrients*, the foods we eat contain a wide variety of *micro*nutrients (vitamins and minerals) that play a crucial role in our subtle bodily functions and cell metabolism — particularly with respect to menstrual cycle health and fertility. Optimal menstrual cycle health and fertility depends on adequate nutrition on both fronts. You'll vastly increase the nutritional value of your meals to support hormone production, menstrual cycle health, and fertility by incorporating specific foods that contain a greater concentration of certain micronutrients:

- Grass-fed and pasture-raised animal products
- Liver and organ meats
- Cod liver oil
- Minimally processed, full-fat dairy products
- Eggs
- Fish, shellfish, and other seafood (including seaweed)
- Bone broth
- Lacto-fermented foods and beverages
- Fruits and vegetables (but mostly vegetables)
- Saturated fat versus vegetable oil (for cooking)

Grass-fed and pasture-raised animal products

When you're sourcing food, it's important to obtain the highest-quality meat and dairy products that your budget will allow. Conventional meat and dairy producers routinely use growth hormones and antibiotics in their operations — a practice that unnecessarily exposes you to hormone and antibiotic residue in your food.[5] The word *conventional* refers to the practices involved in mass meat production. This includes raising animals in confinement (with little or no access to pasture) and using corn and soy (often genetically modified) as the primary type of feed.

Two fatty acids are considered essential for human beings: *linoleic acid* (omega-6) and *alpha-linolenic acid* (omega-3). We can't make them ourselves, so we must get them from food. To maintain optimal health and fertility, we should have a 1:1 balance of omega-6 and omega-3 fatty acids, but it has been estimated that typical Western diets contain ratios as high as 20:1.[6]

Oils such as margarine, canola, safflower, and soybean have largely replaced animal fats such as butter, lard, and tallow (beef fat) in modern food production, dramatically increasing omega-6 consumption. Conventionally raised meat and dairy products have a pro-inflammatory fatty acid profile compared to animals raised on pasture.[7] The use of corn and soy in conventional farming practices produces meat and dairy products that are significantly more inflammatory, containing as much as six times the amount of omega-6s compared to omega-3s.[8] Consistently eating foods that contain a higher ratio of omega-6 fatty acids (compared to omega-3s) contributes to inflammation in the body. Inflammation has been linked to a variety of health issues, from cardiovascular disease and autoimmune disorders to infertility.[9] As a general rule, you'll want to source meat and dairy products from animals that are pasture-raised and grass-fed when possible.

Ancestral populations consumed meat and dairy products along with their naturally-occurring fat. Contrary to the prevailing fear of fat in our modern world, traditional cultures prized animal fat and made no effort to limit their dietary intake of it. The practice of limiting fat consumption is a fairly new one. If you look three or four generations back in your own family history, you'll find that your recent ancestors consumed their meat and dairy products along with their naturally-occurring fat. All ancestral populations consumed animal fat in one form or another.

It may seem strange to think of animal fat as a source of nutrition, but animal fat is an important source of fat-soluble vitamins (A, D, E, and K_2) and cholesterol. These nutrients are essential for optimal menstrual cycle health, hormone production, and fertility. In fact, all your steroid hormones (including estrogen, progesterone, testosterone, and vitamin D) are synthesized directly from cholesterol.[10] Saturated plant fats (like coconut oil) do not contain any cholesterol, so animal fat is your only dietary source. Cholesterol forms a significant portion of your cell membranes, and it's found in every cell in your body.[11] Twenty percent of your total cholesterol is found in your brain (the largest concentration in your body), which makes sense considering 60 percent of your brain is comprised of fat.[12] In practical terms, you'll want to source the best quality meat and animal products you can find and consume them along with their naturally-occurring fat.

Liver and organ meats

Liver is the most nutrient-dense food on the planet. Pound for pound, there's virtually no food that will nourish your body to the same extent as liver and organ meats (see Figure 12–1). By consuming liver, you're taking a direct hit of Mother Nature's most potent multivitamin. Liver far surpasses the nutrient density of all known fruits and vegetables, particularly in its concentration of choline, folate, iron, vitamin A, vitamin K_2, and B vitamins.

Is liver safe to eat? Doesn't it store toxins? The main role of the liver is to filter and detoxify the blood, not to store toxins. If anything, the liver is a storehouse for vitamins and minerals. That's one of the main reasons liver is such a rich source of nutrition. The liver stores vitamins A, D, B_{12}, K_2, iron, copper, and many other micronutrients to ensure you have a good supply on hand if you ever need it. As with any meat you consume, you'll want to opt for the best quality available, preferably grass-fed, pasture-raised, and free from synthetic hormones and antibiotic residue.

	Kale (100g)	Carrots (100g)	Chicken (100g)	Red Meat (100g)	Beef Liver (100g)
Vitamin A (Retinol)	None	None	None	Trace	31 718 IU
Vitamin D	None	None	Trace	Trace	19 IU
Vitamin E	None	0.7 mg	0.4 mg	0.2 mg	0.63 mg
Vitamin C	120.0 mg	5.9 mg	None	None	27.0 mg
Choline	None	8.8 mg	39.4 mg	67.4 mg	426.0 mg
Thiamin (B₁)	0.1 mg	0.1 mg	0.3 mg	0.1 mg	0.26 mg
Riboflavin (B₂)	0.1 mg	0.1 mg	0.1 mg	0.3 mg	4.19 mg
Niacin (B₃)	1.0 mg	1.0 mg	5.6 mg	4.2 mg	16.5 mg
Pantothenic Acid (B₅)	0.1 mg	0.3 mg	0.9 mg	0.42mg	8.8 mg
Pyridoxine (B₆)	0.1 mg	0.1 mg	0.3 mg	0.3 mg	1.0 mg
Biotin (B₇)	0.50 mcg	0.42 mcg	11.0 mcg	2.5 mcg	96.0 mcg
Folate (B₉)	13.0 mcg	19.0 mcg	4.0 mcg	10.0 mcg	253.0 mcg
Cobalamin (B₁₂)	None	None	0.2 mcg	2.0 mcg	70.6 mcg
Calcium	135.0 mg	33.0 mg	14.0 mg	12.0 mg	6.0 mg
Iron	1.7 mg	0.3 mg	1.1 mg	2.0 mg	6.5 mg
Phosphorus	56.0 mg	35.0 mg	210.0 mg	265.0 mg	497.0 mg
Magnesium	34.0 mg	12.0 mg	24.0 mg	26.0 mg	21.0 mg
Potassium	447.0 mg	320.0 mg	218.0 mg	437.0 mg	352.0 mg
Selenium	0.9 mcg	0.1 mcg	24.7 mcg	26.7 mcg	36.1 mcg
Copper	0.3 mg	None	0.2 mg	0.2 mg	14.3 mg
Zinc	0.4 mg	0.2 mg	1.0 mg	10.3 mg	5.3 mg

Figure 12–1: Liver comparison table[13]

Another compelling reason to add liver to your diet is its high concentration of preformed vitamin A (retinol). You may have heard that you can get your vitamin A from carrots, but that's only partially true. Plant foods contain *beta-carotene* — a precursor to vitamin A that our bodies have to convert into retinol before we can fully use it.[14] Beta-carotene does not significantly increase your serum levels of vitamin A.[15] Not to mention that 45 percent of adults aren't capable of converting beta-carotene to retinol at all.[16]

A 2012 study found that about 75 percent of the US population aged 19 to 50 had a vitamin A intake below the recommended level.[17] So unless you're actively eating animal foods that contain sufficient levels of vitamin A, you can be certain you're not getting enough.[18] Preformed vitamin A also plays a central role in the reproductive processes of both men and women.[19] Numerous animal studies have shown that vitamin A deficiency is a reliable way to induce both male and female infertility.[20]

Vitamin A is required for normal sperm production due to the key role it plays in sperm differentiation.[21] Vitamin A is also required for normal testosterone production.[22] One study found that inducing a vitamin A deficiency in male rats brought the normal process of spermatogenesis (sperm production) to a halt.[23] When the researchers introduced vitamin A back into the diet, it was as though they had hit the "on" switch — the rats began producing sperm again, hormone levels began to normalize, and normal reproductive function was restored. Vitamin A plays such a crucial role in sperm production that researchers have been working on a drug that interferes with vitamin A metabolism as a contraceptive for men.[24]

Vitamin A is equally important for female reproduction. Animal studies have shown that severe vitamin A deficiency leads to irregular ovulation and impaired hormone production.[25] When female rats are deprived of vitamin A, they are unable to maintain pregnancies (resulting in miscarriages and stillbirths).[26]

Animal studies have shown that vitamin A deficiency interferes with normal corpus luteum development, impairs progesterone production, and increases the risk of miscarriage and failed implantation.[27] Low progesterone is associated with a number of menstrual cycle irregularities including premenstrual spotting, continuous mucus production, and early miscarriage. Although the association between vitamin A and healthy ovulatory function may sound like a novel concept, it is well established and widely known among dairy farmers. If a dairy farmer wishes to ensure the optimal fertility of his heifers (female cows), it's a fairly standard practice to administer vitamin A via injections or feed supplementation several days prior to ovulation. This administration of vitamin A to cattle prior to ovulation is associated with improvements in ovulatory function, oocyte (egg) production, embryonic survival rates, and progesterone levels.[28]

What other nutrients are found in liver and organ meats? As I've mentioned, eating liver and organ meats is equivalent to taking a food-based multivitamin. Compared to red meat, beef liver contains more than 3 times as much iron, 25 times as much folate, and 35 times as much vitamin B$_{12}$ (to name a few). Liver is not simply a vitamin A supplement (refer to Figure 12-1 for the full micronutrient breakdown). Liver and organ meats contain a high concentration of a variety of micronutrients in their most bioavailable forms (including zinc, selenium, copper, magnesium, and a number of nutritive cofactors and compounds that haven't even been identified yet).

Take iron, for example. You may think you can meet your iron requirements by eating spinach and other leafy green vegetables, but when you eat liver (and other cuts of meat), you're getting *heme* iron, which is more readily absorbed than the *non-heme* iron found in plant foods.[29] Maintaining sufficient iron stores is crucial for maintaining menstrual cycle health and fertility. Iron deficiency can contribute to heavy menstrual bleeding (see Chapter 2), iron deficiency anemia, and a variety of other health issues. Maintaining sufficient iron stores is especially crucial if you're planning to conceive, as your requirements for iron significantly increase during pregnancy (see Chapter 17).[30]

Folate is another important nutrient found in liver and organ meats in its most bioavailable form. You'll notice that I wrote *folate* and not *folic acid*. Folic acid is the synthetic parent compound of folate that does not exist in nature.[31] When you take a vitamin that contains folic acid (or eat foods that have been fortified with folic acid), your body has to convert it into the active form of folate (the form your body can actually use) through a series of metabolic steps — a process called *methylation*.[32] The challenge is that not everyone has the ability to convert folic acid into folate effectively. Your ability to convert folic acid to folate is related to your genes. If you have a certain variation of the *5,10-methylenetetrahydrofolate reductase gene (MTHFR)*, your ability to convert folic acid to folate may be reduced by as much as 70 percent.[33] When you're not able to convert folic acid to folate, you can be deficient in this crucial nutrient even if you're doing all the right things (i.e., taking your vitamins and eating fortified foods). Folate is found in green leafy vegetables, legumes, and a number of other foods, but in much smaller amounts compared to liver and organ meats. To put it into perspective, you'd have to eat 2.5 pounds of spinach to get the same amount of folate as you would from eating 1 oz of chicken liver.

But Lisa, I hate the taste (and texture) of liver and organ meats!
Liver and organ meats have a distinct texture and flavour (to put it mildly). Of all organ meats, liver has the strongest flavour. Liver can have a strong metallic taste due to the high density of vitamins and minerals it contains. The taste and texture can both vary depending on what type of liver you eat. Chicken and turkey liver taste very different from lamb, duck, or beef liver. You may prefer the taste of heart or kidney over liver, but not to worry — there are ways to incorporate organ meats without compromising the flavour of your meals.

You can soften the strong flavour of liver by presoaking it in milk and/or vinegar water for several hours before cooking. A word of caution: if you're adding liver to your favourite ground meat dish for the very first time, *don't overdo it.* Use 4 to 5 parts regular ground meat to 1 part ground liver. Adding too much will overpower the flavour and that's not what you're going for.

If you're not a fan of liver, here are a few other ways you can sneak it in:

- Fry it up the old-fashioned way and season it well using salt, pepper, cloves, curry, thyme, and/or oregano. Add onions and garlic and sauté it in butter or coconut oil.
- Make liver pâté and use it as a spread on bread or crackers.
- Add ground liver to meat sauces for spaghetti, lasagna, chili, taco salad, etc.
- Add ground liver to meat sauce and serve on rice and/or pasta.
- Add ground liver to shepherd's pie and/or meat loaf.
- Add ground liver to your home-made burger patties and/or meatballs.
- Purée liver ahead of time, pour it in an ice cube tray, freeze it, and add to soups, stews, sauces, or ground beef dishes.
- Take desiccated liver capsules.
- Cut raw liver into small pieces, freeze them for two weeks (to kill any microbes), and take them like vitamins.
- Take cod liver oil daily (see below).

Cod liver oil

Cod liver oil was the #1 supplement recommended for pregnant women and young children until the mid-1900s (until vitamins were first synthesized and sold commercially).[34] Since cod liver oil is derived from the liver of codfish (a naturally rich source of vitamins A and D), the main difference between cod liver oil and fish oil lies in the micronutrient profile. Although both fish oil and cod liver oil contain omega-3 fatty acids, only cod liver oil contains vitamins A and D in significant quantities.

Real food sources of nutrition provide a complex assortment of complementary nutrients (as opposed to isolated vitamins and minerals). This means that obtaining vitamin A from food sources is a safer alternative than from supplementation (in most cases) — especially if you're planning for pregnancy (see Chapter 17). For instance, consuming vitamin D alongside vitamin A (as they naturally occur in cod liver oil) counteracts the negative effects associated with excessive vitamin A intake.[35]

Seek a high-quality (minimally processed) brand that contains naturally-occurring vitamins (as opposed to brands that add synthetic vitamins after processing). If you're not keen on the flavour, try combining it with juice or milk to mask the taste, or opt for capsules instead.

Minimally processed, full-fat dairy products

Humans have consumed milk and milk products for at least 8500 years.[36] This speaks to the importance of dairy consumption in human history. However, the milk (and milk products) our ancestors consumed are very different to the milk you'll find on the shelves of your local grocery store. Many traditional cultures consumed a variety of minimally processed (or unprocessed) full-fat dairy products such as raw (unpasteurized) milk, yogurt, butter, and cheese, but today's dairy products are highly processed and bear little resemblance to the dairy products our ancestors consumed. How do traditional versus modern dairy products compare? There are several key differences:

- A2 versus A1
- Full-fat versus low-fat/non-fat

- Unhomogenized versus homogenized
- Grass-fed versus grain-fed
- Raw (unpasteurized) versus pasteurized

A2 versus A1   When someone is unable to digest milk, it's typically referred to as lactose intolerance. However, in most cases, it's their inability to break down one protein in particular — *A1 beta-casein*.[37]

For most of human history, people drank milk that contained the protein *A2 beta-casein*. A few thousand years ago, certain breeds of European cattle developed a gene mutation that caused a subtle difference in the milk they produced.[38] This gene mutation caused certain cows (namely Holsteins) to produce milk that contained A1 beta-casein instead. Holstein cows are today's breed of choice for the dairy industry because they produce more milk, but the milk they produce contains the A1 protein. Breeds that do not have this gene mutation (and produce A2 milk) include Guernsey, Jersey, and Asian and African cattle.[39] Many women report a reduction in period pain upon elimination of A1 milk products (and many children fare better once they switch to goat's milk because goats produce A2 milk).

The main difference between A1 and A2 beta-casein is the structure of the amino acid chain that makes up these two proteins. When you drink A1 milk, it breaks down and releases a peptide called *beta-casomorphin 7* (BCM7).[40] A2 milk, on the other hand, does not release this peptide. If you think about the word *casomorphin*, it combines "caso" (casein) and "morphin" (morphine).[41] BCM7 is known to have opioid and/or narcotic properties, and this subtle difference in protein structure is responsible for many of the common health issues related to milk consumption.

In his book, *Devil in the Milk,* Keith Woodford details the health risks associated with the consumption of A1 milk. The short version is that there's mounting scientific research linking A1 milk and its byproduct BCM7 to heart disease, type 1 diabetes, autism, schizophrenia, allergies, Crohn's disease, colitis, inflammatory conditions, and a variety of autoimmune diseases.[42] By obtaining your milk from a different breed of cow (or sticking with goat's milk), you may find that your issues with dairy products disappear. If you've struggled with a dairy sensitivity, or if you've categorized yourself as lactose intolerant, it may not just be the milk that's the problem. As Woodford puts it in his book, the real issue could be the "devil" *in* the milk.

Full-fat versus low-fat/non-fat   Dairy products used to be consumed in their natural, unadulterated form. The fat was not removed but *prized*. Traditional cultures understood that the butterfat contained in milk had life-giving and fertility-promoting qualities.

Animal fat is particularly essential for optimal hormone production, fertility, and menstrual cycle health. Opting for low-fat alternatives does not support optimal menstrual cycle health, nor fertility. In one study of 18 555 women of reproductive age, women who consumed low-fat dairy products were more than twice as likely to suffer from anovulatory infertility compared to women who consumed high-fat dairy products.[43]

Dairy fat is an important source of fat-soluble vitamins A, D, E, and K_2 (and steroid hormone precursor cholesterol), making it the most nutritious part of any dairy product.[44] It may seem strange to think of dairy fat as a source of nutrition (especially after a lifetime of receiving messages about the dangers of fat), but the bulk of the micronutrients are found in the fat.

Grass-fed versus grain-fed   Grass-fed cattle produce milk with a more favourable fatty acid profile compared to cows fed corn and soy.[45] In particular, the conjugated linoleic acid (CLA) profile of milk from grass-fed cows is significantly higher than that of conventionally raised cattle.[46] CLA is a naturally-occurring fatty acid that has been associated with a number of health benefits, from reducing the risk of heart disease and certain cancers to reducing body fat and promoting weight loss.[47] Not only do grass-fed cows have a better fatty acid composition, but they produce more nutritious milk. In a study published in the *Journal of Dairy Science*, when compared to cows that were taken off pasture and given hay, grass-fed cows produced milk that contained higher levels of vitamin A, beta-carotene, and vitamin E.[48] The researchers found that grass-fed cows produce milk that has a deeper yellow colour, indicating that the colour of milk is directly related to its micronutrient density.

Unhomogenized versus homogenized   As the saying goes, *the cream rises to the top.* Whole milk contains anywhere from 3.8 to 5.2 percent butterfat depending on the breed of cow.[49] A portion of the fat is skimmed off the top and used to produce butter, cream, ice cream, and other dairy products. The remainder of the milk is then sold commercially as 2 percent, 1 percent, or skim milk. Unhomogenized milk naturally separates, leaving a thick layer of cream on top and "skim milk" on the bottom. So why doesn't commercially processed milk separate? In a word: *homogenization.*

Homogenization is a process by which milk is mechanically forced through tiny holes at high pressure to change the size of the fat molecules. When the fat molecules are squeezed through the tiny holes, they break down into smaller particles. This keeps them suspended evenly throughout the milk and prevents the cream from rising to the top.

Milk producers homogenize milk to extend the shelf life of their products.[50] By permanently altering the size and shape of fat molecules, homogenization increases the surface area of the milk as much as 10 times.[51] This dramatic increase in surface area makes homogenized milk much more susceptible to oxidation (meaning it can become damaged by oxygen).[52] The consumption of oxidized fats and cholesterol (like what you find in homogenized milk) has been linked to inflammation and heart disease.[53]

Raw (unpasteurized) versus pasteurized   There's no comparison between commercially processed milk and real (farm fresh) milk. The pasteurization (heat sterilization) process changes the nature of milk by deactivating naturally-occurring enzymes, denaturing milk proteins, killing beneficial bacteria, and altering the interaction of the fat molecules.[54] The heat treatment of milk deactivates an enzyme called *alkaline phosphatase* (an enzyme that plays a role in calcium absorption), and pasteurization has been shown to alter the calcium content of milk.[55] Many people find raw milk to be easier to digest because the naturally-occurring enzymes (including *lactase,* the enzyme you need to break down lactose) remain intact. Not to mention that it just tastes better.

Raw milk is a living food. In addition to enzymes, it's full of beneficial bacteria.[56] In the same way that *you* have a microbiome in your gut flourishing with beneficial microbes, so does raw milk. Consuming milk in its natural form has been shown to improve immune function, as studies have found that raw milk consumption is associated with a lower risk of developing asthma and allergies.[57] With that said, you might wonder if it's safe to consume milk that hasn't been pasteurized. The answer is both yes *and* no.

Big, commercial dairy producers were never set up to produce milk that's clean enough to be consumed raw. As a result, *commercially produced milk requires pasteurization to be fit for human consumption.* Conversely, raw milk farmers run their operations under a completely different paradigm — *one that produces milk that's so clean it doesn't require heat treatment to eliminate pathogens.* To sell unpasteurized milk for human consumption, the milk must be free from pathogens and other contaminants (something readily verified through modern microbial testing).[58] If the milk doesn't contain pathogens, it doesn't require pasteurization to remove them. In his book, *The Raw Truth About Milk*, William Campbell Douglass, MD describes the steps raw milk producers follow to produce what he calls "raw certified milk" — milk that is just as clean (if not cleaner) than pasteurized milk.[59]

The risks associated with consuming raw milk products are highly exaggerated in the media. The US Centers for Disease Control and Prevention (CDC) estimates that about 9.4 million Americans contract an illness from contaminated food each year, with 46 percent of these illnesses linked to produce (i.e., fruits and vegetables).[60] But if you were going to die from eating food, it would most likely be from eating contaminated poultry, which accounts for 28.8 percent of the total death toll.[61] The vast majority of food-borne illnesses associated with dairy are from the consumption of *pasteurized dairy products.*[62] From a statistical standpoint, you're more likely to get food poisoning from eating a green salad than you are from drinking raw milk from a certified operation. If you choose to drink raw milk, choose a producer that operates professionally and routinely tests their milk for contaminants.

Milk can be an incredible source of nutrition, but it can also be a source of inflammation and gastrointestinal discomfort (as is often the case with commercially produced dairy products). Seek minimally processed, pasture-raised, and/or organic dairy products (A2 when possible), and always opt for full-fat varieties. With that said, not everyone is able to consume milk, so this only applies if you're able to tolerate milk and dairy products.

Eggs

Eggs are an important source of choline, folate, B vitamins (including B_{12} and B_6), selenium, zinc, calcium, and vitamin D. However, when it comes to eggs, quality matters. Eggs from hens with access to pasture have been shown to contain twice as much vitamin E, twice as many long-chain omega-3 fatty acids, and a 38 percent higher concentration of vitamin A compared to caged hens.[63] Eggs sourced from hens with access to pasture tend to have yolks that are a deeper yellow-orange color compared to commercially produced eggs — a sign of their micronutrient density.

Eggs are a complete source of protein and can play a role in helping you maintain a healthy body weight. A 2009 study published in *Nutrition Research* found that participants who ate eggs for breakfast felt fuller longer and ate fewer calories for the rest of the day compared to participants who ate a bagel for breakfast.[64] Eggs are known for their ability to stabilize blood sugar and reduce food cravings, making them an important source of nutrition for menstrual cycle health (when tolerated).

Fish, shellfish, and other seafood (including seaweed)

Fish, shellfish, and other seafood are an extremely important source of long-chain omega-3 fatty acids not found in plant foods. Plant foods contain *alpha-linolenic acid* (ALA) and animal foods contain *eicosapentaenoic acid* (EPA) and *docosahexaenoic acid* (DHA).[65] Most of the incredible health benefits associated with omega-3 fatty acids come from EPA and DHA, two fatty acids found in fish and seafood (and in smaller quantities in other animal foods).[66] You can get omega-3s from plant foods (in the form of ALA), but your body has to convert it into EPA and DHA for you to derive the same health benefits. However, our bodies do a poor job converting plant-based omega-3 fats into EPA and DHA.[67] One study measured the conversion rate of participants given flaxseed and sunflower oil, and less than 0.03 percent of the ALA was converted into EPA and DHA.[68] This means that you must obtain EPA and DHA from fish, seafood, fish oil supplements (such as cod liver oil), or microalgae oil.[69]

Omega-3 fatty acids are of great importance for menstrual cycle health and fertility. One animal study found that a diet rich in long-chain omega-3 fatty acids prolonged the female reproductive lifespan and improved overall egg quality.[70] In comparison, the animals who were fed a diet high in omega-6 fatty acids were unable to reproduce into advanced maternal age. Another study found that omega-3 supplementation normalized reproductive hormone levels in women of reproductive age.[71] This is not surprising considering that omega-3 fatty acids have been shown to dramatically reduce inflammation. Inflammation has been shown to interfere with ovulation by suppressing the normal response of your hypothalamic-pituitary-ovarian (HPO) axis.[72] Many traditional cultures made a point of feeding fish and seafood to men and women of reproductive age to boost fertility and encourage normal fetal development.[73] In addition to fish, there are benefits associated with consuming other seafood types including fish roe (eggs), shellfish, and seaweed. Shellfish such as oysters, mussels, crab, shrimp, and lobster are excellent sources of zinc, an important mineral that many women don't get enough of.

A 2012 study published in *Endocrinology* found that ovulatory dysfunction could be induced in mice by feeding them a zinc-deficient diet.[74] This study provides some insight into the critical role zinc plays in maintaining normal ovulatory function and optimizing the health of your menstrual cycle. Whether you're coming off the pill, dealing with painful periods, or you're looking to improve your menstrual cycle parameters, incorporating shellfish is a great way to boost your zinc levels. You're at an increased risk of zinc deficiency if you've used hormonal contraceptives (HCs) for two or more years (see Chapter 7), or if your diet contains very little (or no) red meat.[75] Even if you don't fall into either of these categories, incorporating more foods rich in zinc is a great way to support your menstrual cycle health. If you're allergic to shellfish, you'll have to skip the seafood in favour of other sources of zinc, such as red meat or plant-based sources such as pumpkin or sesame seeds (though animal sources are more readily absorbed).[76]

Seaweed is one of the best food sources of iodine, an essential nutrient that plays a critical role in maintaining optimal menstrual cycle health. Although iodine is often associated *only* with thyroid health, it has profound effects on other systems in the body. Iodine has been shown to support the normal development and maintenance of breast tissue and is essential for normal ovulatory function. A number of animal studies have demonstrated that iodine deficiency causes changes in breast tissue (as seen in fibrocystic breast disease).[77] When similar studies are replicated in women with fibrocystic breasts, iodine replacement therapy has been shown to prevent and reverse the condition.[78] In an article published in the *Journal of Mammary Gland Biology and Neoplasia*, the authors state, "Molecular iodine treatment of patients with benign breast disease is accompanied by a significant bilateral reduction in breast size, in addition to causing remission of disease symptoms."[79]

There are a number of studies on cattle showing the relationship between iodine deficiency and ovulatory dysfunction.[80] A 2006 study published in the *Research Journal of Animal Veterinary Sciences* found that 60 percent of the cows classified as anovulatory (anestrus) began ovulating again within 5 to 10 days of being treated with Lugol's iodine.[81] Of the cows that began ovulating after iodine treatment, 81 percent went on to conceive. The study notes that, "Reproduction is influenced through iodine's action on the thyroid gland. Inadequate thyroid function reduces conception rates and ovarian activity. Thus, iodine deficiency impairs reproduction."[82]

Unfortunately, iodine is the single most contentious nutrient on the planet with practitioners widely disagreeing on what is an appropriate daily dose. The recommended dietary allowance (RDA) for iodine sits at 150 mcg for the general population and 229 mcg for pregnant women. However, many practitioners have found that much higher doses of iodine are required by their patients to achieve optimal health, especially when their patients are iodine deficient.[83] In the same way your practitioner would prescribe additional vitamin D or vitamin B_{12} if a deficiency was identified, you would require additional iodine (in supplement form) if you were found to be deficient.

Specific nutrients are required to optimize thyroid function (in addition to iodine), so if you have a thyroid condition, you'll want to work with a functional medicine practitioner who specializes in thyroid and fertility for best results (see Chapter 16). For more on iodine testing and supplementation, see *Iodine: Why You Need It, Why You Can't Live Without It* by David Brownstein, MD.

Bone broth

Bone broth is deceptively easy to make, and the health benefits associated with incorporating this amazing food into your diet are compelling, to say the least. When you simmer a combination of meat, bones, skin, and connective tissue on low heat for several hours, you're transferring the nutrients from these "leftovers" directly into your broth. The slow cooking of these bones and tissues gently releases gelatin, collagen, and a wide variety of nutrients including calcium, magnesium, potassium, phosphorus, and several amino acids. You'll know you've made a hearty batch of broth when it thickens and takes on a jello-like quality after you've stored it in the refrigerator overnight. If your broth doesn't thicken or gel, you'll want to consider adding in some chicken feet, joint bones, knuckle bones, or any other bony tissues rich in gelatin and collagen; or consider a higher proportion of bones to water (the pot should be at least three-quarters full of bones before adding water).

Bone broth is known as a gut-healing food because of the role it plays in maintaining normal intestinal barrier function. Intestinal permeability (or *leaky gut syndrome*) is characterized by a breakdown in the integrity of your intestinal (gut) barrier. That barrier is the protective layer that separates the outside world (including what you eat and all the microbes and viruses you come into contact with each day) from the rest of your body.[84] When you catch a cold or virus, it most likely entered through your digestive tract. Fortunately, 70 percent of your body's immune cells are found within your intestinal barrier.[85] Your gut plays a critical role in all aspects of your health, from nutrient absorption to immune function and, of course, fertility. When your gut is healthy, there are several layers of protection in place that, together, maintain the integrity of your gut barrier. This includes a physical layer of specialized cells, a layer of mucus (your *gut mucosa*), and an extensive community of beneficial microbes.[86] Studies have shown that when you experience digestive issues such as diarrhea and constipation, the severity of your symptoms is directly related to the degree of your intestinal permeability.[87] The more damaged your gut barrier is, the worse your symptoms will be. This has been seen in cases of irritable bowel syndrome (IBS), inflammatory bowel disease (IBD), ulcerative colitis, Crohn's disease, and other related conditions.[88]

Bone broth contains gelatin and the amino acids glycine and glutamine — three nutrients that are associated with improving digestive function.[89] Glycine and glutamine have been shown to improve intestinal integrity and reduce the gastrointestinal (GI) issues associated with leaky gut syndrome.[90] Bone broth is also rich in collagen, which just happens to be the most abundant protein in the body. Collagen is the main structural component of our connective tissues, and is found in our bones, skin, and fibrous tissues such as our tendons and ligaments.

Maintaining optimal digestive function is especially important for fertility and menstrual cycle health. Digestive issues like IBS and Crohn's disease are associated with increased intestinal permeability, chronic inflammation of the GI tract, and lowered immune function. Women with gut-related health issues are much more likely to have abnormal menstrual cycle patterns ranging from delayed ovulation, to irregular bleeding, to patterns of continuous cervical mucus. Put simply, when your gut is out of balance, your menstrual cycle will be out of balance as well.[91]

In addition to powerful gut-building properties, bone broth contains the amino acids that support your body to produce the most potent antioxidant in the body — *glutathione*. Oxidation is a natural process that damages cell membranes and other structures in the body, including DNA. Oxidative stress is associated with aging, inflammation, increased risk of heart disease, cancer, and infertility. Being the most potent antioxidant in the body, glutathione is critical in reducing oxidative stress, which plays an important role in improving overall health and fertility in the process.

Glutathione is comprised of three amino acids: glycine, glutamine, and cysteine, and as I've mentioned, two of these key precursors to glutathione (glycine and glutamine) can be found right there in your bone broth. A 2011 study released in *The American Journal of Clinical Nutrition* found that dietary supplementation of glutathione precursors cysteine and glycine fully restored normal glutathione synthesis and lowered levels of oxidative stress in the elderly.[92] Another study released in *Molecular Genetics and Metabolism* found that supplementation with glutamine can be used to maintain high levels of glutathione and reduce oxidative stress.[93] This is an important consideration for fertility because excessive oxidative stress has been shown to impair female fertility by interfering with ovulation and reducing egg quality (see Chapter 17).[94]

There's no time like the present to draw from the wisdom of our ancestors and incorporate this healing food into your diet. When you regularly incorporate bone broth into your diet, you're providing your body with the raw materials it needs to maintain a strong gut barrier; and as you can see, the benefits of incorporating bone broth extend well beyond your gut.

Lacto-fermented foods and beverages

For our bodies to function normally, we depend on the actions of trillions of microbes. Your GI tract is lined with approximately *100 trillion bacteria* — that's equal to about 2 to 6 *pounds*.[95] That's a lot of microbes! If you had 100 trillion pennies, you'd have $10 billion. As noted in an article in *Gastroenterology & Hepatology*,

> Within the human gastrointestinal microbiota exists a complex ecosystem of approximately 300 to 500 bacterial species, comprising nearly two million genes (the microbiome). Indeed, the number of bacteria within the gut is approximately 10 times that of all of the cells in the human body, and the collective bacterial genome is vastly greater than the human genome.[96]

Scientists have gone so far as to categorize our gut microbiota as an additional *organ* because of the critical role it plays in our health.

The bottom line is that our bodies are not able to function normally if our gut flora is imbalanced.

You can think of your gut microbiome as a complex and diverse civilization inside your body that is inextricably linked to all areas of your health. The community of bacteria in your gut plays a crucial role in digestion, and without them you wouldn't be able to absorb the nutrients in your food. In addition to digestion, you need a healthy balance of gut microbes for your immune system to function normally.[97] Your gut microbiome keeps pathogens and other potentially harmful bacteria from proliferating. If you've ever taken a round of antibiotics and found that you developed a yeast infection shortly thereafter, you've already experienced this first-hand. A disrupted gut microbiome is linked to:

- Impaired immune function (including autoimmune diseases)
- Bowel diseases like IBS and Crohn's (among others)
- Gut infections like small intestinal bacterial overgrowth (SIBO) and candida
- Obesity
- Diabetes
- Allergies
- Food sensitivities
- Asthma
- Mood disorders like depression and anxiety
- Serious mental illnesses like schizophrenia and autism[98]

Fortunately, you can make a significant positive impact on your gut microbiome by regularly incorporating lacto-fermented foods and drinks into your diet. One 2007 study published in *Proceedings of the National Academy of Sciences* estimates that the total human gut microbiome consists of anywhere from 15 000 to 36 000 species of bacteria.[99] You'll notice that when you buy probiotic supplements you're lucky to see 12 or more different strains of bacteria on the label; however, a single serving of home-made sauerkraut or raw milk kefir may contain a greater number and diversity of microbes than an entire bottle of probiotic pills.[100] If you're looking for a "hack" (although I don't much like that word), regularly consuming fermented foods will greatly increase the number and diversity of the beneficial microbes in your gut. You have to eat anyway, so why not leverage an activity you're already doing in a way that supports your gut health?

Fermentation is a natural process of food preservation. Fermentation promotes the growth of beneficial bacteria while preventing the growth of pathogens, and as the beneficial bacteria grow, they secrete acids that prevent the growth of mould, fungus, and other pathogens. Prior to the days of refrigeration, fermentation allowed ancestral populations to preserve their food for extended periods of time. Fermented food has a characteristically tangy, acidic flavour, which comes from the acids produced by the bacteria. The acidity prevents pathogenic microbes from taking over and rotting your food. What you're left with is an amazing *living* food. Fermented food, much like your body, contains a complex civilization of diverse microbes that we're only beginning to understand. Adding in fermented foods and beverages to your diet is a great way to build and maintain a healthy gut.

Fruits and vegetables (but mostly vegetables)

Fruits and vegetables contain a wide variety of phytonutrients that have significant health benefits. You'll derive benefits from all varieties, but leafy green vegetables and berries are particularly high in phytonutrients and antioxidants. If you have a history of blood sugar problems such as insulin resistance, or polycystic ovary syndrome (PCOS), emphasize green vegetables and low-sugar fruits, i.e., berries (as it *is* possible to overdo it on the sweet fruits).

Plants contain beneficial compounds that decrease blood pressure, reduce inflammation, detoxify heavy metals, and reduce the risk of certain chronic diseases (most notably cancer).[101] Eating a wide variety of colours and types of fruits and vegetables at each meal will boost your total intake of these beneficial compounds. When you sit down to eat a meal, vegetables should make up at least *half* of your plate! It should go without saying that eating a wide variety of brightly-coloured fruits and leafy green vegetables each day is an important part of maintaining optimal menstrual cycle health and fertility.

Saturated fat versus vegetable oil (for cooking)

When you're cooking, you've likely noticed what happens to vegetable oil when it gets hot. It doesn't take much heat for unsaturated vegetable oils to reach their smoke point and start burning. Conversely, saturated fats can better withstand moderate to high heat. This makes saturated fats — such as coconut oil, lard (pork fat), tallow (beef fat), duck fat, and ghee (clarified butter) — a better choice for cooking. (Note: butter is a good choice for cooking at moderate heat, but not high heat, as milk solids burn at high heat.)

From a nutrient density standpoint, vegetable oils are about as nutritious as plastic wrap. Even the term "vegetable oil" is a misnomer. A more accurate term for vegetable oils such as canola, corn, safflower, cottonseed, and soy oils would be *industrial seed oils,* as they are derived from the seeds of these industrially farmed plants.

These oils require extreme processing to manufacture. Producing vegetable oil involves crushing the seeds at an extremely high pressure, followed by high-heat processing and the administration of numerous chemicals and solvents. The oil must then be degummed, bleached, and deodorized before it is deemed suitable for human consumption.[102] Butter, on the other hand, can be made with some heavy cream and a hand mixer in about 5 to 10 minutes.

Industrial seed oils contain a high proportion of omega-6 fats, and very little (if any) omega-3 fats. As you may recall, although omega-6 fatty acids are considered essential, your optimal health is dependent on having a balance of omega-3 and omega-6 fatty acids. When you regularly consume omega-6 oils that have been damaged by heat (or oxidized by processing), they create inflammation in your body. If you're not consuming enough stable saturated fats, your body is forced to incorporate these damaged omega-6 fats into your cells.

Vegetable oils (for the most part) have already been damaged during the manufacturing process. The consumption of these damaged oils contributes to inflammatory conditions such as endometriosis and dysmenorrhea.[103] Replacing these harmful industrial oils with stable saturated fats for cooking will go a long way toward improving your hormone balance and your nutrient intake.

You may be wondering where olive oil fits into all of this. Olive oil is a monounsaturated fat, making it more stable than the industrial seed oils, but not as stable as saturated fat. Like butter, olive oil can withstand some heat, but it cannot withstand high heat for long periods of time. It is best consumed unheated as a wonderful addition to home-made salad dressing or used for cooking at low to moderate heat.

I'll mention trans fat here as an important fat to avoid at all costs. Trans fat is an industrial seed oil that has been turned into a solid through a chemical process called *hydrogenation*. This is how margarine and shortening are made. You'll see it in food products listed as "partially hydrogenated oil."

Eating trans fats on a regular basis is pretty much guaranteed to mess up your cycle in one way or another. One study of women of reproductive age found that for every two percent increase in their trans unsaturated fat consumption, there was a *73 percent* greater risk of ovulatory infertility.[104] Trans fats are found in processed junk food, fake fats such as margarine and shortening, and foods that are fried in unstable oils (like the ones used in fast-food restaurants). Avoiding trans fats isn't always easy, but sticking to real (unprocessed) foods greatly reduces your exposure.

Summary

- You can maximize your nutrient intake by incorporating specific *nutrient-dense fertility foods* containing a high density of key vitamins and minerals that support fertility.
- Liver and organ meats are nature's original multivitamin and contain the micronutrients you require (in their most absorbable forms) for optimal menstrual cycle health and fertility.
- Vitamin A (retinol) plays an essential role in optimal reproductive health for both men and women. The best sources of vitamin A are liver and cod liver oil.
- Modern commercial dairy products bear little resemblance to the milk and dairy products our ancestors consumed. Opt for high quality, minimally processed, full-fat milk and dairy products when possible.
- Pasture-raised (free-range) eggs are an important source of key nutrients that support menstrual cycle health and fertility.
- Fish and other seafood are an important source of long-chain omega-3 fatty acids, shellfish (oysters, mussels, crab, shrimp, and

lobster) are an important source of zinc, and seaweed is an important source of iodine and other trace minerals.

- Bone broth provides key nutrients that support gut health and immune function, and reduce oxidative stress.
- Incorporating lacto-fermented foods and beverages into your diet builds and diversifies your gut flora so you can optimize your gut health, nutrient absorption, and immune function.
- Brightly-coloured fruits and vegetables contain a wide array of phytonutrients that support optimal menstrual cycle health and fertility.
- When cooking at moderate to high heat, avoid industrially processed seed oils, and instead opt for stable saturated fats (animal fats or coconut oil).

Chapter 13
Lifestyle Choices for Healthy Cycles

"Do the best you can until you know better.
Then when you know better, do better."

— Maya Angelou

Your menstrual cycle responds to a wide variety of lifestyle factors. Though you may see improvements after making dietary changes, it's not always enough. In this chapter, I'll take you through lifestyle choices for healthy cycles. It may feel daunting at first, but there's no need to change everything at once. Start with one small change this week and go from there.

Improve Your Sleep Hygiene

Sleep plays a critical role in maintaining a healthy balance of hormones throughout your menstrual cycle, and frankly, if you're not getting enough sleep, your hormones won't be balanced. As the saying goes — *you can't out-supplement sleep.*

Sleep is an essential restorative process your body controls and regulates automatically. We spend about a third of our lives sleeping, so if you live to age 90 you'll have spent about 30 years fast asleep. Although the role of sleep is not completely understood, we know that sleep deprivation negatively affects many different processes including reproduction, immune function, mood regulation, hormone balance, memory, and appetite. If you're not getting enough sleep, you're more likely to develop health conditions such as diabetes, cancer, depression, high blood pressure, and cardiovascular disease.[1]

Your natural sleep cycle is governed by two processes: *sleep pressure* and *circadian rhythm*. Sleep pressure builds the longer you stay awake — it's at its lowest point when you wake up and highest when it's time to sleep. For most of us, this occurs in the mornings and evenings (respectively), but for shift workers it coincides with when they sleep. Your circadian rhythm regulates your reproductive hormone production and your daily sleeping and eating patterns on a rhythmic 24-hour cycle. However, your circadian rhythm is governed by light exposure.

Exposing your body to light at night-time (when it's dark and you're supposed to be sleeping!) disrupts the communication between your hypothalamus, pituitary, and ovaries (your HPO axis), leading to menstrual cycle disturbances. Sleep disruptions and night-time light exposure are associated with an increased risk of menstrual cycle irregularities, pain with menstruation, early miscarriage, preterm birth, low birth weight, and infertility.[2] A study published in *Epidemiology* found that night-time shift work significantly increased endometriosis risk.[3] Women who worked the night shift (at all) were 50 percent more likely to develop endometriosis, and the risk was nearly double for women who worked the night shift regularly (more than half their shifts). It's no wonder that many women see significant improvements in their cycles by simply optimizing their sleep habits.

As a recovering night owl, I'm the first to admit that changing your sleep habits is anything but easy, but the health benefits of regularly getting sufficient (good quality) sleep are worth it — and the improvements you'll see in your cycles are just the tip of the iceberg. To promote and maintain optimal health, we require somewhere between 7 and 9 hours of sleep per night, with an absolute minimum of 7; however, many of us don't even get the bare minimum most nights.[4] According to the National Sleep Foundation, we're getting 6 hours and 55 minutes of sleep on workdays (on average); 86 percent of adults aged 19 to 45 go to sleep later than 10 p.m. on weeknights, 92 percent use electronic devices within an hour of going to bed, 19 percent are woken up by their cell phones a few nights per week, and only 34 percent report regularly feeling refreshed upon waking.[5] The good news is that we can significantly improve the quality (and quantity) of our sleep by adopting a few key habits.

Sleep in complete darkness

Your room should be so dark that you can't see your hand in front of your face! Pitch black — no LED alarm clock, no cell phone, no TV screen, no night light, and no street lights coming in through your window. You may have to move your electronics out of your room (or cover them), and you'll have to find a way to cover your windows at night. Many of my clients use blackout blinds, but you can use a dark sheet or blanket to block out the street lights. Even if you cover your eyes, your skin has a network of photoreceptors that detect the presence or absence of light — so your sleep mask alone won't cut it.[6]

Melatonin and cortisol rise and fall throughout the day based on your circadian rhythm and are very sensitive to the presence or absence of light. Your cortisol levels should be highest in the morning and slowly decline throughout the day, reaching their lowest levels before bedtime. Conversely, your melatonin levels should gradually rise several hours before bedtime, reaching their highest levels while you sleep. Melatonin is necessary for maintaining your normal sleep/wake cycle and is responsible for the sleepy, groggy feeling you have at bedtime — however, night-time light exposure suppresses melatonin.[7] Melatonin also plays a key role in maintaining normal ovulatory function, so if you're not sleeping in complete darkness, your menstrual cycle won't be balanced.[8]

You've got nothing to lose! Sleeping in the dark is one of the simplest and most cost-effective ways to regulate your cycles. Every single client I've worked with who changed her sleep environment reported having deeper and more restful sleep (win-win!).

Minimize your (blue) light exposure at night-time

Imagine going back to a time when night-time was actually dark! The term *light pollution* effectively sums up what we'll be covering here. Blue light refers to bright (daytime) light. Sources of blue light include the sun, digital screens (computers, laptops, cell phones, tablets, etc.), electronic devices, and both fluorescent and LED lights. Daytime blue light exposure is important for maintaining your natural circadian rhythm, but night-time exposure throws off your natural hormone production. Blue light has one of the shortest wavelengths and emits the highest amount of energy. As a result, blue light has the strongest suppressive effect on your melatonin.[9]

According to a study published in the *Journal of Clinical Endocrinology and Metabolism*,

> Compared with dim light, exposure to room light before bedtime suppressed melatonin, resulting in a later melatonin onset in 99 percent of individuals and shortening melatonin duration by about 90 minutes. Also, exposure to room light during the usual hours of sleep suppressed melatonin by greater than 50 percent in most (85 percent) trials. These findings indicate that room light exerts a profound suppressive effect on melatonin levels.[10]

You may not be able to completely avoid night-time blue light exposure, but you can certainly reduce it. Instead of watching TV or staring at your phone before bed, choose a different activity that doesn't expose you to blue light. Turning off your devices two to three hours before bed is ideal, but even 30 minutes is helpful. If ditching your electronics is too much of a stretch, use an app or a special setting that turns your screen orange or red (minimizing your blue light exposure). Opt for dim lighting at home in the evenings and consider buying a pair of orange blue-blocker sunglasses to filter out even more blue light. A simple internet search will get you there, and you'll start feeling the benefits right away — more specifically, you'll feel tired as bedtime approaches.

Get some sunlight first thing in the morning

Sunshine is a free and natural alternative to your morning coffee. Early morning sun exposure elevates your cortisol levels by over 50 percent (while simultaneously suppressing melatonin).[11] Cortisol gives you a natural boost of energy, leaving you feeling more energized and alert (which is why night-time blue light exposure is so problematic!). Exposing yourself to sunshine when you wake up in the morning helps to reset your internal clock and even helps you sleep better at night. Another side benefit of getting some early morning sun is the positive impact it has on your menstrual cycles. Exposure to bright light shortly after waking has been shown to increase ovulation rates and ovarian follicle development in women.[12]

Limit your caffeine consumption

Caffeine increases the time it takes you to fall asleep and decreases your overall sleep time regardless of when you consume it.[13] A study published in the *Journal of Clinical Sleep Medicine* found that consuming caffeine 6 hours before bed doubles the time it takes to fall asleep, whereas consuming caffeine 3 hours before bed triples it.[14] Although the effects of caffeine gradually wear off throughout the day, research shows that having even one cup of coffee first thing in the morning (a full 16 hours before bedtime) negatively affects your sleep patterns. One study compared the sleep patterns of participants who had caffeine first thing in the morning (at 7:10 a.m.) to participants who didn't have any.[15] The participants who had early morning caffeine took longer to fall asleep at bedtime and had significantly different sleep patterns. If getting rid of caffeine is out of the question, consider reducing your consumption, or avoiding it past 3 p.m. to minimize the impact on your sleep.

Get to bed early

If you're not fast asleep by 11 p.m., you're interfering with your body's natural detoxification process. According to traditional Chinese medicine theory, your body's energy circulates through your organ systems each day, with each organ system being most active at a different time. Your gall bladder is most active between 11 p.m. and 1 a.m. and your liver between 1 a.m. and 3 a.m.[16] Your liver is responsible for the smooth flow of blood and vital energy (Qi) throughout your body and is directly associated with your menstrual cycle; therefore getting to bed early helps to support and maintain a balanced and healthy menstrual cycle.

Get some exercise during the day

Regular exercise reduces the time it takes you to fall asleep at bedtime and improves your sleep quality.[17] You can enjoy the additional benefits of natural light exposure by exercising outdoors, but you'll benefit from improvements in sleep quality regardless of where you exercise.

However, if you exercise late at night (and expose yourself to blue LED lights at the gym), the benefits won't outweigh the negative effects of night-time light exposure.[18]

Speaking of exercise, having sex before bedtime (partnered or solo) has been shown to improve sleep quality by reducing the time it takes you to fall asleep and helping you to sleep more soundly throughout the night. Sex reduces blood pressure and cortisol levels, and has even been suggested as treatment for women who suffer from insomnia.[19]

Create a restful night-time routine

Technically you already have a night-time routine, but if you didn't intentionally cultivate your habits, your current routine may not be setting you up for the best possible sleep. A night-time routine doesn't have to be long and involved. It could be as simple as taking a bath, brushing your teeth, shutting off your devices, and spending a few minutes reflecting on what you're grateful for. Try cultivating a few habits that put you into a more restful state as you wind down from your day. Keep it simple so you're more likely to stick with it. Start with one thing that you can do before bed (in five minutes or less) and see how it goes.

Create an ideal sleep environment

Think *sleep sanctuary*. What can you do to make your bedroom feel luxurious? You want your body to automatically associate your room with sleep, and the first step is clarifying which activities are off limits. If you use your bedroom to work, watch TV, eat, or any other non-sleep-related activities, you may need to make some changes. You want your bedroom free of any electronic devices that emit light and any distractions that can interfere with your sleep. By drawing a hard line in the sand and removing your TV, computer, cell phone, and any other electronic devices, you're taking massive strides to improve your overall sleep quality. It may take some getting used to (especially if you're used to falling asleep with the TV on), but I know you can do it.

As we bring the sleep section to a close, I want to stress how important getting good-quality sleep is when you're working to improve your menstrual cycles. It's often easier to run to the store to buy supplements because that doesn't involve making any real changes to your habits. But before you spend hundreds of dollars at the health food store, just humour me. Sleep in the dark for 30 days and see what happens.

Reduce Your Xenoestrogen Exposure

Environmental xenoestrogens fall into two broad categories: natural compounds (found in plants and other natural sources), and synthetically derived chemicals.[20] Xenoestrogens are similar enough to the molecular structure of your natural hormones to trigger hormonal responses; however, they interfere with your natural endocrine processes and are therefore collectively referred to as *endocrine disruptors*.[21] The greater your exposure to xenoestrogens, the greater the negative effect on your menstrual cycles and your fertility.

Here are some common sources of xenoestrogens:

- Hormonal contraceptives (HCs)
- Conventionally produced meat and dairy products
- Non-organic fruits and vegetables containing pesticide residue
- Scented beauty and personal care products
- Scented household cleaning products
- Canned foods
- Plastic food and beverage containers
- Non-stick cookware
- Textiles, furniture, and clothing that have been treated to be stain- or water-resistant
- Environmental toxins (exhaust fumes, flame retardants, PCBs, dioxins, pesticides, etc.)
- Processed soy products

Below are some steps you can take to minimize your exposure. You may be tempted to try them all at once, but most of my clients gradually implement these changes over a period of 3 to 6 months (sometimes a year or more).

Skip the HCs

This should go without saying (especially after reading Chapters 7 and 8), but I wanted to give it an honorary mention. You may have found yourself in the same paradox. You're eating organic food, using natural products, and generally riding a wonderful wave of health consciousness — but you're still using HCs. Before reading this book, you probably didn't classify HCs as endocrine disruptors. For the record, HCs are the atomic bomb of xenoestrogens. While most xenoestrogens impair your endocrine system's ability to function normally, most HCs shut down normal reproductive function by suppressing ovulation. It's like using a jackhammer to scratch an itch. If you're concerned about reducing your xenoestrogen exposure, skip the hormonal birth control.

Switch to pasture-raised, grass-fed meat (and organic dairy products)

Conventional meat and dairy products are highly inflammatory, in part due to the practice of grain feeding. Let's consider where the grain comes from. As of this writing, 94 percent of soybeans and 89 percent of corn produced in the US are genetically modified organisms (GMOs) engineered to be resistant to pesticides, allowing farmers to drench their fields in chemicals without killing these plants.[22] Since the grains fed to conventionally raised animals typically contain pesticide residue, the meat and dairy products from these animals also contain a certain degree of pesticide residue. Conventionally raised cattle are routinely injected with growth hormones to quickly build muscle mass.[23] Growth hormones are also used to increase milk production in dairy cattle (though this practice is illegal in Canada and Europe).[24] By opting for pasture-raised (and/or organic) meat and dairy products, you reduce your exposure to both xenoestrogens and growth hormones.

Eat organic when possible

Conventional fruits and vegetables are heavily sprayed with a variety of pesticides and herbicides (including glyphosate).[25] Glyphosate is a non-specific herbicide toxic to most plants and is the active ingredient in Roundup®. Since 1974, approximately 8.6 billion kg of glyphosate have been sprayed on crops across the world, particularly on GMO crops (also referred to as Roundup Ready® crops).[26] One particularly terrifying use of glyphosate is a practice called desiccation.[27] The word *desiccation* comes from the Latin *desiccatus*, which means "to make very dry." It's standard practice for non-organic wheat farmers to drench their wheat fields in Roundup several days (or weeks) prior to harvest to increase their yields.[28] When Roundup is sprayed on wheat plants before harvest, they dry out and release more seeds as a kind of last stand before they die. More seeds mean a bigger harvest and higher profits; however, this practice leaves increased glyphosate residue on wheat products. Research suggests that this additional exposure to glyphosate may be linked to the increase in gluten sensitivity, irritable bowel syndrome (IBS), and celiac disease.[29]

Glyphosate is only one of hundreds (if not thousands) of endocrine-disrupting chemicals that are routinely used in conventional farming practices, leaving increasing amounts of chemical residue in the food supply.[30] Opting for organic produce (or sourcing local produce from environmentally conscious farmers) allows you to reduce your exposure. You can also look at the Environmental Working Group's *Dirty Dozen*™ (the fruits and vegetables found to contain the highest levels of pesticides) and *Clean Fifteen*™ (those found to contain the lowest).[31] When organic isn't an option, you can reduce your exposure by avoiding the foods highest on the list. A simple internet search will get you there, and it's a great place to start.

Switch to natural, scent-free beauty products

The cosmetics/beauty industry is highly problematic as far as xenoestrogens are concerned. Pretty much all commercially available beauty products contain endocrine-disrupting chemicals. This includes body lotion, hand cream, deodorant, perfume, body wash, soap, shampoo, conditioner, shave gel, make-up ... and the list goes on. Unless you've actively sourced alternative beauty products, your bathroom cabinet is most likely full of them. A wide variety of beauty products (including perfume, nail polish, hairspray, lotion, deodorant, shampoo, conditioner, and even baby care products) contain a group of chemicals called *phthalates*.[32] Phthalates are known to disrupt normal endocrine function and cause estrogenic effects in the body.[33] One study of 337 women over a 3-year period found that women who used conventional beauty products had nearly 3 times the exposure to phthalates compared to women who didn't use them.[34] Given that your skin is your largest organ (and will absorb whatever you put on it), consider this: if you wouldn't put it in your mouth and eat it, you shouldn't put it on your skin! I was able to replace my collection of scented body lotions and face creams with coconut oil and unrefined shea butter. What beauty product could you swap out this week?

Switch to non-toxic and/or organic menstrual products

Conventional pads and tampons are manufactured from a combination of cotton and synthetic fibres such as rayon and polyester. According to the United States Department of Agriculture (USDA), 96 percent of cotton grown in the US is genetically modified (as of 2017), making it one of the most heavily sprayed crops.[35] In 2015, India surpassed China as the top producer of the world's cotton, producing over 8 million tons of cotton fibre by 2017 (93 percent of it was genetically modified).[36] GMO cotton (also known as *Bt cotton*) has been altered to contain a gene that allows the plant to release a toxin that kills certain insect species. *Bt* is short for *Bacillus thuringiensis*, the bacterial strain that naturally produces these toxins.

In addition to the GMO cotton issue, the materials in conventional pads and tampons are bleached and exposed to a wide variety of toxic chemicals during the manufacturing process. The US Food and Drug Administration (FDA) conducted their own review of several brands of conventional pads and tampons, and their analysis confirmed that several of these brands contain dioxins.[37] In case you're not familiar with dioxins, they're a group of highly toxic substances known to cause cancer, damage the immune system, impair reproductive function, and disrupt normal endocrine function.[38] They've been characterized as "persistent organic pollutants" because of their resistance to the natural process of degradation and decomposition — oh, and they're considered to be one of the most toxic substances known to humans.[39] As far as I'm concerned, that's way too many chemicals in my vagina! Your vagina is no place for GMOs, bleach, dioxins, or any other toxic chemicals!

Anecdotally, many women who've replaced their regular pads and tampons with organic versions (or reusable alternatives such as menstrual cups and cloth pads) experience a significant decrease in menstrual cramping and other menstrual cycle issues. Switching to organic and/or reusable alternatives not only reduces your xenoestrogen exposure, but also saves you money and reduces waste. A win-win-*win*!

Clean up your household cleaning routine

Everyday products such as laundry detergent, fabric softener, dryer sheets, fragrant hand soap, dishwasher liquid, and all-purpose cleaner all contain xenoestrogens. The endocrine-disrupting properties of these products are magnified when used inside without proper ventilation, so start by opening the windows when you clean! The next step is to gradually replace your toxic cleaning products with natural alternatives as they run out.

When you run out of dishwashing liquid or laundry detergent, replace it with a non-scented version. Replace your fabric softener and dryer sheets with dryer balls (baseball-sized balls made of wool or plastic that soften your clothes without the added chemicals). Replace your all-purpose cleaner with a home-made mixture of water, vinegar, and a few drops of mint or tea tree essential oil. If you're not able to make your own products, a growing number of companies make non-toxic products for health-conscious consumers (like yourself). Many companies use words like "green" and "natural" but their products still contain chemicals (*fragrance* is fairly common), so start reading labels and only buy from companies that willingly provide an ingredient list.

Reduce your BPA exposure

Bisphenol A (BPA) is a potent xenoestrogen that is known to disrupt normal endocrine function and impair fertility.[40] BPA exposure has been linked to a variety of reproductive disorders including endometriosis, polycystic ovary syndrome (PCOS), and breast cancer.[41] BPA is one of the most widely produced chemicals in the world, with over 6 billion pounds produced each year and over 100 tons released into the atmosphere.[42] The highest concentrations of BPA have been found in canned foods and plastic food and beverage containers, although BPA is found in fast-food, receipts, newspapers, plane tickets, and even household dust.[43] In addition to avoiding plastic, here are a few ways to further reduce your BPA exposure:

- Use glass containers for food storage instead of plastic.
- Buy fresh or frozen fruit and vegetables instead of the canned varieties.
- Use reusable glass or stainless steel containers for water, coffee, and tea.
- Eat real, unprocessed food as much as possible.
- Avoid handling the receipt when you buy things at the store.

Get rid of your non-stick cookware

A group of chemicals referred to as *perfluorinated chemicals* (PFCs) give cookware their convenient non-stick quality. PFCs have a stable chemical structure and create an invisible barrier between two surfaces, which is why they're used in numerous products including non-stick cooking surfaces, stain-resistant and waterproof fabrics, and even firefighting foam. PFCs are potent xenoestrogens that are known to disrupt normal endocrine function.[44] PFCs are also categorized as persistent environmental pollutants because they take an extremely long time to break down. Due to their widespread use, nearly every human being has traces of PFCs in their bloodstream.[45]

It may not be possible to avoid PFCs altogether, but you can certainly minimize your exposure. Consider replacing your non-stick cookware with cast iron, stainless steel, glass, or ceramic cookware. Replacing your pots and pans is a tall order (and can be expensive!) so it may not be the first thing you do, but it's something to consider next time you're looking for new cookware.

Filter your drinking water

In addition to the varying amounts of chlorine and fluoride found in most city water (see the thyroid section in Chapter 6), municipal drinking water often contains natural and synthetic estrogens, pesticide and herbicide residue, detectable levels of various pharmaceutical drugs, and a number of other chemical compounds. One study identified over 250 chemical compounds commonly found in consumer, health, and personal care products (including pharmaceuticals, fragrances, and pesticides), and was able to detect a total of 142 contaminants in treated drinking water.[46] A separate study analyzed the estrogen levels in water both before and after treatment in 25 US drinking water treatment plants, and although water treatment reduced estrogen levels, low levels of estrogen were still detected in several water samples after treatment.[47] You can reduce your exposure by investing in a water filter capable of filtering pesticides, hormones, pharmaceuticals, chlorine, and fluoride (such as a Berkey® water filter).[48] You may also wish to consider using a shower filter.

Limit processed soy products

Soy products fall into the natural compounds category of xeno-estrogens and contain potent *phytoestrogens* that exert an estrogenic effect on the body. In the past, Asian soy preparations included long periods of soaking and simmering that removed much of the *soy isoflavones* and phytoestrogens from traditional soy foods.[49] Modern soy processing doesn't use these traditional methods of preparation, leaving much higher levels of phytoestrogens in processed soy products such as soy milk, tempeh, tofu, and soy-based baby formula (not to mention pesticide residue, given that over 90 percent of soy is genetically modified).[50]

The estrogenic compounds in soy products act as endocrine disruptors and have been shown to alter the menstrual cycle. A study published in the *British Journal of Nutrition* had this finding:

> Long-term ingestion of soybean protein significantly prolonged the length of the menstrual cycle; more specifically, follicular phase length was increased and significant suppression of the mid-cycle surges of gonadotropins, luteinizing hormone (LH), and follicle-stimulating hormone (FSH) occurred.[51]

Soy isoflavones are found in all processed soy products, and they're the most prevalent and potent estrogenic compound found in our food supply.[52] The women in the study experienced a delay in ovulation because the phytoestrogens suppressed their bodies' attempts to ovulate earlier in their cycles. Excess estrogen exposure contributes to other reproductive health issues including estrogen dominance, uterine fibroids, endometriosis, painful or heavy periods, irregular cycles, abnormal cervical mucus patterns, miscarriage, infertility, and cancer.[53] You can minimize your exposure by limiting soy consumption and monitoring your cycles carefully.

Avoid the Junk

In this section I define "junk" as ultra-processed foods, industrial seed oils, trans fats, caffeinated beverages, artificial sweeteners, alcohol, and cigarettes — all items that have very little, if any, inherent nutritional value. We could theoretically refer to them as "anti-nutrients" because they deplete nutrients as your body metabolizes them (instead of replenishing them).[54]

Refined flour, sugar, and processed food

Even though sugar and flour are derived from real food sources, processing strips them of their naturally-occurring nutrients. Vitamins and minerals are then added in afterwards to prevent deficiencies through a process called *fortification*. In Canada the fortification of certain foods is mandatory. The sale of unenriched white flour (or products containing it) is prohibited. In the US, the FDA has developed a fortification policy including strict labelling requirements for any products that are listed as "enriched."[55]

As per Canadian guidelines:

> The standard for flour (also known as "white flour", "enriched flour," or "enriched white flour") ... requires the mandatory addition of thiamin, riboflavin, niacin, folic acid, and iron ... Consequently, all foods sold in Canada that contain white flour must be made with enriched white flour. The sale of unenriched white flour or its use is not permitted.[56]

In other words, even the government knows that processed flour has no nutritional value, and regulations have been enacted to prevent nutrient deficiencies in the population.

In addition, consumption of sugar and refined carbohydrates is associated with weight gain, type 2 diabetes, chronic inflammation, and a number of related health issues.[57] Regular consumption of sugar-sweetened soda and sports drinks has been shown to reduce your chances of conceiving and carrying a pregnancy to term by more than 20 percent.[58] Replacing processed foods with real food alternatives is an important step toward improving your cycles (and your overall health).

Industrial seed oils and trans fats

Industrial seed oils such as soybean, canola, corn, cottonseed, peanut, sunflower, and safflower oil have no nutritional value. They are easily damaged by heat, highly inflammatory, and, like trans fats, are detrimental to menstrual cycle health and fertility (see Chapter 12). Think of them as industrial waste products and aim to avoid using them entirely.

Caffeine

Research shows that caffeine consumption affects menstrual cycle length and reproductive hormone production; it also increases your risk of experiencing fertility challenges.[59] Women who consume moderate to high amounts of caffeine are more likely to experience a delay in their time to conception.[60] One study found that women who consumed 300 mg of caffeine per day (equivalent to about 3 cups of coffee) were 27 percent less likely to conceive during any given menstrual cycle.[61] From a hormonal standpoint, caffeine stimulates cortisol production, which may have a negative impact on your progesterone levels given that your body makes cortisol from progesterone.[62] If you have concerns about how caffeine affects you, remove it for one full cycle and see how your body responds. This doesn't mean you shouldn't ever have coffee (especially if you love it), but an important part of body literacy is understanding how various factors affect your cycles — including caffeine.

Artificial sweeteners

Artificial sweeteners mimic the natural sweetness of sugar without raising blood sugar and are extremely helpful when reducing sugar consumption, but they can cause a variety of health issues. Aspartame, one of the most common artificial sweeteners, breaks down into phenylalanine, aspartic acid, and methanol when ingested.[63] As such, synthetically derived sweeteners (including aspartame, sucralose, and saccharin) are linked to a variety of nasty reactions including memory loss, headaches, dizziness, increased susceptibility to seizures, depression, anxiety, and the list goes on.[64] Fortunately, there are safer alternatives to table sugar.

Stevia is a natural sweetener derived from the leaves of the *Stevia rebaudiana* plant. The leaves are 30 times sweeter than cane sugar but do not raise blood sugar, nor do they break down into harmful compounds when consumed.[65] Erythritol is a non-caloric sugar alcohol that doesn't raise blood sugar; it has been shown to reduce the risk of dental caries (cavities) and improve cardiovascular function in diabetics.[66] Coconut sugar is another natural sweetener with a lower glycemic index compared to table sugar and doesn't raise blood sugar as high.[67] Naturally-occurring sweeteners like honey and maple syrup will still raise blood sugar; however, unlike artificial sweeteners and refined sugar, they contain vitamins, trace minerals, and antioxidants.[68]

Alcohol

Moderate alcohol intake is associated with changes in estrogen, progesterone, testosterone, and LH levels.[69] In a study of 259 women, alcohol consumption significantly increased estradiol levels — each alcoholic drink increased them by over 5 percent, and 4 or more drinks increased them by over 60 percent.[70] Any substance that can cause your estradiol (estrogen) to spike by over 60 percent has the ability to throw off your menstrual cycles! Reducing your alcohol consumption will go a long way toward supporting your hormone balance and improving your menstrual cycles. Of course, you can still enjoy a glass of wine every now and then, but as you track your cycles, you'll gain a greater understanding of how alcohol affects them.

Cigarettes

Just in case you need additional motivation to kick the habit, not only do cigarettes have a negative impact on your health, but they also negatively affect your menstrual cycle. One study found that women who smoked heavily (20 or more cigarettes per day) were nearly 4 times as likely to have short menstrual cycles and more than twice as likely to have a short luteal phase.[71] Moderate smokers (10 or more cigarettes per day) were more than twice as likely to have long, irregular cycles compared to non-smokers. Research also shows that heavy smokers consistently produce about 25 percent less progesterone and are more likely to have elevated levels of estrogen and follicle-stimulating hormone (FSH).[72]

Balance Your Blood Sugar

You'll remember from Chapter 12 that everything you eat falls into one of three macronutrient categories: protein, fat, and carbohydrates — but only carbohydrates significantly raise your blood sugar. Regular consumption of high glycemic carbohydrates (foods that increase blood sugar higher and faster) has been shown to reduce fertility and impair normal ovulatory function.[73] One study found that women who regularly consumed high glycemic foods (including cold breakfast cereals, white rice, and potatoes) were at an increased risk of ovulatory infertility (infertility due to ovulatory dysfunction).[74] Women with the highest total carbohydrate intake were 78 percent more likely to experience ovulatory infertility compared to women with moderate or low carbohydrate intakes.

By opting for low glycemic carbohydrates (such as vegetables and low-sugar fruits) and pairing them with protein and fat at each meal, you slow the release of glucose into your bloodstream, which minimizes blood sugar spikes throughout the day. This balances your blood sugar, reduces cravings, and helps you feel full for longer. By replacing carbohydrate-heavy meals (e.g., oatmeal with a banana on the side) with more balanced meals (e.g., bacon, eggs, and avocado slices with a side of grilled zucchini), you'll find it easier to keep your blood sugar balanced throughout the day.

Identify Food Sensitivities

A food sensitivity (or intolerance) occurs when you have difficulty digesting a specific food, leading to a variety of responses — from bloating and gas to abdominal pain, constipation, or diarrhea. Food allergies, on the other hand, reliably cause an immune response each time you're exposed.[75] When you consume foods you're sensitive to, you'll often notice changes in your menstrual cycle. Some women notice an unhealthy increase in their cervical mucus production, delayed ovulation, or even mid-cycle spotting. Elimination diets have been shown to improve symptoms when sensitivities are identified; for many women, eliminating sensitive foods improves their cycle parameters.[76] If you suspect you have a food sensitivity, consider having your healthcare practitioner test your immune response, or eliminate certain foods and test what happens when you reintroduce them.

Support Your Liver

One of the best ways to support your liver is by reducing your exposure to xenoestrogens, refined sugar, and alcohol.[77] Your liver breaks down your natural estrogens so they can be safely excreted, but this process doesn't always happen smoothly. When your liver needs additional support, you may notice subtle signs in your postovulatory phase including continuous mucus or excessive breast tenderness. Two naturally-occurring compounds, *Indole-3-carbinol* (I3C) and *diindolylmethane* (DIM), have a potent effect on liver function and significantly affect the way estrogen is metabolized in the body.[78]

Estrogen is broken down by your liver by one of two distinct pathways: one leads to the formation of a healthy metabolite of estrogen called *2-hydroxyestrone* and the other leads to the formation of a more potent (and rather dangerous) metabolite of estrogen called *16α-Hydroxyestrone*.[79] The second is associated with fibroids, fibrocystic breasts, breast cancer, cervical cancer, and fertility problems (all associated with excess estrogen). I3C has been shown to support the natural liver detoxification pathways and reduce the harmful effects associated with excess estrogen.[80] You can increase your I3C intake by regularly incorporating cruciferous vegetables into your diet (or via supplementation).

Exercise Smarter (Not Harder)

Exercise has been shown to improve estrogen metabolism (and reduce your exposure to 16α-Hydroxyestrone).[81] Exercise creates an anti-inflammatory response in the body that is associated with a whole host of health benefits, including protection from chronic diseases like diabetes and cardiovascular disease.[82] However, excessive exercise can cause menstrual cycle disruption, and while most women have been taught that static exercise (such as jogging or using an elliptical machine for 30 minutes) will help with weight loss, the research doesn't support this.[83] One study found that women who engaged in high-intensity intermittent exercise experienced significant reductions in total weight and body fat (in a shorter period of time), while women who engaged in steady-state exercise (30 minutes or more of continuous moderate- to high-intensity activity) did not.[84] This challenges what we think we know about exercise and weight loss — that more isn't necessarily better.

If you experience any of these symptoms shortly after starting or modifying your activity level, consider backing off or making some changes:

- Delayed ovulation
- Missed periods
- Premenstrual spotting
- Luteal phase of 10 days or less
- Scant or light periods

Exercise is an important part of achieving and maintaining optimal menstrual cycle health, but it's important not to overdo it. Tracking your cycles offers you a real-time window into the impact of your exercise habits and allows you to quickly identify whether you're doing too much.

Manage Your Stress

Similar to over-exercise, stress can cause ovulatory disruptions, abnormal bleeding patterns, or shorten your luteal phase. It's easy to identify stressful events such as a tight work deadline, driving in heavy traffic, or having a fight with someone you love, but a number of seemingly neutral circumstances can also cause stress:

- Physical stress or trauma
- Travel
- Emotional trauma (past or present)
- Work-related stress
- Hating your job

- Family and relationship stress
- Toxic relationships
- Caring for sick or elderly family members
- Major life events (positive or negative) such as marriage, changing jobs, or moving
- Loneliness
- Having a pessimistic view of the world
- Excessive worrying, negative thinking, and ruminating
- Lingering resentments
- Anger
- Feeling helpless or hopeless
- Excess caffeine and/or sugar consumption
- Consuming foods that trigger an immune response (foods you are allergic or sensitive to)
- Lack of sleep or poor-quality sleep
- Excessive exercise
- Dieting and/or disordered eating patterns
- Rapid weight gain/loss
- Hunger

When you see that having a stressful week at work can delay your ovulation, or that starting a new exercise routine can cause spotting before your period starts, your experience of stress becomes much more tangible. From an evolutionary perspective, your stress response was developed to help you survive, but your body doesn't distinguish between hungry lions and work deadlines. Making sure you're exercising and getting enough sleep is an important part of stress management, and there are a few other practical strategies you can use to reduce stress:

- Cultivate a mindfulness practice
- Reconnect with what makes you happy
- Spend some time in nature
- Practise gratitude
- Ask yourself some big questions

Cultivate a mindfulness practice

Mindfulness involves bringing your full attention to the present moment without passing any judgment.[85] Try focusing on your breathing or following a guided meditation. Each of us has an inner critic or narrator — a constant train of thought (which I often refer to as the *crazy train*) — and focusing on the present allows you to take a break from it. Mindfulness is like exercise for your brain, and I've heard it compared to doing reps at the gym — each time you bring your focus back to the present moment, you've done another rep. Whenever you catch your mind wandering, gently refocus on your breathing (or the guided meditation you're listening to), and bring your attention back to the present moment. Cultivating a mindfulness practice helps you identify when *your* crazy train is taking over, and it allows you to develop a deeper awareness of your thought processes. Research shows that mindfulness actually changes your brain and causes favourable changes to your stress response over time.[86] It has also been shown to improve a number of conditions — from anxiety and depression to psoriasis.[87] If you're looking for a place to start, consider reading *Wherever You Go, There You Are* by Jon Kabat-Zinn or downloading the *Headspace* app on your phone.

Reconnect with what makes you happy

As we get older (and embrace the realities of life), it's far too easy to stop doing the things that used to bring us joy. Take a few minutes to jot down the first five activities or experiences that come to mind. It's cliché to say that it's the simple things in life that spark the most joy, *but it's also true*. The hardest part is finding the time in your already busy day, but we're not aiming for perfection here. If you're serious about managing your stress, you'll have to take it down a notch. Pick one of the activities on your list and spend five minutes doing it today! Don't wait two years until you can plan that family vacation or until you have time to start that class you've been thinking about.

Do you love to dance? Great! Put on your favourite song and let 'er rip! Do you love to draw? Fantastic! Pull out a piece of paper and start sketching. Do you love to travel? Wonderful! Spend five minutes researching the next fun place you want to visit. Keep it simple, or *you won't do it* (otherwise you would have done it already!). Don't overthink it.

I know you're busy ... but I also know that you've earned the right to spend five minutes doing something that brings you joy today.

Spend some time in nature

Spending time in nature has a positive impact on your health and is associated with lower rates of depression, blood pressure, and stress (although we didn't need modern science to tell us that!).[88] One study found that when exposed to stressful stimuli, participants exposed to natural environments recovered faster and more completely than the participants exposed only to urban environments.[89] One way to cope with the stress of daily life is to spend more time outside — even if all you can manage is the walk from your car to your workplace. Pay attention to the feeling of warmth on your skin when the sun is shining, feel the wind on your face, take a moment to smell the flowers, and listen to the sound of birds singing. I'll admit that this may sound a little airy-fairy, but how long has it been since you took a moment to appreciate the beauty of nature?

Practise gratitude

Most of us will naturally focus on the negative in our life and take for granted all of the amazing things. But by taking time to focus on what you're grateful for each day, you can train your mind to focus on what's working in your life. I want you to write down three things you're grateful for each day for the next 30 days (and don't let yourself write the same thing twice!). If I told you to look around and find the colour red, you'd suddenly notice a multitude of red. Nothing changed around you. The red items were there all along, but you only noticed them when you paid attention. Practising gratitude is very similar. By focusing on your blessings, you'll notice how much you have to be thankful for, and when stressful situations arise, you'll be better equipped to manage them.

Ask yourself some big questions

You can eat the healthiest diet, and take all the right supplements, but if you work 80-hour weeks in a high-stress environment, there's a limit to the improvements you'll see on your charts until you acknowledge the elephant in the room. For many women, charting their cycles gives them tangible proof of what their intuition had been telling them all along — *it's not working.* Whether it's the job, the relationship, the commute, that thing you said yes to (that you didn't want to do), or the dreams you've been putting aside for the past 10 years, charting your cycles has a way of nudging you in the right direction.

Do you love your job? Should you look for a different position in the company? What about other companies? Should you start your own business? Are you happy with the relationships in your life? Are you following your dreams? Should you go back to school? Should you take some time off to travel the world? To write that book? Is it time to move? And the list goes on.

Sometimes life gets so busy that when we finally poke our heads up and look around, we realize we're not even close to where we want to be — nor have we taken the necessary steps to figure out what we want from life. There are no easy answers to these big questions. The first step is simply asking them. It may be strange to think that monitoring your menstrual cycles could have such profound implications, but I've seen it happen time and time again. When you have tangible proof that your stressful life situation is affecting your health, it's much harder to turn a blind eye.

Knowing which factors can negatively affect your cycles allows you to start improving them. You may wonder if something as simple as sleeping in the dark, giving up coffee, or managing stress could make that big of a difference in your cycles, but it absolutely can. I encourage you to track your cycles so you can see the changes for yourself!

Summary

- Improving your sleep hygiene can dramatically improve your cycles and your sleep quality.
- Reduce your xenoestrogen exposure.
- Avoid the junk (processed foods, industrial seed oils, caffeine, artificial sweeteners, alcohol, and cigarettes).
- Aim for a balance of protein, fat, and carbohydrates at each meal to maintain a healthy blood sugar balance.
- Identify and address food sensitivities.

- Support your liver by reducing your processed food consumption and xenoestrogen exposure.
- Over-exercise can cause cycle irregularities — pay close attention to how your cycle responds to make sure you're not overdoing it.
- Find practical ways to manage stress, and rediscover what brings you joy in the process.

Chapter 14
Managing Period Pain

"Our whole society is geared towards menstrual denial, and symptoms have a way of disrupting or interrupting the status quo."

— Alexandra Pope and Sjanie Hugo Wurlitzer, *Wild Power*

Period pain (dysmenorrhea) is extremely common, and most women who experience it assume it's just an inescapable part of being a woman. You'll remember from Chapter 2 that any discomfort with your period that goes beyond mild cramping is not normal or healthy — and can be an early warning sign of a more serious condition like endometriosis.

Dysmenorrhea

Primary dysmenorrhea refers to pain and cramping in your lower abdomen during your period. It can start just before your period and often lasts up to three days.[1] The first two days are typically the most severe, and it tends to follow a pretty predictable pattern whenever you get your period. If you experience primary dysmenorrhea, you probably started experiencing it shortly after your very first period, and you may experience secondary symptoms like nausea, vomiting, and diarrhea along with the pain.[2]

Secondary dysmenorrhea is pain that may not be directly related to your period and may be associated with an underlying reproductive disorder or condition such as endometriosis, fibroids, adenomyosis, or pelvic inflammatory disease.[3] What makes secondary dysmenorrhea different is that it can happen at any time during your reproductive life. With secondary dysmenorrhea you might start having painful menstruation several years after you had your first period.[4] You may also experience pain at other times during your cycle — during sex, with bowel movements or urination, or ongoing back or pelvic pain. The most common cause of secondary dysmenorrhea is endometriosis, especially in cases in which ibuprofen or hormonal contraceptives (HCs) have little or no effect on the pain.[5]

Forty-five to 95 percent of menstruating women have some degree of period pain, with 10 to 41 percent of them having such severe symptoms that it limits their daily activities; however, many women don't seek medical support, even when their pain is debilitating.[6] I believe there are three main reasons for this: 1. Most women think painful periods are normal, 2. They fear their pain won't be taken seriously, and 3. They know they'll be offered painkillers and/or the pill (as the only solution) by the vast majority of healthcare practitioners.

What Causes Menstrual Pain?

Your period's painful symptoms are likely related to elevated prostaglandin levels.[7] *Prostaglandins* are a group of lipids (fats) involved in your body's response to inflammation.[8] They play a critical role in menstruation because they initiate the disintegration and shedding of your uterine lining.[9] Inflammation is the way your immune system responds to injury and infection. Think about what happens when you cut your finger — it becomes red, swollen, and sore. That sounds like a bad thing, but inflammation is actually a beneficial and important part of your body's healing process. Inflammation helps to restore damaged tissue and normal physiological function in your body.[10]

Prostaglandins are produced at the sites of damaged or infected tissues in the body, and their job is to cause inflammation, pain, and fever as part of the healing process.[11] Women who experience dysmenorrhea have been shown to have upwards of four times the levels of prostaglandins in their endometrial tissues on the days they experience the most intense pain.[12] High prosta-glandin levels are associated with inflammation, and numerous factors such as consumption of industrial seed oils, sugar, processed foods, conventional meat and dairy products, and exposure to xenoestrogens and toxins therefore increase your risk of having painful periods.

The most effective drugs for reducing the painful symptoms associated with dysmenorrhea fall into the *non-steroidal anti-inflammatory drug (NSAID)* category. NSAIDs (including ibuprofen, aspirin, and naproxen) decrease pain, fever, and inflammation.[13] These drugs suppress the production of prostaglandins, and therefore effectively reduce period pain in most women; however, these drugs are associated with a host of negative side effects including increased cardiovascular risk factors (high blood pressure and increased heart attack risk), fluid retention, stomach ulcers, stomach pain, gastrointestinal bleeding, and kidney problems.[14] Since period pain can be extreme and unrelenting, the only reasonable option for many women is painkillers — regardless of the associated risk factors. They certainly were for me until I was able to eliminate my period pain through a combination of dietary and lifestyle factors. For years I categorized my pain as a 10 out of 10 on the pain scale because it felt like someone was trying to rip my insides out. With that said, I now categorize my pain as a 0 to 0.5 out of 10, and as such, I no longer require pain medication. If you've experienced painful periods, I want you to know that it's possible to reduce, and in some cases, eliminate your pain without drugs.

How Can I Reduce (or Eliminate) My Pain?

First acknowledge that your periods are painful for a reason — your inner guidance system is quite literally screaming at you. It's important to organize your schedule with fewer commitments and more downtime (see Chapter 9). Beyond giving yourself time to relax and retreat, pay attention to dietary and lifestyle factors by addressing nutrient deficiencies, reducing your exposure to endocrine-disrupting chemicals, and reducing your consumption of inflammatory foods. Many women experience a significant reduction in their painful symptoms simply by addressing these factors, but others require additional support.

Know that pain-free periods are possible without medication, but I'll caution you against looking for a magic pill that will get rid of your pain overnight. Allow a few months as you make changes and track your progress by charting your cycles.

Many of my clients have experienced significant reductions in their painful symptoms by following the steps outlined below:

- Avoid vegetable/industrial seed oils (corn, soybean, rapeseed, canola, cottonseed, peanut).
- Use stable saturated fats for cooking (coconut oil, pastured lard, tallow, duck fat, butter, ghee).
- Source pasture-raised, grass-fed meat (free from hormones and antibiotics).
- Opt for minimally processed, organic dairy from grass-fed cows (A2 when possible and raw if available — see Chapter 12).
- Reduce your consumption of refined carbohydrates and processed foods (choose real food instead).
- Avoid xenoestrogens, toxins, and other endocrine-disrupting compounds.
- Avoid plastic food and beverage containers.
- Consider supplementation (particularly magnesium, zinc, and fish oil — see below).
- Consider acupuncture for pain relief, as it has been shown to significantly reduce period pain and improve the painful symptoms associated with endometriosis.[15]
- Consider abdominal massage modalities such as Arvigo® Therapy, Merciér Therapy, or Fertility Massage Therapy™ to improve circulation and the alignment of your uterus and fallopian tubes.
- Consider castor oil packs and/or vaginal steaming.

Seek support from a functional medicine practitioner to help you address the root cause of your period pain (see Chapter 18). If your symptoms are related to an underlying condition such as endometriosis, adenomyosis, fibroids, or pelvic inflammatory disease, you may require additional testing to receive a conclusive diagnosis. In the case of endometriosis, a laparoscopy (a surgical procedure involving the insertion of an instrument called a laparoscope through the abdomen wall) is typically required for diagnosis, whereas other conditions may be diagnosed via ultrasound, endometrial biopsy, or other methods.

Below I've highlighted a few specific nutrients and practices that have been shown to reduce menstrual pain and other related symptoms.

Zinc

Zinc has potent antioxidant and anti-inflammatory properties and has been shown to reduce the severity of dysmenorrhea when taken on the days leading up to your period.[16] Zinc supplementation of 30 to 50 mg daily during the week prior to menstruation has been shown to significantly decrease prostaglandin levels and pain intensity.[17] Women also report a reduction in premenstrual symptoms and menstrual bleeding. Incorporating zinc-rich foods such as red meat, shellfish, oysters, and mussels will increase your intake; or consider supplementing with zinc during the four to five days before your period starts (note: don't take zinc on an empty stomach as it can cause stomach upset).

Magnesium

Magnesium deficiency is associated with an increased inflammatory response in the body, and up to 75 percent of us don't get enough.[18] One study found that women who suffer from dysmenorrhea have significantly lower serum magnesium levels compared to women who don't have painful periods.[19] Magnesium supplementation has been shown to reduce painful symptoms and decrease prostaglandin levels by as much as 45 percent.[20] When choosing an oral magnesium supplement, opt for magnesium glycinate or magnesium citrate for better absorption and less of a laxative effect.[21] You can also improve your magnesium levels by taking Epsom salt baths, using magnesium spray, or making magnesium-infused body lotion — especially if you have difficulty tolerating oral magnesium supplementation (see the Appendix).

Fish oil

Fish oil has an anti-inflammatory effect and has been shown to reduce period pain. Similar to the anti-inflammatory properties of zinc and magnesium, the omega-3 fatty acids in fish oil reduce prostaglandin production, which results in less pain and fewer symptoms.[22] A number of studies have shown that fish oil significantly reduces the intensity of period pain while also decreasing other related symptoms such as back pain, headache, fatigue, and nausea.[23] Fish oil has even been shown to be more effective than ibuprofen in treating severe period pain.[24]

Taking a daily fish oil supplement (such as cod liver oil), and/or incorporating oily fish into your diet at least twice per week is a great way to get more of these beneficial omega-3 oils and reduce your period pain in the process. Consider combining these three anti-inflammatory compounds (zinc, magnesium, and fish oil) as part of your strategy to reduce period pain, particularly during the week before your period (and make sure to track your results on your charts!).

Acupuncture

Acupuncture has been shown to significantly reduce period pain and is considered an effective treatment for women with endometriosis.[25] Although the estimated prevalence of endometriosis is thought to be around 10 percent, an estimated 40 to 60 percent of women who experience dysmenorrhea have endometriosis.[26] Acupuncture is known for its analgesic (pain-reducing) effects, and though not fully understood, acupuncture is thought to have an anti-inflammatory effect and has been shown to significantly reduce prostaglandin levels in women with both primary and secondary dysmenorrhea.[27]

Castor oil packs

Castor oil is derived from the seeds of the *Ricinus communis* plant, and is often used for a variety of conditions including uterine fibroids, migraines, constipation, and dysmenorrhea (just to name a few). Castor oil has a fascinating history; its documented use dates back thousands of years. It has been referred to as *Palma Christi* (the palm of Christ) and is known for its profound healing effects on the body.

Castor oil promotes healing in the body by increasing lymphatic circulation, enhancing immune function, reducing inflammation, stimulating liver function, and enhancing your body's natural detoxification process.[28] In his book *The Oil That Heals*, William McGarey, MD documents the healing power of castor oil in his patients over the 20-plus years he has used it in his practice.[29] It's a fascinating read that may have you running to your local health food store to buy a bottle of castor oil before you even make it to the end. We may not fully understand the inner workings of castor oil from a scientific perspective, but it would be incredibly short-sighted not to consider using castor oil as part of your treatment strategy.

Anecdotally, women have used castor oil to decrease water retention, improve digestive function, improve circulation, and stimulate liver function during the luteal phase of their menstrual cycles in particular. This allows their livers to more effectively break down and metabolize estrogens and clear them from the body. For many women, castor oil has been instrumental in reducing period pain, among other unpleasant menstrual symptoms such as bloating, cramping, breast tenderness, and digestive issues.

Here's what you'll need to make your own castor oil pack:

- A wool or cotton flannel cloth large enough to fold and place over your abdomen,
- A clear plastic bag or plastic wrap (optional)
- A hot water bottle,
- A container large enough to dip your cloth into (preferably with a lid),
- A bath towel and/or an old sheet, and
- Clothes that can get dirty.

Castor oil is thick, messy, and will stain your clothes, so choose a cloth you won't need to use again, wear clothes you don't mind getting dirty, and sit on a big bath towel and/or an old sheet to minimize the mess.

Start by folding the cloth to a size that will fit comfortably over your abdomen and saturate it with castor oil (using the container you chose). It should be wet, but not dripping wet. Find a comfortable place to sit and relax and place the castor oil pack directly on your abdomen. Cover it with plastic wrap and then lay your hot water bottle over it. Relax and enjoy the warm healing power of your castor oil pack for anywhere from 20 minutes to an hour or more. Castor oil packs are great to do when you're reading, watching TV, or while doing meditation or visualization.

The best time to do a castor oil pack is during the luteal phase of your menstrual cycle (after you've ovulated and before your period arrives). Although castor oil packs are relatively safe with few contraindications, they're not recommended if you're pregnant or breastfeeding. If you're trying to conceive, instead of using your castor oil pack in your luteal phase, use it during the first half of your menstrual cycle (before ovulation).

Abdominal therapy modalities

Arvigo Therapy is a non-invasive healing modality that improves many of the negative symptoms associated with menstruation, including dysmenorrhea. It involves the external manipulation of the abdominal region to restore optimal alignment and improve the flow and circulation of blood and lymph to the reproductive organs.[30] The concept behind it is that when your reproductive organs (i.e., your uterus and fallopian tubes) are out of alignment, it can cause painful menstruation, digestive complaints, and even infertility. As outlined in this excerpt,

> When reproductive organs shift, they can constrict normal flow of blood and lymph, and disrupt nerve connections. Just a few extra ounces sitting on blood and lymph vessels can cause havoc throughout the different systems in the body. By shifting the uterus back into place, homeostasis, or the natural balance of the body, is restored in the pelvic area and the surrounding organs. Toxins are flushed and nutrients that help to tone tissue and balance hormones are restored to normal order ... Old adhesions from invasive treatments to the pelvic and abdominal area, including fibroid tumors, endometriosis, and cesarean delivery are diminished when addressed by uterine massage. In addition, digestion, urinary and bladder problems can be helped.[31]

A number of other modalities such as Fertility Massage Therapy and Merciér Therapy use massage therapy in the lower abdomen to improve alignment and circulation.[32] These modalities are far less invasive than surgery, and women often report a dramatic improvement in their menstrual symptoms.[33]

Vaginal steaming

Vaginal steaming is an ancient practice used to cleanse and revitalize the uterus.[34] Think of vaginal steaming as uterine lavage — a gentle way to cleanse the uterus from the inside out, removing any old blood or tissue that has built up over the years.[35] If you haven't heard of vaginal (or yoni) steaming before reading this chapter, it likely sounds pretty strange. Unlike what the title implies, the steam is never uncomfortably hot — it actually feels more like a warm bath (for your vulva) and is quite a relaxing experience.

The first time I heard of vaginal steaming I was reading an article about actress Gwyneth Paltrow, who was talking openly about her experience with it. I remember thinking, *Great, we have to steam our vaginas now? What's next?* (Insert eyeroll). But it turns out that vaginal steams have been an important part of women's healthcare for thousands of years — with records dating back to 12th-century Europe.[36] There are modern-day accounts of vaginal steaming in over 40 countries including Korea, Guatemala, Ghana, Haiti, India, China, Japan, and Vietnam.[37] In the same way colonics cleanse the bowels, vaginal steams cleanse the uterus by eliminating old blood and residue.

Vaginal steaming is used for a variety of reasons:

- Post-partum care (encourages healing and tonifies the uterus following childbirth)
- Uterine cleanse to remove old menses and improve blood flow and circulation
- Pre- and postmenstrual spotting
- Brown or black bleeding and/or abnormal menstrual bleeding
- Blood clots with menses
- Dysmenorrhea (painful periods)
- To improve symptoms associated with uterine fibroids, endometriosis, and ovarian cysts

You'll need the following ingredients:

- 1 to 2 cups of fresh herbs or 1 to 2 oz of dried/ground herbs — you can combine any of the following fresh or dried herbs: oregano, basil, marigold, rosemary, basil, calendula, and lemon balm. Other helpful herbs include burdock leaves, motherwort, yarrow, chamomile, lavender, and thyme.
- 8 cups (2 quarts) water

You can simply use water and sea salt without herbs (note: do not use essential oils, as they are too concentrated). As with castor oil packs, the ideal time for vaginal steaming is during the week before your period starts, unless you're actively trying to conceive, in which case you'd only steam prior to ovulation.

Follow these instructions:

1. Add herbs (or salt) to water and boil for 3 to 5 minutes.
2. Remove from heat and place into a bowl for steaming (or place the pot on a hot plate to retain a steady temperature for steaming).
3. Put your bowl (or hot plate and pot) under your chair.
4. Test the temperature of the steam with your hand before you sit above it. The vaginal steam should feel warm and pleasant to sit over. (If it feels uncomfortable, it's too hot. Allow the water to cool to a comfortable temperature or adjust the temperature of your hot plate.)
5. Take off your pants and underwear and sit comfortably over the steam, using either a steam chair or sitting in a comfortable position (see Figure 14–2).
6. Place a blanket on your lap to keep the steam in and drafts out.
7. Relax, read, or meditate for 20 to 30 minutes to allow the steam to work.

Figure 14-1: Vaginal steam chair

You can buy steam chairs (search "vaginal steam sauna" or "yoni steam seat"), or you can make your own if you're handy (see Figure 14–1). It's nice to have a proper seat if this is something you're planning to do regularly, but you don't need to get all fancy to do a steam. If you don't have a steam chair, you can simply squat comfortably over your steam as shown in Figure 14–2. You may find a local practitioner who offers vaginal steaming by doing a quick internet search (I was surprised to find a local naturopath who offers vaginal steaming in her clinic).

Figure 14-2: Squatting position

Your next period may be heavier, have more clots, or be darker than usual. Don't be alarmed, as it's common for your period to look different after doing a vaginal steam. As the saying goes ... *better out than in.*

Now that we've covered period pain, we'll address PMS in the next chapter.

Summary

- Painful periods are not normal. In a normal period, you should experience either no cramping or very mild cramping or discomfort.
- Menstrual pain is related to inflammation — finding ways to reduce inflammation is key to reducing painful symptoms.
- A number of dietary and lifestyle changes can dramatically help you improve your periods; they include reducing your toxin exposure and incorporating nutrient-dense foods from clean sources.
- Zinc, magnesium, and fish oil have all been shown to reduce period pain by reducing inflammation (and lowering prostaglandin levels), especially when taken during the four to five days leading up to menstruation.
- Acupuncture has been shown to reduce period pain and improve related menstrual symptoms.
- Castor oil packs, abdominal therapy, and vaginal steaming are three non-invasive modalities that have been shown to reduce period pain (and other related symptoms).

Chapter 15
Managing PMS Naturally

"Virtually all women experience some premenstrual signs … the only problem is this: How can 90 percent of menstruating women have a disease?"

— M. Sara Rosenthal, *Managing PMS Naturally*

Premenstrual syndrome (PMS) refers to the mood, behavioural, and physical symptoms women experience during the late luteal phase of the menstrual cycle.[1]
Common PMS symptoms include:

- Mood swings
- Anxiety
- Nervousness
- Irritation
- Impatience
- Neediness
- Depression
- Crying
- Teariness
- Fatigue
- Dizziness
- Fainting

- Headaches
- Heart palpitations
- Sugar cravings
- Insomnia
- Confusion
- Forgetfulness
- Weight gain
- Bloating
- Swelling
- Breast tenderness
- Joint pain
- Back pain

Research suggests that anywhere from 80 to more than 90 percent of women experience PMS symptoms, which begs the question: *If over 90 percent of women experience similar symptoms on the days leading up to their periods, can we really call it a syndrome?*[1]

If 90 percent of women felt tired after running a marathon, would we also call that a syndrome?

When your menstrual cycle is healthy, robust, and normal, you would expect your PMS symptoms (if any) to be mild. Menstrual *molimina* is an older medical term that refers to the normal symptoms that occur following ovulation: breast tenderness, fluid retention, bloating, and negative moods.[2] In women with normal, ovulatory menstrual cycles, molimina occurs so consistently that the symptoms can be used to confirm ovulation (given that these symptoms only occur after ovulation).[3] Understanding molimina allows you to differentiate between normal postovulatory symptoms and PMS.

In her book, *Her Blood Is Gold*, Lara Owen suggests that we should turn the normal way of looking at PMS on its head. While it's often unpleasant and inconvenient to experience premenstrual symptoms, she suggests that we can transform the overall experience into something more meaningful by paying attention to what we can learn from it. She writes:

> It ... makes sense, given the infinite wisdom and inherent balancing capacity of our bodies, that we would have a time of cleansing and emptying before and as we bleed. The body and the psyche work as one, not separately. As the body releases toxins through the blood, so the psyche releases mental and emotional toxins through the expression of feelings.[4]

You may be able to minimize your PMS symptoms by allowing adequate time to rest and retreat, but there's a limit to what we can call "normal" and a point at which rest alone won't resolve them. When you treat your menstrual cycle as a vital sign, you can quickly recognize your symptoms as your body's way of getting your attention. You're not supposed to go into an intense and unrelenting emotional tailspin whenever your period comes around, so in this way, PMS presents an opportunity for healing and growth.

The Role of Estrogen and Progesterone

In a healthy cycle, you produce estrogen before ovulation in your follicular phase and progesterone after ovulation in your luteal phase (see Chapters 2 and 3). Your progesterone starts declining midway through your luteal phase (when pregnancy doesn't occur), and this drop in hormones eventually causes menstruation.[5] However, women with moderate to severe PMS typically experience hormonal imbalances, particularly in the luteal phase.

Research shows that women with significant PMS symptoms often experience a sharp decline in progesterone during the three to five days leading up to their periods and an overall imbalance of estrogen and progesterone during their luteal phase.[6] In contrast, women reporting little or no PMS symptoms have normal hormone profiles. Signs of hormonal imbalances are apparent when you chart your menstrual cycles. Signs of low progesterone include premenstrual spotting, a short luteal phase (less than 10 days), and increased mucus production the week before your period.

Premenstrual Headaches and Migraines

Up to 43 percent of women will experience at least one migraine in their lifetime, making women more than twice as likely as men to experience them.[7] Migraines coincide with menstruation up to 60 percent of the time, indicating a possible relationship between migraines and the cyclical fluctuation of estrogen and progesterone.[8] Menstrual migraines are most likely to happen either during the two days leading up to your period or the first three days of your period, and they're more likely to start around puberty with the onset of the menstrual cycle.[9] However, even though migraines are associated with menstruation, your menstrual cycle doesn't cause them (otherwise every woman would have them with their periods!). Tracking your cycles (and making note of when headaches occur) will help you determine if there's a connection:

- When in your cycle do you experience headaches/migraines?
- Do they happen at other times during your cycle as well?
- Do they fluctuate in severity?
- Are they related to stress?

- Do they worsen with alcohol, caffeine, or sugar consumption?
- Do you notice differences in frequency or severity when you eat certain foods?

Tracking your symptoms over the course of two to three menstrual cycles will provide you with a wealth of information about any link between migraines and your menstrual cycle, and help identify any possible triggers you weren't aware of.

The Four Categories of PMS

The four main categories of PMS, also referred to as *premenstrual tension* (PMT), are anxiety (PMT-A), hyperhydration (PMT-H), carbohydrate cravings (PMT-C), and depression (PMT-D).[10] These categories provide greater insights into the mechanisms that contribute to the most common symptoms — and there's something inherently empowering about giving a name to your experience (especially if your symptoms have never been taken seriously before).

- *Anxiety (PMT-A)* — Anywhere from 66 to 80 percent of women who experience PMS symptoms experience PMT-A, making it the most common category.[11] You know you're experiencing PMT-A if you feel anxious, nervous, and irritable during your luteal phase. These symptoms typically increase in intensity as you approach your period, and you may experience feelings of mild to moderate depression just before your period starts.[12] Once your period starts, these symptoms quickly disappear. PMT-A is categorized by an imbalance of estrogen and progesterone — evident in a shorter than normal luteal phase and low progesterone relative to estrogen.[13]
- *Hyperhydration/bloating (PMT-H)* — About 60 to 66 percent of women who experience PMS symptoms experience PMT-H, making it the second most common category.[14] PMT-H is characterized by water and salt retention and is associated with premenstrual weight gain, abdominal bloating, breast tenderness, or some degree of swelling (edema) in your hands and feet.[15] PMT-H related hyperhydration/bloating is associated with elevated estrogen and aldosterone levels in the late luteal phase.[16]

- *Carbohydrate cravings (PMT-C)* — Anywhere from 24 to 44 percent of women with PMS symptoms experience carbohydrate cravings. PMT-C is characterized by sweet cravings, increased appetite, and an overall increase in your refined carbohydrate consumption that increases in intensity as your period draws near. This often leads to a vicious cycle, as sugar cravings lead you to eat more sweets, and eating more sweets (read: sugar binge) leads to feelings of fatigue, headaches, heart palpitations, dizziness, and even fainting spells — especially in women with blood sugar control issues (such as Polycystic Ovary Syndrome [PCOS]).[17]

- *Depression (PMT-D)* — Up to 23 percent of women experience PMT-D, which is associated with symptoms of depression, social withdrawal, and suicidal ideation in the most serious forms.[18] You may also experience lethargy, forgetfulness, confusion, brain fog, tearfulness, and insomnia.

Though most women identify with one primary category, there's quite a bit of overlap. As we'll cover in more depth below, much of the research aimed at improving PMS symptoms focuses on restoring normal hormone levels.

Treating PMS Naturally

An estimated 18 percent of reproductive-age women experience PMS symptoms severe enough to warrant treatment.[19] PMS is associated with an imbalance of estrogen and progesterone in the luteal phase, as I've mentioned, as well as a number of nutrient deficiencies including magnesium, calcium, vitamin D, and B vitamins. Women who regularly consume foods high in these and other nutrients are less likely to experience PMS symptoms, while women who eat greater amounts of refined sugar, carbohydrates, and conventional dairy products are at a greater risk.[20] Excess refined sugar consumption is also associated with an increased incidence of migraine headaches (especially if you have *hypoglycemia* — a condition characterized by abnormally low blood sugar levels); reducing sugar consumption has been shown to decrease the frequency and severity of migraine headaches by as much as 75 percent.[21] Acupuncture has also been shown to significantly reduce PMS symptoms over the course of one to three menstrual cycles in women with moderate to severe symptoms (in cases in which dietary and lifestyle modifications have been ineffective).[22] Most women wish to seek non-invasive treatment options for PMS prior to seeking medical attention, and many women experience significant improvements by addressing dietary and lifestyle factors (though these changes may not be sufficient for women with severe symptoms).[23] Below I've highlighted a few specific nutrients that have been shown to reduce PMS symptoms.

Magnesium

Research shows that magnesium supplementation significantly reduces PMS symptoms including fluid retention, weight gain, and menstrual migraines, particularly during the luteal phase.[24] Magnesium can be taken orally (magnesium glycinate or citrate), or absorbed transdermally (via Epsom salt baths, magnesium spray, or magnesium-infused body lotion). See the Appendix for details (or refer back to Chapter 14).

Vitamin B₆

Vitamin B_6 deficiency impairs normal tryptophan metabolism, which increases your risk of depression (see Chapter 7), and is also associated with premenstrual symptoms. B_6 supplementation has been shown to significantly reduce PMS symptoms, and women who consume foods rich in B vitamins (including vitamin B_6) have a lower risk of developing PMS.[25] The richest and most bioavailable sources of vitamin B_6 include liver and organ meats (including beef, bison, lamb, chicken, and duck), red meat, fish, and seafood. Vitamin B_6 is heat-sensitive, so consider slow-cooking meat at low temperatures when possible to preserve the nutritional content.[26] Other sources include green vegetables (spinach, broccoli, and Brussels sprouts), chickpeas, bananas, avocados, sweet potatoes, sauerkraut, and raw dairy.

Calcium

Women with PMS tend to have lower overall calcium levels.[27] Your calcium levels fluctuate throughout your cycle; they reach their highest point during your period and their lowest point around ovulation.[28] Calcium supplementation is associated with an overall decrease in PMS symptoms including irritability, depression, anxiety, headaches, water retention, food cravings, and pain during menstruation.[29] One study found that calcium supplementation (1200 mg daily) over a 3-month period resulted in a 48 percent overall reduction in PMS symptoms.[30] However, long-term calcium supplementation (in addition to a high dietary intake) is associated with higher mortality rates from all causes.[31] A study published in *The BMJ* found that women with a high dietary intake of calcium (exceeding 1400 mg per day), who *also* took calcium supplements, were at an increased risk of dying from all causes including cardiovascular disease and ischaemic heart disease (but not stroke).[32] The increased mortality risk was specifically related to the addition of calcium supplements to a diet already high in calcium — meaning that obtaining calcium from food, when possible, is a safer choice.

Milk and other dairy products are an important source of calcium and countless other nutrients; however, pasteurization reduces the overall calcium content and destroys the naturally-occurring enzymes (including phosphatase, which is essential for calcium absorption — see Chapter 12).[33] Other food sources include sardines (with the bones in), dark green leafy vegetables, and almonds.

Vitamin D

Low vitamin D levels are associated with an increased risk of PMS, and as with calcium, your vitamin D levels fluctuate throughout your menstrual cycle.[34] Although you can obtain small amounts of Vitamin D from food sources, the vast majority of your vitamin D comes from the sun (and via supplementation).[35] The amount of vitamin D you produce from sun exposure varies greatly depending on where you live and the colour of your skin.[36] Thirty minutes of full-body sun exposure triggers about 50 000 IUs of vitamin D in a light-skinned person, 8000 to 10 000 IUs in a dark-skinned person, and 20 000 to 30 000 IUs in someone whose skin falls in between.[37] If you have dark skin, your risk of vitamin D deficiency increases the further you live from the equator.[38]

Your skin must be directly exposed to sunlight to synthesize vitamin D — and sunscreen can reduce your vitamin D synthesis by as much as 92.5 percent, depending on how often you reapply.[39] So, expose your bare skin to the sun for at least 15 to 20 minutes per day, depending on your skin tone (60 minutes if you're dark-skinned).

Food sources of vitamin D include dairy products (milk, cheese, yogurt, and kefir), fatty fish (sardines, mackerel, and salmon), cod liver oil, egg yolks, and beef/bison liver; however, without adequate sun exposure, food intake alone won't provide sufficient vitamin D.[40] Consider testing your vitamin D levels and then work with your healthcare practitioner to supplement appropriately (optimal is between 45 and 80 ng/mL).[41]

Vitex

You may already be familiar with vitex because it's one of the most popular natural treatments used for PMS symptoms. *Vitex agnus-castus* (also known as chaste tree) is a shrub that bears fruit (chaste berries) that have been used historically for a variety of reproductive and menstrual conditions associated with an imbalance of hormones.[42] Vitex is thought to act on the hypothalamus and pituitary gland, causing a positive effect on sex hormone balance (particularly during the luteal phase).[43] Vitex has been shown to reduce PMS symptoms such as irritability, anger, headaches, and breast tenderness (when the issue is related to HPO axis dysregulation), but not PMT-H symptoms such as bloating and water retention.[44]

In the next chapter, we'll focus on restoring normal menstrual cycles.

Summary

- From 80 to more than 90 percent of women experience PMS symptoms — a number that calls into question whether or not we can really call it a "syndrome."
- Taking time to rest and retreat during the premenstrual phase can significantly improve your PMS symptoms.
- Severe PMS symptoms often indicate an underlying imbalance of estrogen and progesterone during the luteal phase.
- The four main categories of PMS are PMT-A, H, C, and D: anxiety, hyperhydration/bloating, carbohydrate cravings, and depression.

- Diet and lifestyle factors play significant roles in the severity of your PMS symptoms.
- Premenstrual headaches are associated with fluctuations in estrogen levels and can be reduced by addressing the dietary, lifestyle, and nutritional factors aimed at balancing estrogen and progesterone in the luteal phase.
- A number of nutrients have been shown to reduce PMS symptoms: magnesium, vitamin B_6, calcium, vitamin D, and vitex.

Chapter 16
Restoring Normal Menstrual Cycles

"It is important to remember that symptoms are exactly that: the surface manifestation of a deeper disturbance."

— Lara Owen, *Her Blood Is Gold*

Your menstrual cycle can be used as a diagnostic tool to identify underlying disorders. Persistent disruptions in normal cycling are early warning signs for significant health challenges or conditions including thyroid disorders, polycystic ovary syndrome (PCOS), and hypothalamic amenorrhea (HA). This chapter will increase your awareness of these three conditions and highlight what to watch for as you work toward restoring normal menstrual cycles (also refer back to Chapter 6).

Restoring Normal Cycles with a Thyroid Disorder

Just as a table requires all of its legs to keep it standing, optimal thyroid function depends on the collective action of several nutrients. Although nutritional support doesn't replace the need for thyroid medication (in most cases), it's often necessary in order to improve symptoms (including low BBT) and restore optimal menstrual cycle health.

Iodine

Iodine is required to make thyroid hormones, as each thyroid hormone molecule contains one or more iodine atoms. *Thyroxine* (T_4) and *triiodothyronine* (T_3) are the two main thyroid hormones responsible for maintaining normal cell metabolism. T_4 has four iodine atoms attached to it, while T_3 has three (see Figure 16-1). Making thyroid hormones without iodine is like making coffee without coffee beans — you literally can't do it.

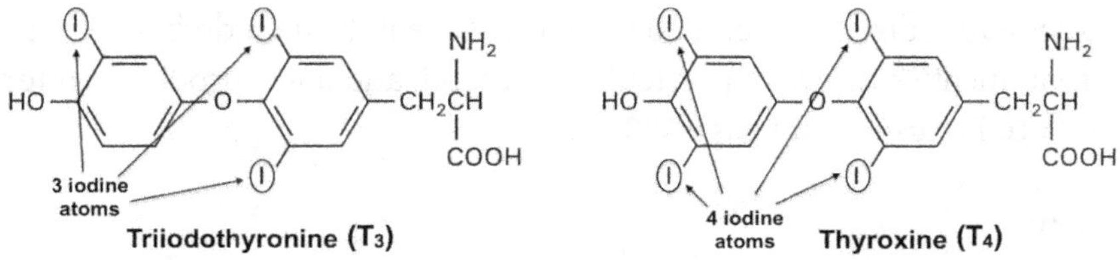

Figure 16-1: Thyroid hormone molecules triiodothyronine (T_3) and thyroxine (T_4). Iodine is an integral part of each thyroid hormone molecule.

Although we generally don't see extreme iodine deficiency (and its detrimental effects) in industrialized nations, mild to moderate deficiency is associated with an increased risk of thyroid disorders, ovulatory disorders, and maternal complications including miscarriage, stillbirth, and congenital abnormalities.[1] Iodine deficiency is the leading (preventable) cause of severe intellectual disability (including *cretinism* — a condition characterized by extreme physical and mental disabilities).[2]

Many practitioners assume their patients' iodine levels are normal instead of testing them, but deficiency is very common. A recent study of pregnant women in the US found that more than half of the women tested had less than adequate iodine levels.[3] Have your healthcare practitioner test your levels via an *iodine loading test* (a urine test done following the administration of iodine) to determine if your levels are adequate.[4]

Selenium

Of all the tissues in the body, the thyroid gland contains the highest concentrations of both iodine and selenium (with breast and ovarian tissue running a close second).[5] Selenium is required for the conversion of T_4 to T_3, which is carried out by a group of enzymes called *deiodinases* (or *selenoenzymes*).[6] Selenium deficiency is associated with increased thyroid antibody production — one of the main factors associated with autoimmune thyroid conditions. Autoimmune disorders are characterized by inflammation, immune system dysregulation, and the development of antibodies to your own tissues.[7] Autoimmune thyroid disorders disproportionately affect women: they represent over 85 percent of cases.[8] Research shows that selenium supplementation reduces the production of thyroid antibodies and counteracts the negative effects associated with excessive iodine intake.[9] Foods high in selenium include brazil nuts, organ meat (kidneys in particular), seafood, and dairy products (refer back to Figure 8-1 on page 130).

Zinc

Zinc is required for the activity of over 300 enzymes in the body and plays a crucial role in the maintenance of normal cell metabolism.[10] Like selenium, adequate levels of zinc are necessary for the conversion of thyroid hormones, and deficiency is associated with low metabolism (as evidenced by low temperatures on your chart).[11] Zinc supplementation has been shown to increase circulating thyroid hormone levels and raise low basal body temperatures (BBTs) in zinc-deficient women.[12] I witnessed this first-hand with my client Sarah. In Chapter 6, we saw how low her BBT was on her chart (even though her lab results were normal — see her original chart repeated in Figure 16-2). See Figure 16-3 for what happened when she started taking zinc.

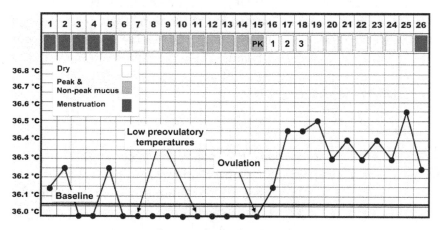

Figure 16-2: Sarah's first chart demonstrates a lower than optimal BBT

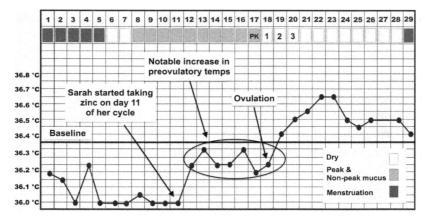

Figure 16-3: Sarah's second chart. Note the increase in her BBT on day 12 of her cycle.

Sarah started taking zinc on day 11 of her second cycle, and from that point forward she experienced a significant change in her BBT. Compared to her first and second charts, Sarah's preovulatory temperatures on following charts are now in the normal range. Her second chart indicates that ovulation took place on day 18. In Sarah's case, the addition of zinc resulted in a significant increase in her BBTs (both before and after ovulation) that persisted over the course of the following three cycles (see Figure 16-4).

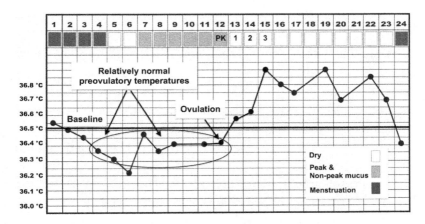

Figure 16-4: Sarah's third chart

Women with a history of hormonal contraceptive (HC) use (and women who limit their consumption of red meat) are at an increased risk of zinc deficiency.[13] If you fall into either category, consider having your levels tested and/or increasing your consumption of zinc-rich foods (see Chapter 12).

Iron

Iron is an essential element with numerous vital functions in the body. Iron carries oxygen from your lungs to your tissues and is required for the production of red blood cells.[14] *Ferritin* is an iron storage protein found in nearly all of your body's tissues, and research shows that thyroid function is affected by your serum ferritin levels.[15] If you have hypothyroidism, you're more likely to have low ferritin levels, and the reverse is true in the case of hyperthyroidism.[16]

Iron deficiency interferes with the normal production and conversion of thyroid hormone, resulting in lower levels of circulating T_4 and T_3.[17] Iron deficiency also impairs your ability to regulate and maintain a normal body temperature and can therefore also contribute to low BBTs.[18] One study found that iron supplementation improved body temperature and partially normalized thyroid hormone concentrations in women who were iron-deficient.[19] Iron deficiency is much more common in women (due to menstruation and the additional iron requirements associated with pregnancy and lactation), so consider testing to confirm that your levels are adequate.

Magnesium

Magnesium is the fourth most abundant mineral in the body and, like zinc, is required for more than 300 enzymatic reactions in the body.[20] Magnesium has been shown to decrease the body's inflammatory response (as seen in thyroid disorders), and individuals with thyroid conditions are more likely to be deficient.[21]

When analyzed via ultrasound, the thyroid glands of both hyper- and hypothyroid individuals show morphological changes including increased vascularization (thick blood vessels), indicating that thyroid disorders negatively affect the thyroid gland itself.[22] Long-term magnesium supplementation has been shown to decrease abnormal thyroid vascularization, improve overall thyroid function, and normalize thyroid hormone levels and antibody counts (see the Appendix for more on magnesium).[23]

Vitamin A

Vitamin A supports the conversion of T_4 to T_3, and has been shown to normalize thyroid hormone production in women of reproductive age.[24] Regularly incorporating food sources of vitamin A (such as liver and cod liver oil) is one way to ensure you're getting enough (refer back to Chapter 12).

Additional nutrients that support thyroid function

Other nutrients that support thyroid function include vitamin C, vitamin D, vitamin E, B vitamins, and other compounds and herbs including inositol and ashwagandha.

- *Vitamins C and E* — Their potent antioxidant qualities protect your thyroid gland from the harmful effects associated with oxidation (tissue damage associated with oxygen exposure).[25]
- *Vitamin D* — Deficiency is associated with autoimmune thyroid disorders, and studies have shown that patients with abnormal thyroid function are more likely to be deficient.[26]
- *B vitamins* — B_{12} deficiency is more common when thyroid disorders are present.[27] Symptoms such as weakness, tiredness, and memory problems typically improve when the deficiency is corrected.[28] In addition to B_{12}, vitamin B_6 deficiency is associated with low thyroid hormone production.[29]
- *Ashwagandha (Withania somnifera)* — Well-known for its ability to help your body cope with stress,[30] ashwagandha has been shown to increase serum T_3 and T_4 levels and normalize thyroid-stimulating hormone (TSH) levels in hypothyroid patients, making it particularly useful in supporting thyroid function.[31]
- *Inositol* — Found in fruits, beans, grains, nuts, and animal foods, inositol is not officially considered a vitamin but is often referred to as "vitamin B_8" (as it falls under the vitamin B category).[32] Inositol has been shown to reduce thyroid antibodies and lower TSH values — two important markers of thyroid dysfunction.[33]

When you begin addressing your thyroid issues, charting your cycles provides a way to track your progress. As is the case with other health-related issues, when your thyroid normalizes, you'll see positive changes in your cycles.

Restoring Normal Cycles with PCOS

Standard treatment for PCOS typically involves HCs, insulin-sensitizing drugs (like metformin), and/or drugs that trigger ovulation, such as clomiphene citrate (Clomid) and letrozole (Femara®).[34] However, metformin is associated with a host of unfavourable gastrointestinal side effects (including nausea, stomach pain, and diarrhea), and ovulation-triggering drugs aren't always effective (see Chapter 17).[35]

In the case of PCOS, elevated androgens, insulin levels, and chronic inflammation work together to disrupt ovulation, often causing long, irregular menstrual cycles. Addressing these factors will allow you to make significant progress in normalizing your cycles.

Stabilize your blood sugar

Given that up to 70 percent of women with PCOS are insulin resistant, stabilizing your blood sugar is an important first step in normalizing your cycles. The more balanced your blood sugar remains throughout the day, the less insulin your pancreas must secrete to control it (and the fewer menstrual cycle disruptions you'll experience). It's normal for your blood sugar to rise after a meal, but when your cells are resistant to insulin, the "fire" (your elevated blood sugar) keeps "burning" much longer that it's supposed to.

Here are three steps to stabilize blood sugar:

1. Consume complex carbohydrates that are low on the glycemic index (think vegetables, berries, and legumes), and avoid refined carbohydrates.
2. Don't consume *unopposed carbohydrates* — always pair carbs with protein and fat at each meal (or snack).
3. Lower your overall carbohydrate intake — use sugar substitutes (like stevia or coconut sugar) and reduce your processed food consumption (see Chapter 13).

When you consume unopposed carbohydrates like orange juice, apples, or a slice of bread (without any protein or fat to slow the blood sugar spike), you're essentially pouring sugar into your bloodstream. This causes a spike in blood sugar followed by a spike in insulin — an effect that's more pronounced in women with PCOS. The most effective (and least invasive) way to address insulin resistance is to modify your carbohydrate intake.[36] Like someone who can't hold their liquor, most women with PCOS can't "hold" their carbohydrates. In her book *Real Food for Pregnancy*, Lily Nichols refers to this phenomenon as "carbohydrate intolerance." She writes, "It's silly when you stop to think about it. If you're given the diagnosis of 'carbohydrate intolerance,' why would you be told to eat a bunch of carbohydrates?"[37] However, today's thinking typically involves finding ways to improve your body's ability to handle carbohydrates (such as giving you drugs that improve your insulin sensitivity) instead of addressing the root of the problem (your carbohydrate intake).[38]

You don't need me to tell you that doughnuts and cookies will raise your blood sugar more rapidly than asparagus and kale, but I'm guessing that when you think of eating carbohydrates, you probably don't picture a green salad or sautéed vegetables. The glycemic index is a ranking system that tells you how different carbohydrate-containing foods affect your blood sugar.[39] Opting for real food carbohydrates that score low on the glycemic index (instead of refined sugar, bread, pasta, and other processed grain products) will go a long way to minimize blood sugar spikes throughout the day; however, it's only part of the equation.

Pay attention to your macronutrient ratio (the relative amount of protein, fat, and carbohydrates you eat at each meal) to ensure you're getting enough protein and fat to offset the effects of the carbs you eat. Here are a few useful strategies:

- Replace your morning oatmeal with a meal that hits all three macronutrient categories (such as eggs, bacon, avocado, grilled zucchini, and a side of fruit).
- In your smoothies, use berries instead of bananas, use full-fat dairy (or an unsweetened alternative), add butter, coconut oil, avocado, and/or pastured egg yolks as a fat source, add protein

(preferably collagen/gelatin powder), and sweeten with stevia (or another low glycemic sweetener) if necessary.

- Change how you arrange your dinner plate — opt for one-half vegetables, one-quarter protein, and one-quarter (or less!) rice, potatoes, or other simple starches/grains.
- Sauté your vegetables in grass-fed butter, coconut oil, and/or pastured lard/tallow.
- Pair your fruits with nuts and/or cheese.
- Choose plain, full-fat yogurt (instead of sweetened varieties that contain little or no fat) — add fruit and/or nuts and sweeten to taste (with coconut sugar, or a low glycemic sweetener like stevia or erythritol).

Once you start eating this way, it quickly becomes second nature. The goal isn't to eat less food, but instead to eat in a way that stabilizes your blood sugar *and* leaves you feeling full and satisfied longer after each meal. Diets higher in fat and lower in refined carbohydrates have been shown to improve insulin sensitivity, hyperandrogenism, and menstrual irregularities in women with PCOS.[40] In one study, a lower-carbohydrate, higher-fat diet reduced insulin resistance, free testosterone levels, and body weight in women with PCOS over a 24-week period — not to mention that 2 of the study participants conceived after previously struggling with infertility.[41] A separate study of 30 women with PCOS found that a lower-carbohydrate, higher-fat diet decreased fasting insulin levels and increased insulin sensitivity over an 8-week period.[42]

Address nutrient deficiencies, insulin resistance, and inflammation

In addition to dietary changes, various nutrients support optimal hormone balance and improve ovulatory function in women with PCOS:

- *Vitamin D deficiency* is extremely common, with 67 to 85 percent of women with PCOS falling below the normal range (less than 20 ng/mL versus the optimal range of 45 to 80 ng/mL).[43] Vitamin D improves insulin sensitivity and blood sugar balance, lowers inflammatory markers, and improves birth outcomes.[44] One study found that PCOS patients deficient in vitamin D were 44 percent less likely to carry their pregnancies to term.[45]

- *Magnesium deficiency* is also common in women with PCOS; it is associated with a variety of metabolic problems including insulin resistance, high blood pressure, and inflammation.[46] Magnesium supplementation has been shown to improve insulin resistance, normalize blood sugar levels, and reduce inflammation.[47]

- *Zinc and selenium levels* are typically lower in women with PCOS.[48] Zinc has potent anti-inflammatory and antioxidant properties and has been shown to improve insulin resistance and reduce testosterone production in women with PCOS.[49] Both zinc and selenium supplementation have been shown to decrease hirsutism and alopecia in women with PCOS, and selenium supplementation has been shown to improve pregnancy rates.[50]

- *Omega-3 fatty acids* (particularly the long-chain DHA and EPA found in fish oil) are particularly important for women with PCOS due to their potent anti-inflammatory properties.[51] In women with PCOS, omega-3 supplementation has been shown to improve metabolic factors (such as cholesterol levels), reduce testosterone levels, and improve ovulatory function.[52]

- *Iodine deficiency* is associated with ovulatory disorders and the formation of cystic tissue (similar to that seen in polycystic ovaries).[53] Consider having your levels tested if you have PCOS.

- *Myo-inositol (MI) and D-chiro-inositol (DCI)* have been shown to improve insulin sensitivity, lower testosterone, normalize reproductive hormone levels, and improve menstrual cycle regularity in women with PCOS.[54] One study found MI more effective than metformin in restoring ovulation, with a spontaneous ovulation rate of 65 percent with MI compared to 50 percent with metformin.[55] Recent research suggests that both MI and DCI play important roles in supporting normal ovulatory function in women with PCOS; they work best when taken together at a ratio of 40:1 (40 parts MI to 1 part DCI).[56]

- *N-acetylcysteine (NAC)* is a potent antioxidant that increases the body's production of glutathione (one of the body's most important antioxidants).[57] NAC has been shown to improve insulin sensitivity, ovulatory dysfunction, and pregnancy rates in women with PCOS.[58]

A number of studies have found that NAC is either equally, or more effective, than metformin in normalizing insulin levels and improving egg quality, ovulation, and pregnancy rates in PCOS cases.[59]

- *Berberine* is a botanical compound found in a number of traditional Chinese medicine herbs, and it has been shown to be as effective as metformin in reducing insulin resistance in women with PCOS.[60] Berberine has also been shown to reduce fasting insulin levels, normalize blood sugar, reduce testosterone levels, and improve ovulatory function in women with PCOS.[61]

- *Cinnamon* is known for its ability to improve insulin and glucose markers in patients with type 2 diabetes, making it an obvious choice for insulin-resistant PCOS patients. In women with PCOS, cinnamon has been shown to decrease insulin resistance and improve menstrual cycle parameters.[62] In one study of 45 women with PCOS, cinnamon supplementation resulted in a significant improvement in menstrual cycle length and ovulatory patterns compared to the control group.[63]

For more information about treating PCOS, see *8 Steps to Reverse Your PCOS* by Fiona McCulloch, ND, and *Healing PCOS* by Amy Medling.

Restoring Normal Cycles with HA

It's possible to get your period back if you have hypothalamic ame-norrhea (HA), but the longer your period has been absent, the longer it will (likely) take to restore normal ovulatory and menstrual function.[64] Recovering your menstrual cycles involves eating more, exercising less, gaining weight, and managing stress — and you'll benefit immensely from having professional support along the way. Follow the guidelines below as you work toward restoring normal cycles:

- *Seek professional support* — You'll benefit from assembling a team of qualified practitioners to support you as you recover. You may require the support of a therapist, naturopath, medical doctor, acupuncturist, dietician, nutritionist, fertility specialist, and/or an HA support group (see Chapter 18).

- *Get enough to eat each day* — Skipping meals is not an option. Not only must you eat breakfast, lunch, and dinner (every day), but you must eat enough at each meal. Every meal should contain a balance of protein, fat, and carbohydrates; it should also contain sufficient calories to sustain your current activity level.

- *Increase your fat intake* — Fat is necessary for normal ovulatory function. One study found that putting women on a low-fat diet significantly delayed ovulation compared to women who consumed a high-fat diet.[65] Since your reproductive hormones (including estrogen and progesterone) are synthesized from cholesterol (and cholesterol is only present in animal fat), you must ensure you incorporate fat into each meal (see Chapter 12).

- *Gain weight* — Many women overcome HA by gaining weight. Ironically, the weight gain usually brings them back to their original weight (before they lost their period). This is often the most difficult step because it involves eating a variety of foods you may have previously restricted — not to mention the change in the size and shape of your body as you gain back the weight.

- *Either exercise less or stop exercising* — Consider cutting down your exercise by half (or less), and replace strenuous workouts with walking when possible. If you're not willing to exercise less, you must ensure you're eating enough to cover your energy deficit by significantly increasing your caloric intake. Consider working with a doctor, naturopath, and/or nutritionist to ensure you're eating an appropriate amount for your energy level.

- *Manage stress* — Whether you decide to develop a daily mindfulness practice, or you get a dog for companionship, find ways to manage stress that make sense for you and fit into your life (refer back to Chapter 13).

- *Address perfectionism* — Striving for perfection has led many women to the hospital. It's not easy to overcome the desire for perfection in every aspect of your life, including (and at times, *especially*) your weight and physical appearance; but the first step is to acknowledge it. For better or worse, we're human beings, and perfection isn't something we were ever designed to attain. Striving for perfection leads to stress, disappointment, and unhappiness — because you'll never get there. Perfectionism doesn't exist in real life, but you, on the other hand, *do* exist in real life — as do the long-term effects of HA. You deserve to be healthy, and a big part of being healthy is having regular periods. It's time for you to put your needs first and your perfectionism second (or take it off the list entirely).

- *Find your tribe* — Connecting with women who are recovering (or have recovered) from HA is so important that I'm mentioning it again. Having a supportive community around you, whether it's in person or online, will show you that you're not the only one who has experienced this, and you definitely don't have to go through it alone.

Andrea's story

I first discovered I had HA when I got off the pill after 12 years straight. A few years into our marriage, we were finally ready to start a family. I had had two and a half years of regular periods when I started the pill for lower back pain during my period, so not having my period resume when I got off the pill was a complete surprise to me, especially since I had always been "very healthy" according to my annual physicals.

The western-medicine-oriented ob-gyn and reproductive endocrinologist that I worked with over the course of over two years offered me no answers and no hope, just higher doses of synthetic hormones and increasingly invasive treatment methods as I progressed from Clomid to IUI [intrauterine insemination] and eventually IVF [in vitro fertilization]. After two rounds of IVF, my body felt so abused that I called it quits and refocused my energy on healing through more holistic means. I worked (unsuccessfully) with an acupuncturist for six months before moving on to a naturopath at an integrative medical practice. That is when things started to become hopeful again. I finally got answers and a treatment protocol that started to heal me. I was diagnosed with Hashimoto's thyroiditis and had a plethora of complications that are commonly associated with Hashimoto's that needed addressing, such as candida, SIBO [small intestinal bacterial overgrowth], adrenal fatigue, and nutrient and vitamin deficiencies among other things.

My healing protocol included supplements, diet changes, reducing my toxin exposure (mainly through filtered water, beauty products, and household cleaning products), sleeping more, working out less, energy healing (reiki and chakra work), emotional healing (which was exponentially accelerated by working with a professional), and some reflection/soul-searching about what my infertility journey was trying to teach me (which led to a career change). Specific diet changes included eliminating gluten, dairy, soy, peanuts, caffeine, alcohol, and refined sugars; switching to high-quality protein sources and organic produce as much as possible; and eating a diet higher in carbohydrates and not restricted in calories. I eventually worked with a chiropractor and a different acupuncturist as well.

When I got my period back, just over four years after getting off the pill and a little over a year of working with my naturopath, it was one of the most amazing moments of my life! I sobbed with relief that all of my efforts had been worth it, and I also felt immense pride that I had successfully healed my body. We were able to get pregnant the first time we tried.

In looking back on my experience, what made the biggest difference for me was giving my body what it needed through food, supplements, sleep, and very limited exercise.

Andrea's journey was long and arduous, but her experience shows us that it's possible to restore normal menstrual cycles — it just doesn't always happen quickly. Andrea's period returned once her body got what it needed through a combination of adequate nutrition, a reduction in exercise, and changes to a variety of her lifestyle factors. For additional information, see *No Period. Now What?* by Nicola Rinaldi, PhD. Not only did Dr. Rinaldi overcome HA herself, she compiled her research into an incredibly detailed and informative resource to help other women do the same.[66]

To identify, address, and overcome these and other health issues that interfere with normal menstruation, you'll often require professional support. These conditions are not DIY projects, and most women benefit from having a team of qualified practitioners — see Chapter 18 for a full discussion on assembling your healthcare team.

Summary

- Thyroid disorders are typically treated with replacement thyroid hormones, but if you continue to have symptoms (including menstrual cycle irregularities), you may require additional nutrients to support optimal thyroid function. Work with a qualified practitioner (such as a naturopath or functional medicine doctor) for best results.
- Dietary changes aimed at stabilizing blood sugar have been shown to effectively reduce insulin resistance, support weight loss, and normalize the menstrual cycle.
- PCOS is associated with certain nutrient deficiencies, and there are several supplements that have been shown to improve symptoms. Work with a qualified practitioner for best results.
- For women with HA, getting their period back involves improving eating patterns, modifying exercise practices, and reducing stress.

Chapter 17
Planning Ahead for Pregnancy

"Reproductive freedom is not just the ability not to have a child through birth control. It's the ability to have one if and when you want."

— Pamela Madsen

There's arguably no other time in a woman's life where she will require as much energy and nutrition as she does during pregnancy. Modern advice for women planning for pregnancy doesn't provide much guidance beyond going off the pill and taking prenatal vitamins; however, in some cases this advice (or rather lack of it) can be harmful. As the mother of two beautiful boys, I can tell you that you'll never regret planning ahead and taking time to prepare your body for pregnancy — and a preconception period of at least 6 to 12 months is ideal.

Preconception Nutrition

If you think of your nutrient stores as a bank account, pregnancy and breastfeeding are two crucial periods of your life when you make massive withdrawals. There will never be a scenario where you go through nine months of pregnancy (followed by several months, or years, of breastfeeding) and have *higher* nutrient stores than you did going in. After all, your body is creating an entirely new life. After giving birth to my first son, I remember looking down at him and thinking, *where did you come from?* In that moment it hit me that my body had used everything I had eaten up to that point to create him.

Building your nutrient stores before pregnancy provides you with the vital energy you'll need to be a mother. If you haven't taken the necessary time to do this ahead of time, your baby will take what she needs directly from *you*. If you spend a minimum of six months to a year preparing, you won't end up overdrawn when your baby arrives ... but you're not the only one who should be planning ahead.

If you're in a relationship with a man, he should be preparing for pregnancy right along with you. Traditional cultures knew this, opting to have both men and women eat special preconception diets during the 6 to 12 months prior to pregnancy.[1] This period of focused nutrition allows both of you to build your nutrient stores so you're both ready (from a nutritional standpoint) when it's time to make a baby.

Nutrient-dense fertility foods

It's not surprising that the foods responsible for improving and maintaining healthy cycles are the same foods that build a healthy baby:

- Liver and organ meats
- Cod liver oil
- Eggs
- Fish, shellfish, and other seafood
- Minimally processed, full-fat dairy products
- Grass-fed and pasture-raised animal products
- Bone broth
- Lacto-fermented foods and beverages
- Fruits and vegetables (but mostly vegetables)
- Saturated fat versus vegetable oil (for cooking)

By regularly incorporating these foods into your preconception diet, you're providing your body with a concentrated source of the nutrients you need — iron, folate, choline, B vitamins, omega-3 fatty acids, vitamin D (in cod liver oil), vitamin A, iodine, and other naturally-occurring nutrients — to build a healthy baby.

I've highlighted below several of the benefits of incorporating these foods during the preconception period, but you can refer back to Chapter 12 for a full discussion.

- *Vitamin A* (retinol) is crucial for fetal heart development and the normal development of your baby's eyes and ears; your requirements significantly increase during pregnancy.[2] The best sources of vitamin A include liver, cod liver oil, eggs, meat, and full-fat dairy.[3]

- Your *iron* requirements dramatically increase during pregnancy, but only about 20 percent of women have sufficient reserves.[4] Iron deficiency increases your risk of premature delivery and having a baby that's small for his gestational age.[5] Regular liver consumption in the preconception phase will help you build up your stores.

- *Folate and choline* are essential for normal neural tube and overall fetal brain development.[6] Neural tube defects and other birth defects occur within the first eight weeks of pregnancy, meaning that preconception intake of these nutrients is required for normal fetal development. These two crucial nutrients are readily available (in their most bioavailable forms) in liver, organ meats, and eggs (if you supplement with folate, choose one that contains the *active* form of folate — methyltetrahydrofolate, methylfolate, or 5-MTHF — see Chapter 12).

- Up to 50 percent of pregnant women are deficient in *vitamin D*.[7] Vitamin D is essential for normal fetal bone development, and deficiency significantly increases your risk of pregnancy complications including pre-eclampsia (high blood pressure) and low birth weight.[8] Women with sufficient preconception levels of vitamin D are more likely to conceive and carry a pregnancy to term, whereas low vitamin D is associated with an increased risk of pregnancy loss.[9] However, many women are deficient despite regular supplementation.[10] Consider having your levels tested to ensure you're getting enough.

- *Omega-3 fatty acids* (DHA and EPA) are crucial for normal visual and neural development, and they are associated with better pregnancy outcomes.[11] Sources include cold-water fatty fish (eaten with the skin), cod liver oil, fish oil, and microalgae oil.

- Sufficient *iodine* is necessary for normal fertility and fetal development.[12] Women deficient in iodine are up to 46 percent less likely to conceive in any given menstrual cycle.[13] Your thyroid hormone production increases by 50 percent during the first few months of pregnancy, thus increasing your requirement for iodine during pregnancy and lactation.[14] Iodine deficiency during pregnancy increases your risk of having a child with attention deficit disorder, hyperactivity disorder, and/or impaired cognitive development.[15] Seaweed is rich in iodine, and other food sources include seafood, eggs, and dairy products (though supplementation may be necessary if a deficiency is identified — see Chapter 16).

- *Lacto-fermented foods and beverages* naturally contain a high density of beneficial microbes (probiotics).[16] Your baby's microbiome is seeded by yours via vaginal delivery and breastfeeding, so your gut health (and the composition of your gut microbiome) is essential.[17] Disruptions in the normal population of an infant's gut microbiome (as in the case of cesarean delivery, the administration of antibiotics, or formula feeding) are associated with an increased risk of allergies, eczema, asthma, childhood obesity, type 1 diabetes, and celiac disease.[18] By regularly consuming fermented foods (and/or supplementing with probiotics), you can optimize what you pass on to your baby through birth and lactation.[19]

Is it safe to eat foods high in vitamin A?

You may wonder if it's safe to consume liver and cod liver oil (or other sources of vitamin A) during pregnancy, and the answer is that it depends on the source. Vitamin A toxicity (also referred to as *hypervitaminosis A*) from food sources is rare, and when it happens, it's usually related to eating the liver of specific animals known to have toxic levels.[20] Polar bear liver, for example, has been found to contain nearly 2 million IUs of vitamin A per 100 grams (beef liver contains 30 000 to 46 000 IUs per 100 grams).[21] If you eat a moderate amount of liver once or twice a week, you'll get the basic nutrients you need for optimal fertility without getting anywhere close to toxic levels.

Most cases of vitamin A toxicity involve supplementation with *synthetic* vitamin A. An article published in *The American Journal of Clinical Nutrition* described a woman who developed symptoms of vitamin A toxicity after taking an average of 400 000 IUs of synthetic vitamin A daily for 8 years.[22] That's the equivalent of eating 3 pounds of beef liver or 6 pounds of chicken liver per day (for the next 8 years!). I'm going to assume you'll never consume that much liver (*smile*).

Megadoses aside, there are significant risks associated with getting your vitamin A from supplements during pregnancy because your body metabolizes it differently from supplements than from food sources. Pregnant women who take large amounts of vitamin A (via supplementation) are more likely to have babies with birth defects.[23] The increased risk of birth defects is linked to a number of specific compounds (called *teratogenic metabolites*) that your body produces as you break down vitamin A. One study found that when women take vitamin A supplements they produce up to *20 times* as much of these harmful metabolites compared to women who consume the same amount of vitamin A from liver.[24] These results strongly suggest that the safest way to get your vitamin A is through food, especially during pregnancy.

Despite all the discussion of getting too much, you're more likely to be deficient in vitamin A. Even though severe deficiency is uncommon in industrialized nations, it's not uncommon for women in Western countries to experience minor vision changes during pregnancy.[25] This may be considered normal by many practitioners, but vision problems during pregnancy may indicate an underlying vitamin A deficiency.[26] Women in developing nations (where vitamin A deficiency is more common) are more likely to experience night blindness during pregnancy than at any other point in their lives, demonstrating the increased need for vitamin A at this critical stage.[27] Regular liver consumption has been shown to prevent this deficiency, and as noted in an article published by the *European Journal of Nutrition*:

> Vitamin A is essential for growth and differentiation of a number of cells and tissues. Notably during pregnancy and throughout the breastfeeding period, vitamin A has an important role in the healthy development of the fetus and the newborn, with lung development and maturation being particularly important. The German Nutrition Society recommends a 40 percent increase in vitamin A intake for pregnant women and a 90 percent increase for breastfeeding women. However, pregnant women or those considering becoming pregnant are generally advised to avoid the intake of vitamin A rich liver and liver foods, based on unsupported scientific findings.[28]

The authors go on to say, "The only relevant dietary source for vitamin A is liver. All other foods containing preformed vitamin A need to be consumed in atypically large amounts in order to meet the vitamin A requirement."[29] Consuming vitamin A rich foods during the preconception period (and while pregnant and breastfeeding) is the safest way to ensure you're getting adequate vitamin A.

How much fish is safe to eat?

When considering how much fish and seafood to eat, it's natural to be concerned about mercury and other chemical contamination (especially during pregnancy). However, research suggests that the benefits of consuming seafood outweigh the risks.[30] A 2007 study reported that "maternal consumption of more than 340 g (12 oz) of seafood per week was beneficial for a child's neurodevelopment."[31] Women who ate the most seafood each week had children with better verbal and communication skills, better fine and gross motor skills, and less social and behavioural issues. In comparison, children of women who ate very little (or no) seafood were more likely to suffer from developmental and behavioural issues. Even when mothers and children consumed fish on a daily basis (and were consequently exposed to higher levels of mercury), there were no reports of adverse developmental effects in the children.[32] The selenium content in most fish binds to mercury and reduces its toxic effects.[33] Large fish such as shark, swordfish, pilot whale, tuna, and kingfish are known to contain higher levels of mercury compared to selenium, so avoid these, and instead opt for smaller fish with a higher selenium-to-mercury ratio.[34]

See *Real Food for Pregnancy* by Lily Nichols and *The Nourishing Traditions Book of Baby & Child Care* by Sally Fallon Morell and Thomas Cowan, MD for more on preconception and pregnancy nutrition.

Hormonal Contraceptives and Pregnancy

Given the well-established temporary delay in the return of normal fertility associated with hormonal contraceptives (HCs), a minimum transition period of 18 months to 2 years is ideal between coming off HCs and trying to conceive. This may sound extreme, but I assure you it's not — and it's even more important as you get older. You may not have the luxury of extra time when you're in your middle to late thirties or early forties, *but that doesn't mean your body doesn't need it.* If you were put on HCs to mask menstrual cycle irregularities, you're at an even greater risk of experiencing a delay in the return of normal cycling post HCs (see Chapter 8).

I urge you to carefully consider your choice of birth control as you get older. Once you reach age 30 and beyond, HCs aren't the best option if you wish to preserve your fertility and avoid unnecessary delays when you're ready to get pregnant. If HCs are your preferred birth control method, recognize that your body will go through a transition period for several months post HCs, and incorporate that time into your decision of when to come off them. This transition period allows you to plan for the worst while hoping for the best. This isn't to say that some women don't conceive immediately when they come off HCs, but given the nutrient deficiencies associated with long-term HC use, getting pregnant right away isn't ideal either.[35]

You'll want to allow your menstrual cycles to normalize and your nutrient stores to fully replenish. When coming off HCs, fertility awareness (FA) charting allows you to track your progress. Ideally, you'll want a minimum of three normal cycles in a row (that fall well within the normal parameters laid out in Chapter 4) prior to conception. As an added bonus, you'll know that you've done everything within your power to give your baby the best possible start. Many women take a year or more to plan their weddings. Why should planning for a baby be any different?

Whenever you take HCs, three distinct events are happening beneath the surface:

1. Endocrine disruption,
2. Nutrient depletion, and
3. Age-related fertility decline.

We've covered endocrine disruption and nutrient depletion in previous chapters, so now we'll focus on the third event — *age-related fertility decline*. If you've been on HCs for 10 years, for example, not only has it suppressed your natural cycles and depleted your nutrient stores, but 10 years have passed — and you are now 10 years older than you were when you started taking them. If you started taking HCs at age 21 you would be 31 now, and most women aren't fully aware of how their age affects their fertility.

Age-Related Fertility Decline

Since most of us spend the majority of our reproductive lives actively avoiding pregnancy, we tend to give little thought to how our fertility changes with age. Many women assume it will be just as easy to conceive at age 35 as it was at 21 — but it's not. Age 35 marks the beginning of a sharp and steady decline in a woman's fertility — in fact, when you reach 35 you're officially considered to be of *advanced maternal age* (and a pregnancy at this stage is referred to as a *geriatric pregnancy*).[36]

At birth, you have an estimated 500 000 to 1 000 000 oocyte-containing follicles (eggs) that are gradually depleted over time.[37] Approximately 25 000 remain at age 37, at which point your follicle count begins declining rapidly (at more than twice the initial rate), leaving an average of 1000 follicles at menopause 12 to 14 years later.[38] In addition to having fewer eggs, your egg quality steadily declines, contributing to higher rates of pregnancy loss.[39] The decline in egg quality is thought to be related to the age of the egg itself and an increased rate of chromosomal and mitochondrial abnormalities.[40]

This is evident in research on the impact of age on pregnancy outcomes. When you reach advanced maternal age, you're at an increased risk of miscarriage, stillbirth, preterm birth, and low birth weight, and your risk of pregnancy-related complications increases exponentially.[41] One study examined the pregnancy outcomes of 634 272 Danish women, and although 13.5 percent of all pregnancies ended in fetal loss (a term that includes pregnancies that end in miscarriage, ectopic pregnancy, and stillbirth), the risk of fetal loss was significantly higher in women aged 35 and older.[42] In women aged 20 to 24, 8.9 percent of pregnancies ended in fetal loss compared to over 20 percent in women aged 35 and above. The risk of fetal loss continued to rise exponentially, with a rate of 54.5 percent in women at age 42 and 74.7 percent in women aged 45 and older. In other words, by the time you reach age 40 more than *half* of all pregnancies end in fetal loss.

With that in mind, the larger question is: What can be done to improve egg quality as you get older?

Improving egg quality

Though you can't reverse the aging process, you can focus on several nutrients associated with improving egg quality during the preconception phase (in addition to addressing the dietary and lifestyle factors outlined in Chapters 12 and 13):

- *Coenzyme Q10* (CoQ10) is an antioxidant that protects the body's tissues from the natural aging process.[43] It has been shown to slow the natural aging process by improving ovarian reserve parameters and reducing oxidative damage to the ovary.[44] Research also suggests CoQ10 improves birth outcomes.[45] The highest concentration of CoQ10 is found in organ meat, specifically heart and liver (though most women opt for supplementation).[46]

- *Omega-3 fatty acids* (DHA and EPA), found in fish, fish oil, cod liver oil, and fish roe, are associated with improved egg quality, embryo morphology, and birth outcomes (higher pregnancy and live birth rates), lending credence to the ancestral practice of consuming seafood (particularly fish eggs) prior to conception. [47]

- *Vitamin A* (retinol) is crucial for reproduction, and is essential for the normal growth and development of your oocytes (eggs).[48] Vitamin A is required to initiate the cell division process that allows you to release a healthy (and fully mature) egg each time you ovulate, and it's best obtained from food sources (see Chapter 12 and page 250 in this chapter).

- *Vitamin D* plays an important role in ovarian function and follicular development.[49] Women with adequate levels of vitamin D are more likely to conceive and carry a pregnancy to term, while women experiencing fertility challenges are more likely to be deficient.[50]

- In women with polycystic ovary syndrome (PCOS), *myo-inositol* and *N-acetylcysteine* (NAC) are associated with improved egg and embryo quality.[51]

- *Dehydroepiandrosterone* (DHEA) is associated with improvements in oocyte quality, embryo quality, and both fertilization and pregnancy rates in women with poor ovarian reserve parameters (note: in most cases DHEA is only available by prescription).[52]

- *Vitamin C, vitamin E, selenium, folate, and zinc* (and other antioxidants) have been shown to reduce oxidative damage and may therefore improve egg quality. Research shows that antioxidants are associated with higher pregnancy and birth rates.[53]

- *Royal jelly* is a white and viscous jelly-like substance that is consumed only by the queen bee and newly hatched honeybee larvae. Although more research is needed, royal jelly is thought to improve egg quality due to its unique role in enhancing the fertility of the queen bee and extending her lifespan.[54]

Navigating Fertility Challenges

Many women discover FA when they start trying to conceive. After years of trying to avoid pregnancy, it can be incredibly jarring to find that pregnancy doesn't always happen immediately after they start trying. In this situation, FA is helpful for two main reasons: accurate timing and identifying underlying health issues.

In a study published in 2012, Kerry Hampton, PhD and her colleagues surveyed 282 women seeking fertility assistance from assisted reproductive technology (ART) clinics in Australia. They found that although 68.2 percent of the women surveyed believed that they were timing sex on the correct days of their cycles, only 12.7 percent had accurately identified the fertile window when tested.[55] FA allows you to accurately identify your fertile days each cycle and provides you with significant insights into your overall health.

Many of my clients have left their doctor's office feeling frustrated because they were not getting the answers they were looking for. No one was investigating *why* they weren't conceiving. They were offered pills, injectables, and a variety of expensive medical procedures, but not much of an explanation as to why they couldn't conceive naturally.

If you've been in this situation, you'll already know what the underlying message is: *Your body is broken, and we don't know why it's broken, but don't worry — we don't need to know why because we can make you ovulate with these fertility drugs!*

I can't promise that tracking your cycles will magically make everything better, but it will give you a much deeper insight into your reproductive health. Tracking your cycles empowers you to start taking control of your fertility and your health. The longer you track your cycles, the more confident and knowledgeable you'll be, and as the saying goes, *knowledge is power.*

When I interviewed Thomas Cowan, MD, author of *The Fourfold Path to Healing*, and asked for his perspective on infertility, he explained it like this:

> If somebody has "infertility," they're not healthy ... the idea that, "Oh, you're perfectly fine, you're just infertile"? I mean, that's nonsense. If you're infertile you're not fine.

If you're infertile you need to do something to get yourself to be healthier — by definition. The idea that there's nothing wrong with you...

It's like going to a doctor, and you say, "I can't have a bowel movement," and he says, "Ah, it's fine, some people have bowel movements, some people don't."

It's not true.[56]

What if fertility challenges are a symptom of an underlying health issue rather than the health issue itself? What if restoring optimal health simultaneously restores normal fertility? But there's another important question you should be asking: What if the issue is related to my partner's sperm quality?

Most women automatically assume the issue lies with them, regardless of the fact that 40 to 50 percent of the time male factor infertility is at play.[57] Before I get into the research on fertility treatments, let's discuss improving sperm quality.

Improving sperm quality

A man's sperm analysis gives him a window into his overall health, similar to what tracking your menstrual cycle does for you. Testing his sperm quality early in the game is crucial for two reasons:

1. If his sperm are fine, you can put your energy into looking for the real problem.
2. If his sperm quality and/or count are low, you have adequate time to improve them.

Men produce sperm every day, but the complete process of spermatogenesis (sperm production) takes approximately 74 days — meaning that when your partner ejaculates you're getting a retrospective measure of his health approximately 3 months ago.[58] In my interview with Marc Sklar, fertility specialist and doctor of acupuncture and Chinese medicine, he identified optimal sperm parameters as a minimum sperm concentration of 40 million sperm per mL, 50 percent normal motility, and 14 percent normal morphology.[59] This is in line with a study published in *The New England Journal of Medicine*, which identified optimal sperm parameters for men as a minimum concentration of 48 million sperm per mL, greater than 63 percent normal motility, and greater than 12 percent normal morphology.[60] These numbers are much higher than the lower reference limit set by the World Health Organization (15 million sperm per mL, 40 percent motility, and 4 percent morphology).[61] Successful fertilization requires sperm of normal motility *and* morphology in sufficient numbers; therefore, 40 percent motility and 4 percent morphology leave a very small number of sperm to work with.[62] For the record, 4 percent morphology means that only *4 out of every 100 sperm are normal*, leaving the other 96 percent with a range of abnormalities that make them unable to fertilize an egg — including sperm with 2 heads, no head, no tail, a short tail, a small (or large) head, and other morphological issues.[63] Always ask for a copy of the test results so you can review the numbers yourself, as there is significant variation in what qualifies as "normal."

Regardless of whether your partner has been tested, I encourage you to adopt several of the following practices *proactively*. As I always say to my clients, six months from now will come regardless of what you do, so you may as well have it arrive with better sperm.

Lifestyle factors for healthy sperm

Numerous lifestyle factors affect sperm quality. As you read through the following list, consider which factors apply to your partner and how you might broach the topic with him. Though most men are receptive to making the necessary changes to improve sperm quality, many are resistant to the idea. If your partner is open to podcasts, consider sharing my interview with Marc Sklar, as some men are more receptive to information presented by other men (you can access the interview here: fertilityfriday.com/134).

- *Follow the preconception diet* — The foods that support optimal fertility and replenish key nutrients for you in the preconception phase are equally important for him in order to optimize his sperm quality. Refer back to the preconception nutrition section earlier in this chapter (and Chapter 12) with him in mind.
- *Keep the boys cool* — Testicles hang outside of the body for a reason. In order for him to produce normal sperm, his testicles need to be

at least 2 to 4 degrees cooler than the rest of his body.[64] Studies have shown that a temperature increase of as little as 1 to 2 degrees can significantly decrease sperm count and quality.[65] Hot tubs, tight clothing, extended periods of sitting (or driving), cycling, and other factors that keep his testicles hot will have a negative impact on his sperm quality.[66]

- *Quit smoking (cigarettes and marijuana)* — Smoking has been shown to lower sperm parameters.[67] One study found that regular marijuana smoking (more than once per week) lowered sperm concentration by 29 percent.[68] Eliminating both of these habits during the preconception phase will have a positive impact on his sperm quality.

- *Reduce (or quit) drinking alcohol* — Similar to smoking, regular alcohol consumption has been shown to reduce all sperm parameters (count, morphology, and motility).[69]

- *Keep cell phones, laptops, and tablets away from the boys* — Cell phone exposure has been shown to reduce sperm count, motility, viability, and normal morphology.[70] To reduce his exposure to electromagnetic radiation from his devices, he should not regularly carry his cell phone in his pocket, nor should he place his laptop directly on his lap.

- *Reduce soy consumption* — Regular soy consumption has been shown to increase chromosomal abnormalities in sperm and decrease overall sperm parameters (including motility and count).[71]

- *Minimize xenoestrogen exposure* — Exposure to xenoestrogens and other estrogenic compounds (such as BPA) have been shown to impair sperm quality, lowering both their motility and motion (see Chapter 13).[72]

- *Exercise regularly (but don't overdo it)* — Finding a balance of regular (but not excessive) exercise is important for sperm health. Excessive training (categorized in two separate studies as either high-intensity exercise for 2 hours at a time 5 days per week, or cycling for 5 or more hours per week) is associated with an overall decrease in sperm quality.[73]

Key nutrients for sperm quality

In addition to the lifestyle factors mentioned above, a variety of specific nutrients have been shown to support optimal sperm health:

- *Vitamin A* is essential for normal sperm development and is ideally obtained from food sources. Vitamin A deficiency is associated with reduced (or lost) sperm production and infertility (see Chapter 12).[74]
- *Folate* and *zinc* are crucial for normal sperm development; deficiency impairs spermatogenesis, increases sperm abnormalities, and lowers testosterone production.[75] In one study of 103 subfertile men (defined as having a sperm concentration of 5 to 20 million sperm/mL with no conception after at least 1 year of trying), supplementation with a combination of zinc and folate over a 3-month study period increased the total count of morphologically normal sperm by 74 percent.[76] Opt for food sources when possible, such as liver and organ meats, eggs, lentils, chickpeas, and green leafy vegetables. Note that the MTHFR gene mutation is associated with male factor infertility as it interferes with folate methylation. If he supplements with folate, opt for the active form (methyltetrahydrofolate, methylfolate, or 5-MTHF — see Chapter 12).[77]
- *Coenzyme Q10* (CoQ10) is an antioxidant that plays a critical role in energy metabolism — an important function of sperm motility.[78] CoQ10 is essential for sperm development and has been shown to improve motility, concentration, and morphology.[79] In one study, 287 infertile men were administered 300 mg of CoQ10 twice daily for 12 months (all men were below normal sperm parameters, had no conception after at least 2 years of trying, and their female partners were assessed as fertile).[80] At the 12-month mark, 48 percent had normal semen parameters, with a 50 percent increase in both sperm concentration (from 17.2 to 31.2 million sperm/mL) and total sperm count (from 54.2 to 81.2 million), a 46 percent increase in morphology (from 8.7 to 12.7 percent), a 74 percent increase in motility (from 26.7 to 46.7 percent), and a pregnancy rate of 31 percent.
- *Vitamin C* supplementation has been shown to significantly improve sperm count, motility, and morphology.[81]
- *Vitamin E* and *selenium* have been shown to improve sperm motility.[82]
- *Omega-3 fatty acids* (DHA and EPA) such as those found in cold-water fatty fish (and cod liver oil/fish oil) have been shown to improve sperm count, concentration, and motility.[83]

- *Vitamin D* plays an important role in sperm quality. Men who are deficient in vitamin D have higher numbers of both abnormal sperm and sperm with poor motility.[84]
- *N-acetylcysteine* (NAC; a precursor to glutathione — the most potent antioxidant in the body) and *L-carnitine* (an amino acid that plays a key role in energy metabolism) have also been shown to improve overall sperm quality, with studies showing improvements in sperm count, morphology, and motility.[85]

Seek professional support when you face a health challenge such as poor sperm quality. You'll get the best results when you work with a qualified practitioner who specializes in male fertility (see Chapter 18).

Fertility Treatments

The media regularly spotlight women conceiving well into their mid-forties and even early fifties. Janet Jackson's pregnancy, for instance, was widely reported on back in 2016 — *and she was 50 at the time*. However, we'll never know the full story of how it happened. I'm not saying we should have access to the details of these women's personal lives (after all, it's none of our business), but without the full backstory it can leave the impression that these women are conceiving *naturally*. In reality, these "miraculous" conceptions are likely a result of a series of complex interventions (not to mention tens of thousands of dollars).

Similar to the way menstrual cycle issues are "treated" with HCs, fertility challenges are "treated" with a combination of powerful drugs and invasive medical procedures, but many women underestimate how much their effectiveness changes with age.[86] I'm thankful these procedures are available to us, but there comes a point when in vitro fertilization (IVF) doesn't work anymore.

In my interview with reproductive endocrinologist and infertility specialist Marjorie Dixon, MD, she said this about supporting clients through fertility treatments at age 40 and beyond:

> The uterus you can organize to accommodate a pregnancy, but the pregnancy will only be healthy based on the quality of the eggs, and after the age of 43 the likelihood of putting

out healthy eggs becomes much less. It's not impossible, but it's much less likely between 43 and 45, and then we don't even offer IVF with your own eggs after 45 years of age.[87]

Fertility treatments can't always save the day, because they can't reverse the natural aging process. When you see fertility-related images and stories in the media, there's a much greater chance that these women conceived using a procedure like IVF using either donor eggs (i.e., eggs from a younger woman that were fertilized with her partner's sperm) or her own previously frozen eggs (i.e., eggs that she froze years ago through a procedure called *fertility preservation* (FP) — more on that later in this chapter). Now let's see what the research has to say about fertility treatments.

Intrauterine insemination (IUI)

IUI completely bypasses your cervix and cervical mucus (CM) by placing sperm directly into your uterus prior to ovulation (thus the term intra*uterine* insemination).[88] IUI is often suggested when there's a known issue with sperm production (i.e., male factor infertility) or when there are issues with CM that prevent sperm from readily passing through.[89] Drugs are typically used to trigger ovulation on a particular date — even in women who are otherwise ovulating normally. Given my background in FA, I've often wondered if this step is necessary for women who track their cycles. If you know when you ovulate (and you ovulate regularly), why would you trigger ovulation with drugs? Furthermore, given the essential role of CM in filtering out defective sperm and preparing them for fertilization, wouldn't you *want* the sperm to pass through your mucus to ensure only the best ones make it through? (But I digress...)

Theoretically, placing sperm directly into the uterus helps sperm make their way into the fallopian tubes (and improves your chances of conceiving), but how does it play out in the real world? There are three important questions to address:

1. How many women conceive after going through IUI treatments?
2. What percentage of these pregnancies go full term (after reconciling the rate of miscarriage/pregnancy loss)?
3. Does your chance of having a successful IUI cycle change with age?

One study analyzed the IUI cycles of 1612 women between the ages of 19 and 45 and found that a woman's age is *highly correlated* with the relative success of IUI.[90] Women under 25 had a significantly higher conception rate — approximately 20 percent, compared to 10 percent for women in their 30s, 7 percent for women aged 40 to 43, and 3 percent for women over age 43. On average, only about one out of every 10 women conceived in any given IUI cycle, making multiple rounds necessary to improve overall pregnancy rates.[91] Note that the above study reports on pregnancy rates, giving us a sense of how many women became pregnant during treatment, but doesn't tell us how many of these women were holding a baby in their arms 9 months later.

The two most common drugs used to stimulate ovulation in an IUI cycle are Clomid and letrozole. Clomid, in particular, is associated with higher rates of miscarriage, the thinning of the endometrial lining, and decreased CM production (see Chapter 11). Additionally, 20 to 25 percent of women are resistant to it (meaning they fail to ovulate when the drug is administered).[92] Compared to Clomid, women who use letrozole are more likely to become pregnant and less likely to miscarry in any given IUI cycle. One study found that women given letrozole were 60 percent more likely to conceive in any given IUI cycle compared to women given Clomid (18.96 versus 11.43 percent).[93] On top of that, the women who conceived using Clomid were 30 percent more likely to miscarry compared to the letrozole group (16.67 versus 12.5 percent). After up to 3 rounds of IUI (and after pregnancy losses were taken into account), 33 percent of the women in the letrozole group experienced an *ongoing pregnancy* (meaning the pregnancy continued beyond 20 weeks of gestation), compared to 19 percent of the women in the Clomid group, which gives us a better idea of how many pregnancies (likely) made it to full term.

You may be able to achieve a similar rate of success by using FA to time sex (also referred to as *fertility-focused* intercourse).[94] With accurate timing, most couples of normal fertility conceive within six months of accurately timed sex (i.e., sex during the five days prior to ovulation).[95]

Even though IUI is often recommended when your partner has poor sperm quality (or a low sperm count), there is another (much less invasive) option to consider in this case — *home insemination*.

Home insemination

Unlike IUI, home insemination involves depositing sperm deep inside the vagina (at the cervix) with the help of a cervical cap, and doesn't require any artificial hormones. If your partner has less than optimal sperm, depositing his ejaculate inside a cervical cap, and placing it directly over your cervix, prolongs the exposure of his sperm to your CM, which increases the chance of a successful pregnancy.[96] Whether you're using fresh semen from your partner, or fresh or frozen semen from a sperm donor, the use of a cervical cap can improve the effectiveness of your home insemination.[97]

Many women spend several minutes (or even an hour or more) lying on their backs after sex to increase their chances of conception, but this common practice is highly ineffective. Unless you have an apparatus in your bedroom that holds you upside down, once ejaculated, semen will flow out of your vagina. Home insemination with a cervical cap is much more effective at prolonging the exposure of your partner's semen to your CM. Cervical caps prevent the backflow of semen through your vagina, keeping it at the opening of your cervix where it needs to be.

One study tested the efficacy of home insemination with the use of a cervical cap in 61 couples with documented infertility.[98] Each couple had been trying to conceive unsuccessfully for anywhere from 1 to 11 years. They were instructed to use a cervical cap 1 to 3 times prior to ovulation each cycle (using FA techniques to identify the fertile window), and to leave it in place for a period of at least 6 hours after sex. Thirty-two of the 61 women achieved pregnancy over the course of 4 to 6 cycles, resulting in a 53 percent pregnancy rate (with 3 pregnancies ending in miscarriage). Another study reported a 44 percent pregnancy rate using cervical cap insemination over a 6-month period.[99] These rates are on par (and in some cases greater) than the success rates of IUI. However, this option is only useful when applied at the correct time of the cycle. Refer back to Chapter 10 for best practices in correctly identifying your fertile window. You may wish to use an ovulation predictor kit (OPK) to time your home insemination closer to ovulation, but remember that peak mucus is the primary sign to watch for.

In vitro fertilization (IVF)

IVF involves extracting eggs, retrieving sperm, putting them together, and creating embryos (fertilized eggs that have started to divide and grow). Sometimes embryos are created by placing the sperm and egg together and letting fertilization happen on its own. Other times a procedure called intracytoplasmic sperm injection (ICSI) is used, which involves injecting an individual sperm directly into each egg using a microscopic needle. Once the embryo is created, it's placed directly into the uterus, where it can go on to implant and grow (assuming the procedure is successful). IVF has a higher overall success rate compared to IUI, but like IUI, the effectiveness is highly correlated with age. See Figure 17–1 for the live birth rates per IVF cycle as reported by the Centers for Disease Control and Prevention.[100]

Under 35	35–37	38–40	41–42	43–44	Over 44
33.1%	26.1%	16.9%	8.3%	3.2%	0.8%

Figure 17–1: Live birth rates per IVF cycle[101]

IVF success rates fall dramatically by age 40, and by age 43 fewer than 4 out of every 100 women will become pregnant using their own eggs. In a study of 2705 women undergoing assisted reproductive treatments, only 1 live birth was recorded in women over age 45, and no live births were recorded for women age 46 and older.[102] The rate of miscarriage ranged from 13.5 percent for women under 35, to 70 percent for women 44 and over.

IVF success is highly correlated with the age of the egg itself — more so than the age of the woman undergoing the procedure. In a study published in *Human Reproduction*, the ongoing pregnancy rate for IVF was 59.1 percent when using eggs from a donor aged 23 or younger and 27.3 percent for egg donors over age 37.[103] The harsh realities of age-related fertility decline have led to a drastic, expensive, and somewhat controversial trend — *fertility preservation* (FP).

Fertility preservation (FP)

Think of FP as "fertility insurance," since it's one of the only known ways to stop the biological clock (so to speak). FP allows you to freeze your eggs (or embryos) for future use if you ever need them. It is often used by women with cancer, as cancer treatments increase the risk of infertility and premature menopause.[104] However, a growing number of young women are starting to proactively undergo this procedure in case they don't find an ideal parenting partner (or significant other) until later in life.[105]

As we covered in the last section, the age of the eggs used in IVF determines how successful the procedure will be; so from that perspective, if you can freeze your eggs in your twenties or early 30s, you'd have the option of using your own — but *younger* — eggs if you were to face fertility challenges in the future.

To be clear, I don't endorse FP, nor am I suggesting that you should or shouldn't do it (given that additional research is required to determine if FP is associated with any long-term health consequences for women who undergo the procedure), but I encourage you to think about how your fertility changes with age. After all, at this very moment, thousands of women are freezing their eggs to preserve their fertility ... just in case. Although I don't think it's necessary for most women to run out and freeze their eggs, we all need to consider how to manage our fertility as we get older.

In an article published in *Global Reproductive Health*, the researchers urge women to carefully consider when to start having children:

> Couples delaying family plans should be aware of the risk of not having any [children] or [having] less children than desired ... couples should start no later than age 32 for a 1-child family, at 27 years for a 2-child family, and at 23 years for 3 children. Even when IVF is an option, couples desiring 1 child should start trying to conceive when the female partner is 35 years of age or younger, for 2 children, the latest starting age is 31 years, and for 3 children 28 years.[106]

The authors are encouraging us to be more conservative in our estimates of how long it will take us to grow our families — a dialogue that's largely missing from our early education about our fertility.

To conclude this chapter, I invite you to consider the importance of assembling a qualified team of healthcare practitioners to support you, whether you're overcoming menstrual cycle irregularities or facing fertility challenges. You deserve to be fully informed about the risks, side effects, and success rates associated with any procedure you choose to have. If your fertility specialist is sharing pregnancy rates with you, ask about the miscarriage rate, and don't forget to ask about the live birth rate. Inflated statistics sound really good, but what matters is how many women bring home a healthy baby.

No one cares more about your fertility and your health than you do. It's up to you to get the care you need. It's not always easy, but it's always worth it. For many women, charting their cycles is what finally gives them a sense of agency and control because it allows them to better understand the underlying factors related to their fertility. In the last chapter, we'll discuss how to assemble your healthcare team.

Summary

- When preparing for pregnancy, consider allowing a 6 to 12 month preconception period to give your baby the best possible start.
- Incorporate specific nutrient-dense fertility foods to help you build up your levels of key nutrients including vitamin A, iron, folate, choline, vitamin D, omega-3s, and iodine.
- When coming off HCs to conceive, allow a minimum transition period of 18 months to 2 years to allow your cycles (and your nutrient stores) to fully normalize.
- When you take HCs, 3 distinct events are happening beneath the surface: 1. endocrine disruption; 2. nutrient depletion; and 3. age-related fertility decline.
- Your fertility declines over time — most notably from age 35 and beyond.
- You and your partner can take several steps toward improving both egg and sperm quality as you get older.
- Male factor infertility is responsible for fertility challenges 40 to 50 percent of the time.
- The success rate of any fertility treatment depends more on the age of the egg than the age of the woman receiving the treatment.
- When seeking a fertility treatment, request full information on its success rates so that you know how many women in your age group have successfully carried a baby to term.

Chapter 18
Getting the Support You Need

"The secret of getting ahead is getting started."

— Sally Berger

If you have problems with your cycles, you might think figuring it out on your own will be easy, but that's not always the case. Unfortunately, it can be extremely difficult to find a practitioner willing to help you identify the root cause of your menstrual cycle issues. Whether you have polycystic ovary syndrome (PCOS), hypothalamic amenorrhea (HA), fibroids, endometriosis, painful periods (or any other type of condition that interferes with your menstrual cycle), the standard solution offered by most healthcare practitioners is hormonal birth control, which doesn't address the underlying problem.

Your Doctor's Perspective on the Pill

To better understand why hormonal contraceptives (HCs) are the go-to "treatment" for all things menstrual, I went right to the source to find out for myself. I connected with Miranda Naylor, DO, an osteopathic and functional medicine doctor practising in California. In our interview, she explained that, in medical school, HCs were presented as a fairly benign class of drugs with very few contra-indications.[1] Dr. Naylor herself used the pill for several years, and like most women, she thought of it more like a vitamin or supplement — not as an actual drug. In terms of side effects, she explained that while she learned that stroke and blood clots were serious risks, the more common side effects (as outlined in Chapter 7) weren't discussed.

Furthermore, it was suggested that the life-threatening side effects only applied to women with specific risk factors (smoking or advanced age) or women who took specific types of HCs.

Dr. Naylor explained that when it comes to birth control, doctors are trained to consider effectiveness above all else. Methods such as sterilization (i.e., getting your tubes tied or a male having a vasectomy), contraceptive implants, IUDs, and the shot have the highest efficacy rates because they don't require any action on the part of the user. These methods make it hard for you to screw it up (no pun intended) because their effectiveness doesn't depend on your ability to remember to take it. Compared to those methods, the pill, the patch, and the (vaginal) ring require you to do something for them to work effectively. Fertility awareness (FA), on the other hand, is entirely *user dependent*. There's more room for error when the effectiveness is dependent on the actions of the user (especially if the user hasn't taken adequate time to learn the method).

In my interview with Marguerite Duane, MD, she explained that most doctors aren't taught anything about fertility awareness-based methods of birth control in medical school:

> I actually didn't hear the term "fertility awareness," or "charting," or "natural family planning" until I was a first-year resident. So I had graduated from medical school and did not learn anything about the whole concept of charting the female cycle.
>
> We did do a research project back in 2012 where we looked at what is being taught in family medicine residency training programs. And at that time about 25 percent of them reported that they did not teach anything at all about fertility awareness-based methods. Which isn't surprising, and as a result, research shows that less than 10 percent of obstetrician gynecologists and family physicians are even familiar and knowledgeable about fertility awareness-based methods.[2]

This means that your doctor isn't out to get you when she discourages you from using fertility awareness-based methods. She's just trying to prevent you from using a birth control method she considers ineffective. Fertility awareness-based methods are lumped in with the rhythm method in medical school, leaving most doctors with the impression that it's pretty much the same as not using a method at all.

Furthermore, when doctors prescribe HCs they're simply following the current Centers for Disease Control and Prevention (CDC) recommendations regarding HC use. The CDC recommendations are based on the guidelines put forth by the World Health Organization (WHO). According to the WHO, it's recommended for women to continue using HCs until age 55 to prevent unplanned pregnancies (as 96 percent of women have reached menopause by then).[3] Put another way, doctors are taught — *in medical school* — that the menstrual cycle serves no purpose outside of reproduction. The continuous suppression of a woman's menstrual cycle is not only thought to be harmless, but is actually considered *advantageous*. From a medical standpoint, the thought is that there's no reason why you *shouldn't* suppress your natural cycles throughout your entire reproductive life (from menarche to menopause).

What I understood from my interview with Dr. Naylor is that most physicians prescribe HCs for three main reasons:

1. HCs are considered to be fairly harmless or benign drugs (in part because most doctors are unaware of the most common side effects).
2. Doctors typically know very little (if anything) about FA and are trained to prescribe HCs to women who wish to prevent pregnancy.
3. In medical school, doctors are trained to prescribe HCs whenever a woman has menstrual cycle irregularities.

When you seek the support of a medical doctor, take some time to consider her perspective. Your doctor is doing her best to support you, and she'll make recommendations based on her knowledge, training, and experience; but that doesn't mean she's fully informed. When you're looking for an answer as to why your cycles are irregular, why your periods are so painful, or why you have cysts on your ovaries, it can be incredibly frustrating to hear your doctor tell you that the pill is your best option — but that's how most doctors are trained.

The first step toward getting answers is to recognize that your doctor may not be able to provide them! Understanding where she's coming from is important. If your doctor only has HCs, painkillers, and other prescription drugs in her tool belt, you can hardly be upset or surprised when she suggests them. You may need to see several healthcare practitioners before you find the right one, but with a little persistence (and patience), *you can do it!*

Finding a Practitioner Who Will Support You

The first step is finding a practitioner whose perspective *already* aligns with yours. Find someone who already provides the type of care you're looking for — someone you don't have to "convince" to see things your way.

If you require support that goes beyond the services your practitioner provides, it's time to see someone else. You wouldn't walk into McDonald's and demand steak and lobster — *they sell burgers there.* And I know you wouldn't take your car to the library for an oil change. It's time to get clear on the fact that different health professionals offer different services.

If you don't feel comfortable moving forward with the recommended treatment options your healthcare practitioner outlines for you, be honest with him. Don't pick a fight, and don't try to change his mind. The more you advocate for yourself, the more you'll realize that no practitioner has all of the answers. Depending on the severity of your health challenges, you may need the support of several healthcare practitioners who specialize in different areas to fully address your issue.

Who's on my team?

Picture yourself sitting at the head of a boardroom table, and around the table are all of your healthcare practitioners — *this is your team.* You may need to seek support from one or several of these practitioners:

- Family doctor or general practitioner (MD)
- Doctor of osteopathic medicine (DO)
- Reproductive endocrinologist/Fertility specialist
- Functional (or integrative) medicine doctor (MD, ND, or DO)
- Nurse practitioner
- Naturopathic doctor (ND)

- Traditional Chinese medicine (TCM) practitioner
- Acupuncturist
- Chiropractor
- Midwife
- Dietician/Nutritionist
- Massage therapist
- Pelvic floor physical or physiotherapist
- Psychologist (therapist, counsellor)
- Fertility awareness charting instructor
- Fertility or health coach
- Doula

Choosing a practitioner

If you were thinking of buying a car, you would likely spend time researching different companies, models, and makes. However, when it comes to choosing a healthcare practitioner, many of us don't realize we can shop around in much the same way. The following guidelines will help you choose the best possible practitioner:

Do your research   Ask your friends and family for referrals. If you can't find a practitioner that way, search online with keywords such as "functional medicine," "integrative practice," "holistic health," and "women's health" (plus the name of the city you live in). Get a sense of your practitioner's specialization to see if their approach aligns with what you're looking for. Once you've found a few options and prepared a few questions, call the office directly. You probably won't be able to speak directly to the practitioner, but don't skip this step. By the time you've contacted three to four possible healthcare practitioners, you'll have a sense of which one feels like the best fit.

Find a practitioner who specializes in the issue you have   All practitioners receive general training that allows them to support a wide variety of patients, but you'll want a practitioner who specializes in *your* specific issue. For instance, if you're struggling with long, irregular periods associated with your PCOS, you'll need a naturopath or functional medicine doctor who specializes in female fertility, menstrual cycle disorders, or PCOS (specifically). This way your practitioner will be more knowledgeable, have more clinical experience, and be abreast of the latest research and clinical developments. Many practitioners have an online presence, which will allow you to identify their areas of specialization. Has your practitioner written a book or published any articles on the topic you need support with? Does your practitioner regularly work with patients with the same issue? What type of results do their patients typically get?

Consider seeing a functional practitioner in addition to your doctor   It would be so nice if one health professional could give you all the answers you need, but it doesn't work like that. When you need your teeth cleaned you go to the dentist, when you need your eyes examined you go to an ophthalmologist, and when you experience emotional issues you see a therapist. In other words, you may need the additional support of a specialized practitioner to help you address your reproductive health issues. If you need a practitioner to help you identify the root cause of your issues and support you through a combination of dietary and lifestyle changes, make plans to see a naturopathic doctor (ND), functional medicine doctor (MD, ND, or DO), traditional Chinese medicine (TCM) doctor, acupuncturist, or other qualified health professional (in addition to your regular doctor).

Interview your new practitioner   Use your first appointment to interview your new provider. Approach it like a first date or a job interview. Prepare a short list of questions so that you will better understand your practitioner's area of specialization, experience, and approach to patient care. The answers you get to questions like, "What are the most common conditions you see in your practice?" and, "Have any of your patients successfully reversed issue 'X' after working with you?" as well as, "How long does it typically take your patients to see improvements?" will help you confirm that you're working with the right person.

Know when it's time to move on   You might have the nicest doctor you've seen for 20 years, but you could develop a new health condition she's not able to help with. Or perhaps your practitioner just doesn't know enough about your specific condition to best support you. If you feel like you know more than your practitioner or you don't feel supported — *you're in the wrong office!* You deserve to be heard, respected, and supported by your healthcare practitioners; if that's not happening, it's time to take your business elsewhere.

Remember, you're sitting at the head of the table. Your practitioners will make recommendations based on their specific training and experience, but you *always* get the final say:

- You get to decide what treatment options are appropriate for you.
- You can agree or disagree with anything your practitioners recommend.
- You have the right to do your own independent research prior to making any decisions.
- When your practitioner makes a recommendation, you have the right to think it over for a few days before making a decision.
- You have the right to get a second opinion from another practitioner before moving forward with any recommenddation.
- You have the right to fire your practitioner (and find a new one) if you're not satisfied with your care.

When I was pregnant with my first son, my midwife helped me realize that I had the right to decline (or accept) any treatment that was recommended to me by my practitioners. When she mentioned that I could choose whether or not to have an ultrasound, I remember asking, "You mean I have a choice?" It had never occurred to me that having an ultrasound during pregnancy was a choice (and that I could choose *not* to have one). I did choose to have an ultrasound, but the experience taught me that I don't have to follow every course of treatment recommended by my practitioners.

Many women have assembled an incredible team of health professionals who treat them respectfully, take them seriously, and offer phenomenal support and encouragement. However, it doesn't always start out that way. I've spoken to countless women whose healthcare practitioners warned them not to use FA (because they thought it was the rhythm method) or told them that pill is the only way to resolve menstrual cycle problems.

Women are socialized to be nice, polite, and compliant. It's often easier to smile, say thank you, and take home a prescription (that you have no intention of ever taking) than to tell your doctor you don't want medication. However, the onus is on you to advocate for yourself, and in case you needed to hear this, I give you full permission to do so. You deserve to have the best possible support on your fertility journey — don't settle for anything less.

Where Do I Go from Here?

In the introduction to this book, I asked if you were ready to go down the rabbit hole with me, and now you've made it all the way to the end. You now know that your menstrual cycle contains an incredible wealth of information that can help you take control of your fertility. You also know that FA is an incredible tool for natural birth control, preserving your fertility, and identifying potential health issues.

I came to the knowledge I've shared with you in this book over a period of nearly 20 years. I can only imagine how it feels if you've just stumbled across it. If this is all new to you, you're likely experiencing a flood of different emotions, from excitement and relief to anger and frustration.

You're probably wondering why we're not all taught this as we grow up, and you may already be thinking of ways to tell every single girl and woman you know. As far as I'm concerned, that's the only way this information will ever become mainstream — through word of mouth.

That's why I spent nearly two years (and countless hours) poring over thousands of research articles in the process of writing this book. Not only did I want to share the importance of your *fifth vital sign*, but I wanted to show you the science behind it. I also wanted to illustrate the gap between the latest research and clinical practice.

Thousands of new research papers are published each day, but it takes anywhere from 10 to 20 *years* for original research to be translated into routine medical practice in your doctor's office.[4] For this reason, seeking informed support for menstrual cycle and fertility-related issues is often incredibly challenging. If you wish to achieve optimal menstrual cycle health and fertility, the first step is to empower yourself through FA. Educating yourself helps you better understand and identify the underlying issues. It also empowers you to select the most suitable healthcare practitioners when you need support.

I'll admit that it's a lot to take in, but I know you picked up this book for a reason. Somehow you knew there is more to your menstrual cycle than meets the eye. Since you've made it all the way to the end of the book, I'm fairly certain that you're passionate about this topic, and you're ready to discover what you can learn from your cycles. You want to take back control of your fertility, your health, and ultimately, your life as well. *Your menstrual cycle is the fifth vital sign of your health and your fertility.* This simple truth has the power to change your whole life. I know it did for me.

The knowledge contained in this book has empowered me to make informed choices about my health, advocate for the care I need, and manage my fertility naturally throughout my entire adult life. I hope it does the same for you.

Sending you love and light as you embark on your own fertility awareness journey.

Summary

- Most doctors are trained to prescribe HCs, painkillers, and other drugs to help you manage complaints about your menstrual cycle.
- In medical school, doctors are encouraged to prioritize the effectiveness of birth control methods above all else, making them far less likely to recommend fertility awareness-based methods (as user dependent methods have a higher risk of failure).
- Most health professionals have very little (if any) knowledge about fertility awareness-based methods, leaving many of them under the impression that they're the same as the rhythm method.
- When facing health challenges, assemble a team of qualified healthcare practitioners to support you.
- Your practitioners will share their recommendations, but you *always* get the final say.
- When choosing a practitioner, first do your research. Find someone who specializes in the specific area you need support with, consider working with a functional medicine practitioner (in addition to your medical doctor), interview them to ensure they're a good fit, but most importantly, know when it's time to move on.

Afterword

This book will always hold a special place in my heart, not only because it's my very first book, but because it represents a significant milestone in my fertility awareness journey. Like most women who discover fertility awareness, I firmly believe that every woman deserves to know exactly how her body and her fertility work. I wish I'd had this book when I first embarked on my own fertility awareness journey.

In the nearly two decades since I first discovered fertility awareness, I've gradually replaced my initial feelings of anger, outrage, and sadness (at not having been taught this vital information in school) with a fierce commitment to sharing this important knowledge with as many women as possible. With that said, I actively refrain from harassing my unsuspecting friends and family members (unless they ask me about it!). As much as we might want to force the women in our lives to learn about fertility awareness, they'll only be receptive to it when they're ready. This book provides you with an additional tool to *gently* share this knowledge with others when the time is right.

The biggest gift fertility awareness has given me over the years is the ability to trust my intuition. By paying attention to my *fifth vital sign*, I have gained the courage, confidence, and audacity to question the status quo, advocate for myself, and make informed decisions about my health — *and now it's your turn.*

Appendix: Magnesium

Magnesium deficiency causes an increased inflammatory response in the body, and up to 75 percent of us aren't getting enough of it from our diet. [1] Women who suffer from dysmenorrhea have significantly lower serum magnesium levels compared to women without dysmenorrhea, and magnesium supplementation has been found to significantly reduce PMS symptoms including fluid retention and weight gain.

Note that magnesium in large enough doses will loosen your stool. If you choose to supplement with magnesium orally, opt for magnesium glycinate or magnesium citrate; these forms absorb more readily and have less of a laxative effect.[2] If you're unable to tolerate oral magnesium supplementation, consider increasing your magnesium levels by taking Epsom salt baths, particularly during the week before your period. Epsom salt is comprised of magnesium sulphate, and adding Epsom salt to your bathwater and soaking in it is not only relaxing, but it increases your serum magnesium levels as it absorbs through your skin. You may find that you sleep better after taking an Epsom salt bath before bed due to the muscle-relaxing effects of magnesium. If you live near the ocean, going for a swim in natural salt water will also raise your magnesium levels.[3]

But since you can increase your magnesium stores transdermally (i.e., through the skin), I've provided recipes for magnesium spray and magnesium-infused body lotion. Magnesium spray is often referred to as "magnesium oil spray" but it does not actually contain any oil. It's referred to as magnesium oil because of the oily texture the water develops once it's saturated with magnesium. Making your own magnesium spray at home is easy and relatively inexpensive. All you need are magnesium flakes and water. You can use magnesium chloride flakes or Epsom salt (magnesium sulphate) to make your mixture. Magnesium chloride flakes may be a better choice because they're less likely to cause skin irritation, and more effective at raising your serum magnesium levels.[4]

Magnesium Spray

You only need two ingredients to make magnesium spray: 1 cup water and ¾ to 1 cup magnesium chloride flakes (or Epsom salt).

1. Boil the water and add the magnesium flakes or Epsom salt. Boiling the water helps the magnesium flakes dissolve quickly. Once the flakes are dissolved, let the mixture cool.
2. Pour your magnesium spray into a spray bottle and keep it in your bathroom.

Spray the mixture on your skin after you shower. Wait a few minutes for it to dry and lotion your skin as usual — I use a mixture of shea butter and coconut oil on my skin, and it helps the magnesium to absorb. You might find that the magnesium spray irritates your skin a little the first time you use it. This should go away once you've used it a few times and your body gets used to it. You can always dilute the mixture a bit if you find that it's too strong.

Magnesium-Infused Body Lotion

You can use your magnesium spray to make magnesium-infused body lotion. Since magnesium does not dissolve in oil, dissolve it in water first, and then add it to your lotion mixture. I make lotion that contains three parts shea butter to two parts coconut oil, and a few tablespoons of olive oil.

- 1 cup shea butter
- ⅔ cup coconut oil
- 2 tbsp olive oil
- 2 to 4 tbsp magnesium spray (see above recipe)
- One or two glass jars for storage

Follow these instructions:

1. Melt the coconut oil on low heat.
2. Add the shea butter to the melted oil and allow it to melt gradually (keep stirring!). Once the coconut oil and shea butter have both melted, add the olive oil.
3. Remove from heat and add the magnesium spray.
4. Stir once more and transfer the lotion into the glass storage container(s).
5. Let the mixture cool. If you're in a rush, you can refrigerate it.
6. To ensure your magnesium spray is fully mixed (oil rises, so you may find that your magnesium spray sinks to the bottom of your container), you may have to stir your lotion a few times before it sets.

Voilà! You now have magnesium-infused body lotion.

Resources

Fertility Awareness Resources

The Fifth Vital Sign: Master Your Cycles and Optimize Your Fertility — thefifthvitalsignbook.com

- Free training videos, *Cervical Mucus 101, and BBT 101*: thefifthvitalsignbook.com/bonuses
- *Fertility Awareness Mastery Charting Workbook: A Companion to The Fifth Vital Sign* thefifthvitalsignbook.com/chartingworkbook
- *Fertility Awareness Mastery Online Study Course*: thefifthvitalsignbook.com/fam
- *Fertility Awareness Mastery Live Coaching Course*: thefifthvitalsignbook.com/live

Fertility Friday — fertilityfriday.com

- *The Fertility Friday Podcast*: fertilityfriday.com/podcast

Taking Charge of Your Fertility — tcoyf.com

- *Taking Charge of Your Fertility: The Definitive Guide to Natural Birth Control, Pregnancy Achievement, and Reproductive Health* by Toni Weschler

Justisse College — justisse.ca

- *Justisse Method Fertility Awareness and Body Literacy: A User's Guide* by Geraldine Matus

The Garden of Fertility — gardenoffertility.com

- *The Garden of Fertility: A Guide to Charting Your Fertility Signals to Prevent or Achieve Pregnancy — Naturally — and to Gauge Your Reproductive Health* by Katie Singer

FACTS: Fertility Appreciation Collaborative to Teach the Science — factsaboutfertility.org

Grace of the Moon by Sarah Bly — graceofthemoon.com

Fertility UK — fertilityuk.org

The Kindara Charting App — kindara.com

Suggested Reading

- *Taking Charge of Your Fertility* by Toni Weschler, MPH
- *Justisse Method Fertility Awareness and Body Literacy* by Geraldine Matus, PhD
- *The Garden of Fertility* by Katie Singer
- *The Complete Guide to Fertility Awareness* by Jane Knight
- *Period Repair Manual* by Lara Briden, ND
- *Women's Bodies, Women's Wisdom* by Christiane Northrup, MD
- *8 Steps to Reverse Your PCOS* by Fiona McCulloch, ND
- *Healing PCOS* by Amy Medling
- *No Period. Now What?* by Nicola Rinaldi, PhD
- *Overcoming Thyroid Disorders* and *Iodine* by David Brownstein, MD
- *Real Food for Pregnancy* by Lily Nichols, RDN, CDE
- *The Nourishing Traditions Book of Baby and Childcare* by Sally Fallon Morell and Thomas Cowan, MD
- *Pathways to Pregnancy* by Mary Wong, R.TCMP, R.Ac
- *The Infertility Cure* by Randine Lewis, PhD
- *How to Conceive Naturally* by Christa Orecchio and Willow Buckley
- *The Pill Problem* by Ross Pelton, RPh, CCN
- *The Pill: Are You Sure It's for You?* by Jane Bennett and Alexandra Pope
- *Sweetening the Pill* by Holly Grigg-Spall
- *Her Blood Is Gold* by Lara Owen
- *Wild Power* by Alexandra Pope and Sjanie Hugo Wurlitzer
- *Managing PMS Naturally* by M. Sara Rosenthal
- *Cunt* by Inga Muscio

Quick Favour

If you enjoyed this book, may I ask a quick favour?

Would you take a moment to share how this book has resonated with you by reviewing it on Amazon?

Book reviews are one of the best ways to share *The Fifth Vital Sign* with others. Follow the link below to share your thoughts.

I also invite you to share your biggest takeaways from this book with other women in your life. Consider how your friends, family, and clients could benefit from the information contained here.

Thank you for helping me share this important message!

thefifthvitalsignbook.com/review

Your Very Own Charting Workbook

Fertility Awareness Mastery Charting Workbook: A Companion to The Fifth Vital Sign

"This knowledge is so empowering, I only wish FAM is something I would've learned as a teenager."
— Karen G.

"I feel so empowered to know what my body's up to and how it reacts to the lifestyle changes that I make."
— Holly L.

"The Fifth Vital Sign is a tool to improve your health, transform your life, and become the best version of yourself. I'm recommending it to all of my clients."
— Chloe Skerlak, Justisse holistic reproductive health practitioner

Grab your copy today!

thefifthvitalsignbook.com/chartingworkbook

Ready to Start Charting Your Cycles?

Learning how to chart your cervical mucus and understanding your basal body temperature and cervical position is complex, especially if you've recently come off hormonal birth control (or had a baby). Shave months (and in some cases ... *years!*) off the learning process.

Fertility Awareness Mastery Online Course and Live Coaching Programs!

Learn how to chart your cycles, monitor your fifth vital sign with confidence, and gain a unique window into your health and fertility.

Master your three main fertile signs — cervical mucus, basal body temperature, and cervical position — and benefit from this highly effective *non-hormonal* method of birth control for the rest of your life!

"I can't properly explain how empowering it is to feel so utterly in control of your body and your health. To work with someone who is so passionate and dedicated to helping you get there is beyond a pleasure."

— Emily W.

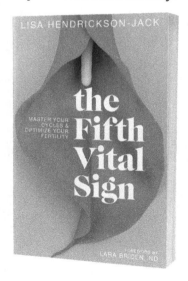

Lisa Hendrickson-Jack has taught hundreds of women to chart their cycles and gain confidence using fertility awareness for birth control, conception, and overall health. Learn how you can do the same!

thefifthvitalsignbook.com/fam

References

Introduction

[1] Muscio, Inga. (1998). *Cunt: A Declaration of Independence*. New York, NY: Seal Press, 61.

[2] Ibid, 68.

Chapter 1

[1] ACOG Committee on Adolescent Health Care. "ACOG Committee Opinion No. 349, November 2006: Menstruation in girls and adolescents: using the menstrual cycle as a vital sign." *Obstetrics & Gynecology* 108, no. 5 (2006): 1323–1328; American Academy of Pediatrics and American College of Obstetricians and Gynecologists. "Menstruation in girls and adolescents: using the menstrual cycle as a vital sign." *Pediatrics* 118, no. 5 (2006): 2245–2250.

[2] American Academy of Pediatrics and American College of Obstetricians and Gynecologists. "Menstruation in girls and adolescents: using the menstrual cycle as a vital sign." *Pediatrics* 118, no. 5 (2006): 2248.

[3] Vigil, Pilar, Carolina Lyon, Betsi Flores, Hernán Rioseco, and Felipe Serrano. "Ovulation, a sign of health." *The Linacre Quarterly* 84, no. 4 (2017): 343–355.

[4] National Heart Lung and Blood Institute. "Electrocardiogram." Accessed October 26, 2017.www.nhlbi.nih.gov/health/health-topics/topics/ekg.

[5] Depares, J., R.E. Ryder, S.M. Walker, M.F. Scanlon, and C.M. Norman. "Ovarian ultrasonography highlights precision of symptoms of ovulation as markers of ovulation." *British Medical Journal (Clinical Research Ed.)* 292, no. 6535 (1986): 1562.

[6] Fehring, Richard J., Mary Schneider, and Kathleen Raviele. "Variability in the phases of the menstrual cycle." *Journal of Obstetric, Gynecologic, & Neonatal Nursing* 35, no. 3 (2006): 376–384.

[7] Stein, I.R., and Melvin R. Cohen. "Sperm survival at estimated ovulation time: prognostic significance." *Fertility and Sterility* 1, no. 2 (1950): 169–75; Ahlgren, Mats. "Sperm transport to and survival in the human fallopian tube." *Gynecologic and Obstetric Investigation* 6, no. 3–4 (1975): 206–214.

[8] Frank-Herrmann, Petra, J. Heil, C. Gnoth, E. Toledo, S. Baur, C. Pyper, E. Jenetzky, T. Strowitzki, and G. Freundl. "The effectiveness of a fertility awareness based method to avoid pregnancy in relation to a couples' sexual behaviour during the fertile time: a prospective longitudinal study." *Human Reproduction* 22, no. 5 (2007).

[9] Andrist, Linda C., Raquel D. Arias, Deborah Nucatola, Andrew M. Kaunitz, B. Lynn Musselman, Suzanne Reiter, Jennifer Boulanger, Linda Dominguez, and Steven Emmert. "Women's and providers' attitudes toward menstrual suppression with extended use of oral contraceptives." *Contraception* 70, no. 5 (2004): 359–363; Coutinho, E.M., and S.J. Segal. (1999). *Is Menstruation Obsolete?* Oxford University Press.

[10] Steinem, Gloria. "If Men Could Menstruate." Accessed September 10, 2017. ww3.haverford.edu/psychology/ddavis/p109g/steinem.menstruate.html

[11] Lin, Valerie Chun-Ling, Rongxian Jin, Puay-Hoon Tan, Swee-Eng Aw, Chow-Thai Woon, and Boon-Huat Bay. "Progesterone induces cellular differentiation in MDA-MB-231 breast cancer cells transfected with progesterone receptor complementary DNA." *The American Journal of Pathology* 162, no. 6 (2003): 1781–1787.

[12] Ali, Simak, and R. Charles Coombes. "Estrogen receptor alpha in human breast cancer: occurrence and significance." *Journal of Mammary Gland Biology and Neoplasia* 5, no. 3 (2000): 271–281.

[13] Mohammed, Hisham, I. Alasdair Russell, Rory Stark, Oscar M. Rueda, Theresa E. Hickey, Gerard A. Tarulli, Aurelien A. Serandour et al. "Progesterone receptor modulates ERα action in breast cancer." *Nature* 523, no. 7560 (2015): 313; Lange, Carol A., Jennifer K. Richer, and Kathryn B. Horwitz. "Hypothesis: progesterone primes breast cancer cells for cross-talk with proliferative or antiproliferative signals." *Molecular Endocrinology* 13, no. 6 (1999): 829–836; Chang, King-Jen, Tigris T.Y. Lee, Gustavo Linares-Cruz, Sabine Fournier, and Bruno de Ligniéres. "Influences of percutaneous administration of estradiol and progesterone on human breast epithelial cell cycle in vivo." *Fertility and Sterility* 63, no. 4 (1995): 785–791.

[14] Kumar, Nirmala S., Jennifer Richer, Gareth Owen, Elizabeth Litman, Kathryn B. Horwitz, and Kimberly K. Leslie. "Selective down-regulation of progesterone receptor isoform B in poorly differentiated human endometrial cancer cells: implications for unopposed estrogen action." *Cancer Research* 58, no. 9 (1998): 1860–1865.

[15] Dumesic, Daniel A., and Rogerio A. Lobo. "Cancer risk and PCOS." *Steroids* 78, no. 8 (2013): 782–785.

[16] Haoula, Zeina, Maisa Salman, and William Atiomo. "Evaluating the association between endometrial cancer and polycystic ovary syndrome." *Human Reproduction* 27, no. 5 (2012): 1327–1331; Chittenden, B.G., G. Fullerton, A. Maheshwari, and S. Bhattacharya. "Polycystic ovary syndrome and the risk of gynaecological cancer: a systematic review." *Reproductive Biomedicine Online* 19, no. 3 (2009): 398–405.

[17] Clavel-Chapelon, Françoise. "Cumulative number of menstrual cycles and breast cancer risk: results from the E3N cohort study of French women." *Cancer Causes & Control* 13, no. 9 (2002): 831–838.

[18] Chang, King-Jen, Tigris T.Y. Lee, Gustavo Linares-Cruz, Sabine Fournier, and Bruno de Ligniéres. "Influences of percutaneous administration of estradiol and progesterone on human breast epithelial cell cycle in vivo." *Fertility and Sterility* 63, no. 4 (1995): 785–791; Prior, Jerilynn C. "Preventive Powers of Ovulation and Progesterone: Ovulation and Breast Health." Accessed January 8, 2017. www.cemcor.ca/files/uploads/6_Ovulation_and_Breast_Health.pdf

[19] Whelan, Elizabeth A., Dale P. Sandler, Jan L. Root, Ken R. Smith, and Clarice R. Weinberg. "Menstrual cycle patterns and risk of breast cancer." *American Journal of Epidemiology* 140, no. 12 (1994): 1081–1090.

[20] Seifert-Klauss, Vanadin, and Jerilynn C. Prior. "Progesterone and bone: actions promoting bone health in women." *Journal of Osteoporosis* (2010): 1–18.

[21] Hergenroeder, Albert C. "Bone mineralization, hypothalamic amenorrhea, and sex steroid therapy in female adolescents and young adults." *The Journal of Pediatrics* 126, no. 5 (1995): 683–689; Cann, Christopher E., Mary C. Martin, Harry K. Genant, and Robert B. Jaffe. "Decreased spinal mineral content in amenorrheic women." *JAMA* 251, no. 5 (1984): 626–629; Chou, Sharon H., and Christos Mantzoros. "Bone metabolism in anorexia nervosa and hypothalamic amenorrhea." *Metabolism* 80 (2018): 91–104.

[22] Hart, Roger, and Dorota A. Doherty. "The potential implications of a PCOS diagnosis on a woman's long-term health using data linkage." *The Journal of Clinical Endocrinology & Metabolism* 100, no. 3 (2015): 911–919; Orio Jr., Francesco, Stefano Palomba, Letizia Spinelli, Teresa Cascella, Libuse Tauchmanova, Fulvio Zullo, Gaetano Lombardi, and Annamaria Colao. "The cardiovascular risk of young women with polycystic ovary syndrome: an observational, analytical, prospective case-control study." *The Journal of Clinical Endocrinology & Metabolism* 89, no. 8 (2004): 3696–3701.

[23] Cheng, Wanli, Ontario D. Lau, and Nada A. Abumrad. "Two antiatherogenic effects of progesterone on human macrophages; inhibition of cholesteryl ester synthesis and block of its enhancement by glucocorticoids." *The Journal of Clinical Endocrinology & Metabolism* 84, no. 1 (1999): 265–271; Prior, Jerilynn C. "Progesterone within ovulatory menstrual cycles needed for cardiovascular protection: an evidence-based hypothesis." *Journal of Restorative Medicine* 3, no. 1 (2014): 85–103.

Chapter 2

[1] Groothuis, P.G., H.H.N.M. Dassen, A. Romano, and C. Punyadeera. "Estrogen and the endometrium: lessons learned from gene expression profiling in rodents and human." *Human Reproduction Update* 13, no. 4 (2007): 405–417.

[2] Kumar, Nirmala S., Jennifer Richer, Gareth Owen, Elizabeth Litman, Kathryn B. Horwitz, and Kimberly K. Leslie. "Selective down-regulation of progesterone receptor isoform B in poorly differentiated human endometrial cancer cells: implications for unopposed estrogen action." *Cancer Research* 58, no. 9 (1998): 1860–1865.

[3] Hilgers, Thomas W. (2010). *The NaPro Technology Revolution: Unleashing the Power in a Woman's Cycle*. New York, NY: Beaufort Books, 331–335.

[4] Ibid, 332; Fehring, Richard J., Mary Schneider, and Kathleen Raviele. "Variability in the phases of the menstrual cycle." *Journal of Obstetric, Gynecologic, & Neonatal Nursing* 35, no. 3 (2006): 376–377.

[5] Fehring, Richard J., Mary Schneider, and Kathleen Raviele. "Variability in the phases of the menstrual cycle." *Journal of Obstetric, Gynecologic, & Neonatal Nursing* 35, no. 3 (2006): 376–377.

[6] Guttorm, Eigil. "Menstrual bleeding with intrauterine contraceptive devices." *Acta Obstetricia et Gynecologica Scandinavica* 50, no. 1 (1971): 9–16; Dasharathy, Sonya S., Sunni L. Mumford, Anna Z. Pollack, Neil J. Perkins, Donald R. Mattison, Jean Wactawski-Wende, and Enrique F. Schisterman. "Menstrual bleeding patterns among regularly menstruating women." *American Journal of Epidemiology* 175, no. 6 (2012): 536–545; Livingstone, Mark, and Ian S. Fraser. "Mechanisms of abnormal uterine bleeding." *Human Reproduction Update* 8, no. 1 (2002): 60–67.

[7] Fehring, Richard J., Mary Schneider, and Kathleen Raviele. "Variability in the phases of the menstrual cycle." *Journal of Obstetric, Gynecologic, & Neonatal Nursing* 35, no. 3 (2006): 376–377.

[8] Price, D.C., E.M. Forsyth, S.H. Cohn, and E.P. Cronkite. "The study of menstrual and other blood loss, and consequent iron deficiency, by Fe59 whole-body counting." *Canadian Medical Association Journal* 90, no. 2 (1964): 51; Fraser, Ian S., H.O.D. Critchley, M.G. Munro, and M. Broder. "Can we achieve international agreement on terminologies and definitions used to describe abnormalities of menstrual bleeding?" *Human Reproduction* 22, no. 3 (2007): 635–643; Dasharathy, Sonya S., Sunni L. Mumford, Anna Z. Pollack, Neil J. Perkins, Donald R. Mattison, Jean Wactawski-Wende, and Enrique F. Schisterman. "Menstrual bleeding patterns among regularly menstruating women." *American Journal of Epidemiology* 175, no. 6 (2012): 536–545; Hallberg, Leif, Ann-Marie Högdahl, Lennart Nilsson, and Göran Rybo. "Menstrual blood loss — a population study." *Acta Obstetricia et Gynecologica Scandinavica* 45, no. 3 (1966): 320–351; Hallberg, Leif, Ann-Marie Högdahl, Lennart Nilsson, and Göran Rybo. "Menstrual blood loss and iron deficiency." *Acta Medica Scandinavica* 180, no. 5 (1966): 639–650.

[9] Hallberg, Leif, and Lennart Nilsson. "Constancy of individual menstrual blood loss." *Acta Obstetricia et Gynecologica Scandinavica* 43, no. 4 (1964): 352–359; Cheong, Revelita L., Miriam D. Kuizon, and Rosario T. Tajaon. "Menstrual blood loss and iron nutrition in Filipino women." *The Southeast Asian Journal of Tropical Medicine and Public Health* 22, no. 4 (1991): 595–604; Dasharathy, Sonya S., Sunni L. Mumford, Anna Z. Pollack, Neil J. Perkins, Donald R. Mattison, Jean Wactawski-Wende, and Enrique F. Schisterman. "Menstrual bleeding patterns among regularly menstruating women." *American Journal of Epidemiology* 175, no. 6 (2012): 536–545; Barer, Adelaide P., and W.M. Fowler. "The blood loss during normal menstruation." *American Journal of Obstetrics and Gynecology* 31, no. 6 (1936): 979–986; Price, D.C., E.M. Forsyth, S.H. Cohn, and E.P. Cronkite. "The study of menstrual and other blood loss, by Fe59 whole-body counting." *Canadian Medical Association Journal* 90, no. 2 (1964): 51; Chen, Bertha H., and Linda C. Giudice. "Dysfunctional uterine bleeding." *Western Journal of Medicine* 169, no. 5 (1998): 280.

[10] Fraser, Ian S., H.O.D. Critchley, M.G. Munro, and M. Broder. "Can we achieve international agreement on terminologies and definitions used to describe abnormalities of menstrual bleeding?" *Human Reproduction* 22, no. 3 (2007): 635–643.

[11] Kovacs, Peter, S.Z. Matyas, K. Boda, and S.G. Kaali. "The effect of endometrial thickness on IVF/ICSI outcome." *Human Reproduction* 18, no. 11 (2003): 2337–2341; Israel, Robert, John D. Isaacs, Carla S. Wells, Daniel B. Williams, Randall R. Odem, Michael J. Gast, and Ronald C. Strickler. "Endometrial thickness is a valid monitoring parameter in cycles of ovulation induction with menotropins alone." *Fertility and Sterility* 65, no. 2 (1996): 262–266; Alborzi, S., M.

Momtahan, J. Zolghadri, and M.E. Parsanezhad. "The effect of endometrial pattern and thickness on pregnancy rate in controlled ovarian hyperstimulation-intrauterine insemination." *Medical Journal of the Islamic Republic of Iran (MJIRI)* 19, no. 3 (2005): 189–193; Oliveira, J.B.A., R.L.R. Baruffi, A.L. Mauri, C.G. Petersen, M.C. Borges, and J.G. Franco. "Endometrial ultrasonography as a predictor of pregnancy in an in-vitro fertilization programme after ovarian stimulation and gonadotrophin-releasing hormone and gonadotrophins." *Human Reproduction* 12, no. 11 (1997): 2515–2518; Dickey, Richard P., Terry T. Olar, Steven N. Taylor, David N. Curole, and Ellen M. Matulich. "Relationship of endometrial thickness and pattern to fecundity in ovulation induction cycles: effect of clomiphene citrate alone and with human menopausal gonadotropin." *Fertility and Sterility* 59, no. 4 (1993): 756–760; Habibzadeh, Victoria, Sayed Noureddin Nematolahi Mahani, and Hadiss Kamyab. "The correlation of factors affecting the endometrial thickness with pregnancy outcome in the IUI cycles." *Iranian Journal of Reproductive Medicine* 9, no. 1 (2011): 41.

[12] Dickey, Richard P., Terry T. Olar, Steven N. Taylor, David N. Curole, and Ellen M. Matulich. "Relationship of endometrial thickness and pattern to fecundity in ovulation induction cycles: effect of clomiphene citrate alone and with human menopausal gonadotropin." *Fertility and Sterility* 59, no. 4 (1993): 756–760; Israel, Robert, John D. Isaacs, Carla S. Wells, Daniel B. Williams, Randall R. Odem, Michael J. Gast, and Ronald C. Strickler. "Endometrial thickness is a valid monitoring parameter in cycles of ovulation induction with menotropins alone." *Fertility and Sterility* 65, no. 2 (1996): 262–266; Alborzi, S., M. Momtahan, J. Zolghadri, and M.E. Parsanezhad. "The effect of endometrial pattern and thickness on pregnancy rate in controlled ovarian hyperstimulation-intrauterine insemination." *Medical Journal of the Islamic Republic of Iran (MJIRI)* 19, no. 3 (2005): 191; Oliveira, J.B.A., R.L.R. Baruffi, A.L. Mauri, C.G. Petersen, M.C. Borges, and J.G. Franco. "Endometrial ultrasonography as a predictor of pregnancy in an in-vitro fertilization programme after ovarian stimulation and gonadotrophin-releasing hormone and gonadotrophins." *Human Reproduction* 12, no. 11 (1997): 2517; Habibzadeh, Victoria, Sayed Noureddin Nematolahi Mahani, and Hadiss Kamyab. "The correlation of factors affecting the endometrial thickness with pregnancy outcome in the IUI cycles." *Iranian Journal of Reproductive Medicine* 9, no. 1 (2011): 45.

[13] Dickey, Richard P., Terry T. Olar, Steven N. Taylor, David N. Curole, and Ellen M. Matulich. "Relationship of endometrial thickness and pattern to fecundity in ovulation induction cycles: effect of clomiphene citrate alone and with human menopausal gonadotropin." *Fertility and Sterility* 59, no. 4 (1993): 756–760.

[14] Kovacs, Peter, S.Z. Matyas, K. Boda, and S.G. Kaali. "The effect of endometrial thickness on IVF/ICSI outcome." *Human Reproduction* 18, no. 11 (2003): 2339.

[15] Chen, Bertha H., and Linda C. Giudice. "Dysfunctional uterine bleeding." *Western Journal of Medicine* 169, no. 5 (1998): 280–284.

[16] Livingstone, Mark, and Ian S. Fraser. "Mechanisms of abnormal uterine bleeding." *Human Reproduction Update* 8, no. 1 (2002): 60–67.

[17] Ibid, 61.

[18] Silberzweig, James E., Daniel K. Powell, Alan H. Matsumoto, and James B. Spies. "Management of uterine fibroids: a focus on uterine-sparing interventional techniques." *Radiology* 280, no. 3 (2016): 675–692; Donnez, Jacques, and Marie-Madeleine Dolmans. "Uterine fibroid management: from the present to the future." *Human Reproduction Update* 22, no. 6 (2016): 665–686.

[19] Munro, Malcolm G., Hilary O.D. Critchley, Michael S. Broder, Ian S. Fraser, and FIGO Working Group on Menstrual Disorders. "FIGO classification system (PALM-COEIN) for causes of abnormal uterine bleeding in nongravid women of reproductive age." *International Journal of Gynecology & Obstetrics* 113, no. 1 (2011): 3–13; Chen, Bertha H., and Linda C. Giudice. "Dysfunctional uterine bleeding." *Western Journal of Medicine* 169, no. 5 (1998): 280–284.

[20] Peric, H., and I. S. Fraser. "The symptomatology of adenomyosis." *Best Practice & Research: Clinical Obstetrics & Gynaecology* 20, no. 4 (2006): 547–555; Livingstone, Mark, and Ian S. Fraser. "Mechanisms of abnormal uterine bleeding." *Human Reproduction Update* 8, no. 1 (2002): 62.

[21] Beebeejaun, Yusuf, and Rajesh Varma. "Heavy menstrual flow: current and future trends in management." *Reviews in Obstetrics & Gynecology* 6 (2013): 155–164.

[22] Livingstone, Mark, and Ian S. Fraser. "Mechanisms of abnormal uterine bleeding." *Human Reproduction Update* 8, no. 1 (2002): 62.

[23] Vigil, Pilar, Leonard F. Blackwell, and Manuel E. Cortés. "The importance of fertility awareness in the assessment of a woman's health a review." *The Linacre Quarterly* 79, no. 4 (2012): 426–450; Krassas, G.E., N. Pontikides, T.H. Kaltsas, P.H. Papadopoulou, J. Paunkovic, N. Paunkovic, and LH Duntas. "Disturbances of menstruation in hypothyroidism." *Clinical Endocrinology* 50, no. 5 (1999): 655–659.

[24] Livingstone, Mark, and Ian S. Fraser. "Mechanisms of abnormal uterine bleeding." *Human Reproduction Update* 8, no. 1 (2002): 63.

[25] The Centre for Menstrual Cycle and Ovulation Research. "Very Heavy Menstrual Flow." Accessed January 8, 2017. www.cemcor.ubc.ca/resources/very-heavy-menstrual-flow; Livingstone, Mark, and Ian S. Fraser. "Mechanisms of abnormal uterine bleeding." *Human Reproduction Update* 8, no. 1 (2002): 60.

[26] Cole, Susan K., W.Z. Billewicz, and A.M. Thomson. "Sources of variation in menstrual blood loss." *BJOG: An International Journal of Obstetrics and Gynaecology* 78, no. 10 (1971): 933–939.

[27] Rosenthal, M. Sara. (2001). *Managing PMS Naturally: A Sourcebook of Natural Solutions.* Toronto: Prentice Hall Canada.

[28] Dasharathy, Sonya S., Sunni L. Mumford, Anna Z. Pollack, Neil J. Perkins, Donald R. Mattison, Jean Wactawski-Wende, and Enrique F. Schisterman. "Menstrual bleeding patterns among regularly menstruating women." *American Journal of Epidemiology* 175, no. 6 (2012): 536–545.

[29] Ibid, 538.

[30] Jabbour, Henry N., Kurt J. Sales, Rob D. Catalano, and Jane E. Norman. "Inflammatory pathways in female reproductive health and disease." *Reproduction* 138, no. 6 (2009): 903–919.

31 Ibid.

32 Ibid, 907–909.

33 Hadfield, Ruth, Helen Mardon, David Barlow, and Stephen Kennedy. "Delay in the diagnosis of endometriosis: a survey of women from the USA and the UK." *Human Reproduction* 11, no. 4 (1996): 878–880.

34 Ibid.

35 Hendrickson-Jack, Lisa. "[On-Air Client Session] FFP 220 | Managing Intense Period Pain | Maria & Lisa." *Fertility Friday Podcast.* Podcast Audio, September 7, 2018. fertilityfriday.com/220

36 Moradi, Maryam, Melissa Parker, Anne Sneddon, Violeta Lopez, and David Ellwood. "Impact of endometriosis on women's lives: a qualitative study." *BMC Women's Health* 1, no. 14 (2014): 1–12.

37 Wu, Meng-Hsing, Yutaka Shoji, Pei-Chin Chuang, and Shaw-Jenq Tsai. "Endometriosis: disease pathophysiology and the role of prostaglandins." *Expert Reviews in Molecular Medicine* 9, no. 2 (2007): 2.

38 García, Celso-Ramón, and Sami S. David. "Pelvic endometriosis: infertility and pelvic pain." *American Journal of Obstetrics and Gynecology* 129, no. 7 (1977): 740–744; Farquhar, Cynthia. "Endometriosis." *The BMJ* 334 (2007): 249–253.

Chapter 3

1 Odeblad, Erik. "The discovery of different types of cervical mucus and the Billings Ovulation Method." *Bulletin of the Natural Family Planning Council of Victoria* 21, no. 3 (1994): 4; Klaus, Hanna. "Natural Family Planning — Is it Scientific? Is it Effective?" *Newman Lecture Series* 1 (2000): 6.

2 Odeblad, Erik. "The discovery of different types of cervical mucus and the Billings Ovulation Method." *Bulletin of the Natural Family Planning Council of Victoria* 21, no. 3 (1994): 3–31; Hilgers, Thomas W. (2004). *The Medical & Surgical Practice of NaPro Technology.* Omaha, NE: Pope Paul VI Institute Press, 203–205; Matus, Geraldine (Ed.). "Statistical Parameters of the Menstrual Cycle." *Justisse HRHP Training Program.* Justisse College. Accessed January 23, 2017. www.justisse.ca/index.php/college/courseware/page/1074.

3 Odeblad, Erik. "The discovery of different types of cervical mucus and the Billings Ovulation Method." *Bulletin of the Natural Family Planning Council of Victoria* 21, no. 3 (1994): 2; *Human Embryology Embryogenesis.* "The path of the sperm cells to the oocyte — capacitation." Accessed January 23, 2017. www.embryology.ch/anglais/dbefruchtung/weg02.html

4 Moghissi, Kamran S. "The function of the cervix in fertility." *Fertility and Sterility* 23, no. 4 (1972): 295–306; Klaus, Hanna. "Natural Family Planning — Is it Scientific? Is it Effective?" *Newman Lecture Series* 1 (2000): 4; Viergiver, Ellenmae, and W.T. Pommerenke. "Measurement of the cyclic variations in the quantity of cervical mucus and its correlation with basal temperature." *American Journal of Obstetrics and Gynecology* 48, no. 3 (1944): 321–328.

5 Pommerenke, W.T. "Cyclic changes in the physical and chemical properties of cervical mucus." *American Journal of Obstetrics and Gynecology* 52, no. 6 (1946): 1023–1031.

6 Hilgers, Thomas W. (2004). *The Medical & Surgical Practice of NaPro Technology.* Omaha, NE: Pope Paul VI Institute Press, 185–186.

7 Ravel, Jacques, Pawel Gajer, Zaid Abdo, G. Maria Schneider, Sara S.K. Koenig, Stacey L. McCulle, Shara Karlebach. "Vaginal microbiome of reproductive-age women." *Proceedings of the National Academy of Sciences* 108, no. Supplement 1 (2011): 4680–4687.

8 Miller, Elizabeth A., DeAnna E. Beasley, Robert R. Dunn, and Elizabeth A. Archie. "Lactobacilli dominance and vaginal pH: why is the human vaginal microbiome unique?" *Frontiers in Microbiology* 7 (2016): 1–13.

9 Zhou, Xia, Stephen J. Bent, Maria G. Schneider, Catherine C. Davis, Mohammed R. Islam, and Larry J. Forney. "Characterization of vaginal microbial communities in adult healthy women using cultivation-independent methods." *Microbiology* 150, no. 8 (2004): 2565–2573; Donders, Gilbert G.G., Eugene Bosmans, Alfons Dekeersmaeckerb, Annie Vereecken, Ben Van Bulck, and Bernard Spitz. "Pathogenesis of abnormal vaginal bacterial flora." *American Journal of Obstetrics and Gynecology* 182, no. 4 (2000): 872–878; Linhares, Iara M., Paul R. Summers, Bryan Larsen, Paulo C. Giraldo, and Steven S. Witkin. "Contemporary perspectives on vaginal ph and lactobacilli." *American Journal of Obstetrics and Gynecology* 204, no. 2 (2011): 120e1–120e5.

10 O'Hanlon, Deirdre E., Thomas R. Moench, and Richard A. Cone. "Vaginal pH and microbicidal lactic acid when lactobacilli dominate the microbiota." *PLOS One* 8, no. 11 (2013): e80074; Rakoff, A.E., Louis G. Feo, and Leopold Goldstein. "The biologic characteristics of the normal vagina." *American Journal of Obstetrics and Gynecology* 47, no. 4 (1944): 467–494; Ravel, Jacques, Pawel Gajer, Zaid Abdo, G. Maria Schneider, Sara S.K. Koenig, Stacey L. McCulle, and Shara Karlebach. "Vaginal microbiome of reproductive-age women." *Proceedings of the National Academy of Sciences* 108, no. Supplement 1 (2011): 4680–4687; Miller, Elizabeth A., DeAnna E. Beasley, Robert R. Dunn, and Elizabeth A. Archie. "Lactobacilli dominance and vaginal pH: why is the human vaginal microbiome unique?" *Frontiers in Microbiology* 7 (2016): 1–13.

11 Haugen, T.B., and T. Grotmol. "pH of human semen." *International Journal of Andrology* 21, no. 2 (1998): 105–108; Eggert-Kruse, Waltraud, Andreas Köhler, Gerhard Rohr, and Benno Runnebaum. "The pH as an important determinant of sperm-mucus interaction." *Fertility and Sterility* 59, no. 3 (1993): 617–628; Stein, Irving F., and Melvin R. Cohen. "Sperm survival at estimated ovulation time: prognostic significance." *Fertility and Sterility* 1, no. 2 (1950): 169–175; Ahlgren, Mats. "Sperm transport to and survival in the human fallopian tube." *Gynecologic and Obstetric Investigation* 6, no. 3–4 (1975): 206–214.

12 Lambert, Hovey, James W. Overstreet, Patricio Morales, Frederick W. Hanson, and Ryuzo Yanagimachi. "Sperm capacitation in the human female reproductive tract." *Fertility and Sterility* 43, no. 2 (1985): 325–327.

13 De Jonge, Christopher. "Biological basis for human capacitation—revisited." *Human Reproduction Update* 23, no. 3 (2017): 290.

[14] López-Torres, Aideé S., María E. González-González, Esperanza Mata-Martínez, Fernando Larrea, Claudia L. Treviño, and Mayel Chirinos. "Luteinizing hormone modulates intracellular calcium, protein tyrosine phosphorylation and motility during human sperm capacitation." *Biochemical and Biophysical Research Communications* 483, no. 2 (2017): 834–839.

[15] Hilgers, Thomas W. (2004). *The Medical & Surgical Practice of NaPro Technology.* Omaha, NE: Pope Paul VI Institute Press, 107; Matus, Geraldine. "Justisse Method: Fertility Awareness and Body Literacy: A User's Guide." *Justisse-Healthworks for Women* (2009): 27.

[16] Frank-Herrmann, Petra, J. Heil, C. Gnoth, E. Toledo, S. Baur, C. Pyper, E. Jenetzky, T. Strowitzki, and G. Freundl. "The effectiveness of a fertility awareness based method to avoid pregnancy in relation to a couple's sexual behaviour during the fertile time: a prospective longitudinal study." *Human Reproduction* 22, no. 5 (2007): 1310–1319.

[17] Katz, David F., Patricio Morales, Steven J. Samuels, and James W. Overstreet. "Mechanisms of filtration of morphologically abnormal human sperm by cervical mucus." *Fertility and Sterility* 54, no. 3 (1990): 513–516; Kunz, G., D. Beil, H. Deininger, L. Wildt, and G. Leyendecker. "The dynamics of rapid sperm transport through the female genital tract: evidence from vaginal sonography of uterine peristalsis and hysterosalpingoscintigraphy." *Human Reproduction* 11, no. 3 (1996): 627–632.

[18] Fehring, Richard J. "Accuracy of the peak day of cervical mucus as a biological marker of fertility." *Contraception* 66, no. 4 (2002): 231–235; Hilgers, Thomas W. (2004). *Reproductive Anatomy & Physiology: A Primer for FertilityCare Professionals,* 2nd edition. Omaha, NE: Pope Paul VI Institute Press, 68–69; Odeblad, Erik. "The discovery of different types of cervical mucus and the Billings Ovulation Method." *Bulletin of the Natural Family Planning Council of Victoria* 21, no. 3 (1994): 2; Klaus, Hanna. "Natural Family Planning — Is it Scientific? Is it Effective?" *Newman Lecture Series* 1 (2000): 5.

[19] Mitchell, Leia, Michelle King, Heather Brillhart, and Andrew Goldstein. "Cervical ectropion may be a cause of desquamative inflammatory vaginitis." *Sexual Medicine* 5, no. 3 (2017): e212–e214.

[20] Hendrickson-Jack, Lisa. "FFP 106 | What You Need to Know About Progesterone and Pregnancy | Using Your Cycle to Time Hormone Testing | Fertility Awareness Method | Dr. Nora Pope." *Fertility Friday Podcast.* Podcast Audio, November 11, 2016. fertilityfriday.com/106

[21] Pastor, Zlatko, and Roman Chmel. "Differential diagnostics of female 'sexual' fluids: a narrative review." *International Urogynecology Journal* (2017): 1–9.

[22] Levin, Roy J. "The ins and outs of vaginal lubrication." *Sexual and Relationship Therapy* 18, no. 4 (2003): 509–513.

[23] Nejat, Edward J., and Judi L. Chervenak. "The continuum of ovarian aging and clinicopathologies associated with the menopausal transition." *Maturitas* 66, no. 2 (2010): 187–190; Strauss, Jerome F., and Robert L. Barbieri (2009). *Yen & Jaffe's Reproductive Endocrinology: Physiology, Pathophysiology, and Clinical Management,* 6th edition. Philadelphia, PA: Elsevier: 155–189; Wikipedia. "Folliculogenesis." Accessed October 12, 2017. en.wikipedia.org/wiki/Folliculogenesis#Primordial

[24] Hilgers, Thomas W. (2004). *Reproductive Anatomy & Physiology: A Primer for FertilityCare Professionals,* 2nd edition. Omaha, NE: Pope Paul VI Institute Press, 88–89.

[25] Strauss, Jerome F., and Robert L. Barbieri (2009). *Yen & Jaffe's Reproductive Endocrinology: Physiology, Pathophysiology, and Clinical Management,* 6th edition. Philadelphia, PA: Elsevier: 165–171.

[26] Odeblad, Erik. "The discovery of different types of cervical mucus and the Billings Ovulation Method." *Bulletin of the Natural Family Planning Council of Victoria* 21, no. 3 (1994): 8–13; Moghissi, Kamran S. "The function of the cervix in fertility." *Fertility and Sterility* 23, no. 4 (1972): 295–306.

[27] Strauss, Jerome F., and Robert L. Barbieri (2009). *Yen & Jaffe's Reproductive Endocrinology: Physiology, Pathophysiology, and Clinical Management,* 6th edition. Philadelphia, PA: Elsevier, 174–178.

[28] Aspillaga, Margaret O., Paul G. Whittaker, Christina E. Grey, and Tom Lind. "Endocrinologic events in early pregnancy failure." *American Journal of Obstetrics and Gynecology* 147, no. 8 (1983): 903–908; McNeilly, A.S., J. Kerin, I.A. Swanston, T.A. Bramley, and D.T. Baird. "Changes in the binding of human chorionic gonadotrophin/luteinizing hormone, follicle-stimulating hormone and prolactin to human corpora lutea during the menstrual cycle and pregnancy." *Journal of Endocrinology* 87, no. 3 (1980): 315–325; Tuckey, Robert C. "Progesterone synthesis by the human placenta." *Placenta* 26, no. 4 (2005): 273–281.

[29] Strauss, Jerome F., and Robert L. Barbieri (2009). *Yen & Jaffe's Reproductive Endocrinology: Physiology, Pathophysiology, and Clinical Management,* 6th edition. Philadelphia, PA: Elsevier, 174–178.

[30] Brucker, Mary C. (2015). *Pharmacology for Women's Health.* Jones & Bartlett Publishers: 372–373.

[31] Odeblad, Erik. "The functional structure of human cervical mucus." *Acta Obstetricia et Gynecologica Scandinavica* 47, no. S1 (1968): 57–79.

[32] Odeblad, Erik. "The discovery of different types of cervical mucus and the Billings Ovulation Method." *Bulletin of the Natural Family Planning Council of Victoria* 21, no. 3 (1994):13.

[33] Ibid,1–31.

[34] Ibid, 13.

[35] Odeblad, E. "Investigation on the physiological basis for fertility awareness method." *Bulletin of the Ovulation Method Research and Reference Centre of Australia* 29, no. 1 (2002): 2–11.

[36] Pommerenke, W.T. "Cyclic changes in the physical and chemical properties of cervical mucus." *American Journal of Obstetrics and Gynecology* 52, no. 6 (1946): 1023–1031; Moghissi, Kamran S. "The function of the cervix in fertility." *Fertility and Sterility* 23, no. 4 (1972): 295–306; Daunter, B., and C. Counsilman. "Cervical mucus: its structure and possible biological functions." *European Journal of Obstetrics & Gynecology and Reproductive Biology* 10, no. 3 (1980): 141–161.

[37] Odeblad, E., A. Ingelman-Sundberg, L. Hallstrom, A. Hoglund, U. Leppanen, K. Lisspers, E. Perenyi, K. Rudolfsson-Asberg, K. Sahlin, and C. Lindstrom-Sjogren. "The biophysical properties of the cervical-vaginal secretions." *International Review of Natural Family Planning* 7, no. 1 (1983): 1–56.

[38] Ibid, 1–17.

[39] Menarguez, Mikaela, Erik Odeblad, and Helvia Temprano. "Recent Research in Cervical Secretion: Some Biophysical Aspects." *Sveikatos Mokslai/Health Sciences* 21, no. 3 (75) (2011): 55–60.

[40] Kunz, G., D. Beil, H. Deininger, L. Wildt, and G. Leyendecker. "The dynamics of rapid sperm transport through the female genital tract: evidence from vaginal sonography of uterine peristalsis and hysterosalpingoscintigraphy." *Human Reproduction* 11, no. 3 (1996): 627–632; Suarez, S.S., and A.A. Pacey. "Sperm transport in the female reproductive tract." *Human Reproduction Update* 12, no. 1 (2006): 27.

[41] Odeblad, E. "Investigation on the physiological basis for fertility awareness method." *Bulletin of the Ovulation Method Research and Reference Centre of Australia* 29, no. 1 (2002): 4.

[42] Klaus, Hanna. "Natural family planning: a review." *Obstetrical & Gynecological Survey* 37, no. 2 (1982): 3.

[43] Hunter, Ronald H.F. "Human sperm reservoirs and Fallopian tube function: a role for the intra-mural portion?" *Acta Obstetricia et Gynecologica Scandinavica* 74, no. 9 (1995): 677–681.

[44] Odeblad, E., A. Ingelman-Sundberg, L. Hallstrom, A. Hoglund, U. Leppanen, K. Lisspers, E. Perenyi, K. Rudolfsson-Asberg, K. Sahlin, and C. Lindstrom-Sjogren. "The biophysical properties of the cervical-vaginal secretions." *International Review of Natural Family Planning* 7, no. 1 (1983): 1–56.

[45] Odeblad, Erik. "The discovery of different types of cervical mucus and the Billings Ovulation Method." *Bulletin of the Natural Family Planning Council of Victoria* 21, no. 3 (1994): 8.

[46] Ibid, 13; Odeblad, E. "Investigation on the physiological basis for fertility awareness method." *Bulletin of the Ovulation Method Research and Reference Centre of Australia* 29, no. 1 (2002): 6.

[47] Hilgers, Thomas W. (2004). *Reproductive Anatomy & Physiology: A Primer for FertilityCare Professionals*, 2nd edition. Omaha, NE: Pope Paul VI Institute Press, 54–55.

[48] Odeblad, Erik. "The discovery of different types of cervical mucus and the Billings Ovulation Method." *Bulletin of the Natural Family Planning Council of Victoria* 21, no. 3 (1994): 14.

[49] Ibid.

[50] Ibid, 26.

Chapter 4

[1] Treloar, Alan E., Ruth E. Boynton, Borghild G. Behn, and Byron W. Brown. "Variation of the human menstrual cycle through reproductive life." *International Journal of Fertility* 12, no. 1 Pt 2 (1967): 77–126.

[2] Harlow, Siobán D., and Sara A. Ephross. "Epidemiology of menstruation and its relevance to women's health." *Epidemiologic Reviews* 17, no. 2 (1995): 265–286.

[3] Treloar, Alan E., Ruth E. Boynton, Borghild G. Behn, and Byron W. Brown. "Variation of the human menstrual cycle through reproductive life." *International Journal of Fertility* 12, no. 1 Pt 2 (1967): 77–126.

[4] Ibid, 99.

[5] Fehring, Richard J., Mary Schneider, and Kathleen Raviele. "Variability in the phases of the menstrual cycle." *Journal of Obstetric, Gynecologic, & Neonatal Nursing* 35, no. 3 (2006): 376–384; Creinin, Mitchell D., Sharon Keverline, and Leslie A. Meyn. "How regular is regular? An analysis of menstrual cycle regularity." *Contraception* 70, no. 4 (2004): 289–292; Münster, Kirstine, Lone Schmidt, and Peter Helm. "Length and variation in the menstrual cycle — a cross-sectional study from a Danish county." *BJOG: An International Journal of Obstetrics and Gynaecology* 99, no. 5 (1992): 422–429; Treloar, Alan E., Ruth E. Boynton, Borghild G. Behn, and Byron W. Brown. "Variation of the human menstrual cycle through reproductive life." *International Journal of Fertility* 12, no. 1 Pt 2 (1967): 77–126; Harlow, Siobán D., and Sara A. Ephross. "Epidemiology of menstruation and its relevance to women's health." *Epidemiologic Reviews* 17, no. 2 (1995): 265–286; Cole, Laurence A., Donald G. Ladner, and Francis W. Byrn. "The normal variabilities of the menstrual cycle." *Fertility and Sterility* 91, no. 2 (2009): 522–527.

[6] Fehring, Richard J., Mary Schneider, and Kathleen Raviele. "Variability in the phases of the menstrual cycle." *Journal of Obstetric, Gynecologic, & Neonatal Nursing* 35, no. 3 (2006): 376–384.

[7] Ibid; Odeblad, Erik. "The discovery of different types of cervical mucus and the Billings Ovulation Method." *Bulletin of the Natural Family Planning Council of Victoria* 21, no. 3 (1994): 1–31; Harlow, Siobán D., and Sara A. Ephross. "Epidemiology of Menstruation and its Relevance to Women's Health." *Epidemiologic Reviews* 17, no. 2 (1995): 265–286; Treloar, Alan E., Ruth E. Boynton, Borghild G. Behn, and Byron W. Brown. "Variation of the human menstrual cycle through reproductive life." *International Journal of Fertility* 12, no. 1 Pt 2 (1967): 77–126; Chiazze, Leonard, Franklin T. Brayer, John J. Macisco, Margaret P. Parker, and Benedict J. Duffy. "The length and variability of the human menstrual cycle." *JAMA* 203, no. 6 (1968): 377–380; Mumford, Sunni L, Anne Z. Steiner, Anna Z. Pollack, Neil J. Perkins, Amanda C. Filiberto, Paul S. Albert, Donald R. Mattison, Jean Wactawski-Wende, and Enrique F. Schisterman. "The utility of menstrual cycle length as an indicator of cumulative hormonal exposure." *The Journal of Clinical Endocrinology & Metabolism* 97, no. 10 (2012): E1871–E1879; Landgren, B.-M., A.-L. Unden, and Egon Diczfalusy. "Hormonal profile of the cycle in 68 normally menstruating women." *Acta Endocrinologica* 94, no. 1 (1980): 89–98; Cole, Laurence A., Donald G. Ladner, and Francis W. Byrn. "The normal variabilities of the menstrual cycle." *Fertility and Sterility* 91, no. 2 (2009): 522–527; Creinin, Mitchell D., Sharon Keverline, and Leslie A. Meyn. "How regular is regular? An analysis of menstrual cycle regularity." *Contraception* 70, no. 4 (2004): 289–292; Lenton, E.A., B.M. Landgren, L. Sexton, and R. Harper. "Normal variation in the length of the follicular phase of the menstrual cycle: effect of chronological age." *British Journal of Obstetrics and Gynaecology* 91, no. 7 (1984): 681–684, 685–689; Hilgers, Thomas W. (2004). *The Medical & Surgical Practice of NaPro Technology*. Omaha, NE: Pope Paul VI Institute Press, 203–205; Matus, Geraldine (Ed.). "Statistical parameters of the menstrual cycle." *Justisse HRHP Training Program*. Justisse College. Accessed January 23. 2017. www.justisse.ca/index.php/college/courseware/page/1074.

[8] Harlow, Siobán D., and Sara A. Ephross. "Epidemiology of menstruation and its relevance to women's health." *Epidemiologic Reviews* 17, no. 2 (1995): 265–286; Landgren, B.-M., A.-L. Unden, and Egon Diczfalusy. "Hormonal profile of

the cycle in 68 normally menstruating women." *Acta Endocrinologica* 94, no. 1 (1980): 89–98; Mumford, Sunni L., Anne Z. Steiner, Anna Z. Pollack, Neil J. Perkins, Amanda C. Filiberto, Paul S. Albert, Donald R. Mattison, Jean Wactawski-Wende, and Enrique F. Schisterman. "The utility of menstrual cycle length as an indicator of cumulative hormonal exposure." *The Journal of Clinical Endocrinology & Metabolism* 97, no. 10 (2012): E1871–E1879; Fehring, Richard J., Mary Schneider, and Kathleen Raviele. "Variability in the phases of the menstrual cycle." *Journal of Obstetric, Gynecologic, & Neonatal Nursing* 35, no. 3 (2006): 376–384.

9 Creinin, Mitchell D., Sharon Keverline, and Leslie A. Meyn. "How regular is regular? An analysis of menstrual cycle regularity." *Contraception* 70, no. 4 (2004): 289–292; Fehring, Richard J., Mary Schneider, and Kathleen Raviele. "Variability in the phases of the menstrual cycle." *Journal of Obstetric, Gynecologic, & Neonatal Nursing* 35, no. 3 (2006): 376–384; Odeblad, Erik. "The discovery of different types of cervical mucus and the Billings Ovulation Method." *Bulletin of the Natural Family Planning Council of Victoria* 21, no. 3 (1994): 1–31.

10 Odeblad, Erik. "The discovery of different types of cervical mucus and the Billings Ovulation Method." *Bulletin of the Natural Family Planning Council of Victoria* 21, no. 3 (1994): 1–31; Fehring, Richard J., Mary Schneider, and Kathleen Raviele. "Variability in the phases of the menstrual cycle." *Journal of Obstetric, Gynecologic, & Neonatal Nursing* 35, no. 3 (2006): 376–384.

11 Fehring, Richard J., Mary Schneider, and Kathleen Raviele. "Variability in the phases of the menstrual cycle." *Journal of Obstetric, Gynecologic, & Neonatal Nursing* 35, no. 3 (2006): 376–384; Harlow, Siobán D., and Sara A. Ephross. "Epidemiology of menstruation and its relevance to women's health." *Epidemiologic Reviews* 17, no. 2 (1995): 265–286; Lenton, E.A., B.M. Landgren, L. Sexton, and R. Harper. "Normal variation in the length of the follicular phase of the menstrual cycle: effect of chronological age." *British Journal of Obstetrics and Gynaecology* 91, no. 7 (1984): 681–684; Mumford, Sunni L., Anne Z. Steiner, Anna Z. Pollack, Neil J. Perkins, Amanda C. Filiberto, Paul S. Albert, Donald R. Mattison, Jean Wactawski-Wende, and Enrique F. Schisterman. "The utility of menstrual cycle length as an indicator of cumulative hormonal exposure." *The Journal of Clinical Endocrinology & Metabolism* 97, no. 10 (2012): E1871–E1879; Landgren, B.-M., A.-L. Unden, and Egon Diczfalusy. "Hormonal profile of the cycle in 68 normally menstruating women." *Acta Endocrinologica* 94, no. 1 (1980): 89–98.

12 Fehring, Richard J., Mary Schneider, and Kathleen Raviele. "Variability in the phases of the menstrual cycle." *Journal of Obstetric, Gynecologic, & Neonatal Nursing* 35, no. 3 (2006): 376–384.

13 Ibid; Harlow, Siobán D., and Sara A. Ephross. "Epidemiology of menstruation and its relevance to women's health." *Epidemiologic Reviews* 17, no. 2 (1995): 269; Lenton, Elizabeth A., Brut Landgren, and Lynne Sexton. "Normal variation in the length of the luteal phase of the menstrual cycle: identification of the short luteal phase." *BJOG: An International Journal of Obstetrics and Gynaecology* 91, no. 7 (1984): 685–689; Crawford, Natalie M., David A. Pritchard, Amy H. Herring, and Anne Z. Steiner. "A prospective evaluation of luteal phase length and natural fertility." *Fertility and Sterility* (2017); Mumford, Sunni L., Anne Z. Steiner, Anna Z. Pollack, Neil J. Perkins, Amanda C. Filiberto, Paul S. Albert, Donald R. Mattison, Jean Wactawski-Wende, and Enrique F. Schisterman. "The utility of menstrual cycle length as an indicator of cumulative hormonal exposure." *The Journal of Clinical Endocrinology & Metabolism* 97, no. 10 (2012): E1871–E1879; Cole, Laurence A., Donald G. Ladner, and Francis W. Byrn. "The normal variabilities of the menstrual cycle." *Fertility and Sterility* 91, no. 2 (2009): 522–527; Hilgers, Thomas W. (2004). *The Medical & Surgical Practice of NaProTechnology*. Omaha, NE: Pope Paul VI Institute Press, 203–205; Landgren, B.-M., A.-L. Unden, and Egon Diczfalusy. "Hormonal profile of the cycle in 68 normally menstruating women." *Acta Endocrinologica* 94, no. 1 (1980): 89–98.

14 Mesen, Tolga B., and Steven L. Young. "Progesterone and the luteal phase: a requisite to reproduction." *Obstetrics and Gynecology Clinics of North America* 42, no. 1 (2015): 135.

15 Strauss, Jerome F., and Robert L. Barbieri (2009). *Yen & Jaffe's Reproductive Endocrinology: Physiology, Pathophysiology, and Clinical Management*, 6th edition. Philadelphia, PA: Elsevier, 213–214; Tabibzadeh, S., and A. Babaknia. "The signals and molecular pathways involved in implantation, a symbiotic interaction between blastocyst and endometrium involving adhesion and tissue invasion." *MHR: Basic Science of Reproductive Medicine* 1, no. 4 (1995): 179–202; Matus, Geraldine (Ed.). "Female sexual anatomy and physiology." *Justisse HRHP Training Program*. Justisse College. Accessed February 20, 2017. www.justisse.ca/index.php/college/courseware/page/1059.

16 Gnoth, Christian, P. Frank-Herrmann, A. Schmoll, E. Godehardt, and G. Freundl. "Cycle characteristics after discontinuation of oral contraceptives." *Gynecological Endocrinology* 16, no. 4 (2002): 307–317.

17 Qublan, H., Z. Amarin, M. Nawasreh, F. Diab, S. Malkawi, N. Al-Ahmad, and M. Balawneh. "Luteinized unruptured follicle syndrome: incidence and recurrence rate in infertile women with unexplained infertility undergoing intrauterine insemination." *Human Reproduction* 21, no. 8 (2006): 2110–2113.

18 Cutler, Winnifred Berg. "Lunar and menstrual phase locking." *American Journal of Obstetrics and Gynecology* 137, no. 7 (1980): 834–839.

19 Law, Sung Ping. "The regulation of menstrual cycle and its relationship to the moon." *Acta Obstetricia et Gynecologica Scandinavica* 65, no. 1 (1986): 45–48.

20 Dewan, Edmond M. "On the possibility of a perfect rhythm method of birth control by periodic light stimulation." *American Journal of Obstetrics and Gynecology* 99, no. 7 (1967): 1016–1019; Lin, May C., Daniel F. Kripke, Barbara L. Perry, and Sarah L. Berga. "Night light alters menstrual cycles." *Psychiatry Research* 33, no. 2 (1990): 135–138; Rex, Katharine M., Daniel F. Kripke, Roger J. Cole, and Melville R. Klauber. "Nocturnal light effects on menstrual cycle length." *The Journal of Alternative and Complementary Medicine* 3, no. 4 (1997): 387–390.

21 Rex, Katharine M., Daniel F. Kripke, Roger J. Cole, and Melville R. Klauber. "Nocturnal light effects on menstrual cycle length." *The Journal of Alternative and Complementary Medicine* 3, no. 4 (1997): 387–390; Lin, May C., Daniel F. Kripke, Barbara L. Perry, and Sarah L. Berga. "Night light alters menstrual cycles." *Psychiatry Research* 33, no. 2 (1990): 135–138.

22 Harlow, Siobán D., and Genevieve M. Matanoski. "The association between weight, physical activity, and stress and variation in the length of the menstrual cycle." *American Journal of Epidemiology* 133, no. 1 (1991): 38–49.

Chapter 5

1 "UNESCO UIS. Literacy." Accessed November 11, 2017. uis.unesco.org/en/topic/literacy

2 Global Industry Analysis, Size, Share, Growth, Trends and Forecast 2015–2023. "Oral Contraceptive Pills Market — Global Industry Analysis, Size, Share, Growth, Trends and Forecast 2015–2023." Accessed November 13, 2017. www.transparencymarketresearch.com/oral-contraceptive-pills-market.html

3 "Body Literacy – Justisse for Women." Accessed August 25, 2018. www.justisse.ca/index.php/pages/page/body-literacy

4 Frank-Herrmann, P., J. Heil, C. Gnoth, E. Toledo, S. Baur, C. Pyper, E. Jenetzky, T. Strowitzki, and G. Freundl. "The effectiveness of a fertility awareness based method to avoid pregnancy in relation to a couple's sexual behaviour during the fertile time: a prospective longitudinal study." Human Reproduction (2007).

5 Urrutia, Rachel Peragallo, Chelsea B. Polis, Elizabeth T. Jensen, Margaret E. Greene, Emily Kennedy, and Joseph B. Stanford. "Effectiveness of fertility awareness–based methods for pregnancy prevention: a systematic review." Obstetrics & Gynecology 132, no. 3 (2018): 591–604.

6 Hilgers, Thomas W. (2004). The Medical & Surgical Practice of NaPro Technology. Omaha, NE: Pope Paul VI Institute Press, 67–72; Matus, Geraldine. "Justisse Method: Fertility Awareness and Body Literacy: A User's Guide." Justisse-Healthworks for Women (2009): 15–17.

7 McNab, Brian K. "On the definition of uniformity in the definition of basal rate of metabolism." Physiological Zoology 70, no. 6 (1997): 718–720; Henry, C.J.K. "Basal metabolic rate studies in humans: measurement and development of new equations." Public Health Nutrition 8, no. 7a (2005): 1133–1152.

8 Hilgers, Thomas W. (2010). The NaPro Technology Revolution: Unleashing the Power in a Woman's Cycle. New York, NY: Beaufort Books, 122–156.

9 Su, Hsiu-Wei, Yu-Chiao Yi, Ting-Yen Wei, Ting-Chang Chang, and Chao-Min Cheng. "Detection of ovulation, a review of currently available methods." Bioengineering & Translational Medicine (2017): 238–246.

10 Kambic, R.T., and V. Lamprecht. "Calendar rhythm efficacy: a review." Advances in Contraception 12, no. 2 (1996): 123–128.

11 Brayer, Franklin T., Leonard Chiazze, and Benedict J. Duffy. "Calendar rhythm and menstrual cycle range." Fertility and Sterility 20, no. 2 (1969): 279–288.

Chapter 6

1 Kim, Brian. "Thyroid hormone as a determinant of energy expenditure and the basal metabolic rate." Thyroid 18, no. 2 (2008): 141–144; Al-Adsani, Hana, L. John Hoffer, and J. Enrique Silva. "Resting energy expenditure is sensitive to small dose changes in patients on chronic thyroid hormone replacement." The Journal of Clinical Endocrinology & Metabolism 82, no. 4 (1997): 1118–1125.

2 Giorda, Carlo B., Paolo Carnà, Francesco Romeo, Giuseppe Costa, Barbara Tartaglino, and Roberto Gnavi. "Prevalence, incidence and associated comorbidities of treated hypothyroidism: an update from a European population." European Journal of Endocrinology 176, no. 5 (2017): 533–542; Vanderpump, Mark P.J., and W. Michael G. Tunbridge. "Epidemiology and prevention of clinical and subclinical hypothyroidism." Thyroid 12, no. 10 (2002): 839–847.

3 Tunbridge, W.M.G., D.C. Evered, R. Hall, D. Appleton, M. Brewis, F. Clark, J. Grimley Evans, E. Young, T. Bird, and P.A. Smith. "The spectrum of thyroid disease in a community: the Whickham survey." Clinical Endocrinology 7, no. 6 (1977): 481–493; Canaris, Gay J., Neil R. Manowitz, Gilbert Mayor, and E. Chester Ridgway. "The Colorado thyroid disease prevalence study." Archives of Internal Medicine 160, no. 4 (2000): 526–534.

4 Garber, Jeffrey R., Rhoda H. Cobin, Hossein Gharib, James V. Hennessey, Irwin Klein, Jeffrey I. Mechanick, Rachel Pessah-Pollack, Peter A. Singer, and Kenneth A. Woeber for the American Association of Clinical Endocrinologists and American Thyroid Association Taskforce on Hypothyroidism in Adults. "Clinical practice guidelines for hypothyroidism in adults: cosponsored by the American Association of Clinical Endocrinologists and the American Thyroid Association." Thyroid 22, no. 12 (2012): 1200–1235; Wartofsky, Leonard, and Richard A. Dickey. "The evidence for a narrower thyrotropin reference range is compelling." The Journal of Clinical Endocrinology & Metabolism 90, no. 9 (2005): 5483–5488.

5 Negro, Roberto, and Alex Stagnaro-Green. "Diagnosis and management of subclinical hypothyroidism in pregnancy." The BMJ 349 (2014): 1–10.

6 Joshi, J.V., S.D. Bhandarkar, M. Chadha, D. Balaiah, and R. Shah. "Menstrual irregularities and lactation failure may precede thyroid dysfunction or goitre." Journal of Postgraduate Medicine 39, no. 3 (1993): 137–41.

7 Krassas, Gerasimos E. "Thyroid disease and female reproduction." Fertility and Sterility 74, no. 6 (2000): 1063–1070.

8 Krassas, G.E., Kris Poppe, and Daniel Glinoer. "Thyroid function and human reproductive health." Endocrine Reviews 31, no. 5 (2010): 702–755.

9 Krassas, Gerasimos E. "Thyroid disease and female reproduction." Fertility and Sterility 74, no. 6 (2000): 1063–1070.

10 Jacobson, Melanie H., Penelope P. Howards, Lyndsey A. Darrow, Juliana W. Meadows, James S. Kesner, Jessica B. Spencer, Metrecia L. Terrell, and Michele Marcus. "Thyroid hormones and menstrual cycle function in a longitudinal cohort of premenopausal women." Paediatric and Perinatal Epidemiology (2018): 1–10.

11 Hess, Sonja Y. "The impact of common micronutrient deficiencies on iodine and thyroid metabolism: the evidence from human studies." Best Practice & Research: Clinical Endocrinology & Metabolism 24, no. 1 (2010): 117–132.

12 Peckham, Stephen, David Lowery, and Sarah Spencer. "Are fluoride levels in drinking water associated with hypothyroidism prevalence in England? A large observational study of GP practice data and fluoride levels in drinking water." Journal of Epidemiol Community Health 69, no. 7 (2015): 619–624.

13 Pearce, Elizabeth N., and Lewis E. Braverman. "Environmental pollutants and the thyroid." Best Practice & Research; Clinical Endocrinology & Metabolism 23, no. 6 (2009): 801–813; Kashiwagi, Keiko, Nobuaki Furuno, Shigeyuki Kitamura, Shigeru Ohta, Kazumi Sugihara, Kozo Utsumi, Hideki Hanada, Kikuyo Taniguchi, Ken-ichi Suzuki, and

Akihiko Kashiwagi. "Disruption of thyroid hormone function by environmental pollutants." *Journal of Health Science* 55, no. 2 (2009): 147–160.

14 Rice, Kevin M., Ernest M. Walker Jr., Miaozong Wu, Chris Gillette, and Eric R. Blough. "Environmental mercury and its toxic effects." *Journal of Preventive Medicine and Public Health* 47, no. 2 (2014): 74–83.

15 Liontiris, Michael I., and Elias E. Mazokopakis. "A concise review of Hashimoto thyroiditis (HT) and the importance of iodine, selenium, vitamin D and gluten on the autoimmunity and dietary management of HT patients. Points that need more investigation." *Hellenic Journal of Nuclear Medicine* 20, no. 1 (2017): 51–56.

16 Fröhlich, Eleonore, and Richard Wahl. "Thyroid autoimmunity: role of anti-thyroid antibodies in thyroid and extra-thyroidal diseases." *Frontiers in Immunology* 8 (2017): 521: 1–16.

17 Paynter, O.E., G.J. Burin, R.B. Jaeger, and C.A. Gregorio. "Goitrogens and thyroid follicular cell neoplasia: evidence for a threshold process." *Regulatory Toxicology and Pharmacology* 8, no. 1 (1988): 102–119.

18 Bianco, Antonio C., Domenico Salvatore, Balázs Gereben, Marla J. Berry, and P. Reed Larsen. "Biochemistry, cellular and molecular biology, and physiological roles of the iodothyronine selenodeiodinases." *Endocrine Reviews* 23, no. 1 (2002): 59–60; Brownstein, David. (2008). *Overcoming Thyroid Disorders*. Arden, NC: Medical Alternatives Press.

19 Ingbar, S.H., and L.E. Braverman. "Active form of the thyroid hormone." *Annual Review of Medicine* 26, no. 1 (1975): 443–449.

20 Danforth Jr., Elliot, and A.G. Burger. "The impact of nutrition on thyroid hormone physiology and action." *Annual Review of Nutrition* 9, no. 1 (1989): 201–227.

21 Abdalla, Sherine M., and Antonio C. Bianco. "Defending plasma T_3 is a biological priority." *Clinical Endocrinology* 81, no. 5 (2014): 633–641; Pascual, Angel, and Ana Aranda. "Thyroid hormone receptors, cell growth and differentiation." *Biochimica et Biophysica Acta (BBA)–General Subjects* 1830, no. 7 (2013): 3908–3916.

22 Bianco, Antonio C., Domenico Salvatore, Balázs Gereben, Marla J. Berry, and P. Reed Larsen. "Biochemistry, cellular and molecular biology, and physiological roles of the iodothyronine selenodeiodinases." *Endocrine Reviews* 23, no. 1 (2002): 38–89; Abdalla, Sherine M., and Antonio C. Bianco. "Defending plasma T_3 is a biological priority." *Clinical Endocrinology* 81, no. 5 (2014): 633–641.

23 Garber, Jeffrey R., Rhoda H. Cobin, Hossein Gharib, James V. Hennessey, Irwin Klein, Jeffrey I. Mechanick, Rachel Pessah-Pollack, Peter A. Singer, and Kenneth A. Woeber for the American Association of Clinical Endocrinologists and American Thyroid Association Taskforce on Hypothyroidism in Adults. "Clinical practice guidelines for hypothyroidism in adults: cosponsored by the American Association of Clinical Endocrinologists and the American Thyroid Association." *Thyroid* 22, no. 12 (2012): 1200–1235.

24 Hoang, Thanh D., Cara H. Olsen, Vinh Q. Mai, Patrick W. Clyde, and Mohamed K.M. Shakir. "Desiccated thyroid extract compared with levothyroxine in the treatment of hypothyroidism: a randomized, double-blind, crossover study." *The Journal of Clinical Endocrinology & Metabolism* 98, no. 5 (2013): 1982–1990; Friedman, Michael, Jorge R. Miranda-Massari, and Michael J. González. "Supraphysiological cyclic dosing of sustained release T3 in order to reset low basal body temperature." *Puerto Rico Health Sciences Journal* 25, no. 1 (2006): 23–29; Wilson, E. Denis. "Reversing hypometabolic symptoms by normalizing low body temperatures with sustained-release T3 in patients with euthyroid TSH levels." *Journal of Restorative Medicine* 1, no. 1 (2012): 64–74.

25 McCook, Judy G., Beth A. Bailey, Stacey L. Williams, Sheeba Anand, and Nancy E. Reame. "Differential contributions of polycystic ovary syndrome (PCOS) manifestations to psychological symptoms." *The Journal of Behavioral Health Services & Research* 42, no. 3 (2015): 383–394; Padmanabhan, Vasantha. "Polycystic ovary syndrome — 'a riddle wrapped in a mystery inside an enigma.'" *The Journal of Clinical Endocrinology & Metabolism* 94, no. 6 (2009): 1883–1885.

26 Sirmans, Susan M., and Kristen A. Pate. "Epidemiology, diagnosis, and management of polycystic ovary syndrome." *Clinical Epidemiology* 6 (2014): 1–13.

27 Chang, J., R. Azziz, R. Legro, D. Dewailly, S. Franks, R. Tarlatzis, B. Fauser et al. "Revised 2003 consensus on diagnostic criteria and long-term health risks related to polycystic ovary syndrome." *Fertility and Sterility* 81, no. 1 (2004): 19–25.

28 Azziz, Ricardo, Enrico Carmina, Didier Dewailly, Evanthia Diamanti-Kandarakis, Hector F. Escobar-Morreale, Walter Futterweit, Onno E. Janssen et al. "Criteria for defining polycystic ovary syndrome as a predominantly hyperandrogenic syndrome: an androgen excess society guideline." *The Journal of Clinical Endocrinology & Metabolism* 91, no. 11 (2006): 4237–4245.

29 Ibid.

30 Hendrickson-Jack, Lisa. "FFP 111 | 8 Steps to Reverse Your PCOS | Inflammation, Gut Health, Thyroid Disorders & PCOS | Infertility | Autoimmunity | Dr. Fiona McCulloch, ND." *Fertility Friday Podcast*. Podcast Audio, December 2, 2016. fertilityfriday.com/Fiona-McCulloch-ND

31 Wild, Robert A. "Long-term health consequences of PCOS." *Human Reproduction Update* 8, no. 3 (2002): 231–241; Barry, John A., Mallika M. Azizia, and Paul J. Hardiman. "Risk of endometrial, ovarian and breast cancer in women with polycystic ovary syndrome: a systematic review and meta-analysis." *Human Reproduction Update* 20, no. 5 (2014): 748–758; Harris, Holly R., and Kathryn L. Terry. "Polycystic ovary syndrome and risk of endometrial, ovarian, and breast cancer: a systematic review." *Fertility Research and Practice* 1, no. 2 (2016): 1–9.

32 Maslyanskaya, Sofya, Hina J. Talib, Jennifer L. Northridge, Amanda M. Jacobs, Chanelle Coble, and Susan M. Coupey. "Polycystic ovary syndrome: an under-recognized cause of abnormal uterine bleeding in adolescents admitted to a children's hospital." *Journal of Pediatric and Adolescent Gynecology* 30, no. 3 (2017): 349–355.

33 Kirchengast, S., and J. Huber. "Body composition characteristics and body fat distribution in lean women with polycystic ovary syndrome." *Human Reproduction* 16, no. 6 (2001): 1255–1260.

34 Azziz, Ricardo, Enrico Carmina, Didier Dewailly, Evanthia Diamanti-Kandarakis, Héctor F. Escobar-Morreale, Walter Futterweit, Onno E. Janssen et al. "The Androgen Excess and PCOS Society criteria for the polycystic ovary syndrome: the complete task force report." Fertility and Sterility 91, no. 2 (2009): 456–488.

35 Azziz, Ricardo, Enrico Carmina, Didier Dewailly, Evanthia Diamanti-Kandarakis, Hector F. Escobar-Morreale, Walter Futterweit, Onno E. Janssen et al. "Criteria for defining polycystic ovary syndrome as a predominantly hyperandrogenic syndrome: an androgen excess society guideline." The Journal of Clinical Endocrinology & Metabolism 91, no. 11 (2006): 4237–4245.

36 Balen, Adam H., Joop S.E. Laven, Seang-Lin Tan, and Didier Dewailly. "Ultrasound assessment of the polycystic ovary: international consensus definitions." Human Reproduction Update 9, no. 6 (2003): 505–514.

37 Azziz, Ricardo, Enrico Carmina, Didier Dewailly, Evanthia Diamanti-Kandarakis, Héctor F. Escobar-Morreale, Walter Futterweit, Onno E. Janssen et al. "The Androgen Excess and PCOS Society criteria for the polycystic ovary syndrome: the complete task force report." Fertility and Sterility 91, no. 2 (2009): 456–488.

38 Azziz, Ricardo, Enrico Carmina, Didier Dewailly, Evanthia Diamanti-Kandarakis, Hector F. Escobar-Morreale, Walter Futterweit, Onno E. Janssen et al. "Criteria for defining polycystic ovary syndrome as a predominantly hyperandrogenic syndrome: an androgen excess society guideline." The Journal of Clinical Endocrinology & Metabolism 91, no. 11 (2006): 4237–4245.

39 Dumesic, Daniel A., Sharon E. Oberfield, Elisabet Stener-Victorin, John C. Marshall, Joop S. Laven, and Richard S. Legro. "Scientific statement on the diagnostic criteria, epidemiology, pathophysiology, and molecular genetics of polycystic ovary syndrome." Endocrine Reviews 36, no. 5 (2015): 487–525.

40 Azziz, Ricardo, Enrico Carmina, Didier Dewailly, Evanthia Diamanti-Kandarakis, Héctor F. Escobar-Morreale, Walter Futterweit, Onno E. Janssen et al. "The Androgen Excess and PCOS Society criteria for the polycystic ovary syndrome: the complete task force report." Fertility and Sterility 91, no. 2 (2009): 456–488.

41 Rao, Ujvala, and Roy Homburg. (2018). "Anovulation in Women with PCOS." Infertility in Women with Polycystic Ovary Syndrome. Springer, Cham, 23–30; Cadagan, David, Raheela Khan, and Saad Amer. "Thecal cell sensitivity to luteinizing hormone and insulin in polycystic ovarian syndrome." Reproductive Biology 16, no. 1 (2016): 53–60.

42 Azziz, Ricardo, Enrico Carmina, Didier Dewailly, Evanthia Diamanti-Kandarakis, Héctor F. Escobar-Morreale, Walter Futterweit, Onno E. Janssen et al. "The Androgen Excess and PCOS Society criteria for the polycystic ovary syndrome: the complete task force report." Fertility and Sterility 91, no. 2 (2009): 456–488.

43 Ibid

44 Kelly, Christopher J.G., John Connell, Iain T. Cameron, Gwyn W. Gould, and Helen Lyall. "The long term health consequences of polycystic ovary syndrome." BJOG: An International Journal of Obstetrics and Gynaecology 107, no. 11 (2000): 1327–1338.

45 Rojas, Joselyn, Mervin Chávez, Luis Olivar, Milagros Rojas, Jessenia Morillo, José Mejías, María Calvo, and Valmore Bermúdez. "Polycystic ovary syndrome, insulin resistance, and obesity: navigating the pathophysiologic labyrinth." International Journal of Reproductive Medicine (2014): 1–17.

46 Hotamisligil, Gökhan S. "Inflammation and metabolic disorders." Nature 444, no. 7121 (2006): 860–867.

47 Kelly, Chris C.J., Helen Lyall, John R. Petrie, Gwyn W. Gould, John M.C. Connell, and Naveed Sattar. "Low grade chronic inflammation in women with polycystic ovarian syndrome." The Journal of Clinical Endocrinology & Metabolism 86, no. 6 (2001): 2453–2455; Ridker, Paul M., Charles H. Hennekens, Julie E. Buring, and Nader Rifai. "C-reactive protein and other markers of inflammation in the prediction of cardiovascular disease in women." New England Journal of Medicine 342, no. 12 (2000): 836–843.

48 O'Neill, S., and L. O'Driscoll. "Metabolic syndrome: a closer look at the growing epidemic and its associated pathologies." Obesity Reviews 16, no. 1 (2015): 1–12; Franks, Stephen. "Polycystic ovary syndrome: not just a fertility problem." Women's Health. (2015): 433–436.

49 Dunaif, Andrea, and Bart C.J.M. Fauser. "Renaming PCOS — a two-state solution." The Journal of Clinical Endocrinology & Metabolism 98, no. 11 (2013): 4325–4328; Rosenwaks, Zev. "Polycystic ovary syndrome, an enigmatic syndrome begging for a name change." Fertility and Sterility 108, no. 5 (2017): 748–749.

50 Diamanti-Kandarakis, Evanthia, Jean-Patrice Baillargeon, Maria J. Iuorno, Daniela J. Jakubowicz, and John E. Nestler. "A modern medical quandary: polycystic ovary syndrome, insulin resistance, and oral contraceptive pills." The Journal of Clinical Endocrinology & Metabolism 88, no. 5 (2003): 1927–1932; de Melo, Anderson Sanches, Rosana Maria dos Reis, Rui Alberto Ferriani, and Carolina Sales Vieira. "Hormonal contraception in women with polycystic ovary syndrome: choices, challenges, and noncontraceptive benefits." Open Access Journal of Contraception 8 (2017): 13–23.

51 Gordon, Catherine M. "Functional hypothalamic amenorrhea." New England Journal of Medicine 363, no. 4 (2010): 365–371.

52 Chou, Sharon H., and Christos Mantzoros. "Bone metabolism in anorexia nervosa and hypothalamic amenorrhea." Metabolism (2017).

53 Frisch, Rose E., and Janet W. McArthur. "Menstrual cycles: fatness as a determinant of minimum weight for height necessary for their maintenance or onset." Science 185, no. 4155 (1974): 949–951.

54 Winkler, Laura Al-Dakhiel, Jacob Stampe Frølich, Maya Schulpen, and René Klinkby Støving. "Body composition and menstrual status in adults with a history of anorexia nervosa — at what fat percentage is the menstrual cycle restored?" International Journal of Eating Disorders 50, no. 4 (2017): 370–377.

55 Beals, Katherine A., and Amanda K. Hill. "The prevalence of disordered eating, menstrual dysfunction, and low bone mineral density among US collegiate athletes." International Journal of Sport Nutrition and Exercise Metabolism 16, no. 1 (2006): 1–23.

56 Hobart, Julie A., and Douglas R. Smucker. "The female athlete triad." American Family Physician 61, no. 11 (2000): 3357–3364.

[57] Deimel, Jay F., and Bradley J. Dunlap. "The female athlete triad." *Clinics in Sports Medicine* 31, no. 2 (2012): 247–254.

[58] Ong, Jun Liang, and Iain A. Brownlee. "Energy expenditure, availability, and dietary intake assessment in competitive female dragon boat athletes." *Sports* 5, 45, no. 2 (2017): 1–7.

[59] Cialdella-Kam, Lynn, Charlotte P. Guebels, Gianni F. Maddalozzo, and Melinda M. Manore. "Dietary intervention restored menses in female athletes with exercise-associated menstrual dysfunction with limited impact on bone and muscle health." *Nutrients* 6, no. 8 (2014): 3018–3039.

[60] Biller, Beverly M.K., Howard J. Federoff, James I. Koenig, and Anne Klibanski. "Abnormal cortisol secretion and responses to corticotropin-releasing hormone in women with hypothalamic amenorrhea." *The Journal of Clinical Endocrinology & Metabolism* 70, no. 2 (1990): 311–317.

[61] Hergenroeder, Albert C. "Bone mineralization, hypothalamic amenorrhea, and sex steroid therapy in female adolescents and young adults." *The Journal of Pediatrics* 126, no. 5 (1995): 683–689.

[62] Cann, Christopher E., Mary C. Martin, Harry K. Genant, and Robert B. Jaffe. "Decreased spinal mineral content in amenorrheic women." *JAMA* 251, no. 5 (1984): 626–629.

[63] Hergenroeder, Albert C. "Bone mineralization, hypothalamic amenorrhea, and sex steroid therapy in female adolescents and young adults." *The Journal of Pediatrics* 126, no. 5 (1995): 683–689.

[64] Berger, Claudie, David Goltzman, Lisa Langsetmo, Lawrence Joseph, Stuart Jackson, Nancy Kreiger, Alan Tenenhouse, K. Shawn Davison, Robert G. Josse, Jerilynn C. Prior, and David A. Hanley. "Peak bone mass from longitudinal data: implications for the prevalence, pathophysiology, and diagnosis of osteoporosis." *Journal of Bone and Mineral Research* 25, no. 9 (2010): 1948–1957.

[65] Hergenroeder, Albert C., E. O'Brian Smith, Roman Shypailo, Lovell A. Jones, William J. Klish, and Kenneth Ellis. "Bone mineral changes in young women with hypothalamic amenorrhea treated with oral contraceptives, medroxyprogesterone, or placebo over 12 months." *American Journal of Obstetrics and Gynecology* 176, no. 5 (1997): 1017–1025.

[66] Warren, Michelle P., Jeanne Brooks-Gunn, Richard P. Fox, Claire C. Holderness, Emily P. Hyle, William G. Hamilton, and Linda Hamilton. "Persistent osteopenia in ballet dancers with amenorrhea and delayed menarche despite hormone therapy: a longitudinal study." *Fertility and Sterility* 80, no. 2 (2003): 398–404.

[67] Altayar, Osama, Alaa Al Nofal, B. Gisella Carranza Leon, Larry J. Prokop, Zhen Wang, and M. Hassan Murad. "Treatments to prevent bone loss in functional hypothalamic amenorrhea: a systematic review and meta-analysis." *Journal of the Endocrine Society* 1, no. 5 (2017): 500–511.

Chapter 7

[1] Wiley, T.S., Julie Taguchi, and Bent Formby. (2009). *Sex, Lies, and Menopause: The Shocking Truth about Synthetic Hormones and the Benefits of Natural Alternatives*. New York, NY: Harper Collins.

[2] Watkins, E.S. "How the pill became a lifestyle drug: The pharmaceutical industry and birth control in the United States since 1960." *American Journal of Public Health* 102, no. 8 (2012): 1462–1472.

[3] Liao, Pamela Verma, and Janet Dollin. "Half a century of the oral contraceptive pill: historical review and view to the future." *Canadian Family Physician* 58, no. 12 (2012): e757–e760.

[4] Marsh, Margaret S., and Wanda Ronner. (2008). *The Fertility Doctor: John Rock and the Reproductive Revolution*. Baltimore, MD: Johns Hopkins University Press, 140.

[5] Roberts, William C. "Facts and ideas from anywhere: 'The pill' and its four major developers." *Proceedings (Baylor University Medical Centre)* 28, no. 3 (2015): 421–432.

[6] Chasan-Taber, Lisa, Walter C. Willett, Meir J. Stampfer, Donna Spiegelman, Bernard A. Rosner, David J. Hunter, Graham A. Colditz, and JoAnn E. Manson. "Oral contraceptives and ovulatory causes of delayed fertility." *American Journal of Epidemiology* 146, no. 3 (1997): 264.

[7] Lefebvre, Yves. "Anatomical and functional changes induced by oral contraception." *Canadian Medical Association Journal* 102, no. 6 (1970): 622.

[8] Korver, Tjeerd, Christine Klipping, Doris Heger-Mahn, Ingrid Duijkers, Gonnie van Osta, and Thom Dieben. "Maintenance of ovulation inhibition with the 75-μg desogestrel-only contraceptive pill (Cerazette®) after scheduled 12-h delays in tablet intake." *Contraception* 71, no. 1 (2005): 8–13; Rice, C.F., S.R. Killick, T. Dieben, and H. Coelingh Bennink. "A comparison of the inhibition of ovulation achieved by desogestrel 75 μg and levonorgestrel 30 μg daily." *Human Reproduction* 14, no. 4 (1999): 982–985; Xiao, Bilian, Liying Zhou, Xuling Zhang, Tapani Luukkainen, and Hannu Allonen. "Pharmacokinetic and pharmacodynamic studies of levonorgestrel-releasing intrauterine device." *Contraception* 41, no. 4 (1990): 353–362.

[9] Xiao, Bilian, Tao Zeng, Shangchun Wu, Hongzhu Sun, and Na Xiao. "Effect of levonorgestrel-releasing intrauterine device on hormonal profile and menstrual pattern after long-term use." *Contraception* 51, no. 6 (1995): 359–365.

[10] Grow, Daniel R., and Khosro Iromloo. "Oral contraceptives maintain a very thin endometrium before operative hysteroscopy." *Fertility and Sterility* 85, no. 1 (2006): 204–207; Benagiano, Giuseppe, Alessandra Pera, and Francesco M. Primiero. "The endometrium and hormonal contraceptives." *Human Reproduction* 15, no. suppl 1 (2000): 101–118.

[11] Hatcher, Robert Anthony, and Anita L. Nelson. (2007). *Contraceptive Technology*. London: Ardent Media; Nassaralla, Claudia L., Joseph B. Stanford, K. Diane Daly, Mary Schneider, Karen C. Schliep, and Richard J. Fehring. "Characteristics of the menstrual cycle after discontinuation of oral contraceptives." *Journal of Women's Health* 20, no. 2 (2011): 169–177.

[12] Oliveira, J.B.A., R.L.R. Baruffi, A.L. Mauri, C.G. Petersen, M.C. Borges, and J.G. Franco. "Endometrial ultrasonography as a predictor of pregnancy in an in-vitro fertilization programme after ovarian stimulation and gonadotrophin-releasing hormone and gonadotrophins." *Human Reproduction* 12, no. 11 (1997): 2515–2518; Dickey, Richard P., Terry T. Olar, Steven N. Taylor, David N. Curole, and Ellen M. Matulich. "Relationship of endometrial thickness and pattern to

fecundity in ovulation induction cycles: effect of clomiphene citrate alone and with human menopausal gonadotropin." *Fertility and Sterility* 59, no. 4 (1993): 756–760.

13 Oliveira, J.B.A., R.L.R. Baruffi, A.L. Mauri, C.G. Petersen, M.C. Borges, and J.G. Franco. "Endometrial ultrasonography as a predictor of pregnancy in an in-vitro fertilization programme after ovarian stimulation and gonadotrophin-releasing hormone and gonadotrophins." *Human Reproduction* 12, no. 11 (1997): 2517.

14 Dickey, Richard P., Terry T. Olar, Steven N. Taylor, David N. Curole, and Ellen M. Matulich. "Relationship of endometrial thickness and pattern to fecundity in ovulation induction cycles: effect of clomiphene citrate alone and with human menopausal gonadotropin." *Fertility and Sterility* 59, no. 4 (1993): 756–760; Al Mohammady, Maged, Ghada Abdel Fattah, and Mostafa Mahmoud. "The impact of combined endometrial thickness and pattern on the success of intracytoplasmic sperm injection (ICSI) cycles." *Middle East Fertility Society Journal* 18, no. 3 (2013): 165–170.

15 Grow, Daniel R., and Khosro Iromloo. "Oral contraceptives maintain a very thin endometrium before operative hysteroscopy." *Fertility and Sterility* 85, no. 1 (2006): 204–207; Mascarenhas, Lawrence, Agaath van Beek, H. Coelingh Bennink, and John Newton. "A 2-year comparative study of endometrial histology and cervical cytology of contraceptive implant users in Birmingham, UK." *Human Reproduction* 13, no. 11 (1998): 3059; Benagiano, Giuseppe, Alessandra Pera, and Francesco M. Primiero. "The endometrium and hormonal contraceptives." *Human Reproduction* 15, no. suppl 1 (2000): 101–118; Wright, Kristen Page, and Julia V. Johnson. "Evaluation of extended and continuous use oral contraceptives." *Therapeutics and Clinical Risk Management* (2008): 905–911.

16 Hidalgo, Maria M., Creusa Hidalgo-Regina, M. Valeria Bahamondes, Ilza Monteiro, Carlos A. Petta, and Luis Bahamondes. "Serum levonorgestrel levels and endometrial thickness during extended use of the levonorgestrel-releasing intrauterine system." *Contraception* 80, no. 1 (2009): 84–89; Lakha, F., P.C. Ho, Z.M. Van der Spuy, K. Dada, R. Elton, A.F. Glasier, H.O.D. Critchley, A.R.W. Williams, and D.T. Baird. "A novel estrogen-free oral contraceptive pill for women: multicentre, double-blind, randomized controlled trial of mifepristone and progestogen-only pill (levonorgestrel)." *Human Reproduction* 22, no. 9 (2007): 2428–2436.

17 Wright, Kristen Page, and Julia V. Johnson. "Evaluation of extended and continuous use oral contraceptives." *Therapeutics and Clinical Risk Management* (2008): 906.

18 Ibid, 907.

19 "YAZ (Drospirenone/Ethinyl Estradiol) — Official Website." Accessed March 18, 2017. www.yaz-us.com

20 Helmerhorst, F.M., J.P. Vandenbroucke, C.J.M. Doggen, and F.R. Rosendaal. "The venous thrombotic risk of oral contraceptives, effects of oestrogen dose and progestogen type: results of the MEGA case-control study." *The BMJ* 339 (2009): 1–8.

21 "Thrombosis." Wikipedia. Accessed August 23, 2017. en.wikipedia.org/wiki/Thrombosis

22 Hendrickson-Jack, Lisa. "FFP 007 | What the Pill Really Does to Your Hormones | PCOS & Menstrual Irregularities | Dr. Lara Briden." *Fertility Friday Podcast*. Podcast Audio, January 30, 2015. fertilityfriday.com/lara

23 Castle, S., and I. Askew. "Contraceptive discontinuation: reasons, challenges, and solutions." *New York: Population Council* (2015): 1–33; Berenson, Abbey B., and Constance M. Wiemann. "Contraceptive use among adolescent mothers at 6 months postpartum." *Obstetrics & Gynecology* 89, no. 6 (1997): 999–1005; Westhoff, Carolyn L., Stephen Heartwell, Sharon Edwards, Mimi Zieman, Gretchen Stuart, Carrie Cwiak, Anne Davis, Tina Robilotto, Linda Cushman, and Debra Kalmuss. "Oral contraceptive discontinuation: do side effects matter?" *American Journal of Obstetrics and Gynecology* 196, no. 4 (2007): 412-e1; Peipert, Jeffrey F., Qiuhong Zhao, Jenifer E. Allsworth, Emiko Petrosky, Tessa Madden, David Eisenberg, and Gina Secura. "Continuation and satisfaction of reversible contraception." *Obstetrics and Gynecology* 117, no. 5 (2011): 1105.

24 Castle, S., and I. Askew. "Contraceptive discontinuation: reasons, challenges, and solutions." *New York: Population Council* (2015): 2–3; Westhoff, Carolyn L, Stephen Heartwell, Sharon Edwards, Mimi Zieman, Gretchen Stuart, Carrie Cwiak, Anne Davis, Tina Robilotto, Linda Cushman, and Debra Kalmuss. "Oral contraceptive discontinuation: do side effects matter?" *American Journal of Obstetrics and Gynecology* 196, no. 4 (2007): 412e1–412e7.

25 Westfall, John M., Deborah S. Main, and Lynn Barnard. "Continuation rates among injectable contraceptive users." *Family Planning Perspectives* (1996): 275–277.

26 Test ID: TTFB Testosterone, Total, Bioavailable, and Free, Serum. TTFB – Clinical: Testosterone, Total, Bioavailable, and Free, Serum. Accessed December 21, 2017. www.mayomedicallaboratories.com/test-catalog/Clinical and Interpretive/83686

27 Davis, Susan. "Testosterone and sexual desire in women." *Journal of Sex Education and Therapy* 25, no. 1 (2000): 25–32.

28 Davis, Susan R., and Jane Tran. "Testosterone influences libido and well being in women." *Trends in Endocrinology & Metabolism* 12, no. 1 (2001): 33–37.

29 Zimmerman, Y., M.J.C. Eijkemans, H.J.T. Coelingh Bennink, M.A. Blankenstein, and B.C.J.M. Fauser. "The effect of combined oral contraception on testosterone levels in healthy women: a systematic review and meta-analysis." *Human Reproduction Update* 20, no. 1 (2014): 76–105; Crewther, Blair T., Dave Hamilton, Kathleen Casto, Liam P. Kilduff, and Christian J. Cook. "Effects of oral contraceptive use on the salivary testosterone and cortisol responses to training sessions and competitions in elite women athletes." *Physiology & Behavior* 147 (2015): 84–90; Greco, Teri, Cynthia A. Graham, John Bancroft, Amanda Tanner, and Helen A. Doll. "The effects of oral contraceptives on androgen levels and their relevance to premenstrual mood and sexual interest: a comparison of two triphasic formulations containing norgestimate and either 35 or 25 μg of ethinyl estradiol." *Contraception* 76, no. 1 (2007): 8–17; Biswas, Arijit, Osborne A.C. Viegas, Herjan J.T. Coeling Bennink, Tjeerd Korver, and Shan S. Ratnam. "Effect of Implanon use on selected parameters of thyroid and adrenal function." *Contraception* 62, no. 5 (2000): 247–251; Segall-Gutierrez, Penina, Joanna Du, Chunying Niu, Marshall Ge, Ian Tilley, Kelly Mizraji, and Frank Z. Stanczyk. "Effect of subcutaneous depo-medroxyprogesterone acetate (DMPA-SC) on serum androgen markers in normal-weight, obese, and extremely obese women." *Contraception* 86, no. 6 (2012): 739–745.

30 Zimmerman, Y., M.J.C. Eijkemans, H.J.T. Coelingh Bennink, M.A. Blankenstein, and B.C.J.M. Fauser. "The effect of combined oral contraception on testosterone levels in healthy women: a systematic review and meta-analysis." *Human Reproduction Update* 20, no. 1 (2014): 76–105.

31 Anderson, David C. "Sex-hormone-binding globulin." *Clinical Endocrinology* 3, no. 1 (1974): 72.

32 Panzer, Claudia, Sarah Wise, Gemma Fantini, Dongwoo Kang, Ricardo Munarriz, Andre Guay, and Irwin Goldstein. "Impact of oral contraceptives on sex hormone-binding globulin and androgen levels: a retrospective study in women with sexual dysfunction." *The Journal of Sexual Medicine* 3, no. 1 (2006): 104–113; Zimmerman, Y., M.J.C. Eijkemans, H.J.T. Coelingh Bennink, M.A. Blankenstein, and B.C.J.M. Fauser. "The effect of combined oral contraception on testosterone levels in healthy women: a systematic review and meta-analysis." *Human Reproduction Update* 20, no. 1 (2014): 76–105; Hugon-Rodin, Justine, Martine Alhenc-Gelas, H. Coenraad Hemker, Sylvie Brailly-Tabard, Anne Guiochon-Mantel, Geneviève Plu-Bureau, and Pierre-Yves Scarabin. "Sex hormone-binding globulin and thrombin generation in women using hormonal contraception." *Biomarkers* (2016): 1–5; Van Vliet, Huib A.A.M., Marijke Frolich, M. Christella, LG.D. Thomassen, Carine J.M. Doggen, Frits R. Rosendaal, Jan Rosing, and Frans M. Helmerhorst. "Association between sex hormone-binding globulin levels and activated protein C resistance in explaining the risk of thrombosis in users of oral contraceptives containing different progestogens." *Human Reproduction* 20, no. 2 (2005): 563–568.

33 Panzer, Claudia, Sarah Wise, Gemma Fantini, Dongwoo Kang, Ricardo Munarriz, Andre Guay, and Irwin Goldstein. "Impact of oral contraceptives on sex hormone-binding globulin and androgen levels: a retrospective study in women with sexual dysfunction." *The Journal of Sexual Medicine* 3, no. 1 (2006): 108.

34 Ibid, 110.

35 Ibid, 110.

36 Mes-Krowinkel, Miranda G., Yvonne V. Louwers, Annemarie G.M.G.J. Mulders, Frank H. de Jong, Bart C.J.M. Fauser, and Joop S.E. Laven. "Influence of oral contraceptives on anthropomorphometric, endocrine, and metabolic profiles of anovulatory polycystic ovary syndrome patients." *Fertility and Sterility* 101, no. 6 (2014): 1757–1765.

37 Bouchard, Céline, Jacques Brisson, Michel Fortier, Carol Morin, and Caty Blanchette. "Use of oral contraceptive pills and vulvar vestibulitis: a case-control study." *American Journal of Epidemiology* 156, no. 3 (2002): 254–261; Bohm-Starke, Nina, Ulrika Johannesson, Marita Hilliges, Eva Rylander, and Erik Torebjörk. "Decreased mechanical pain threshold in the vestibular mucosa of women using oral contraceptives: A contributing factor in vulvar vestibulitis?" *The Journal of Reproductive Medicine* 49, no. 11 (2004): 888–892; Battaglia, Cesare, Elena Morotti, Nicola Persico, Bruno Battaglia, Paolo Busacchi, Paolo Casadio, Roberto Paradisi, and Stefano Venturoli. "Clitoral vascularization and sexual behavior in young patients treated with drospirenone–ethinyl estradiol or contraceptive vaginal ring: a prospective, randomized, pilot study." *The Journal of Sexual Medicine* 11, no. 2 (2014): 471–480.

38 Bouchard, Céline, Jacques Brisson, Michel Fortier, Carol Morin, and Caty Blanchette. "Use of oral contraceptive pills and vulvar vestibulitis: a case-control study." *American Journal of Epidemiology* 156, no. 3 (2002): 254–261.

39 Battaglia, Cesare, Elena Morotti, Nicola Persico, Bruno Battaglia, Paolo Busacchi, Paolo Casadio, Roberto Paradisi, and Stefano Venturoli. "Clitoral vascularization and sexual behavior in young patients treated with drospirenone–ethinyl estradiol or contraceptive vaginal ring: a prospective, randomized, pilot study." *The Journal of Sexual Medicine* 11, no. 2 (2014): 471–480.

40 Battaglia, Cesare, Bruno Battaglia, Fulvia Mancini, Paolo Busacchi, Maria Chiara Paganotto, Elena Morotti, and Stefano Venturoli. "Sexual behavior and oral contraception: A pilot study." *The Journal of Sexual Medicine* 9, no. 2 (2012): 550–557.

41 Battaglia, Cesare, Elena Morotti, Nicola Persico, Bruno Battaglia, Paolo Busacchi, Paolo Casadio, Roberto Paradisi, and Stefano Venturoli. "Clitoral vascularization and sexual behavior in young patients treated with drospirenone–ethinyl estradiol or contraceptive vaginal ring: a prospective, randomized, pilot study." *The Journal of Sexual Medicine* 11, no. 2 (2014): 471–480.

42 Hendrickson-Jack, Lisa. "FFP 007 | What the Pill Really Does to Your Hormones | PCOS & Menstrual Irregularities | Dr. Lara Briden." *Fertility Friday Podcast*. Podcast Audio, January 30, 2015. fertilityfriday.com/lara

43 Lee, Joo Yong, and Kang Su Cho. "Chemical castration for sexual offenders: physicians' views." *Journal of Korean Medical Science* 28, no. 2 (2013): 171–172; Heim, Nikolaus. "Sexual behavior of castrated sex offenders." *Archives of Sexual Behavior* 10, no. 1 (1981): 11–19.

44 Skovlund, Charlotte Wessel, Lina Steinrud Mørch, Lars Vedel Kessing, and Øjvind Lidegaard. "Association of hormonal contraception with depression." *JAMA Psychiatry* 73, no. 11 (2016): 1154–1162; Lundin, Cecilia, Kristina Gemzell Danielsson, Marie Bixo, Lena Moby, Hanna Bengtsdotter, Izabella Jawad, Lena Marions et al. "Combined oral contraceptive use is associated with both improvement and worsening of mood in the different phases of the treatment cycle — A double-blind, placebo-controlled randomized trial." *Psychoneuroendocrinology* 76 (2017): 135–143; Sirakov, M., and E. Tomova. "Oral contraceptives and mood/sexual disorders in women." *Akusherstvo I Ginekologiia* 54, no. 5 (2014): 34–40; Oinonen, Kirsten A., and Dwight Mazmanian. "To what extent do oral contraceptives influence mood and affect?" *Journal of Affective Disorders* 70, no. 3 (2002): 229–240; Herzberg, Brenda N., Anthony L. Johnson, and Susannah Brown. "Depressive symptoms and oral contraceptives." *The BMJ* 4, no. 5728 (1970): 142–145.

45 Skovlund, Charlotte Wessel, Lina Steinrud Mørch, Lars Vedel Kessing, and Øjvind Lidegaard. "Association of hormonal contraception with depression." *JAMA Psychiatry* 73, no. 11 (2016): 1161.

46 Cowen, Philip J., and Michael Browning. "What has serotonin to do with depression?" *World Psychiatry* 14, no. 2 (2015): 158–160; Adams, P.W., V. Wynn, D.P. Rose, M. Seed, J. Folkard, and R. Strong. "Effect of pyridoxine hydrochloride (vitamin B6) upon depression associated with oral contraception." *The Lancet* 301, no. 7809 (1973): 897–904; Birdsall, Timothy C. "5-Hydroxytryptophan: a clinically-effective serotonin precursor." *Alternative Medicine Review: A Journal of Clinical Therapeutic* 3, no. 4 (1998): 271–280.

[47] Var, Chivorn, Sheryl Keller, Rathavy Tung, Dylan Freeland, and Alessandra N. Bazzano. "Supplementation with vitamin B6 reduces side effects in Cambodian women using oral contraception." *Nutrients* 6, no. 9 (2014): 3353–3362; Leeton, John. "Depression induced by oral contraception and the role of vitamin B6 in its management." *Australian and New Zealand Journal of Psychiatry* 8, no. 2 (1974): 85–88; Shaarawy, M., M. Fayad, A.R. Nagui, and S. Abdel-Azim. "Serotonin metabolism and depression in oral contraceptive users." *Contraception* 26, no. 2 (1982): 193–204.

[48] Pelton, Ross. "The pill problem: how to protect your health from the side effects of oral contraceptives. *Natural Pharmacist*, 2013; Owens, Michael J., and Charles B. Nemeroff. "Role of serotonin in the pathophysiology of depression: focus on the serotonin transporter." *Clinical Chemistry* 40, no. 2 (1994): 288–295.

[49] Leeton, John. "Depression induced by oral contraception and the role of vitamin B6 in its management." *Australian and New Zealand Journal of Psychiatry* 8, no. 2 (1974): 87; Kishi, H., T. Kishi, R.H. Williams, T. Watanabe, K. Folkers, and M.L. Stahl. "Deficiency of vitamin B6 in women taking contraceptive formulations." *Research Communications in Chemical Pathology and Pharmacology* 17, no. 2 (1977): 283–293; Webb, J.L. "Nutritional effects of oral contraceptive use: a review." *The Journal of Reproductive Medicine* 25, no. 4 (1980): 150–156; Luhby, A. Leonard, Myron Brin, Myron Gordon, Patricia Davis, Maureen Murphy, and Herbert Spiegel. "Vitamin B6 metabolism in users of oral contraceptive agents. I. Abnormal urinary xanthurenic acid excretion and its correction by pyridoxine." *The American Journal of Clinical Nutrition* 24, no. 6 (1971): 684–693; Winston, F. "Oral contraceptives pyridoxine and depression." *American Journal of Psychiatry* 130, no. 11 (1973): 1217–1221; Adams, P. W., V. Wynn, D.P. Rose, M. Seed, J. Folkard, and R. Strong. "Effect of pyridoxine hydrochloride (vitamin B6) upon depression associated with oral contraception." *The Lancet* 301, no. 7809 (1973): 897–904.

[50] Skovlund, Charlotte Wessel, Lina Steinrud Mørch, Lars Vedel Kessing, and Øjvind Lidegaard. "Association of hormonal contraception with depression." *JAMA Psychiatry* 73, no. 11 (2016): 1154–1162; Gingnell, Malin, Jonas Engman, Andreas Frick, Lena Moby, Johan Wikström, Mats Fredrikson, and Inger Sundström-Poromaa. "Oral contraceptive use changes brain activity and mood in women with previous negative affect on the pill — a double-blinded, placebo-controlled randomized trial of a levonorgestrel-containing combined oral contraceptive." *Psychoneuroendocrinology* 38, no. 7 (2013): 1133–1144.

[51] Schaffir, Jonathan, Brett L. Worly, and Tamar L. Gur. "Combined hormonal contraception and its effects on mood: a critical review." *The European Journal of Contraception & Reproductive Health Care* 21, no. 5 (2016): 347–355.

[52] Wiebe, Ellen R., Lori A. Brotto, and Jacqueline MacKay. "Characteristics of women who experience mood and sexual side effects with use of hormonal contraception." *Journal of Obstetrics and Gynaecology Canada* 33, no. 12 (2011): 1234–1240.

[53] Ibid, 1236.

[54] Ibid, 1234.

[55] Ibid, 1237.

[56] Ibid, 1237.

[57] Ibid, 1239.

[58] Behre, Hermann M., Michael Zitzmann, Richard A. Anderson, David J. Handelsman, Silvia W. Lestari, Robert I. McLachlan, M. Cristina Meriggiola et al. "Efficacy and safety of an injectable combination hormonal Contraceptive for men." *The Journal of Clinical Endocrinology & Metabolism* 101, no. 12 (2016): 4779–4788.

[59] Ibid, 4782.

[60] Ibid, 4781.

[61] Ibid, 4784.

[62] Ibid, 4783.

[63] Ibid, 4781.

[64] Ibid, 4781.

[65] Havlicek, Jan, S. Craig Roberts, and Jaroslav Flegr. "Women's preference for dominant male odour: effects of menstrual cycle and relationship status." *Biology Letters* 1, no. 3 (2005): 256–259; Havlicek, Jan, and S. Craig Roberts. "MHC-correlated mate choice in humans: a review." *Psychoneuroendocrinology* 34, no. 4 (2009): 497–512; Wedekind, Claus, and Sandra Füri. "Body odour preferences in men and women: do they aim for specific MHC combinations or simply heterozygosity?" *Proceedings of the Royal Society of London B: Biological Sciences* 264, no. 1387 (1997): 1473–1478; Thornhill, Randy, Steven W. Gangestad, Robert Miller, Glenn Scheyd, Julie K. McCollough, and Melissa Franklin. "Major histocompatibility complex genes, symmetry, and body scent attractiveness in men and women." *Behavioral Ecology* 14, no. 5 (2003): 668–678; Little, Anthony C., Benedict C. Jones, and Robert P. Burriss. "Preferences for masculinity in male bodies change across the menstrual cycle." *Hormones and Behavior* 51, no. 5 (2007): 633–639.

[66] Havlicek, Jan, and S. Craig Roberts. "MHC-correlated mate choice in humans: a review." *Psychoneuroendocrinology* 34, no. 4 (2009): 498; Wedekind, Claus, and Sandra Füri. "Body odour preferences in men and women: do they aim for specific MHC combinations or simply heterozygosity?" *Proceedings of the Royal Society of London B: Biological Sciences* 264, no. 1387 (1997): 1471; Penn, Dustin J. "The scent of genetic compatibility: sexual selection and the major histocompatibility complex." *Ethology* 108, no. 1 (2002): 1–21.

[67] Thornhill, Randy, Steven W. Gangestad, Robert Miller, Glenn Scheyd, Julie K. McCollough, and Melissa Franklin. "Major histocompatibility complex genes, symmetry, and body scent attractiveness in men and women." *Behavioral Ecology* 14, no. 5 (2003): 668–678.

[68] Havlicek, Jan, S. Craig Roberts, and Jaroslav Flegr. "Women's preference for dominant male odour: effects of menstrual cycle and relationship status." *Biology Letters* 1, no. 3 (2005): 256–257; Wedekind, Claus, and Sandra Füri. "Body odour preferences in men and women: do they aim for specific MHC combinations or simply heterozygosity?" *Proceedings of the Royal Society of London B: Biological Sciences* 264, no. 1387 (1997): 1476–1477; Alvergne, Alexandra, and Virpi Lummaa. "Does the contraceptive pill alter mate choice in humans?" *Trends in Ecology & Evolution* 25, no. 3 (2010):

171–179; Roberts, S. Craig, Anthony C. Little, L. Morris Gosling, David I. Perrett, Vaughan Carter, Benedict C. Jones, Ian Penton-Voak, and Marion Petrie. "MHC-heterozygosity and human facial attractiveness." *Evolution and Human Behavior* 26, no. 3 (2005): 213–226; Penn, Dustin J. "The scent of genetic compatibility: sexual selection and the major histocompatibility complex." *Ethology* 108, no. 1 (2002): 5–8; Ober, Carole, Lowell R. Weitkamp, Nancy Cox, Harvey Dytch, Donna Kostyu, and Sherman Elias. "HLA and mate choice in humans." *The American Journal of Human Genetics* 61, no. 3 (1997): 497–504.

69 Little, Anthony C., Benedict C. Jones, and Robert P. Burriss. "Preferences for masculinity in male bodies change across the menstrual cycle." *Hormones and Behavior* 51, no. 5 (2007): 637; O'Connor, Jillian J.M., David R. Feinberg, Paul J. Fraccaro, Diana J. Borak, Cara C. Tigue, Daniel E. Re, Benedict C. Jones, Anthony C. Little, and Bernard Tiddeman. "Female preferences for male vocal and facial masculinity in videos." *Ethology* 118, no. 4 (2012): 321–330; Little, Anthony C., Benedict C. Jones, D. Michael Burt, and David I. Perrett. "Preferences for symmetry in faces change across the menstrual cycle." *Biological Psychology* 76, no. 3 (2007): 209–216; Debruine, LM., B.C. Jones, D.A. Frederick, M.G. Haselton, I.S. Penton-Voak, and D.I. Perrett. "Evidence for menstrual cycle shifts in women's preferences for masculinity: a response to Harris (in press) 'menstrual cycle and facial preferences reconsidered.'" *Evolutionary Psychology* 8, no. 4 (2010): 768–775; Little, Anthony C., Robert P. Burriss, Marion Petrie, Benedict C. Jones, and S. Craig Roberts. "Oral contraceptive use in women changes preferences for male facial masculinity and is associated with partner facial masculinity." *Psychoneuroendocrinology* 38, no. 9 (2013): 1777–1785; Peterson, Ashley, Rachael Carmen, and Glenn Geher. "Ovulatory shifts in mating intelligence." *Journal of Social, Evolutionary, and Cultural Psychology* 7, no. 1 (2013): 66.

70 Ober, C., S. Elias, D.D. Kostyu, and W.W. Hauck. "Decreased fecundability in Hutterite couples sharing HLA-DR." *American Journal of Human Genetics* 50, no. 1 (1992): 9–13.

71 Ober, Carole, Terry Hyslop, Sherman Elias, Lowell R. Weitkamp, and Walter W. Hauck. "Human leukocyte antigen matching and fetal loss: results of a 10 year prospective study." *Human Reproduction* 13, no. 1 (1998): 35–37; Beydoun, H., and A.F. Saftlas. "Association of human leucocyte antigen sharing with recurrent spontaneous abortions." *Tissue Antigens* 65, no. 2 (2005): 123–35.

72 Alvergne, Alexandra, and Virpi Lummaa. "Does the contraceptive pill alter mate choice in humans?" *Trends in Ecology & Evolution* 25, no. 3 (2010): 2–4; Kuukasjärvi, Seppo, C.J. Peter Eriksson, Esa Koskela, Tapio Mappes, Kari Nissinen, and Markus J. Rantala. "Attractiveness of women's body odors over the menstrual cycle: the role of oral contraceptives and receiver sex." *Behavioral Ecology* 15, no. 4 (2004): 579–584; Puts, David A., Drew H. Bailey, Rodrigo A. Cárdenas, Robert P. Burriss, Lisa LM. Welling, John R. Wheatley, and Khytam Dawood. "Women's attractiveness changes with estradiol and progesterone across the ovulatory cycle." *Hormones and Behavior* 63, no. 1 (2013): 13–19.

73 Rosvall, Kimberly A. "Intrasexual competition in females: evidence for sexual selection?" *Behavioral Ecology* (2011): arr106; Cobey, Kelly D., Christine Klipping, and Abraham P. Buunk. "Hormonal contraceptive use lowers female intrasexual competition in pair-bonded women." *Evolution and Human Behavior* 34, no. 4 (2013): 294–298.

74 Miller, Geoffrey, Joshua M. Tybur, and Brent D. Jordan. "Ovulatory cycle effects on tip earnings by lap dancers: economic evidence for human estrus?" *Evolution and Human Behavior* 28, no. 6 (2007): 375–381.

75 Webb, J.L. "Nutritional effects of oral contraceptive use: a review." *The Journal of Reproductive Medicine* 25, no. 4 (1980): 150–156; Shojania, A. Majid. "Oral contraceptives: effect of folate and vitamin B_{12} metabolism." *Canadian Medical Association Journal* 126, no. 3 (1982): 244; Li, X., J. Ran, and H. Rao. "Megaloblastic changes in cervical epithelium associated with oral contraceptives and changes after treatment with folic acid." *Chinese Journal of Obstetrics and Gynecology* 30, no. 7 (1995): 410–413; Albright, F., A.M. Butler, A.O. Hampton, P. Smith, M.B. Dockerty, R.K. Ghormley, R.L.J. Kennedy, and D.G. Pugh. "The pill and folate metabolism." *The BMJ* (1971); Shere, Mahvash, Priya Bapat, Cheri Nickel, Bhushan Kapur, and Gideon Koren. "Association between use of oral contraceptives and folate status: a systematic review and meta-analysis." *Journal of Obstetrics and Gynaecology Canada* 37, no. 5 (2015): 430–438; Bielenberg, J. "Folic acid and vitamin deficiency caused by oral contraceptives." *Medizinische Monatsschrift fur Pharmazeuten* 14, no. 8 (1991): 244–247.

76 Shere, Mahvash, Priya Bapat, Cheri Nickel, Bhushan Kapur, and Gideon Koren. "Association between use of oral contraceptives and folate status: a systematic review and meta-analysis." *Journal of Obstetrics and Gynaecology Canada* 37, no. 5 (2015): 430–438.

77 Ibid.

78 Green, Timothy J., Lisa A. Houghton, Ursula Donovan, Rosalind S. Gibson, and Deborah L. O'Connor. "Oral contraceptives did not affect biochemical folate indexes and homocysteine concentrations in adolescent females." *Journal of the American Dietetic Association* 98, no. 1 (1998): 49–55; McWilson, Stephanie, Brittney N. Bivins, Katelyn A. Russell, and Lynn B. Bailey. "Oral contraceptive use: impact on folate, vitamin B_6, and vitamin B_{12} status." *Nutrition Reviews* 69, no. 10 (2011): 572–583; McArthur, Jennifer O., HoMan Tang, Peter Petocz, and Samir Samman. "Biological variability and Impact of oral contraceptives on vitamins B_6, B_{12} and folate status in women of reproductive age." *Nutrients* 5, no. 9 (2013): 3634–3645; Sütterlin, Marc W., Stefanie S. Bussen, Lorenz Rieger, Johannes Dietl, and Thomas Steck. "Serum folate and Vitamin B_{12} levels in women using modern oral contraceptives (OC) containing 20 µg ethinyl estradiol." *European Journal of Obstetrics & Gynecology and Reproductive Biology* 107, no. 1 (2003): 57–61; Mountifield, J.A. "Serum vitamin B_{12} and folate levels in women taking oral contraceptives." *Canadian Family Physician* 32 (1986): 862–865.

79 Mountifield, J.A. "Serum vitamin B_{12} and folate levels in women taking oral contraceptives." *Canadian Family Physician* 32 (1986): 863; McArthur, Jennifer O., HoMan Tang, Peter Petocz, and Samir Samman. "Biological variability and Impact of oral contraceptives on vitamins B_6, B_{12} and folate status in women of reproductive age." *Nutrients* 5, no. 9 (2013): 3639–3643; Palmery, M., A. Saraceno, A. Vaiarelli, and G. Carlomagno. "Oral contraceptives and changes in nutritional requirements." *European Review for Medical and Pharmacological Sciences* 17, no. 13 (2013): 1804–1813.

80 McArthur, Jennifer O., HoMan Tang, Peter Petocz, and Samir Samman. "Biological variability and Impact of oral contraceptives on vitamins B_6, B_{12} and folate status in women of reproductive age." *Nutrients* 5, no. 9 (2013): 3634–3645;

Sütterlin, Marc W., Stefanie S. Bussen, Lorenz Rieger, Johannes Dietl, and Thomas Steck. "Serum folate and Vitamin B_{12} levels in women using modern oral contraceptives (OC) containing 20 μg ethinyl estradiol." *European Journal of Obstetrics & Gynecology and Reproductive Biology* 107, no. 1 (2003): 57–61; Green, Timothy J., Lisa A. Houghton, Ursula Donovan, Rosalind S. Gibson, and Deborah L. O'Connor. "Oral contraceptives did not affect biochemical folate indexes and homocysteine concentrations in adolescent females." *Journal of the American Dietetic Association* 98, no. 1 (1998): 49–55.

[81] Lassi, Zohra S., and Zulfiqar A. Bhutta. "Clinical utility of folate-containing oral contraceptives." *International Journal of Women's Health* 4 (2012): 185–190; Taylor, Thomas N., Raymond A. Farkouh, Jonathan B. Graham, Antje Colligs, Marion Lindemann, Richard Lynen, and Sean D. Candrilli. "Potential reduction in neural tube defects associated with use of Metafolin-fortified oral contraceptives in the United States." *American Journal of Obstetrics and Gynecology* 205, no. 5 (2011): 460-e1; Holzgreve, Wolfgang, Klaus Pietrzik, Berthold Koletzko, and Christel Eckmann-Scholz. "Adding folate to the contraceptive pill: a new concept for the prevention of neural tube defects." *The Journal of Maternal-Fetal & Neonatal Medicine* 25, no. 9 (2012): 1529–1536; Wiesinger, Herbert, Urte Eydeler, Frank Richard, Dietmar Trummer, Hartmut Blode, Beate Rohde, and Konstanze Diefenbach. "Bioequivalence evaluation of a folate-supplemented oral contraceptive containing ethinylestradiol/drospirenone/levomefolate calcium versus ethinylestradiol/drospirenone and levomefolate calcium alone." *Clinical Drug Investigation* 32, no. 10 (2012): 673–684.

[82] Shere, Mahvash, Priya Bapat, Cheri Nickel, Bhushan Kapur, and Gideon Koren. "Motherisk rounds: the effectiveness of folate-fortified oral contraceptives in maintaining optimal folate levels to protect against neural tube defects: a systematic review." *Journal of Obstetrics and Gynaecology Canada* 37, no. 6 (2015): 527–533.

[83] Leeton, John. "Depression induced by oral contraception and the role of vitamin B_6 in its management." *Australian and New Zealand Journal of Psychiatry* 8, no. 2 (1974): 85–88; Webb, J.L. "Nutritional effects of oral contraceptive use: a review." *The Journal of Reproductive Medicine* 25, no. 4 (1980): 150–156; Rose, D.P., J.E. Leklem, R.R. Brown, and C. Potera. "Effect of oral contraceptives and vitamin B_6 supplements on alanine and glycine metabolism." *The American Journal of Clinical Nutrition* 29, no. 9 (1976): 956–960; Rios-Avila, Luisa, Bonnie Coats, Maria Ralat, Yueh-Yun Chi, Øivind Midttun, Per M. Ueland, Peter W. Stacpoole, and Jesse F. Gregory. "Pyridoxine supplementation does not alter in vivo kinetics of one-carbon metabolism but modifies patterns of one-carbon and tryptophan metabolites in vitamin B_6-insufficient oral contraceptive users." *The American Journal of Clinical Nutrition* 102, no. 3 (2015): 616–625.

[84] Ibid; Palmery, M., A. Saraceno, A. Vaiarelli, and G. Carlomagno. "Oral contraceptives and changes in nutritional requirements." *European Review for Medical and Pharmacological Sciences* 17, no. 13 (2013): 1805–1808.

[85] Akinloye, O., T.O. Adebayo, O.O. Oguntibeju, D.P. Oparinde, and E.O. Ogunyemi. "Effects of contraceptives on serum trace elements, calcium and phosphorus levels." *West Indian Medical Journal* 60, no. 3 (2011): 308–315; Dante, Giulia, Alberto Vaiarelli, and Fabio Facchinetti. "Vitamin and mineral needs during the oral contraceptive therapy: a systematic review." *International Journal of Reproduction, Contraception, Obstetrics and Gynecology* 3, no. 1 (2016): 1–10; Hess, Frances M., Janet C. King, and Sheldon Margen. "Zinc excretion in young women on low zinc intakes and oral contraceptive agents." *The Journal of Nutrition* 107, no. 9 (1977): 1610–1620.

[86] Palmery, M., A. Saraceno, A. Vaiarelli, and G. Carlomagno. "Oral contraceptives and changes in nutritional requirements." *European Review for Medical and Pharmacological Sciences* 17, no. 13 (2013): 1808–1810; Webb, J.L. "Nutritional effects of oral contraceptive use: a review." *The Journal of Reproductive Medicine* 25, no. 4 (1980): 150–156.

[87] Akinloye, O., T.O. Adebayo, O.O. Oguntibeju, D.P. Oparinde, and E.O. Ogunyemi. "Effects of contraceptives on serum trace elements, calcium and phosphorus levels." *West Indian Medical Journal* 60, no. 3 (2011): 310–315.

[88] Hendrickson-Jack, Lisa. "FFP 203 | The Pill Problem | Ross Pelton." *Fertility Friday Podcast.* Podcast Audio, June 1, 2018. fertilityfriday.com/203

[89] International Collaboration of Epidemiological Studies of Cervical Cancer. "Cervical cancer and hormonal contraceptives: collaborative reanalysis of individual data for 16 573 women with cervical cancer and 35 509 women without cervical cancer from 24 epidemiological studies." *The Lancet* 370, no. 9599 (2007): 1609–1621; Smith, Jennifer S., Jane Green, Amy Berrington De Gonzalez, Paul Appleby, Julian Peto, Martyn Plummer, Silvia Franceschi, and Valerie Beral. "Cervical cancer and use of hormonal contraceptives: a systematic review." *The Lancet* 361, no. 9364 (2003): 1159–1167; Madeleine, Margaret M., Janet R. Daling, Stephen M. Schwartz, Katherine Shera, Barbara McKnight, Joseph J. Carter, Gregory C. Wipf. "Human papillomavirus and long-term oral contraceptive use increase the risk of adenocarcinoma in situ of the cervix." *Cancer Epidemiology and Prevention Biomarkers* 10, no. 3 (2001): 171–177.

[90] Hendrickson-Jack, Lisa. "FFP 095 | Cervical Cancer & The Pill | Menstrual Suppression | Cervical Dysplasia | Abnormal Pap | No More Periods? The Blessings of the Curse | Dr. Susan Rako." *Fertility Friday Podcast.* Podcast Audio, September 9, 2016. fertilityfriday.com/95

[91] Braaten, Kari P., and Marc R. Laufer. "Human papillomavirus (HPV), HPV-related disease, and the HPV vaccine." *Reviews in Obstetrics and Gynecology* 1, no. 1 (2008): 2–10; Centers for Disease Control and Prevention. *Genital HPV Infection Fact Sheet.* (2004). Rockville, MD: CDC National Prevention Information Network.

[92] Marks, Morgan, Patti E. Gravitt, Swati B. Gupta, Kai-Li Liaw, Amha Tadesse, Esther Kim, Chailert Phongnarisorn et al. "Combined oral contraceptive use increases HPV persistence but not new HPV detection in a cohort of women from Thailand." *Journal of Infectious Diseases* (2011): 1509.

[93] Beral, Valerie, Carol Hermon, Clifford Kay, Philip Hannaford, Sarah Darby, and Gillian Reeves. "Mortality associated with oral contraceptive use: 25 year follow up of cohort of 46 000 women from Royal College of General Practitioners' oral contraception study." *The BMJ* 318, no. 7176 (1999): 96–100.

[94] Piyathilake, Chandrika J., Olga L. Henao, Maurizio Macaluso, Phillip E. Cornwell, Sreelatha Meleth, Douglas C. Heimburger, and Edward E. Partridge. "Folate is associated with the natural history of high-risk human papillomaviruses." *Cancer Research* 64, no. 23 (2004): 8788–8793; Piyathilake, Chandrika J., Maurizio Macaluso, Ilene Brill, Douglas C. Heimburger, and Edward E. Partridge. "Lower red blood cell folate enhances the HPV-16–associated risk of cervical intraepithelial neoplasia." *Nutrition* 23, no. 3 (2007): 203–210; Zhao, W., M. Hao, Y. Wang, N. Feng, Z. Wang, W. Wang,

J. Wang, and L. Ding. "Association between folate status and cervical intraepithelial neoplasia." *European Journal of Clinical Nutrition* (2016); Jia, W.L., L. Ding, Z.Y. Ren, T.T. Wu, W.M. Zhao, S.L. Fan, and J.T. Wang. "Effects of both folic acid, p16 protein expression and their interaction on progression of cervical cancerization." *Chinese Journal of Epidemiology* 37, no. 12 (2016): 1647–1652; Hao, Min, Weihong Zhao, Lili Zhang, Honghong Wang, and Xin Yang. "Low folate levels are associated with methylation-mediated transcriptional repression of miR-203 and miR-375 during cervical carcinogenesis." *Oncology Letters* 11, no. 6 (2016): 3863–3869; Li, Q.L., L. Ding, J. Nan, C.L. Liu, Z.K. Yang, F. Chen, Y.L. Liang, and J.T. Wang. "Relationship and interaction between folate and expression of methyl-CpG-binding protein 2 in cervical cancerization." *Chinese Journal of Epidemiology* 37, no. 7 (2016): 985–991; Bai, Li-Xia, Jin-Tao Wang, Ling Ding, Shi-Wen Jiang, Hui-Jie Kang, Chen-Fei Gao, Xiao Chen, Chen Chen, and Qin Zhou. "Folate deficiency and FHIT hypermethylation and HPV 16 infection promote cervical cancerization." *Asian Pacific Journal of Cancer Prevention* 15, no. 21 (2014): 9313–9317.

95 Iversen, Lisa, Selvaraj Sivasubramaniam, Amanda J. Lee, Shona Fielding, and Philip C. Hannaford. "Lifetime cancer risk and combined oral contraceptives: the Royal College of General Practitioners' Oral Contraception Study." *American Journal of Obstetrics and Gynecology* 216, no. 6 (2017): 580-e1; Cogliano, Vincent, Yann Grosse, Robert Baan, Kurt Straif, Béatrice Secretan, and Fatiha El Ghissassi. "Carcinogenicity of combined oestrogen-progestagen contraceptives and menopausal treatment." *The Lancet Oncology* 6, no. 8 (2005): 552–553; Urban, Margaret, Emily Banks, Sam Egger, Karen Canfell, Dianne O'Connell, Valerie Beral, and Freddy Sitas. "Injectable and oral contraceptive use and cancers of the breast, cervix, ovary, and endometrium in black South African women: case–control study." *PLOS Medicine* 9, no. 3 (2012): e1001182: 1–11; Forman, D., T.J. Vincent, and R. Doll. "Cancer of the liver and the use of oral contraceptives." *The BMJ (Clinical Research Edition)* 292, no. 6532 (1986): 1357–1361; Henderson, B.E., S. Preston-Martin, H.A. Edmondson, R.L. Peters, and M.C. Pike. "Hepatocellular carcinoma and oral contraceptives." *British Journal of Cancer* 48, no. 3 (1983): 437; Bassuk, Shari S., and JoAnn E. Manson. "Oral contraceptives and menopausal hormone therapy: relative and attributable risks of cardiovascular disease, cancer, and other health outcomes." *Annals of Epidemiology* 25, no. 3 (2015): 193–200.

96 Gierisch, Jennifer M., Remy R. Coeytaux, Rachel Peragallo Urrutia, Laura J. Havrilesky, Patricia G. Moorman, William J. Lowery, Michaela Dinan et al. "Oral contraceptive use and risk of breast, cervical, colorectal, and endometrial cancers: a systematic review." *Cancer Epidemiology and Prevention Biomarkers* (2013): 1931–1943; Bassuk, Shari S., and JoAnn E. Manson. "Oral contraceptives and menopausal hormone therapy: relative and attributable risks of cardiovascular disease, cancer, and other health outcomes." *Annals of Epidemiology* 25, no. 3 (2015): 193–200; Fernandez, E., C. La Vecchia, A. Balducci, L. Chatenoud, S. Franceschi, and E. Negri. "Oral contraceptives and colorectal cancer risk: a meta-analysis." *British Journal of Cancer* 84, no. 5 (2001): 722–727; Bosetti, Cristina, Francesca Bravi, Eva Negri, and Carlo La Vecchia. "Oral contraceptives and colorectal cancer risk: a systematic review and meta-analysis." *Human Reproduction Update* 15, no. 5 (2009): 489–498.

97 Urban, Margaret, Emily Banks, Sam Egger, Karen Canfell, Dianne O'Connell, Valerie Beral, and Freddy Sitas. "Injectable and oral contraceptive use and cancers of the breast, cervix, ovary, and endometrium in black South African women: case-control study." *PLOS Medicine* 9, no. 3 (2012): 9; Iversen, Lisa, Selvaraj Sivasubramaniam, Amanda J. Lee, Shona Fielding, and Philip C. Hannaford. "Lifetime cancer risk and combined oral contraceptives: the Royal College of General Practitioners' Oral Contraception Study." *American Journal of Obstetrics and Gynecology* (2017); Grevers, Xin, Anne Grundy, Abbey E. Poirier, Farah Khandwala, Matthew Feldman, Christine M. Friedenreich, and Darren R. Brenner. "Cancer incidence attributable to the use of oral contraceptives and hormone therapy in Alberta in 2012." *CMAJ Open* 4, no. 4 (2016): E757–E759.

98 Cogliano, Vincent, Yann Grosse, Robert Baan, Kurt Straif, Béatrice Secretan, and Fatiha El Ghissassi. "Carcinogenicity of combined oestrogen-progestagen contraceptives and menopausal treatment." *The Lancet Oncology* 6, no. 8 (2005): 553.

99 Franceschi, Silvia. (2005) "The IARC commitment to cancer prevention: the example of papillomavirus and cervical cancer." *Tumor Prevention and Genetics III*. Springer Berlin Heidelberg, 277–297.

100 Ibid.

101 Ibid, 283.

102 Beral, Valerie, Carol Hermon, Clifford Kay, Philip Hannaford, Sarah Darby, and Gillian Reeves. "Mortality associated with oral contraceptive use: 25 year follow up of cohort of 46 000 women from Royal College of General Practitioners' oral contraception study." *The BMJ* 318, no. 7176 (1999): 99.

103 Maletzky, Barry M., Arthur Tolan, and Bentson McFarland. "The Oregon depo-provera program: a five-year follow-up." *Sexual Abuse: A Journal of Research and Treatment* 18, no. 3 (2006): 303–316; Prentky, Robert A. "Arousal reduction in sexual offenders: A review of antiandrogen interventions." *Sexual Abuse: A Journal of Research and Treatment* 9, no. 4 (1997): 335–347; Lee, Joo Yong, and Kang Su Cho. "Chemical castration for sexual offenders: physicians' views." *Journal of Korean Medical Science* 28, no. 2 (2013): 171–17; Scott, Charles L., and Trent Holmberg. "Castration of sex offenders: prisoners' rights versus public safety." *Journal of the American Academy of Psychiatry and the Law* 31 (2003): 502–509.

Chapter 8

1 Nilsson, Carl Gustaf, Pekka Lähteenmäki, and Tapani Luukkainen. "Levonorgestrel plasma concentrations and hormone profiles after insertion and after one year of treatment with a levonorgestrel-IUD." *Contraception* 21, no. 3 (1980): 225–233; Xiao, Bilian, Tao Zeng, Shangchun Wu, Hongzhu Sun, and Na Xiao. "Effect of levonorgestrel-releasing intrauterine device on hormonal profile and menstrual pattern after long-term use." *Contraception* 51, no. 6 (1995): 359–365; Jeppsson, S., and E.D.B. Johansson. "Medroxyprogesterone acetate, estradiol, FSH and LH in peripheral blood after intramuscular administration of Depo-Provera to women." *Contraception* 14, no. 4 (1976): 461–469; Duijkers, Ingrid J.M., Doris Heger-Mahn, Dominique Drouin, and Sven Skouby. "A randomised study comparing the effect on ovarian activity

of a progestogen-only pill (POP) containing desogestrel and a new POP containing drospirenone in a 24/4 regimen." *The European Journal of Contraception & Reproductive Health Care* 20, no. 6 (2015): 419–427; Lakha, F., P.C. Ho, Z.M. Van der Spuy, K. Dada, R. Elton, A.F. Glasier, H.O.D. Critchley, A.R.W. Williams, and D.T. Baird. "A novel estrogen-free oral contraceptive pill for women: multicentre, double-blind, randomized controlled trial of mifepristone and progestogen-only pill (levonorgestrel)." *Human Reproduction* 22, no. 9 (2007): 2428–2436.

[2] Nassaralla, Claudia L., Joseph B. Stanford, K. Diane Daly, Mary Schneider, Karen C. Schliep, and Richard J. Fehring. "Characteristics of the menstrual cycle after discontinuation of oral contraceptives." *Journal of Women's Health* 20, no. 2 (2011): 169–177; Jukic, Anne Marie Zaura, Clarice R. Weinberg, Donna D. Baird, and Allen J. Wilcox. "Lifestyle and reproductive factors associated with follicular phase length." *Journal of Women's Health* 16, no. 9 (2007): 1340–1347; Larsson-Cohn, Ulf. "The length of the first three menstrual cycles after combined oral contraceptive treatment." *Acta Obstetricia et Gynecologica Scandinavica* 48, no. 3 (1969): 416–422.

[3] Gnoth, Christian, P. Frank-Herrmann, A. Schmoll, E. Godehardt, and G. Freundl. "Cycle characteristics after discontinuation of oral contraceptives." *Gynecological Endocrinology* 16, no. 4 (2002): 311–313.

[4] Jacobs, H.S., U.A. Knuth, M.G. Hull, and S. Franks. "'Post-pill' amenorrhoea — cause or coincidence?" *The BMJ* 2, no. 6092 (1977): 940–942; Steele, S.J., Bridgett Mason, and Ann Brett. "Amenorrhoea after discontinuing combined oestrogen-progestogen oral contraceptives." *The BMJ* 4, no. 5888 (1973): 343; Rojas-Walsson, R., and R. Cardoso. "Diagnosis and management of post-pill amenorrhea." *The Journal of Family Practice* 13, no. 2 (1981): 165–169.

[5] Larsson-Cohn, Ulf. "The length of the first three menstrual cycles after combined oral contraceptive treatment." *Acta Obstetricia et Gynecologica Scandinavica* 48, no. 3 (1969): 416–422.

[6] Ibid.

[7] Kushnir, Vitaly A., David H. Barad, and Norbert Gleicher. "Ovarian reserve screening before contraception?" *Reproductive Biomedicine Online* 29, no. 5 (2014): 527–529.

[8] Steele, S.J., Bridgett Mason, and Ann Brett. "Amenorrhoea after discontinuing combined oestrogen-progestogen oral contraceptives." *The BMJ* 4, no. 5888 (1973): 343.

[9] Ibid.

[10] Deb, S., B.K. Campbell, C. Pincott-Allen, J.S. Clewes, G. Cumberpatch, and N.J. Raine-Fenning. "Quantifying effect of combined oral contraceptive pill on functional ovarian reserve as measured by serum anti-Müllerian hormone and small antral follicle count using three-dimensional ultrasound." *Ultrasound in Obstetrics & Gynecology* 39, no. 5 (2012): 574–580; Bentzen, J G., Julie Lyng Forman, Anja Pinborg, Ø. Lidegaard, E.C. Larsen, L. Friis-Hansen, Trine Holm Johannsen, and A. Nyboe Andersen. "Ovarian reserve parameters: a comparison between users and non-users of hormonal contraception." *Reproductive Biomedicine Online* 25, no. 6 (2012): 612–619; D'Arpe, Stella, Mara Di Feliciantonio, Miriam Candelieri, Silvia Franceschetti, Maria Grazia Piccioni, and Carlo Bastianelli. "Ovarian function during hormonal contraception assessed by endocrine and sonographic markers: a systematic review." *Reproductive Biomedicine Online* 33, no. 4 (2016): 436–448; Birch Petersen, K., H.W. Hvidman, J.L. Forman, A. Pinborg, E.C. Larsen, K.T. Macklon, R. Sylvest, and A. Nyboe Andersen. "Ovarian reserve assessment in users of oral contraception seeking fertility advice on their reproductive lifespan." *Human Reproduction* 30, no. 10 (2015): 2364–2375; Christensen, Jeanette T., Jesper Boldsen, and Jes G. Westergaard. "Ovarian volume in gynecologically healthy women using no contraception, or using IUD or oral contraception." *Acta Obstetricia et Gynecologica Scandinavica* 76, no. 8 (1997): 784–789.

[11] Birch Petersen, K., H.W. Hvidman, J.L. Forman, A. Pinborg, E.C. Larsen, K.T. Macklon, R. Sylvest, and A. Nyboe Andersen. "Ovarian reserve assessment in users of oral contraception seeking fertility advice on their reproductive lifespan." *Human Reproduction* 30, no. 10 (2015): 2364–2375.

[12] Deb, S., B.K. Campbell, C. Pincott-Allen, J.S. Clewes, G. Cumberpatch, and N.J. Raine-Fenning. "Quantifying effect of combined oral contraceptive pill on functional ovarian reserve as measured by serum anti-Müllerian hormone and small antral follicle count using three-dimensional ultrasound." *Ultrasound in Obstetrics & Gynecology* 39, no. 5 (2012): 574–580.

[13] Wu, Cheng-Hsuan, Yu-Ching Chen, Hsin-Hung Wu, Jyuer-Ger Yang, Yu-Jun Chang, and Horng-Der Tsai. "Serum anti-Müllerian hormone predicts ovarian response and cycle outcome in IVF patients." *Journal of Assisted Reproduction and Genetics* 26, no. 7 (2009): 383–389.

[14] Bentzen, J.G., Julie Lyng Forman, Anja Pinborg, Ø. Lidegaard, E.C. Larsen, L. Friis-Hansen, Trine Holm Johannsen, and A. Nyboe Andersen. "Ovarian reserve parameters: a comparison between users and non-users of hormonal contraception." *Reproductive Biomedicine Online* 25, no. 6 (2012): 612–619; Deb, S., B.K. Campbell, C. Pincott-Allen, J.S. Clewes, G. Cumberpatch, and N.J. Raine-Fenning. "Quantifying effect of combined oral contraceptive pill on functional ovarian reserve as measured by serum anti-Müllerian hormone and small antral follicle count using three-dimensional ultrasound." *Ultrasound in Obstetrics & Gynecology* 39, no. 5 (2012): 574–580; Birch Petersen, K., H.W. Hvidman, J.L. Forman, A. Pinborg, E.C. Larsen, K.T. Macklon, R. Sylvest, and A. Nyboe Andersen. "Ovarian reserve assessment in users of oral contraception seeking fertility advice on their reproductive lifespan." *Human Reproduction* 30, no. 10 (2015): 2364–2375.

[15] Ibid.

[16] Letourneau, Joseph M., Hakan Cakmak, Molly Quinn, Nikita Sinha, Marcelle I. Cedars, and Mitchell P. Rosen. "Long-term hormonal contraceptive use is associated with a reversible suppression of antral follicle count and a break from hormonal contraception may improve oocyte yield." *Journal of Assisted Reproduction and Genetics* 34, no. 9 (2017): 1137–1144.

[17] Barnhart, Kurt T., and Courtney A. Schreiber. "Return to fertility following discontinuation of oral contraceptives." *Fertility and Sterility* 91, no. 3 (2009): 659–663; Mikkelsen, Ellen M., Anders H. Riis, Lauren A. Wise, Elizabeth E. Hatch, Kenneth J. Rothman, and Henrik Toft Sørensen. "Pre-gravid oral contraceptive use and time to pregnancy: a Danish prospective cohort study." *Human Reproduction* 28, no. 5 (2013): 1398–1405; Bracken, Michael B., Karen G. Hellenbrand, and Theodore R. Holford. "Conception delay after oral contraceptive use: the effect of estrogen dose."

Fertility and Sterility 53, no. 1 (1990): 21–27; Linn, S., S.C. Schoenbaum, R.R. Monson, B. Rosner, and K.J. Ryan. "Delay in conception for former 'pill' users." *JAMA* 247, no. 5 (1982): 629; Doll, Helen, Martin Vessey, and Rosemary Painter. "Return of fertility in nulliparous women after discontinuation of the intrauterine device: comparison with women discontinuing other methods of contraception." *BJOG: An International Journal of Obstetrics and Gynaecology* 108, no. 3 (2001): 304–314.

[18] Hassan, M A.M., and S.R. Killick. "Is previous use of hormonal contraception associated with a detrimental effect on subsequent fecundity?" *Human Reproduction* 19, no. 2 (2004): 344–351.

[19] Ibid.

[20] Bracken, Michael B., Karen G. Hellenbrand, and Theodore R. Holford. "Conception delay after oral contraceptive use: the effect of estrogen dose." *Fertility and Sterility* 53, no. 1 (1990): 25.

[21] Linn, Shai, Stephen C. Schoenbaum, Richard R. Monson, Bernard Rosner, and Kenneth J. Ryan. "Delay in conception for former 'pill' users." *JAMA* 247, no. 5 (1982): 629–632.

[22] Berg, J.M., J.L. Tymoczko, and L. Stryer. (2002). *Biochemistry*, 5th edition. Section 26.4, Important Derivatives of Cholesterol Include Bile Salts and Steroid Hormones. New York, NY: W.H. Freeman.

[23] Suwa, Hiroto, Hiroshi Kishi, Fumiharu Imai, Kohshiro Nakao, Takashi Hirakawa, and Takashi Minegishi. "Retinoic acid enhances progesterone production via the cAMP/PKA signaling pathway in immature rat granulosa cells." *Biochemistry and Biophysics Reports* 8 (2016): 62–67; Talavera, F., and B. P. Chew. "Comparative role of retinol, retinoic acid and β-carotene on progesterone secretion by pig corpus luteum in vitro." *Journal of Reproduction and Fertility* 82, no. 2 (1988): 611–615; Pethes, G., E. Horvath, M. Kulcsar, Gy Huszenicza, Gy Somorjai, B. Varga, and J. Haraszti. "In vitro progesterone production of corpus luteum cells of cows fed low and high levels of beta-carotene." *Transboundary and Emerging Diseases* 32, no. 1–10 (1985): 289–296; Mumford, Sunni L, Richard W. Browne, Karen C. Schliep, Jonathan Schmelzer, Torie C. Plowden, Kara A. Michels, Lindsey A. Sjaarda et al. "Serum antioxidants are associated with serum reproductive hormones and ovulation among healthy women–3." *The Journal of Nutrition* 146, no. 1 (2015): 98–106; Byrd, J.A., S.L. Pardue, and B.M. Hargis. "Effect of ascorbate on luteinizing hormone stimulated progesterone biosynthesis in chicken granulosa cells in vitro." *Comparative Biochemistry and Physiology — Part A: Physiology* 104, no. 2 (1993): 279–281; Miszkiel, Grazyna, Dariusz Skarzynski, Marek Bogacki, and Jan Kotwica. "Concentrations of catecholamines, ascorbic acid, progesterone and oxytocin in the corpora lutea of cyclic and pregnant cattle." *Reproduction Nutrition Development* 39, no. 4 (1999): 509–516; Soheila, S., K. Faezeh, S. Kourosh, S. Fatemeh, N. Nasrollah, G. Mahin, M. Asadi-Samani, and M. Bahmani. "Effects of vitamin B6 on premenstrual syndrome: A systematic review and meta-Analysis." *Journal of Chemical and Pharmaceutical Sciences* 9, no. 3 (2016): 1346–1353; Doll, H., S. Brown, A. Thurston, and M. Vessey. "Pyridoxine (vitamin B6) and the premenstrual syndrome: a randomized crossover trial." *The Journal of the Royal College of General Practitioners* 39, no. 326 (1989): 364; Williams, Melanie J., Raymond I. Harris, and Bernard C. Dean. "Controlled trial of pyridoxine in the premenstrual syndrome." *Journal of International Medical Research* 13, no. 3 (1985): 174–179; Parikh, G., M. Varadinova, P. Suwandhi, T. Araki, Z. Rosenwaks, L. Poretsky, and D. Seto-Young. "Vitamin D regulates steroidogenesis and insulin-like growth factor binding protein-1 (IGFBP-1) production in human ovarian cells." *Hormone and Metabolic Research* 42, no. 10 (2010): 754–757.

[24] Data adapted from nutritiondata.self.com.

[25] Kuhl, H., G. Gahn, G. Romberg, P.-H. Althoff, and H.-D. Taubert. "A randomized cross-over comparison of two low-dose oral contraceptives upon hormonal and metabolic serum parameters: II. Effects upon thyroid function, gastrin, STH, and glucose tolerance." *Contraception* 32, no. 1 (1985): 97–107; Weeke, Jørgen, and Aage Prange Hansen. "Serum TSH and serum T_3 levels during normal menstrual cycles and during cycles on oral contraceptives." *Acta Endocrinologica* 79, no. 3 (1975): 431–438.

[26] Arthur, John R., Fergus Nicol, and Geoffrey J. Beckett. "Selenium deficiency, thyroid hormone metabolism, and thyroid hormone deiodinases." *The American Journal of Clinical Nutrition* 57, no. 2 (1993): 236S–239S; Mahmoodianfard, Salma, Mohammadreza Vafa, Fatemeh Golgiri, Mohsen Khoshniat, Mahmoodreza Gohari, Zahra Solati, and Mahmood Djalali. "Effects of zinc and selenium supplementation on thyroid function in overweight and obese hypothyroid female patients: a randomized double-blind controlled trial." *Journal of the American College of Nutrition* 34, no. 5 (2015): 391–399; Maxwell, Christy, and Stella Lucia Volpe. "Effect of zinc supplementation on thyroid hormone function." *Annals of Nutrition and Metabolism* 51, no. 2 (2007): 188–194.

[27] Khalili, Hamed, Leslie M. Higuchi, Ashwin N. Ananthakrishnan, James M. Richter, Diane Feskanich, Charles C. Fuchs, and Andrew T. Chan. "Oral contraceptives, reproductive factors and risk of inflammatory bowel disease." *Gut* (2012): gutjnl-2012; Cornish, Julie A., Emile Tan, Constantinos Simillis, Susan K. Clark, Julian Teare, and Paris P. Tekkis. "The risk of oral contraceptives in the etiology of inflammatory bowel disease: a meta-analysis." *The American Journal of Gastroenterology* 103, no. 9 (2008): 2394–2400.

[28] Looijer-van Langen, Mirjam, Naomi Hotte, Levinus A. Dieleman, Eric Albert, Chris Mulder, and Karen L. Madsen. "Estrogen receptor-β signaling modulates epithelial barrier function." *American Journal of Physiology: Gastrointestinal and Liver Physiology* 300, no. 4 (2011): G621–G626; Braniste, Viorica, Aurore Jouault, Eric Gaultier, Arnaud Polizzi, Claire Buisson-Brenac, Mathilde Leveque, Pascal G. Martin, Vassilia Theodorou, Jean Fioramonti, and Eric Houdeau. "Impact of oral bisphenol A at reference doses on intestinal barrier function and sex differences after perinatal exposure in rats." *Proceedings of the National Academy of Sciences* 107, no. 1 (2010): 448–453.

[29] Rezk, Mohamed, Tarek Sayyed, Alaa Masood, and Ragab Dawood. "Risk of bacterial vaginosis, Trichomonas vaginalis and Candida albicans infection among new users of combined hormonal contraception vs LNG-IUS." *The European Journal of Contraception & Reproductive Health Care* 22, no. 5 (2017): 344–348.

[30] Scaldaferri, Franco, Loris Riccardo Lopetuso, Valentina Petito, Valerio Cufino, Mirna Bilotta, Vincenzo Arena, Egidio Stigliano et al. "Gelatin tannate ameliorates acute colitis in mice by reinforcing mucus layer and modulating gut microbiota composition: Emerging role for 'gut barrier protectors' in IBD?" *United European Gastroenterology Journal* 2,

no. 2 (2014): 113–122; Li, Wei, Kaiji Sun, Yun Ji, Zhenlong Wu, Weiwei Wang, Zhaolai Dai, and Guoyao Wu. "Glycine regulates expression and distribution of claudin-7 and ZO-3 proteins in intestinal porcine epithelial cells." *The Journal of Nutrition* 146, no. 5 (2016): 964–969.

31 "How Does the Liver Work?" National Center for Biotechnology Information. Accessed April 13, 2017. www.ncbi.nlm.nih.gov/pubmedhealth/PMH0072577

32 "How the Liver Works." How the Liver Works – Liver Functions | Canadian Liver Foundation. Accessed April 13, 2017. www.liver.ca/liver-health/how-liver-works.aspx

33 Michnovicz, Jon J., Herman Adlercreutz, and H. Leon Bradlow. "Changes in levels of urinary estrogen metabolites after oral indole-3-carbinol treatment in humans." *Journal of the National Cancer Institute* 89, no. 10 (1997): 718–723.

34 Thomson, Cynthia A., Emily Ho, and Meghan B. Strom. "Chemopreventive properties of 3, 3'-diindolylmethane in breast cancer: evidence from experimental and human studies." *Nutrition Reviews* 74, no. 7 (2016): 432–443.

Chapter 9

1 Hendrickson-Jack, Lisa. "FFP 173 | Reclaiming Menstruation | The Wisdom and Power of Your Menstrual Cycle | Lara Owen." *Fertility Friday Podcast.* Podcast Audio, December 15, 2017. fertilityfriday.com/173

2 Hendrickson-Jack, Lisa. "FFP 150 | Harnessing the Power of Your Menstrual Cycle | Wild Power | Alexandra Pope & Sjanie Hugo Wurlitzer." *Fertility Friday Podcast.* Podcast Audio, August 2, 2017. fertilityfriday.com/150

3 Ibid.

4 Ibid.

5 Government of Canada Statistics. "Women in Canada: A Gender-based Statistical Report — Women and Paid Work." Accessed February 3, 2018. www.statcan.gc.ca/pub/89-503-x/2015001/article/14694-eng.htm

6 Hendrickson-Jack, Lisa. "FFP 071 | Connecting with the Wisdom of Your Menstrual Cycle | Fertility Massage Therapy | Clare Blake." *Fertility Friday Podcast.* Podcast Audio, April 1, 2016. fertilityfriday.com/71

7 Ibid.

8 Pope, Alexandra, and Sjanie Hugo Wurlitzer. (2017). *Wild Power: Discover the Magic of Your Menstrual Cycle and Awaken the Feminine Path to Power.* London: Hay House, 51.

9 Hendrickson-Jack, Lisa. "FFP 150 | Harnessing the Power of Your Menstrual Cycle | Wild Power | Alexandra Pope & Sjanie Hugo Wurlitzer." *Fertility Friday Podcast.* Podcast Audio, August 2, 2017. fertilityfriday.com/150

10 Hampson, Elizabeth. "Estrogen-related variations in human spatial and articulatory-motor skills." *Psychoneuroendocrinology* 15, no. 1 (1990): 97–111; Romans, Sarah E., David Kreindler, Gillian Einstein, Sheila Laredo, Michele J. Petrovic, and James Stanley. "Sleep quality and the menstrual cycle." *Sleep Medicine* 16, no. 4 (2015): 489–495; Krug, Rosemarie, Ursula Stamm, Reinhard Pietrowsky, Horst L. Fehm, and Jan Born. "Effects of menstrual cycle on creativity." *Psychoneuroendocrinology* 19, no. 1 (1994): 21–31.

11 Alvergne, Alexandra, and Virpi Lummaa. "Does the contraceptive pill alter mate choice in humans?" *Trends in Ecology & Evolution* 25, no. 3 (2010): 2–4; Kuukasjärvi, Seppo, C.J. Peter Eriksson, Esa Koskela, Tapio Mappes, Kari Nissinen, and Markus J. Rantala. "Attractiveness of women's body odors over the menstrual cycle: the role of oral contraceptives and receiver sex." *Behavioral Ecology* 15, no. 4 (2004): 579–584; Puts, David A., Drew H. Bailey, Rodrigo A. Cárdenas, Robert P. Burriss, Lisa LM. Welling, John R. Wheatley, and Khytam Dawood. "Women's attractiveness changes with estradiol and progesterone across the ovulatory cycle." *Hormones and Behavior* 63, no. 1 (2013): 13–19.

12 Pope, Alexandra, and Sjanie Hugo Wurlitzer. (2017). *Wild Power: Discover the Magic of Your Menstrual Cycle and Awaken the Feminine Path to Power.* London: Hay House, 51.

13 Owen, Lara. (2008). *Her Blood Is Gold: Awakening to the Wisdom of Menstruation.* Wimborne, UK: Archive Publishing, 55.

Chapter 10

1 Hilgers, Thomas W. (2004). *The Medical & Surgical Practice of NaPro Technology.* Omaha, NE: Pope Paul VI Institute Press, 136–137; Matus, Geraldine. "Justisee Method: Fertility Awareness and Body Literacy: A User's Guide." *Justisee-Healthworks for Women* (2009): 34–35.

2 Frank-Herrmann, P., J. Heil, C. Gnoth, E. Toledo, S. Baur, C. Pyper, E. Jenetzky, T. Strowitzki, and G. Freundl. "The effectiveness of a fertility awareness based method to avoid pregnancy in relation to a couple's sexual behaviour during the fertile time: a prospective longitudinal study." *Human Reproduction* (2007).

3 Hatcher, Robert Anthony, and Anita L. Nelson. *Contraceptive Technology.* Ardent Media, 2007: 337–342; Trussell, James, and Kathryn Kost. "Contraceptive failure in the United States: a critical review of the literature." *Studies in Family Planning* 18, no. 5 (1987): 237–283.

4 Zukerman, Zvi, David B. Weiss, and Raoul Orvieto. "Does preejaculatory penile secretion originating from Cowper's gland contain sperm?" *Journal of Assisted Reproduction and Genetics* 20, no. 4 (2003): 157–159.

5 Ibid; Pudney, Jeffrey, Monica Oneta, Kenneth Mayer, George Seage III, and Deborah Anderson. "Pre-ejaculatory fluid as potential vector for sexual transmission of HIV-1." *The Lancet* 340, no. 8833 (1992): 1470; Ilaria, Gerard, Jonathan L Jacobs, Bruce Polsky, Brian Koll, Penny Baron, Clarinda Maclow, Donald Armstrong, and Peter N Schlegel. "Detection of HIV-1 DNA sequences in pre-ejaculatory fluid." *The Lancet* 340, no. 8833 (1992): 1469;

6 Killick, Stephen R., Christine Leary, James Trussell, and Katherine A. Guthrie. "Sperm content of pre-ejaculatory fluid." *Human Fertility* 14, no. 1 (2011): 48–52.

7 Mauck, Christine K., Vivian Brache, Thomas Kimble, Andrea Thurman, Leila Cochon, Sarah Littlefield, Kim Linton, Gustavo F. Doncel, and Jill L. Schwartz. "A phase I randomized postcoital testing and safety study of the Caya diaphragm used with 3% nonoxynol-9 gel, ContraGel or no gel." *Contraception* 96, no. 2 (2017): 124–130; Chakraborty, Debanjana, Arindam Maity, Tarun Jha, and Nirup Bikash Mondal. "Spermicidal and contraceptive potential of desgalactotigonin: a

prospective alternative of nonoxynol-9." *PloS One* 9, no. 9 (2014): e107164; Stafford, Michael K., Helen Ward, Adrienne Flanagan, Isobel J. Rosenstein, David Taylor-Robinson, J. Richard Smith, Jonathan Weber, and Valerie S. Kitchen. "Safety study of nonoxynol-9 as a vaginal microbicide: evidence of adverse effects." *Journal of Acquired Immune Deficiency Syndromes* 17, no. 4 (1998): 327–331; Niruthisard, Somchai, Ronald E. Roddy, and Supawat Chutivongse. "The effects of frequent nonoxynol-9 use on the vaginal and cervical mucosa." *Sexually Transmitted Diseases* 18, no. 3 (1991): 176–179.

[8] Frank-Herrmann, P., J. Heil, C. Gnoth, E. Toledo, S. Baur, C. Pyper, E. Jenetzky, T. Strowitzki, and G. Freundl. "The effectiveness of a fertility awareness based method to avoid pregnancy in relation to a couple's sexual behaviour during the fertile time: a prospective longitudinal study." *Human Reproduction* (2007).

[9] Guermandi, Ellade, Walter Vegetti, Massimiliano M. Bianchi, Anna Uglietti, Guido Ragni, and Piergiorgio Crosignani. "Reliability of ovulation tests in infertile women." *Obstetrics & Gynecology* 97, no. 1 (2001): 92–96.

[10] Johnson, Sheri L., Jessica Dunleavy, Neil J. Gemmell, and Shinichi Nakagawa. "Consistent age-dependent declines in human semen quality: a systematic review and meta-analysis." *Ageing Research Reviews* 19 (2015): 22–33; Swan, Shanna H., Eric P. Elkin, and Laura Fenster. "The question of declining sperm density revisited: an analysis of 101 studies published 1934-1996." *Environmental Health Perspectives* 108, no. 10 (2000): 961–966.

[11] Carlsen, Elisabeth, Aleksander Giwercman, Niels Keiding, and Niels E. Skakkebaek. "Evidence for decreasing quality of semen during past 50 years." *The BMJ* 305, no. 6854 (1992): 609–613.

[12] Levine, Hagai, Niels Jørgensen, Anderson Martino-Andrade, Jaime Mendiola, Dan Weksler-Derri, Irina Mindlis, Rachel Pinotti, and Shanna H. Swan. "Temporal trends in sperm count: a systematic review and meta-regression analysis." *Human Reproduction Update* 23, no. 6 (2017): 646–659.

[13] Ibid.

[14] Rolland, Matthieu, J.l. Le Moal, V. Wagner, Dominique Royère, and J. De Mouzon. "Decline in semen concentration and morphology in a sample of 26 609 men close to general population between 1989 and 2005 in France." *Human Reproduction* 28, no. 2 (2012): 462–470; Geoffroy-Siraudin, Cendrine, Anderson Dieudonné Loundou, Fanny Romain, Vincent Achard, Blandine Courbiere, Marie-Hélène Perrard, Philippe Durand, and Marie-Roberte Guichaoua. "Decline of semen quality among 10 932 males consulting for couple infertility over a 20-year period in Marseille, France." *Asian Journal of Andrology* 14, no. 4 (2012): 584–590; Chen, Z., K.B. Isaacson, T.L. Toth, L. Godfrey-Bailey, I. Schiff, and R. Hauser. "Temporal trends in human semen parameters in New England in the United States, 1989–2000." *Archives of Andrology* 49, no. 5 (2003): 369–374; Auger, Jacques, Jean Marie Kunstmann, Francoise Czyglik, and Pierre Jouannet. "Decline in semen quality among fertile men in Paris during the past 20 years." *New England Journal of Medicine* 332, no. 5 (1995): 281–285; Huang, Chuan, Baishun Li, Kongrong Xu, Dan Liu, Jing Hu, Yang Yang, Hongchuan Nie, Liqing Fan, and Wenbing Zhu. "Decline in semen quality among 30,636 young Chinese men from 2001 to 2015." *Fertility and Sterility* 107, no. 1 (2017): 83–88; Irvine, Stewart, Elizabeth Cawood, David Richardson, Eileen MacDonald, and John Aitken. "Evidence of deteriorating semen quality in the United Kingdom: birth cohort study in 577 men in Scotland over 11 years." *The BMJ* 312, no. 7029 (1996): 467–471.

[15] Kumar, Naina, and Amit Kant Singh. "Trends of male factor infertility, an important cause of infertility: a review of literature." *Journal of Human Reproductive Sciences* 8, no. 4 (2015): 191–196.

Chapter 11

[1] Viergiver, Ellenmae, and W.T. Pommerenke. "Measurement of the cyclic variations in the quantity of cervical mucus and its correlation with basal temperature." *American Journal of Obstetrics and Gynecology* 48, no. 3 (1944): 321–328.

[2] Odeblad, Erik. "The discovery of different types of cervical mucus and the Billings Ovulation Method." *Bulletin of the Natural Family Planning Council of Victoria* 21, no. 3 (1994): 14; Klaus, Hanna. "Natural family planning: a review." *Obstetrical & Gynecological Survey* 37, no. 2 (1982): 4–6.

[3] Odeblad, Erik. "The discovery of different types of cervical mucus and the Billings Ovulation Method." *Bulletin of the Natural Family Planning Council of Victoria* 21, no. 3 (1994): 14.

[4] Matus, Geraldine Ed. "Atypical Mucus Patterns Accompanying Ovulation." *Justisse HRHP Training Program*. Justisse College. Accessed February 5, 2017. www.justisse.ca/index.php/college/courseware/page/1308

[5] Elkind-Hirsch, Karen E., Kathy Phillips, Sandra M. Bello, Milton McNicho, and Dominique de Ziegler. "Sequential hormonal supplementation with vaginal estradiol and progesterone gel corrects the effect of clomiphene on the endometrium in oligo-ovulatory women." *Human Reproduction* 17, no. 2 (2002): 295; Glud, Eva, Susanne Krüger Kjaer, Rebecca Troisi, and Louise A. Brinton. "Fertility drugs and ovarian cancer." *Epidemiologic Reviews* 20, no. 2 (1998): 238.

[6] Van der Merwe, J.V. "The effect of clomiphene and conjugated oestrogens on cervical mucus." *South African Medical Journal* 60, no. 9 (1981): 347-349; Massai, Maria Rebecca, Dominique de Ziegler, Valerie Lesobre, Christine Bergeron, René Frydman, and Philippe Bouchard. "Clomiphene citrate affects cervical mucus and endometrial morphology independently of the changes in plasma hormonal levels induced by multiple follicular recruitment." *Fertility and Sterility* 59, no. 6 (1993): 1179–1186; Acharya, U., D.S. Irvine, M.P.R. Hamilton, and A.A. Templeton. "The effect of three anti-oestrogen drugs on cervical mucus quality and in-vitro sperm — cervical mucus interaction in ovulatory women." *Human Reproduction* 8, no. 3 (1993): 437–441; Roumen, F.J. "Decreased quality of cervix mucus under the influence of clomiphene: a meta-analysis." *Nederlands Tijdschrift voor Geneeskunde* 141, no. 49 (1997): 2401–2405.

[7] Randall, John M., and Allan Templeton. "Cervical mucus score and in vitro sperm mucus interaction in spontaneous and clomiphene citrate cycles." *Fertility and Sterility* 56, no. 3 (1991): 467–468.

[8] Ibid.

[9] Ibid, 468.

[10] Oktay, Kutluk, Erkan Buyuk, Natalie Libertella, Munire Akar, and Zev Rosenwaks. "Fertility preservation in breast cancer patients: a prospective controlled comparison of ovarian stimulation with tamoxifen and letrozole for embryo cryopreservation." *Journal of Clinical Oncology* 23, no. 19 (2005): 4347–4353; Oktay, K., E. Buyuk, O. Davis, I. Yermakova,

L. Veeck, and Z. Rosenwaks. "Fertility preservation in breast cancer patients: IVF and embryo cryopreservation after ovarian stimulation with tamoxifen." *Human Reproduction* 18, no. 1 (2003): 90–95; Acharya, U., D.S. Irvine, M.P.R. Hamilton, and A.A. Templeton. "The effect of three anti-oestrogen drugs on cervical mucus quality and in-vitro sperm — cervical mucus interaction in ovulatory women." *Human Reproduction* 8, no. 3 (1993): 440.

11 Massai, Maria Rebecca, Dominique de Ziegler, Valerie Lesobre, Christine Bergeron, René Frydman, and Philippe Bouchard. "Clomiphene citrate affects cervical mucus and endometrial morphology independently of the changes in plasma hormonal levels induced by multiple follicular recruitment." *Fertility and Sterility* 59, no. 6 (1993): 1179–1186.

12 Asemi, Zatollah, Zahra Vahedpoor, Mehri Jamilian, Fereshteh Bahmani, and Ahmad Esmaillzadeh. "Effects of long-term folate supplementation on metabolic status and regression of cervical intraepithelial neoplasia: a randomized, double-blind, placebo-controlled trial." *Nutrition* 32, no. 6 (2016): 681–686.

13 International Collaboration of Epidemiological Studies of Cervical Cancer. "Cervical cancer and hormonal contraceptives: collaborative reanalysis of individual data for 16 573 women with cervical cancer and 35 509 women without cervical cancer from 24 epidemiological studies." *The Lancet* 370, no. 9599 (2007): 1609–1621; Smith, Jennifer S., Jane Green, Amy Berrington De Gonzalez, Paul Appleby, Julian Peto, Martyn Plummer, Silvia Franceschi, and Valerie Beral. "Cervical cancer and use of hormonal contraceptives: a systematic review." *The Lancet* 361, no. 9364 (2003): 1159–1167; Madeleine, Margaret M., Janet R. Daling, Stephen M. Schwartz, Katherine Shera, Barbara McKnight, Joseph J. Carter, Gregory C. Wipf. "Human papillomavirus and long-term oral contraceptive use increase the risk of adenocarcinoma in situ of the cervix." *Cancer Epidemiology and Prevention Biomarkers* 10, no. 3 (2001): 171–177.

14 Braaten, Kari P., and Marc R. Laufer. "Human papillomavirus (HPV), HPV-related disease, and the HPV vaccine." *Reviews in Obstetrics and Gynecology* 1, no. 1 (2008): 2–10; Centers for Disease Control and Prevention. Genital HPV Infection Fact Sheet. Rockville, MD: CDC National Prevention Information Network, 2004.

15 Marks, Morgan, Patti E. Gravitt, Swati B. Gupta, Kai-Li Liaw, Amha Tadesse, Esther Kim, Chailert Phongnarisorn. "Combined oral contraceptive use increases HPV persistence but not new HPV detection in a cohort of women from Thailand." *Journal of Infectious Diseases* 204, no. 10 (2011): 1505–1513.

16 Zhao, W., M. Hao, Y. Wang, N. Feng, Z. Wang, W. Wang, J. Wang, and L. Ding. "Association between folate status and cervical intraepithelial neoplasia." *European Journal of Clinical Nutrition* 70, no. 7 (2016): 837–842; Piyathilake, Chandrika J., Maurizio Macaluso, Michelle M. Chambers, Suguna Badiga, Nuzhat R. Siddiqui, Walter C. Bell, Jeffrey C. Edberg, Edward E. Partridge, Ronald D. Alvarez, and Gary L. Johanning. "Folate and vitamin B12 may play a critical role in lowering the HPV 16 methylation–associated risk of developing higher grades of CIN." *Cancer Prevention Research* 7, no. 11 (2014): 1128–1137; Shimizu, H., C. Nagata, S. Komatsu, N. Morita, H. Higashiiwai, N. Sugahara, and S. Hisamichi. "Decreased serum retinol levels in women with cervical dysplasia." *British Journal of Cancer* 73, no. 12 (1996): 1600.

17 Butterworth, C.E., Kenneth D. Hatch, Hazel Gore, Helmut Mueller, and Carlos L. Krumdieck. "Improvement in cervical dysplasia associated with folic acid therapy in users of oral contraceptives." *The American Journal of Clinical Nutrition* 35, no. 1 (1982): 73–82.

18 Ibid.

19 Asemi, Zatollah, Zahra Vahedpoor, Mehri Jamilian, Fereshteh Bahmani, and Ahmad Esmaillzadeh. "Effects of long-term folate supplementation on metabolic status and regression of cervical intraepithelial neoplasia: A randomized, double-blind, placebo-controlled trial." *Nutrition* 32, no. 6 (2016): 681–686.

20 Meyskens, Frank L., and Alberto Manetta. "Prevention of cervical intraepithelial neoplasia and cervical cancer." *The American Journal of Clinical Nutrition* 62, no. 6 (1995): 1417S–1419S.

21 Graham, Vivian, Earl S. Surwit, Sheldon Weiner, and Frank L. Meyskens Jr. "Phase II trial of β-all-trans-retinoic acid for cervical intraepithelial neoplasia delivered via a collagen sponge and cervical cap." *Western Journal of Medicine* 145, no. 2 (1986): 192.

22 Bell, Maria C., Peg Crowley-Nowick, H. Leon Bradlow, Daniel W. Sepkovic, Delf Schmidt-Grimminger, Patti Howell, E. J. Mayeaux, Angela Tucker, Elba A. Turbat-Herrera, and J. Michael Mathis. "Placebo-controlled trial of indole-3-carbinol in the treatment of CIN." *Gynecologic Oncology* 78, no. 2 (2000): 123–129.

23 Odeblad, Erik. "The discovery of different types of cervical mucus and the Billings Ovulation Method." *Bulletin of the Natural Family Planning Council of Victoria* 21, no. 3 (1994): 14.

Chapter 12

1 Health Canada. "Get Your Copy." Accessed August 12, 2018. www.canada.ca/en/health-canada/services/food-nutrition/canada-food-guide/get-your-copy.html#a1

2 Price, Weston A. (2016). *Nutrition and Physical Degeneration*, 8th edition. Lemon Grove, CA: Price-Pottenger Nutrition Foundation, 362.

3 Ibid.

4 Monteiro, C.A. "Nutrition and health. The issue is not food, nor nutrients, so much as processing." *Public Health Nutrition* 12, no. 5 (2009): 729–731.

5 Landers, Timothy F., Bevin Cohen, Thomas E. Wittum, and Elaine L. Larson. "A review of antibiotic use in food animals: perspective, policy, and potential." *Public Health Reports* 127, no. 1 (2012): 4–22; Thomas, Ashley Dawn. "Supplementation of two novel probiotics in the diet of lactating dairy cows." *Iowa State University Digital Repository: Graduate Theses and Dissertations* (2017): 1–41; Donovan, Christine. "If FDA does not regulate food, who will? A study of hormones and antibiotics in meatproduction." *American Journal of Law & Medicine* 41, no. 2–3 (2015): 459–482.

6 Simopoulos, Artemis P. "The importance of the ratio of omega-6/omega-3 essential fatty acids." *Biomedicine & Pharmacotherapy* 56, no. 8 (2002): 365–379.

7 Średnicka-Tober, Dominika, Marcin Barański, Chris J. Seal, Roy Sanderson, Charles Benbrook, Håvard Steinshamn, Joanna Gromadzka-Ostrowska et al. "Higher PUFA and n-3 PUFA, conjugated linoleic acid, α-tocopherol and iron, but

lower iodine and selenium concentrations in organic milk: a systematic literature review and meta-and redundancy analyses." *British Journal of Nutrition* 115, no. 6 (2016): 1043–1060; Daley, Cynthia A., Amber Abbott, Patrick S. Doyle, Glenn A. Nader, and Stephanie Larson. "A review of fatty acid profiles and antioxidant content in grass-fed and grain-fed beef." *Nutrition Journal* 9, no. 1 (2010): 1–12.

[8] Ibid.

[9] Simopoulos, Artemis P. "The importance of the ratio of omega-6/omega-3 essential fatty acids." *Biomedicine & Pharmacotherapy* 56, no. 8 (2002): 365–379; Halis, Gülden, and Aydin Arici. "Endometriosis and inflammation in infertility." *Annals of the New York Academy of Sciences* 1034, no. 1 (2004): 300–315.

[10] Berg, J.M., J.L. Tymoczko, and L. Stryer. (2002). *Biochemistry*, 5th edition. Section 26.4, Important Derivatives of Cholesterol Include Bile Salts and Steroid Hormones. New York: W.H. Freeman; Payne, Anita H., and Dale B. Hales. "Overview of steroidogenic enzymes in the pathway from cholesterol to active steroid hormones." *Endocrine Reviews* 25, no. 6 (2004): 947–970.

[11] Alberts, B., A. Johnson, J. Lewis et al. (2002). *Molecular Biology of the Cell*, 4th edition, The Lipid Bilayer. New York, NY: Garland Science.

[12] Zhang, Juan, and Qiang Liu. "Cholesterol metabolism and homeostasis in the brain." *Protein & Cell* 6, no. 4 (2015): 254–264; Mutka, Aino-Liisa, and Elina Ikonen. "Genetics and molecular biology: brain cholesterol balance—not such a closed circuit after all." *Current Opinion in Lipidology* 21, no. 1 (2010): 93–94.

[13] Data adapted from nutritiondata.self.com

[14] Borel, Patrick, and Charles Desmarchelier. "Genetic variations associated with vitamin A status and vitamin A bioavailability." *Nutrients* 9, no. 3 (2017): 246.

[15] Dimitrov, Nikolay V., C. Meyer, D.E. Ullrey, W. Chenoweth, A. Michelakis, W. Malone, C. Boone, and G. Fink. "Bioavailability of beta-carotene in humans." *The American Journal of Clinical Nutrition* 48, no. 2 (1988): 298–304.

[16] Lin, Yumei, Stephen R. Dueker, Betty J. Burri, Terry R. Neidlinger, and Andrew J. Clifford. "Variability of the conversion of β-carotene to vitamin A in women measured by using a double-tracer study design." *The American Journal of Clinical Nutrition* 71, no. 6 (2000): 1545–1554; Hickenbottom, Sabrina J., Jennifer R. Follett, Yumei Lin, Stephen R. Dueker, Betty J. Burri, Terry R. Neidlinger, and Andrew J. Clifford. "Variability in conversion of β-carotene to vitamin A in men as measured by using a double-tracer study design." *The American Journal of Clinical Nutrition* 75, no. 5 (2002): 900–907.

[17] Troesch, Barbara, Birgit Hoeft, Michael McBurney, Manfred Eggersdorfer, and Peter Weber. "Dietary surveys indicate vitamin intakes below recommendations are common in representative Western countries." *British Journal of Nutrition* 108, no. 04 (2012): 692–698.

[18] Weber, Daniela, and Tilman Grune. "The contribution of β-carotene to vitamin A supply of humans." *Molecular Nutrition & Food Research* 56, no. 2 (2012): 251–258.

[19] Clagett-Dame, Margaret, and Danielle Knutson. "Vitamin A in reproduction and development." *Nutrients* 3, no. 4 (2011): 385–428.

[20] Li, Hui, Krzysztof Palczewski, Wolfgang Baehr, and Margaret Clagett-Dame. "Vitamin A deficiency results in meiotic failure and accumulation of undifferentiated spermatogonia in prepubertal mouse testis." *Biology of Reproduction* 84, no. 2 (2011): 336–341; Thompson, J.N., J. McC. Howell, and G.A.J. Pitt. "Vitamin A and reproduction in rats." *Proceedings of the Royal Society B* 159, no. 976 (1964): 510–535; Lamb, Adrian J., Piyaratana Apiwatanaporn, and James A. Olson. "Induction of rapid, synchronous vitamin A deficiency in the rat." *The Journal of Nutrition* 104, no. 9 (1974): 1140–1148.

[21] Hogarth, Cathryn A., and Michael D. Griswold. "The key role of vitamin A in spermatogenesis." *The Journal of Clinical Investigation* 120, no. 4 (2010): 956–962; Busada, Jonathan T., and Christopher B. Geyer. "The role of retinoic acid (RA) in spermatogonial differentiation." *Biology of Reproduction* 94, no. 1 (2016): 1–10; Chung, S.S.W., and D.J. Wolgemuth. "Role of retinoid signaling in the regulation of spermatogenesis." *Cytogenetic and Genome Research* 105, no. 2–4 (2004): 189–202.

[22] Huang, H.F.S., and W.C. Hembree. "Spermatogenic response to vitamin A in vitamin A deficient rats." *Biology of Reproduction* 21, no. 4 (1979): 891–904.

[23] Ibid.

[24] Hogarth, Cathryn A., John K. Amory, and Michael D. Griswold. "Inhibiting vitamin A metabolism as an approach to male contraception." *Trends in Endocrinology & Metabolism* 22, no. 4 (2011): 136–144.

[25] Clagett-Dame, Margaret, and Danielle Knutson. "Vitamin A in reproduction and development." *Nutrients* 3, no. 4 (2011): 385–428; Talavera, F., and B.P. Chew. "Comparative role of retinol, retinoic acid and β-carotene on progesterone secretion by pig corpus luteum in vitro." *Journal of Reproduction and Fertility* 82, no. 2 (1988): 611–615.

[26] Thompson, J.N., J. McC. Howell, and G.A.J. Pitt. "Vitamin A and reproduction in rats." *Proceedings of the Royal Society B* 159, no. 976 (1964): 510–535.

[27] Ganguly, J., G.S. Pope, S.Y. Thompson, Joyce Toothill, J.D. Edwards-Webb, and H.B. Waynforth. "Studies on metabolism of vitamin A. The effect of vitamin A status on the secretion rates of some steroids into the ovarian venous blood of pregnant rats." *Biochemical Journal* 122, no. 2 (1971): 235–239; Jayaram, M., S. K. Murthy, and J. Ganguly. "Effect of vitamin A deprivation on the cholesterol side-chain cleavage enzyme activity of testes and ovaries of rats." *Biochemical Journal* 136, no. 1 (1973): 221–223; Best, Monica W., Juanjuan Wu, Samuel A. Pauli, Maureen A. Kane, Keely Pierzchalski, Donna R. Session, Dori C. Woods, Weirong Shang, Robert N. Taylor, and Neil Sidell. "A role for retinoids in human oocyte fertilization: regulation of connexin 43 by retinoic acid in cumulus granulosa cells." *Molecular Human Reproduction* 21, no. 6 (2015): 527–534.

[28] Whaley, S.L., V.S. Hedgpeth, C.E. Farin, N.S. Martus, F.C. Jayes, and J.H. Britt. "Influence of vitamin A injection before mating on oocyte development, follicular hormones, and ovulation in gilts fed high-energy diets." *Journal of Animal Science* 78, no. 6 (2000): 1598–1607; Ikeda, Shuntaro, Masayuki Kitagawa, Hiroshi Imai, and Masayasu Yamada. "The roles of

vitamin A for cytoplasmic maturation of bovine oocytes." *Journal of Reproduction and Development* 51, no. 1 (2005): 23–35; Trojačanec, Snježana, Stanko Boboš, and Marija Pajić. "Influence of β-carotene and vitamin A supplementation on the ovarian activity of dairy cows with chronic fertility impairment." *Veterinarski Arhiv* 82, no. 6 (2012): 567–575.

[29] Charlton, Robert W., and Thomas H. Bothwell. "Iron absorption." *Annual Review of Medicine* 34, no. 1 (1983): 55–68; Layrisse, Miguel, J.D. Cook, C. Martinez, M. Roche, I.N. Kuhn, R.B. Walker, and C.A. Finch. "Food iron absorption: a comparison of vegetable and animal foods." *Blood* 33, no. 3 (1969): 430–443.

[30] Charlton, Robert W., and Thomas H. Bothwell. "Iron absorption." *Annual Review of Medicine* 34, no. 1 (1983): 55–68.

[31] Scaglione, Francesco, and Giscardo Panzavolta. "Folate, folic acid and 5-methyltetrahydrofolate are not the same thing." *Xenobiotica* 44, no. 5 (2014): 480–488.

[32] Ibid.

[33] McEwen, Bradley J. "Methylenetetrahydrofolate reductase (MTHFR): mythology or polymorphism (ology)?" *Advances in Integrative Medicine* 3, no. 3 (2016): 79–81; Liew, Siaw-Cheok, and Esha Das Gupta. "Methylenetetrahydrofolate reductase (MTHFR) C677T polymorphism: epidemiology, metabolism and the associated diseases." *European Journal of Medical Genetics* 58, no. 1 (2015): 1–10.

[34] Fallon Morell, Sally, and Thomas S. Cowan. (2015). *The Nourishing Traditions Book of Baby & Child Care.* Washington, DC: New Trends Publishing, Inc.

[35] Metz, Alan L., Mary M. Walser, and William G. Olson. "The interaction of dietary vitamin A and vitamin D related to skeletal development in the turkey poult." *The Journal of Nutrition* 115, no. 7 (1985): 929–935.

[36] Warinner, Christina, Jessica Hendy, Camilla Speller, Enrico Cappellini, Roman Fischer, Christian Trachsel, Jette Arneborg et al. "Direct evidence of milk consumption from ancient human dental calculus." *Scientific Reports* 4 (2014): 7104.

[37] Jianqin, Sun, Xu Leiming, Xia Lu, Gregory W. Yelland, Jiayi Ni, and Andrew J. Clarke. "Effects of milk containing only A2 beta casein versus milk containing both A1 and A2 beta casein proteins on gastrointestinal physiology, symptoms of discomfort, and cognitive behavior of people with self-reported intolerance to traditional cows' milk." *Nutrition Journal* 15, no. 1 (2015): 35.

[38] Pal, Sebely, Keith Woodford, Sonja Kukuljan, and Suleen Ho. "Milk intolerance, beta-casein and lactose." *Nutrients* 7, no. 9 (2015): 7285–7297.

[39] Woodford, Keith. (2009). *Devil in the Milk: Illness, Health and the Politics of A1 and A2 Milk.* Hartford, VT: Chelsea Green Publishing.

[40] De Noni, Ivano. "Release of β-casomorphins 5 and 7 during simulated gastro-intestinal digestion of bovine β-casein variants and milk-based infant formulas." *Food Chemistry* 110, no. 4 (2008): 897–903.

[41] Woodford, Keith. (2009). *Devil in the Milk: Illness, Health and the Politics of A1 and A2 Milk.* Hartford, VT: Chelsea Green Publishing.

[42] Jianqin, Sun, Xu Leiming, Xia Lu, Gregory W. Yelland, Jiayi Ni, and Andrew J. Clarke. "Effects of milk containing only A2 beta casein versus milk containing both A1 and A2 beta casein proteins on gastrointestinal physiology, symptoms of discomfort, and cognitive behavior of people with self-reported intolerance to traditional cows' milk." *Nutrition Journal* 15, no. 1 (2016): 35; Fiedorowicz, Ewa, Maciej Kaczmarski, Anna Cieślińska, Edyta Sienkiewicz-Szłapka, Beata Jarmołowska, Barbara Chwała, and Elżbieta Kostyra. "β-casomorphin-7 alters μ-opioid receptor and dipeptidyl peptidase IV genes expression in children with atopic dermatitis." *Peptides* 62 (2014): 144–149; Kamiński, Stanisław, Anna Cieślińska, and Elżbieta Kostyra. "Polymorphism of bovine beta-casein and its potential effect on human health." *Journal of Applied Genetics* 48, no. 3 (2007): 189–198; Cade, Robert, Malcolm Privette, Melvin Fregly, Neil Rowland, Zhongjie Sun, Virginia Zele, Herbert Wagemaker, and Charlotte Edelstein. "Autism and schizophrenia: intestinal disorders." *Nutritional Neuroscience* 3, no. 1 (2000): 57–72; Tailford, Kristy A., Celia L. Berry, Anita C. Thomas, and Julie H. Campbell. "A casein variant in cow's milk is atherogenic." *Atherosclerosis* 170, no. 1 (2003): 13–19; Laugesen, Murray, and Robert Elliott. "Ischaemic heart disease, Type 1 diabetes, and cow milk A1 beta-casein." *The New Zealand Medical Journal (Online)* 116, no. 1168 (2003).

[43] Chavarro, J.E., J.W. Rich-Edwards, B. Rosner, and W.C. Willett. "A prospective study of dairy foods intake and anovulatory infertility." *Human Reproduction* 22, no. 5 (2007): 1340–1347.

[44] Ravisankar, Panchumarthy, A. Abhishekar Reddy, B. Nagalakshmi, O. Sai Koushik, B. Vijaya Kumar, and P. Sai Anvith. "The comprehensive review on fat soluble vitamins." *IOSR Journal of Pharmacy* 5, no. 11 (2015): 12–28.

[45] Elgersma, A., S. Tamminga, and G. Ellen. "Modifying milk composition through forage." *Animal Feed Science and Technology* 131, no. 3 (2006): 207–225.

[46] Dhiman, T.R., G.R. Anand, L.D. Satter, and M.W. Pariza. "Conjugated linoleic acid content of milk from cows fed different diets." *Journal of Dairy Science* 10, no. 82 (1999): 2146–2156; Staszak, Ewa. "Conjugated linoleic acid (CLA) content of milk from cows fed different diets." *Folia Biologica* 53, no. 4 (2005): 103–106.

[47] Smit, Liesbeth A., Ana Baylin, and Hannia Campos. "Conjugated linoleic acid in adipose tissue and risk of myocardial infarction." *The American Journal of Clinical Nutrition* 92, no. 1 (2010): 34–40; Bhattacharya, Arunabh, Jameela Banu, Mizanur Rahman, Jennifer Causey, and Gabriel Fernandes. "Biological effects of conjugated linoleic acids in health and disease." *The Journal of Nutritional Biochemistry* 17, no. 12 (2006): 789–810; Gaullier, Jean-Michel, Johan Halse, Kjetil Høye, Knut Kristiansen, Hans Fagertun, Hogne Vik, and Ola Gudmundsen. "Conjugated linoleic acid supplementation for 1 y reduces body fat mass in healthy overweight humans." *The American Journal of Clinical Nutrition* 79, no. 6 (2004): 1118–1125.

[48] Nozière, P., P. Grolier, D. Durand, A. Ferlay, P. Pradel, and B. Martin. "Variations in carotenoids, fat-soluble micronutrients, and color in cows' plasma and milk following changes in forage and feeding level." *Journal of Dairy Science* 89, no. 7 (2006): 2634–2648.

[49] Schutz, M.M., L.B. Hansen, G.R. Steuernagel, and A.L. Kuck. "Variation of milk, fat, protein, and somatic cells for dairy cattle." *Journal of Dairy Science* 73, no. 2 (1990): 484–493.

[50] Pereda, Julieta, V. Ferragut, J.M. Quevedo, B. Guamis, and A.J. Trujillo. "Effects of ultra-high pressure homogenization on microbial and physicochemical shelf life of milk." *Journal of Dairy Science* 90, no. 3 (2007): 1081–093.

[51] Wiking, Lars, and Jonatan A. Dickow. "Effect of homogenization temperature and pressure on lipoprotein lipase activity and free fatty acids accumulation in milk." *Food and Nutrition* 4 (2013): 101–108.

[52] Douglass II, William Campbell. (2007). *The Raw Truth About Milk: How Science is Destroying Nature's Nearly Perfect Food and Why Animal Protein and Animal Fat in Your Diet Can Save Your Life.* Republic of Panama: Rhino Publishing, S.A.

[53] Kanner, J. "Dietary advanced lipid oxidation endproducts are risk factors to human health." *Molecular Nutrition & Food Research* 51, no. 9 (2007): 1094–1101; Staprans, Ilona, Xian-Mang Pan, Joseph H. Rapp, and Kenneth R. Feingold. "The role of dietary oxidized cholesterol and oxidized fatty acids in the development of atherosclerosis." *Molecular Nutrition & Food Research* 49, no. 11 (2005): 1075–1082; Staprans, Ilona, Xian-Mang Pan, Joseph H. Rapp, and Kenneth R. Feingold. "Oxidized cholesterol in the diet accelerates the development of aortic atherosclerosis in cholesterol-fed rabbits." *Arteriosclerosis, Thrombosis, and Vascular Biology* 18, no. 6 (1998): 977–983.

[54] Raikos, Vassilios. "Effect of heat treatment on milk protein functionality at emulsion interfaces. A review." *Food Hydrocolloids* 24, no. 4 (2010): 259–265; Vasbinder, Astrid J., and Cornelis G. De Kruif. "Casein–whey protein interactions in heated milk: the influence of pH." *International Dairy Journal* 13, no. 8 (2003): 669–677.

[55] Rankin, S.A., A. Christiansen, W. Lee, D.S. Banavara, and A. Lopez-Hernandez. "Invited review: the application of alkaline phosphatase assays for the validation of milk product pasteurization." *Journal of Dairy Science* 93, no. 12 (2010): 5538–5551; Brun, Lucas R., María L. Brance, Mercedes Lombarte, Maela Lupo, Verónica E. Di Loreto, and Alfredo Rigalli. "Regulation of intestinal calcium absorption by luminal calcium content: role of intestinal alkaline phosphatase." *Molecular Nutrition & Food Research* 58, no. 7 (2014): 1546–1551; Wasserman, R.H., and C.S. Fullmer. "Calcium transport proteins, calcium absorption, and vitamin D." *Annual Review of Physiology* 45, no. 1 (1983): 375–390; Seiquer, I., C. Delgado-Andrade, A. Haro, and M.P. Navarro. "Assessing the effects of severe heat treatment of milk on calcium bioavailability: in vitro and in vivo studies." *Journal of Dairy Science* 93, no. 12 (2010): 5635–5643; Demott, B.J. "Ionic calcium in milk and whey." *Journal of Dairy Science* 51, no. 7 (1968): 1008–1012; Reykdal, Olafur, and Ken Lee. "Soluble, dialyzable and ionic calcium in raw and processed skim milk, whole milk and spinach." *Journal of Food Science* 56, no. 3 (1991): 864–866.

[56] Li, Nan, Yuezhu Wang, Chunping You, Jing Ren, Wanyi Chen, Huajun Zheng, and Zhenmin Liu. "Variation in raw milk microbiota throughout 12 months and the impact of weather conditions." *Scientific Reports* 8, no. 1 (2018): 2371.

[57] Waser, M., K.B. Michels, C. Bieli, H. Flöistrup, G. Pershagen, E. Von Mutius, M. Ege et al. "Inverse association of farm milk consumption with asthma and allergy in rural and suburban populations across Europe." *Clinical & Experimental Allergy* 37, no. 5 (2007): 661–670; Loss, Georg, Silvia Apprich, Marco Waser, Wolfgang Kneifel, Jon Genuneit, Gisela Büchele, Juliane Weber et al. "The protective effect of farm milk consumption on childhood asthma and atopy: the GABRIELA study." *Journal of Allergy and Clinical Immunology* 128, no. 4 (2011): 766–773.

[58] Douglass II, William Campbell. (2007). *The Raw Truth About Milk: How Science is Destroying Nature's Nearly Perfect Food and Why Animal Protein and Animal Fat in Your Diet Can Save Your Life.* Republic of Panama: Rhino Publishing, S.A.

[59] Ibid.

[60] Scallan, Elaine, Robert M. Hoekstra, Frederick J. Angulo, Robert V. Tauxe, Marc-Alain Widdowson, Sharon L. Roy, Jeffery L. Jones, and Patricia M. Griffin. "Foodborne illness acquired in the United States—major pathogens." *Emerging Infectious Diseases* 17, no. 1 (2011).

[61] Painter, John A., Robert M. Hoekstra, Tracy Ayers, Robert V. Tauxe, Christopher R. Braden, Frederick J. Angulo, and Patricia M. Griffin. "Attribution of foodborne illnesses, hospitalizations, and deaths to food commodities by using outbreak data, United States, 1998–2008." *Emerging Infectious Diseases* 19, no. 3 (2013): 407.

[62] Olsen, Sonja J., Michelle Ying, Meghan F. Davis, Marshall Deasy, Ben Holland, Larry Iampietro, C. Michael Baysinger et al. "Multidrug-resistant Salmonella Typhimurium infection from milk contaminated after pasteurization." *Emerging Infectious Diseases* 10, no. 5 (2004): 932–935; Ryan, Caroline A., Mary K. Nickels, Nancy T. Hargrett-Bean, Tomy Endo, Leonard Mayer, M.S.P.H. Langkop, M.D. Kenney, and Nancy D. Puhr. "Massive outbreak of antimicrobial-resistant salmonellosis traced to pasteurized milk." *JAMA* 258 (1987): 3269–3274.

[63] Karsten, H.D., P.H. Patterson, R. Stout, and G. Crews. "Vitamins A, E and fatty acid composition of the eggs of caged hens and pastured hens." *Renewable Agriculture and Food Systems* 25, no. 1 (2010): 45–54.

[64] Ratliff, Joseph, Jose O. Leite, Ryan de Ogburn, Michael J. Puglisi, Jaci VanHeest, and Maria Luz Fernandez. "Consuming eggs for breakfast influences plasma glucose and ghrelin, while reducing energy intake during the next 24 hours in adult men." *Nutrition Research* 30, no. 2 (2010): 96–103.

[65] Swanson, Danielle, Robert Block, and Shaker A. Mousa. "Omega-3 fatty acids EPA and DHA: health benefits throughout life." *Advances in Nutrition* 3, no. 1 (2012): 1–7.

[66] Innis, Sheila M. "Dietary (n-3) fatty acids and brain development." *The Journal of Nutrition* 137, no. 4 (2007): 855–859; Calder, Philip C. "Marine omega-3 fatty acids and inflammatory processes: effects, mechanisms and clinical relevance." *Biochimica et Biophysica Acta (BBA)–Molecular and Cell Biology of Lipids* 1851, no. 4 (2015): 469–484.

[67] Goyens, Petra L.L., Mary E. Spilker, Peter L. Zock, Martijn B. Katan, and Ronald P. Mensink. "Compartmental modeling to quantify α-linolenic acid conversion after longer term intake of multiple tracer boluses." *Journal of Lipid Research* 46, no. 7 (2005): 1474–1483.

[68] Hussein, Nahed, Eric Ah-Sing, Paul Wilkinson, Clare Leach, Bruce A. Griffin, and D. Joe Millward. "Long-chain conversion of [13C] linoleic acid and α-linolenic acid in response to marked changes in their dietary intake in men." *Journal of Lipid Research* 46, no. 2 (2005): 269–280.

[69] Doughman, Scott D., Srirama Krupanidhi, and Carani B. Sanjeevi. "Omega-3 fatty acids for nutrition and medicine: considering microalgae oil as a vegetarian source of EPA and DHA." *Current Diabetes Reviews* 3, no. 3 (2007): 198–203.

[70] Nehra, Deepika, Hau D. Le, Erica M. Fallon, Sarah J. Carlson, Dori Woods, Yvonne A. White, Amy H. Pan et al. "Prolonging the female reproductive lifespan and improving egg quality with dietary omega-3 fatty acids." *Aging Cell* 11, no. 6 (2012): 1046–1054.

[71] Al-Safi, Zain A., Huayu Liu, Nichole E. Carlson, Justin Chosich, Mary Harris, Andrew P. Bradford, Celeste Robledo, Robert H. Eckel, and Alex J. Polotsky. "Omega-3 fatty acid supplementation lowers serum FSH in normal weight but not obese women." *The Journal of Clinical Endocrinology & Metabolism* 101, no. 1 (2016): 324–333.

[72] Karsch, Fred J., Deborah F. Battaglia, Kellie M. Breen, Nathalie Debus, and Thomas G. Harris. "Mechanisms for ovarian cycle disruption by immune/inflammatory stress." *Stress* 5, no. 2 (2002): 101–112.

[73] Price, Weston A. (2016). *Nutrition and Physical Degeneration*, 8th edition. Lemon Grove, CA: Price-Pottenger Nutrition Foundation, 366.

[74] Tian, X., and F.J. Diaz. "Zinc depletion causes multiple defects in ovarian function during the periovulatory period in mice." *Endocrinology* 153, no. 2 (2012): 873–886.

[75] Hunt, Janet R. "Bioavailability of iron, zinc, and other trace minerals from vegetarian diets." *The American Journal of Clinical Nutrition* 78, no. 3 (2003): 633S–639S.

[76] Harland, Barbara F., and Donald Oberleas. "Phytate in foods." *World Review of Nutrition and Dietetics* 52 (1987): 235–259; Hunt, Janet R. "Bioavailability of iron, zinc, and other trace minerals from vegetarian diets." *The American Journal of Clinical Nutrition* 78, no. 3 (2003): 633S–639S.

[77] Eskin, Bernard A., Carolyn E. Grotkowski, Christopher P. Connolly, and William R. Ghent. "Different tissue responses for iodine and iodide in rat thyroid and mammary glands." *Biological Trace Element Research* 49, no. 1 (1995): 9–19; Eskin, Bernard A., Doris G. Bartuska, Marvin R. Dunn, Ginette Jacob, and Mary B. Dratman. "Mammary Gland Dysplasia in Iodine Deficiency: Studies in Rats." *JAMA* 200, no. 8 (1967): 691–695; Eskin, Bernard A., Richard Shuman, Theodore Krouse, and Judith A. Merion. "Rat mammary gland atypia produced by iodine blockade with perchlorate." *Cancer Research* 35, no. 9 (1975): 2332–2339.

[78] Ghent, W.R., Bernard A. Eskin, D.A. Low, and L.P. Hill. "Iodine replacement in fibrocystic disease of the breast." *Canadian Journal of Surgery* 36, no 5 (1993): 453–60.

[79] Aceves, Carmen, Brenda Anguiano, and Guadalupe Delgado. "Is iodine a gatekeeper of the integrity of the mammary gland?" *Journal of Mammary Gland Biology and Neoplasia* 10, no. 2 (2005): 189–196.

[80] Sarkar, A.K. "Therapeutic management of anoestrus cows with diluted Logul's iodine and massage on reproductive organs — uncontrolled case study." *Research Journal of Animal and Veterinary Sciences* 1, no. 1 (2006): 30–32; Gupta, Raman, M.S. Thakur, and Arvind Sharma. "Estrus induction and fertility response in true anestrus buffaloes using lugol's iodine." *Animal Reproduction* 20, no. 1 (2011): 12–14; Ahlawat, A.R., P.U. Gajbhiye, M.D. Odedra, V.B. Dongre, and S.N. Ghodasara. "Effect of Lugol's iodine on estrus induction and fertility response in true anestrus Jaffrabadi buffaloes." *Buffalo Bulletin* 35, no. 3 (2016): 303–305.

[81] Sarkar, A.K. "Therapeutic management of anoestrus cows with diluted Logul's iodine and aassage on reproductive organs — uncontrolled case study." *Research Journal of Animal and Veterinary Sciences* 1, no. 1 (2006): 30–32.

[82] Ibid.

[83] Brownstein, David. (2008). *Iodine: Why You Need It, Why You Can't Live Without It.* Arden, NC: Medical Alternatives Press.

[84] Scaldaferri, Franco, Marco Pizzoferrato, Viviana Gerardi, Loris Lopetuso, and Antonio Gasbarrini. "The gut barrier: new acquisitions and therapeutic approaches." *Journal of Clinical Gastroenterology* 46 (2012): S12–S17.

[85] Lopetuso, Loris Riccardo, Franco Scaldaferri, G. Bruno, V. Petito, F. Franceschi, and A. Gasbarrini. "The therapeutic management of gut barrier leaking: the emerging role for mucosal barrier protectors." *European Review for Medical and Pharmacological Sciences* 19, no. 6 (2015): 1068–1076.

[86] Bischoff, Stephan C., Giovanni Barbara, Wim Buurman, Theo Ockhuizen, Jörg-Dieter Schulzke, Matteo Serino, Herbert Tilg, Alastair Watson, and Jerry M. Wells. "Intestinal permeability–a new target for disease prevention and therapy." *BMC Gastroenterology* 14, no. 1 (2014): 189.

[87] Chang, Jeff, Rupert W. Leong, Valerie C. Wasinger, Matthew Ip, Michael Yang, and Tri Giang Phan. "Impaired intestinal permeability contributes to ongoing bowel symptoms in patients with inflammatory bowel disease and mucosal healing." *Gastroenterology* 153, no. 3 (2017): 723–731.

[88] Odenwald, Matthew A., and Jerrold R. Turner. "Intestinal permeability defects: is it time to treat?" *Clinical Gastroenterology and Hepatology* 11, no. 9 (2013): 1075–1083.

[89] Scaldaferri, Franco, Loris Riccardo Lopetuso, Valentina Petito, Valerio Cufino, Mirna Bilotta, Vincenzo Arena, Egidio Stigliano et al. "Gelatin tannate ameliorates acute colitis in mice by reinforcing mucus layer and modulating gut microbiota composition: Emerging role for 'gut barrier protectors' in IBD?" *United European Gastroenterology Journal* 2, no. 2 (2014): 113–122.

[90] Li, Wei, Kaiji Sun, Yun Ji, Zhenlong Wu, Weiwei Wang, Zhaolai Dai, and Guoyao Wu. "Glycine regulates expression and distribution of Claudin-7 and ZO-3 proteins in intestinal porcine epithelial cells, 2." *The Journal of Nutrition* 146, no. 5 (2016): 964–969; Bertrand, Julien, Ibtissem Ghouzali, Charlène Guérin, Christine Bôle-Feysot, Mélodie Gouteux, Pierre Déchelotte, Philippe Ducrotté, and Moïse Coëffier. "Glutamine restores tight junction protein claudin-1 expression in colonic mucosa of patients with diarrhea-predominant irritable bowel syndrome." *Journal of Parenteral and Enteral Nutrition* 40, no. 8 (2016): 1170–1176; Wang, Bin, Zhenlong Wu, Yun Ji, Kaiji Sun, Zhaolai Dai, and Guoyao Wu. "L-glutamine enhances tight junction integrity by activating CaMK kinase 2–AMP-activated protein kinase signaling in intestinal porcine epithelial cells, 2." *The Journal of Nutrition* 146, no. 3 (2016): 501–508.

⁹¹ Weber, Anne M., Cleve Ziegler, Jerome L. Belinson, Allison R. Mitchinson, Theresa Widrich, and Victor Fazio. "Gynecologic history of women with inflammatory bowel disease." *Obstetrics & Gynecology* 86, no. 5 (1995): 843–847; Saha, Sumona, Ying-Qi Zhao, Samir A. Shah, Silvia Degli Esposti, Sheldon Lidofsky, Sana Salih, Renee Bright et al. "Menstrual cycle changes in women with inflammatory bowel disease: a study from the ocean state Crohn's and colitis area registry." *Inflammatory Bowel Diseases* 20, no. 3 (2014): 534–540.

⁹² Sekhar, Rajagopal V., Sanjeet G. Patel, Anuradha P. Guthikonda, Marvin Reid, Ashok Balasubramanyam, George E. Taffet, and Farook Jahoor. "Deficient synthesis of glutathione underlies oxidative stress in aging and can be corrected by dietary cysteine and glycine supplementation." *The American Journal of Clinical Nutrition* 94, no. 3 (2011): 847–853.

⁹³ Amores-Sánchez, María Isabel, and Miguel Ángel Medina. "Glutamine, as a precursor of glutathione, and oxidative stress." *Molecular Genetics and Metabolism* 67, no. 2 (1999): 100–105.

⁹⁴ Agarwal, Ashok, Anamar Aponte-Mellado, Beena J. Premkumar, Amani Shaman, and Sajal Gupta. "The effects of oxidative stress on female reproduction: a review." *Reproductive Biology and Endocrinology* 10, no. 1 (2012): 10–49; Ruder, Elizabeth H., Terryl J. Hartman, and Marlene B. Goldman. "Impact of oxidative stress on female fertility." *Current Opinion in Obstetrics & Gynecology* 21, no. 3 (2009): 219–222.

⁹⁵ Hao, Wei-Long, and Yuan-Kun Lee. (2004). "Microflora of the gastrointestinal tract." *Public Health Microbiology.* New York, NY: Humana Press, 491–502.

⁹⁶ Quigley, E.M. "Gut bacteria in health and disease." *Gastroenterology & Hepatology* 9, no. 9 (2013): 560–569.

⁹⁷ Guarner, Francisco, and Juan-R. Malagelada. "Gut flora in health and disease." *The Lancet* 361, no. 9356 (2003): 512–519; Jandhyala, Sai Manasa, Rupjyoti Talukdar, Chivkula Subramanyam, Harish Vuyyuru, Mitnala Sasikala, and D. Nageshwar Reddy. "Role of the normal gut microbiota." *World Journal of Gastroenterology* 21, no. 29 (2015): 8787.

⁹⁸ Forsythe, Paul, Nobuyuki Sudo, Timothy Dinan, Valerie H. Taylor, and John Bienenstock. "Mood and gut feelings." *Brain, Behavior, and Immunity* 24, no. 1 (2010): 9–16; Kinross, James M., Ara W. Darzi, and Jeremy K. Nicholson. "Gut microbiome-host interactions in health and disease." *Genome Medicine* 3, no. 3 (2011): 14–26; Dash, Sarah, Gerard Clarke, Michael Berk, and Felice N. Jacka. "The gut microbiome and diet in psychiatry: focus on depression." *Current Opinion in Psychiatry* 28, no. 1 (2015): 1–6; Strati, Francesco, Duccio Cavalieri, Davide Albanese, Claudio De Felice, Claudio Donati, Joussef Hayek, Olivier Jousson et al. "New evidences on the altered gut microbiota in autism spectrum disorders." *Microbiome* 5, no. 1 (2017): 24–35; Severance, Emily G., Emese Prandovszky, James Castiglione, and Robert H. Yolken. "Gastroenterology issues in schizophrenia: why the gut matters." *Current Psychiatry Reports* 5, no. 17 (2015): 1–10.

⁹⁹ Frank, Daniel N., Allison L. St Amand, Robert A. Feldman, Edgar C. Boedeker, Noam Harpaz, and Norman R. Pace. "Molecular-phylogenetic characterization of microbial community imbalances in human inflammatory bowel diseases." *Proceedings of the National Academy of Sciences* 104, no. 34 (2007): 13780–13785.

¹⁰⁰ Marco, Maria L., Dustin Heeney, Sylvie Binda, Christopher J. Cifelli, Paul D. Cotter, Benoit Foligné, Michael Gänzle et al. "Health benefits of fermented foods: microbiota and beyond." *Current Opinion in Biotechnology* 44 (2017): 94–102; Hendrickson-Jack, Lisa. "FFP 066 | Gut Health and Fertility | Preconception Nutrition | GAPS Diet | Dr. Natasha Campbell-McBride." *Fertility Friday Podcast.* Podcast Audio, February 26, 2016. fertilityfriday.com/166

¹⁰¹ Roche, Andrea, Erika Ross, Nicole Walsh, Kierin O'Donnell, Alyssa Williams, Marjorie Klapp, Nova Fullard, and Sari Edelstein. "Representative literature on the phytonutrients category: Phenolic acids." *Critical Reviews in Food Science and Nutrition* 57, no. 6 (2017): 1089–1096; Zhu, Fengmei, Bin Du, and Baojun Xu. "Anti-inflammatory effects of phytochemicals from fruits, vegetables, and food legumes: A review." *Critical Reviews in Food Science and Nutrition* (2017): 1–11; Chung, Raymond Tsz Man. "Detoxification effects of phytonutrients against environmental toxicants and sharing of clinical experience on practical applications." *Environmental Science and Pollution Research* 24, no. 10 (2017): 8946–8956; Aga, Miho, Kanso Iwaki, Yasuto Ueda, Shimpei Ushio, Naoya Masaki, Shigeharu Fukuda, Tetsuo Kimoto, Masao Ikeda, and Masashi Kurimoto. "Preventive effect of Coriandrum sativum (Chinese parsley) on localized lead deposition in ICR mice." *Journal of Ethnopharmacology* 77, no. 2–3 (2001): 203–208.

¹⁰² Fallon Morell, Sally. (2017). *Nourishing Fats: Why We Need Animal Fats for Health and Happiness.* New York, NY: Grand Central Life & Style.

¹⁰³ Hansen, S.O., and Ulla Breth Knudsen. "Endometriosis, dysmenorrhoea and diet." *European Journal of Obstetrics & Gynecology and Reproductive Biology* 169, no. 2 (2013): 162–171.

¹⁰⁴ Chavarro, Jorge E., Janet W. Rich-Edwards, Bernard A. Rosner, and Walter C. Willett. "Dietary fatty acid intakes and the risk of ovulatory infertility." *The American Journal of Clinical Nutrition* 85, no. 1 (2007): 231–237.

Chapter 13

¹ Mullington, Janet M., Monika Haack, Maria Toth, Jorge M. Serrador, and Hans K. Meier-Ewert. "Cardiovascular, inflammatory, and metabolic consequences of sleep deprivation." *Progress in Cardiovascular Diseases* 51, no. 4 (2009): 294–302; Knutson, Kristen L., Karine Spiegel, Plamen Penev, and Eve Van Cauter. "The metabolic consequences of sleep deprivation." *Sleep Medicine Reviews* 11, no. 3 (2007): 163–178; Nakata A. "Work hours, sleep sufficiency, and prevalence of depression among full-time employees: a community-based cross-sectional study." *Journal of Clinical Psychiatry* 72 (2011): 605–14; Kakizaki, M., S. Kuriyama, T. Sone, et al. "Sleep duration and the risk of breast cancer: the Ohsaki Cohort Study." *British Journal of Cancer* 99 (2008):1502–1505; Alvarenga, Tathiana A., Camila Hirotsu, Renata Mazaro-Costa, Sergio Tufik, and Monica L. Andersen. "Impairment of male reproductive function after sleep deprivation." *Fertility and Sterility* 103, no. 5 (2015): 1355–1362.

² Lawson, Christina C., Elizabeth A. Whelan, Eileen N. Lividoti Hibert, Donna Spiegelman, Eva S. Schernhammer, and Janet W. Rich-Edwards. "Rotating shift work and menstrual cycle characteristics." *Epidemiology* 22, no. 3 (2011): 305–312; Stocker, Linden J., Nicholas S. Macklon, Ying C. Cheong, and Susan J. Bewley. "Influence of shift work on early reproductive outcomes: a systematic review and meta-analysis." *Obstetrics & Gynecology* 124, no. 1 (2014): 99–110;

Chung, Fen-Fang, Chuan-Chiang Chou Yao, and Gwo-Hwa Wan. "The associations between menstrual function and lifestyle/working conditions among nurses in Taiwan." *Journal of Occupational Health* 47, no. 2 (2005): 149–156; Goldstein, Cathy A., and Yolanda R. Smith. "Sleep, Circadian Rhythms, and Fertility." *Current Sleep Medicine Reports* 2, no. 4 (2016): 206–217; Lauria, Laura, Terri J. Ballard, Massimiliano Caldora, Clelia Mazzanti, and Arduino Verdecchia. "Reproductive disorders and pregnancy outcomes among female flight attendants." *Aviation, Space, and Environmental Medicine* 77, no. 5 (2006): 533–539; Grajewski, Barbara, Elizabeth A. Whelan, Christina C. Lawson, Misty J. Hein, Martha A. Waters, Jeri L. Anderson, Leslie A. MacDonald et al. "Miscarriage among flight attendants." *Epidemiology* 26, no. 2 (2015): 192–203.

3 Marino, Jennifer L., Victoria L. Holt, Chu Chen, and Scott Davis. "Shift Work, hCLOCK T3111C polymorphism, and endometriosis risk." *Epidemiology* (2008): 477–484.

4 Watson, Nathaniel F., M. Safwan Badr, Gregory Belenky, Donald L. Bliwise, Orfeu M. Buxton, Daniel Buysse, David F. Dinges et al. "Joint consensus statement of the American Academy of Sleep Medicine and Sleep Research Society on the recommended amount of sleep for a healthy adult: methodology and discussion." *Journal of Clinical Sleep Medicine* 11, no. 8 (2015): 931–952; Ford, Earl S., Timothy J. Cunningham, and Janet B. Croft. "Trends in self-reported sleep duration among US adults from 1985 to 2012." *Sleep* 38, no. 5 (2015): 829–832.

5 Gradisar, Michael, Amy R. Wolfson, Allison G. Harvey, Lauren Hale, Russell Rosenberg, and Charles A. Czeisler. "The sleep and technology use of Americans: findings from the National Sleep Foundation's 2011 Sleep in America poll." *Journal of Clinical Sleep Medicine* 9, no. 12 (2013): 1291–1299.

6 Iyengar, Bhanu. "The melanocyte photosensory system in the human skin." *Springer Plus* 1, no. 2 (2013): 1–18; Tsutsumi, Moe, Kazuyuki Ikeyama, Sumiko Denda, Jotaro Nakanishi, Shigeyoshi Fuziwara, Hirofumi Aoki, and Mitsuhiro Denda. "Expressions of rod and cone photoreceptor-like proteins in human epidermis." *Experimental Dermatology* 18, no. 6 (2009): 567–570.

7 Graham, Charles, Mary R. Cook, Mary M. Gerkovich, and Antonio Sastre. "Examination of the Melatonin Hypothesis in Women Exposed at Night to EMF or Bright Light." *Environmental Health Perspectives* (2001): 501–507; Bojkowski, C.J., M.E. Aldhous, J. English, C. Franey, A.L. Poulton, D.J. Skene, and J. Arendt. "Suppression of nocturnal plasma melatonin and 6-sulfatoxymelatonin by bright and dim light in man." *Hormone and Metabolic Research* 19, no. 09 (1987): 437–440.

8 DeFelice, Joy, R. Kambic, and R. DeFelice. "Light elimination therapy for the treatment of infertility: A pilot study." Paper presented at the Billings Ovulation Method of America Meeting, Spokane, WA (2002): 1–4; Lee Barron, Mary. "Light exposure, melatonin secretion, and menstrual cycle parameters: an integrative review." *Biological Research for Nursing* 9, no. 1 (2007): 49–69; Gamble, K.L., D. Resuehr, and C.H. Johnson. "Shift work and circadian dysregulation of reproduction." *Frontiers in Endocrinology* 4 (2013): 92.

9 Figueiro, M.G., and M.S. Rea. "The effects of red and blue lights on circadian variations in cortisol, alpha amylase, and melatonin." *International Journal of Endocrinology* 2010 (2009): 829351–829351.

10 Gooley, Joshua J., Kyle Chamberlain, Kurt A. Smith, Sat Bir S. Khalsa, Shantha M.W. Rajaratnam, Eliza Van Reen, Jamie M. Zeitzer, Charles A. Czeisler, and Steven W. Lockley. "Exposure to room light before bedtime suppresses melatonin onset and shortens melatonin duration in humans." *The Journal of Clinical Endocrinology & Metabolism* 96, no. 3 (2010): E463—E472.

11 Leproult, Rachel, Egidio F. Colecchia, Mireille L'Hermite-Balériaux, and Eve Van Cauter. "Transition from dim to bright light in the morning induces an immediate elevation of cortisol levels." *The Journal of Clinical Endocrinology & Metabolism* 86, no. 1 (2001): 151–157; Scheer, F.A.J.L., and Ruud M. Buijs. "Light affects morning salivary cortisol in humans." *The Journal of Clinical Endocrinology & Metabolism* 84 (1999): 3395–3398.

12 Danilenko, Konstantin V., and Elena A. Samoilova. "Stimulatory Effect of Morning Bright Light on Reproductive Hormones and Ovulation: Results of a Controlled Crossover Trial." *PLOS Clinical Trials* 4, no. 2 (2007).

13 Burke, Tina M., Rachel R. Markwald, Andrew W. McHill, Evan D. Chinoy, Jesse A. Snider, Sara C. Bessman, Christopher M. Jung, John S. O'Neill, and Kenneth P. Wright. "Effects of caffeine on the human circadian clock in vivo and in vitro." *Science Translational Medicine* 7, no. 305 (2015): 305ra146; Landolt, Hans-Peter, Esther Werth, Alexander A. Borbély, and Derk-Jan Dijk. "Caffeine intake (200 mg) in the morning affects human sleep and EEG power spectra at night." *Brain Research* 675, no. 1 (1995): 67–74.

14 Drake, C., T. Roehrs, J. Shambroom, and T. Roth. "Caffeine effects on sleep taken 0, 3, or 6 hours before going to bed." *Journal of Clinical Sleep Medicine* 9, no. 11 (2013): 1195-1200.

15 Landolt, Hans-Peter, Esther Werth, Alexander A. Borbély, and Derk-Jan Dijk. "Caffeine intake (200 mg) in the morning affects human sleep and EEG power spectra at night." *Brain Research* 675, no. 1 (1995): 67–74.

16 Lee, Bruce Y., Patrick J. LaRiccia, and Andrew B. Newberg. "Acupuncture in theory and practice part 1: theoretical basis and physiologic effects." *Hospital Physician* 40, no. 4 (2004): 11-18.

17 Yang, Pei-Yu, Ka-Hou Ho, Hsi-Chung Chen, and Meng-Yueh Chien. "Exercise training improves sleep quality in middle-aged and older adults with sleep problems: a systematic review." *Journal of Physiotherapy* 58, no. 3 (2012): 157–163; Reid, Kathryn J., Kelly Glazer Baron, Brandon Lu, Erik Naylor, Lisa Wolfe, and Phyllis C. Zee. "Aerobic exercise improves self-reported sleep and quality of life in older adults with insomnia." *Sleep Medicine* 11, no. 9 (2010): 934–940; Youngstedt, Shawn D., and Christopher E. Kline. "Epidemiology of exercise and sleep." *Sleep and Biological Rhythms* 4, no. 3 (2006): 215–221.

18 Myllymäki, Tero, Heikki Kyröläinen, Katri Savolainen, Laura Hokka, Riikka Jakonen, Tanja Juuti, Kaisu Martinmäki, Jukka Kaartinen, Marja-Liisa Kinnunen, and Heikki Rusko. "Effects of vigorous late-night exercise on sleep quality and cardiac autonomic activity." *Journal of Sleep Research* 20, no. 1pt2 (2011): 146–153; Yoshida, Hironori, Tohru Ishikawa, Fumio Shiraishi, and Toshinori Kobayashi. "Effects of the timing of exercise on the night sleep." *Psychiatry and Clinical Neurosciences* 52, no. 2 (1998): 139–140.

19 Khodr, Amy, Caroline Awada, Massoot Mohammed, and Reabal Najjar. "Bump and sleep: how sexual intercourse can improve sleep of women with insomnia." Accessed August 18, 2017. ruor.uottawa.ca/handle/10393/35554?mode=full

20 Singleton, David W., and Sohaib A. Khan. "Xenoestrogen exposure and mechanisms of endocrine disruption." *Frontiers in Bioscience* 8 (2003): s110–s118.

21 Gore, A.C., D. Crews, L.L. Doan, M. La Merrill, H. Patisaul, and A. Zota. "Introduction to endocrine disrupting chemicals (EDCs)—a guide for public interest organizations and policy makers." *Endocrine Society Reports and White Papers* 1 (2014): 1–69.

22 "Recent Trends in GE Adoption." Accessed August 22, 2017. www.ers.usda.gov/data-products/adoption-of-genetically-engineered-crops-in-the-us/recent-trends-in-ge-adoption.aspx

23 USDA Food Safety and Inspection Service. "FSIS." Accessed September 10, 2018. www.fsis.usda.gov/wps/portal/fsis/topics/food-safety-education/get-answers/food-safety-fact-sheets/meat-preparation/beef-from-farm-to-table; Health Canada. "Questions and Answers - Hormonal Growth Promoters." Accessed September 10, 2018. www.canada.ca/en/health-canada/services/drugs-health-products/veterinary-drugs/factsheets-faq/hormonal-growth-promoters.html

24 Health Canada. "Questions and Answers - Hormonal Growth Promoters." Accessed September 10, 2018. www.canada.ca/en/health-canada/services/drugs-health-products/veterinary-drugs/factsheets-faq/hormonal-growth-promoters.html; Social Protection Statistics - Unemployment Benefits - Statistics Explained. "Hormones in Meat - Food Safety - European Commission." Accessed September 10, 2018. ec.europa.eu/food/safety/chemical_safety/meat_hormones_en

25 Mnif, Wissem, Aziza Ibn Hadj Hassine, Aicha Bouaziz, Aghleb Bartegi, Olivier Thomas, and Benoit Roig. "Effect of endocrine disruptor pesticides: a review." *International Journal of Environmental Research and Public Health* 8, no. 6 (2011): 2265–2303.

26 Benbrook, Charles M. "Trends in glyphosate herbicide use in the United States and globally." *Environmental Sciences Europe* 28, no. 1 (2016): 1–15.

27 Monsanto International S.A.R.L. and Monsanto Europe S.A. "The agronomic benefits of glyphosate in Europe: review of the benefits of glyphosate per market use." *Review* (2010): 1–82.

28 Darwent, A.L., K.J. Kirkland, L. Townley-Smith, K.N. Harker, A.J. Cessna, O.M. Lukow, and L.P. Lefkovitch. "Effect of preharvest applications of glyphosate on the drying, yield and quality of wheat." *Canadian Journal of Plant Science* 74, no. 2 (1994): 221–230.

29 Samsel, Anthony, and Stephanie Seneff. "Glyphosate, pathways to modern diseases II: Celiac sprue and gluten intolerance." *Interdisciplinary Toxicology* 6, no. 4 (2013): 159–184.

30 Bøhn, Thomas, Marek Cuhra, Terje Traavik, Monica Sanden, J. Fagan, and R. Primicerio. "Compositional differences in soybeans on the market: glyphosate accumulates in Roundup Ready GM soybeans." *Food Chemistry* 153 (2014): 207–215.

31 "EWG." Accessed March 30, 2018. www.ewg.org

32 Center for Food Safety and Applied Nutrition. "Ingredients - Phthalates." US Food and Drug Administration Home Page. Accessed August 21, 2017. www.fda.gov/cosmetics/productsingredients/ingredients/ucm128250.htm

33 Chen, Xueping, Shisan Xu, Tianfeng Tan, Sin Ting Lee, Shuk Han Cheng, Fred Wang Fat Lee, Steven Jing Liang Xu, and Kin Chung Ho. "Toxicity and estrogenic endocrine disrupting activity of phthalates and their mixtures." *International Journal of Environmental Research and Public Health* 11, no. 3 (2014): 3156–3168.

34 Parlett, Lauren E., Antonia M. Calafat, and Shanna H. Swan. "Women's exposure to phthalates in relation to use of personal care products." *Journal of Exposure Science & Environmental Epidemiology* 23, no. 2 (2013): 197–206.

35 USDA. "Adoption of Genetically Engineered Crops in the US." Accessed August 21, 2017. www.ers.usda.gov/data-products/adoption-of-genetically-engineered-crops-in-the-us.aspx

36 Biotech Country Facts and Trends–ISAAA Publications. "Biotech Country Facts and Trends–India." Accessed August 21, 2017. www.isaaa.org/resources/publications/biotech_country_facts_and_trends/download/Facts%20and%20Trends%20-%20India.pdf

37 US Food and Drug Administration Home Page. "Women's Health Research–Dioxin in Tampons." Accessed August 21, 2017. www.fda.gov/scienceresearch/specialtopics/womenshealthresearch/ucm134825.htm

38 Gibson, Douglas A., and Philippa T.K. Saunders. "Endocrine disruption of oestrogen action and female reproductive tract cancers." *Endocrine-Related Cancer* 21, no. 2 (2014): T13–T31; Hutz, R.J., M.J. Carvan III, J.K. Larson, Q. Liu, R.V. Stelzer, T.C. King-Heiden, M.G. Baldridge, N. Shahnoor, and K. Julien. "Familiar and novel reproductive endocrine disruptors: xenoestrogens, dioxins and nanoparticles." *Current Trends in Endocrinology* 7 (2014): 111–122; Marshall, Nikki B., and Nancy I. Kerkvliet. "Dioxin and immune regulation." *Annals of the New York Academy of Sciences* 1183, no. 1 (2010): 25–37; Hutz, R.J., M.J. Carvan, M.G. Baldridge, L.K. Conley, and T.K. Heiden. "Environmental toxicants and effects on female reproductive function." *Trends in Reproductive Biology* 2 (2006): 1–11.

39 Hutz, R.J., M.J. Carvan, M.G. Baldridge, L.K. Conley, and T.K. Heiden. "Environmental toxicants and effects on female reproductive function." *Trends in Reproductive Biology* 2 (2006): 1–11.

40 Alonso-Magdalena, Paloma, Ana Belén Ropero, Sergi Soriano, Marta García-Arévalo, Cristina Ripoll, Esther Fuentes, Iván Quesada, and Ángel Nadal. "Bisphenol-A acts as a potent estrogen via non-classical estrogen triggered pathways." *Molecular and Cellular Endocrinology* 355, no. 2 (2012): 201–207; Mileva, Guergana, Stephanie L. Baker, Anne Konkle, and Catherine Bielajew. "Bisphenol-A: epigenetic reprogramming and effects on reproduction and behavior." *International Journal of Environmental Research and Public Health* 11, no. 7 (2014): 7537–7561; Richter, Catherine A., Linda S. Birnbaum, Francesca Farabollini, Retha R. Newbold, Beverly S. Rubin, Chris E. Talsness, John G. Vandenbergh, Debby R. Walser-Kuntz, and Frederick S. vom Saal. "In vivo effects of bisphenol A in laboratory rodent studies." *Reproductive Toxicology* 24, no. 2 (2007): 199-224; Caserta, Donatella, Noemi Di Segni, Maddalena Mallozzi, Valentina Giovanale, Alberto Mantovani, Roberto Marci, and Massimo Moscarini. "Bisphenol A and the female reproductive tract: an overview of recent laboratory evidence and epidemiological studies." *Reproductive Biology and Endocrinology* 12 (2014): 12–37.

41 Kandaraki, Eleni, Antonis Chatzigeorgiou, Sarantis Livadas, Eleni Palioura, Frangiscos Economou, Michael Koutsilieris, Sotiria Palimeri, Dimitrios Panidis, and Evanthia Diamanti-Kandarakis. "Endocrine disruptors and polycystic ovary syndrome (PCOS): elevated serum levels of bisphenol A in women with PCOS." *The Journal of Clinical Endocrinology & Metabolism* 96, no. 3 (2010): E480–E484; Cobellis, Luigi, Nicola Colacurci, Elisabetta Trabucco, Carmen Carpentiero, and Lucia Grumetto. "Measurement of bisphenol A and bisphenol B levels in human blood sera from healthy and endometriotic women." *Biomedical Chromatography* 23, no. 11 (2009): 1186–1190; Signorile, Pietro G., Enrico P. Spugnini, Luigi Mita, Pasquale Mellone, Alfredo D'Avino, Mariangela Bianco, Nadia Diano et al. "Prenatal exposure of mice to bisphenol A elicits an endometriosis-like phenotype in female offspring." *General and Comparative Endocrinology* 168, no. 3 (2010): 318–325; Bhan, Arunoday, Imran Hussain, Khairul I. Ansari, Samara AM Bobzean, Linda I. Perrotti, and Subhrangsu S. Mandal. "Bisphenol-A and diethylstilbestrol exposure induces the expression of breast cancer associated long noncoding RNA HOTAIR in vitro and in vivo." *The Journal of Steroid Biochemistry and Molecular Biology* 141 (2014): 160–170.
42 Vandenberg, Laura N., Maricel V. Maffini, Carlos Sonnenschein, Beverly S. Rubin, and Ana M. Soto. "Bisphenol-A and the great divide: a review of controversies in the field of endocrine disruption." *Endocrine Reviews* 30, no. 1 (2009): 75–95.
43 Cao, X-L., C. Perez-Locas, G. Dufresne, G. Clement, S. Popovic, F. Beraldin, R. W. Dabeka, and M. Feeley. "Concentrations of bisphenol A in the composite food samples from the 2008 Canadian total diet study in Quebec City and dietary intake estimates." *Food Additives and Contaminants* 28, no. 6 (2011): 791–798; Liao, Chunyang, and Kurunthachalam Kannan. "Widespread occurrence of bisphenol A in paper and paper products: implications for human exposure." *Environmental Science & Technology* 45, no. 21 (2011): 9372–9379; Wang, Wei, Khalid O. Abualnaja, Alexandros G. Asimakopoulos, Adrian Covaci, Bondi Gevao, Boris Johnson-Restrepo, Taha A. Kumosani et al. "A comparative assessment of human exposure to tetrabromobisphenol A and eight bisphenols including bisphenol A via indoor dust ingestion in twelve countries." *Environment International* 83 (2015): 183–191.
44 Biegel, Lisa B., Raymond CM Liu, Mark E. Hurtt, and Jon C. Cook. "Effects of ammonium perfluorooctanoate on Leydig-cell function: in vitro, in vivo, and ex vivo studies." *Toxicology and Applied Pharmacology* 134, no. 1 (1995): 18–25; Shi, Zhimin, Hongxia Zhang, Yang Liu, Muqi Xu, and Jiayin Dai. "Alterations in gene expression and testosterone synthesis in the testes of male rats exposed to perfluorododecanoic acid." *Toxicological Sciences* 98, no. 1 (2007): 206–215; Wei, Yanhong, Jiayin Dai, Min Liu, Jianshe Wang, Muqi Xu, Jinmiao Zha, and Zijian Wang. "Estrogen-like properties of perfluorooctanoic acid as revealed by expressing hepatic estrogen-responsive genes in rare minnows (Gobiocypris rarus)." *Environmental Toxicology and Chemistry* 26, no. 11 (2007): 2440–2447; White, Sally S., Suzanne E. Fenton, and Erin P. Hines. "Endocrine disrupting properties of perfluorooctanoic acid." *The Journal of Steroid Biochemistry and Molecular Biology* 127, no. 1 (2011): 16–26.
45 Jensen, Allan Astrup, and Henrik Leffers. "Emerging endocrine disrupters: perfluoroalkylated substances." *International Journal of Andrology* 31, no. 2 (2008): 161–169.
46 Glassmeyer, Susan T., Edward T. Furlong, Dana W. Kolpin, Angela L. Batt, Robert Benson, J. Scott Boone, Octavia Conerly et al. "Nationwide reconnaissance of contaminants of emerging concern in source and treated drinking waters of the United States." *Science of the Total Environment* 581 (2017): 909–922.
47 Conley, Justin M., Nicola Evans, Heath Mash, Laura Rosenblum, Kathleen Schenck, Susan Glassmeyer, E.T. Furlong, Dana W. Kolpin, and Vickie S. Wilson. "Comparison of in vitro estrogenic activity and estrogen concentrations in source and treated waters from 25 US drinking water treatment plants." *Science of the Total Environment* 579 (2017): 1610–1617.
48 Wang, H., Z. Yang, B. Zhou, H. Gao, X. Yan, and J. Wang. "Fluoride-induced thyroid dysfunction in rats: roles of dietary protein and calcium level." *Toxicology and Industrial Health* 25, no. 1 (2009): 49–57.
49 Bennetau-Pelissero, Catherine. "Risks and benefits of phytoestrogens: where are we now?" *Current Opinion in Clinical Nutrition & Metabolic Care* 19, no. 6 (2016): 477–483.
50 James, Clive. "Global status of commercialized biotech/GM crops: 2014." *ISAAA Brief* 49 (2015).
51 Cassidy, Aedin, Sheila Bingham, and Kenneth Setchell. "Biological effects of isoflavones in young women: importance of the chemical composition of soyabean products." *British Journal of Nutrition* 74, no. 4 (1995): 588.
52 Fernandez-Lopez, Adrian, Valérie Lamothe, Mathieu Delample, Muriel Denayrolles, and Catherine Bennetau-Pelissero. "Removing isoflavones from modern soyfood: Why and how?" *Food Chemistry* 210 (2016): 286–294.
53 Fucic, Aleksandra, Marija Gamulin, Zeljko Ferencic, Jelena Katic, Martin Krayer von Krauss, Alena Bartonova, and Domenico F. Merlo. "Environmental exposure to xenoestrogens and oestrogen related cancers: reproductive system, breast, lung, kidney, pancreas, and brain." *Environmental Health* 11 (2012): 1–9; Fernandez, Sandra Viviana, and Jose Russo. "Estrogen and xenoestrogens in breast cancer." *Toxicologic Pathology* 38, no. 1 (2010): 110–122; Diamanti-Kandarakis, Evanthia, Jean-Pierre Bourguignon, Linda C. Giudice, Russ Hauser, Gail S. Prins, Ana M. Soto, R. Thomas Zoeller, and Andrea C. Gore. "Endocrine-disrupting chemicals: an Endocrine Society scientific statement." *Endocrine Reviews* 30, no. 4 (2009): 293–342.
54 Monteiro, Carlos Augusto, Geoffrey Cannon, Jean-Claude Moubarac, Renata Bertazzi Levy, Maria Laura C. Louzada, and Patricia Constante Jaime. "The UN Decade of Nutrition, the NOVA food classification and the trouble with ultra-processing." *Public Health Nutrition* 21, no. 1 (2018): 5–17; Leevy, Carroll M., and Şerban A. Moroianu. "Nutritional aspects of alcoholic liver disease." *Clinics in Liver Disease* 9, no. 1 (2005): 67–81.
55 Rosenberg, I.H., S.A. Abrams, G.R. Beecher, Catherine Champagne, Fergus Clydesdale, Jeanne Goldberg, Penny Kris-Etherton et al. "Dietary reference intakes: guiding principles for nutrition labeling and fortification." Washington (DC): National Academies Press (US); 2003. 3, *Overview of Food Fortification in the United States and Canada*: 45–55.

56 Government of Canada, Canadian Food Inspection Agency. "Prohibition against the sale of unenriched white flour and products containing unenriched flour." Accessed September 4, 2017. www.inspection.gc.ca/food/labelling/food-labelling-for-industry/grain-and-bakery-products/unenriched-flour/eng/1415915977878/1415915979471

57 Schulze, Matthias B., Kurt Hoffmann, JoAnn E. Manson, Walter C. Willett, James B. Meigs, Cornelia Weikert, Christin Heidemann, Graham A. Colditz, and Frank B. Hu. "Dietary pattern, inflammation, and incidence of type 2 diabetes in women." *The American Journal of Clinical Nutrition* 82, no. 3 (2005): 675–684; Ludwig, David S., Joseph A. Majzoub, Ahmad Al-Zahrani, Gerard E. Dallal, Isaac Blanco, and Susan B. Roberts. "High glycemic index foods, overeating, and obesity." *Pediatrics* 103, no. 3 (1999): e26; Malik, Vasanti S., Matthias B. Schulze, and Frank B. Hu. "Intake of sugar-sweetened beverages and weight gain: a systematic review." *The American Journal of Clinical Nutrition* 84, no. 2 (2006): 274–288.

58 Hatch, Elizabeth E., Amelia K. Wesselink, Kristen A. Hahn, James J. Michiel, Ellen M. Mikkelsen, Henrik Toft Sorensen, Kenneth J. Rothman, and Lauren A. Wise. "Intake of sugar-sweetened beverages and fecundability in a North American preconception cohort." *Epidemiology* 29, no. 3 (2018): 369–378.

59 Fenster, Laura, Chris Quale, Kirsten Waller, Gayle C. Windham, Eric P. Elkin, Neal Benowitz, and Shanna H. Swan. "Caffeine consumption and menstrual function." *American Journal of Epidemiology* 149, no. 6 (1999): 550–557; Kotsopoulos, Joanne, A. Heather Eliassen, Stacey A. Missmer, Susan E. Hankinson, and Shelley S. Tworoger. "Relationship between caffeine intake and plasma sex hormone concentrations in premenopausal and postmenopausal women." *Cancer* 115, no. 12 (2009): 2765–2774.

60 Stanton, Cynthia K., and Ronald H. Gray. "Effects of caffeine consumption on delayed conception." *American Journal of Epidemiology* 142, no. 12 (1995): 1322–1329; Wilcox, Allen, Clarice Weinberg, and Donna Baird. "Caffeinated beverages and decreased fertility." *The Lancet* 332, no. 8626–8627 (1988): 1453–1456.

61 Hatch, Elizabeth E., and Michael B. Bracken. "Association of delayed conception with caffeine consumption." *American Journal of Epidemiology* 138, no. 12 (1993): 1082–1092.

62 Lovallo, William R., Thomas L. Whitsett, Bong Hee Sung, Andrea S. Vincent, and Michael F. Wilson. "Caffeine stimulation of cortisol secretion across the waking hours in relation to caffeine intake levels." *Psychosomatic Medicine* 67, no. 5 (2005): 734–739; Strauss III, Jerome F., and Robert L. Barbieri (2013). *Yen and Jaffe's Reproductive Endocrinology*, 7th edition. Philadelphia, PA: Elsevier Health Sciences, 88–89.

63 Humphries, P., E. Pretorius, and H. Naudé. "Direct and indirect cellular effects of aspartame on the brain." *European Journal of Clinical Nutrition* 62 (2008): 451–462.

64Ibid; Chattopadhyay, Sanchari, Utpal Raychaudhuri, and Runu Chakraborty. "Artificial sweeteners–a review." *Journal of Food Sciences and Technology* 51, no. 4 (2014): 611–621.

65 Goyal, S.K., and R.K. Goyal. "Stevia (Stevia rebaudiana) a bio-sweetener: a review." *International Journal of Food Sciences and Nutrition* 61, no. 1 (2010): 1–10.

66 de Cock, P. "Erythritol functional roles in oral-systemic health." *Advances in Dental Research* 29, no. 1 (2018): 104–109.

67 Trinidad, Trinidad P., Aida C. Mallillin, Rosario S. Sagum, and Rosario R. Encabo. "Glycemic index of commonly consumed carbohydrate foods in the Philippines." *Journal of Functional Foods* 2, no. 4 (2010): 271–274.

68 Phillips, Katherine M., Monica H. Carlsen, and Rune Blomhoff. "Total antioxidant content of alternatives to refined sugar." *Journal of the American Dietetic Association* 109, no. 1 (2009): 64–71.

69 Gill, Jan. "The effects of moderate alcohol consumption on female hormone levels and reproductive function." *Alcohol and Alcoholism* 35, no. 5 (2000): 417–423; Schliep, Karen C., Shvetha M. Zarek, Enrique F. Schisterman, Jean Wactawski-Wende, Maurizio Trevisan, Lindsey A. Sjaarda, Neil J. Perkins, and Sunni L. Mumford. "Alcohol intake, reproductive hormones, and menstrual cycle function: a prospective cohort study." *The American Journal of Clinical Nutrition* 102, no. 4 (2015): 933–942.

70 Schliep, Karen C., Shvetha M. Zarek, Enrique F. Schisterman, Jean Wactawski-Wende, Maurizio Trevisan, Lindsey A. Sjaarda, Neil J. Perkins, and Sunni L. Mumford. "Alcohol intake, reproductive hormones, and menstrual cycle function: a prospective cohort study." *The American Journal of Clinical Nutrition* 102, no. 4 (2015): 933–942.

71 Windham, G.C., E.P. Elkin, S.H. Swan, K.O. Waller, and L. Fenster. "Cigarette smoking and effects on menstrual function." *Obstetrics & Gynecology* 93, no. 1 (1999): 61–62.

72 Windham, Gayle C., Patrick Mitchell, Meredith Anderson, and Bill L. Lasley. "Cigarette smoking and effects on hormone function in premenopausal women." *Environmental Health Perspectives* 113, no. 10 (2005): 1285–1290.

73 Chavarro, Jorge E., Janet W. Rich-Edwards, Bernard A. Rosner, and Walter C. Willett. "Diet and lifestyle in the prevention of ovulatory disorder infertility." *Obstetrics & Gynecology* 110, no. 5 (2007): 1050–1058; Chavarro, Jorge E., Janet W. Rich-Edwards, Bernard A. Rosner, and Walter C. Willett. "A prospective study of dietary carbohydrate quantity and quality in relation to risk of ovulatory infertility." *European Journal of Clinical Nutrition* 63, no. 1 (2009): 78–86; Douglas, Crystal C., Leigh E. Norris, Robert A. Oster, Betty E. Darnell, Ricardo Azziz, and Barbara A. Gower. "Difference in dietary intake between women with polycystic ovary syndrome and healthy controls." *Fertility and Sterility* 86, no. 2 (2006): 411–417.

74 Chavarro, Jorge E., Janet W. Rich-Edwards, Bernard A. Rosner, and Walter C. Willett. "A prospective study of dietary carbohydrate quantity and quality in relation to risk of ovulatory infertility." *European Journal of Clinical Nutrition* 63, no. 1 (2009): 78–86.

75 Chafen, Jennifer J. Schneider, Sydne J. Newberry, Marc A. Riedl, Dena M. Bravata, Margaret Maglione, Marika J. Suttorp, Vandana Sundaram et al. "Diagnosing and managing common food allergies: a systematic review." *JAMA* 303, no. 18 (2010): 1848–1856.

76 Agata, Hiroatsu, Naomi Kondo, Osamu Fukutomi, Shinji Shinoda, and Tadao Orii. "Effect of elimination diets on food-specific IgE antibodies and lymphocyte proliferative responses to food antigens in atopic dermatitis patients exhibiting sensitivity to food allergens." *Journal of Allergy and Clinical Immunology* 91, no. 2 (1993): 668–679.

[77] Ouyang, Xiaosen, Pietro Cirillo, Yuri Sautin, Shannon McCall, James L. Bruchette, Anna Mae Diehl, Richard J. Johnson, and Manal F. Abdelmalek. "Fructose consumption as a risk factor for non-alcoholic fatty liver disease." *Journal of Hepatology* 48, no. 6 (2008): 993–999; Zelber-Sagi, Shira, Dorit Nitzan-Kaluski, Rebecca Goldsmith, Muriel Webb, Laurie Blendis, Zamir Halpern, and Ran Oren. "Long term nutritional intake and the risk for non-alcoholic fatty liver disease (NAFLD): a population based study." *Journal of Hepatology* 47, no. 5 (2007): 711–717; Thuy, Sabine, Ruth Ladurner, Valentina Volynets, Silvia Wagner, Stefan Strahl, Alfred Königsrainer, Klaus-Peter Maier, Stephan C. Bischoff, and Ina Bergheim. "Nonalcoholic fatty liver disease in humans is associated with increased plasma endotoxin and plasminogen activator inhibitor 1 concentrations and with fructose intake." *The Journal of Nutrition* 138, no. 8 (2008): 1452–1455; Maddrey, Willis C. "Alcohol-induced liver disease." *Clinics in Liver Disease* 4, no. 1 (2000): 115–131; Lackner, Carolin, Walter Spindelboeck, Johannes Haybaeck, Philipp Douschan, Florian Rainer, Luigi Terracciano, Josef Haas, Andrea Berghold, Ramon Bataller, and Rudolf E. Stauber. "Histological parameters and alcohol abstinence determine long-term prognosis in patients with alcoholic liver disease." *Journal of Hepatology* 66, no. 3 (2017): 610–618.

[78] Michnovicz, Jon J., Herman Adlercreutz, and H. Leon Bradlow. "Changes in levels of urinary estrogen metabolites after oral indole-3-carbinol treatment in humans." *Journal of the National Cancer Institute* 89, no. 10 (1997): 718–723; Michnovicz, Jon J., and H. Leon Bradlow. "Altered estrogen metabolism and excretion in humans following consumption of indole-3-carbinol." *Nutrition and Cancer* (1991): 59–66.

[79] Surushe, Priyanka, Mayuri Bari, Rahul Hajare, and Anil Chandewar Swapnil Surushe. "Breast cancer and dietary Indole 3 carbinol — a review." *Asian Journal of Pharmacy & Life Science ISSN* 2231 (2012): 72–80; Jain, Mohit M., Nirmala Kumari, and Geeta Rai. "A novel formulation of veggies with potent liver detoxifying activity." *International Journal of Computational Biology and Drug Design* 8, no. 1 (2015): 75–86.

[80] Weng, Jing-Ru, Chen-Hsun Tsai, Samuel K. Kulp, and Ching-Shih Chen. "Indole-3-carbinol as a chemopreventive and anti-cancer agent." *Cancer Letters* 262, no. 2 (2008): 153–163.

[81] Smith, Alma J., William R. Phipps, William Thomas, Kathryn H. Schmitz, and Mindy S. Kurzer. "The effects of aerobic exercise on estrogen metabolism in healthy premenopausal women." *Cancer Epidemiology and Prevention Biomarkers* 22, no. 5 (2013): 756–764.

[82] Petersen, Anne Marie W., and Bente Klarlund Pedersen. "The anti-inflammatory effect of exercise." *Journal of Applied Physiology* 98, no. 4 (2005): 1154–1162; Jelleyman, Charlotte, Thomas Yates, Gary O'Donovan, Laura J. Gray, James A. King, Kamlesh Khunti, and Melanie J. Davies. "The effects of high-intensity interval training on glucose regulation and insulin resistance: a meta-analysis." *Obesity Reviews* 16, no. 11 (2015): 942–961; Almenning, Ida, Astrid Rieber-Mohn, Kari Margrethe Lundgren, Tone Shetelig Løvvik, Kirsti Krohn Garnæs, and Trine Moholdt. "Effects of high intensity interval training and strength training on metabolic, cardiovascular and hormonal outcomes in women with polycystic ovary syndrome: a pilot study." *PLOS One* 10, no. 9 (2015): e0138793.

[83] Warren, Michelle P., and Abigail T. Chua. "Exercise-induced amenorrhea and bone health in the adolescent athlete." *Annals of the New York Academy of Sciences* 1135, no. 1 (2008): 244–252; Sokoloff, Natalia Cano, Madhusmita Misra, and Kathryn E. Ackerman. (2016). "Exercise, training, and the hypothalamic-pituitary-gonadal axis in men and women." *Sports Endocrinology*, vol. 47. Basel: Karger Publishers, 27–43; Wu, T., X. Gao, M. Chen, and R.M. Van Dam. "Long-term effectiveness of diet-plus-exercise interventions vs. diet-only interventions for weight loss: a meta-analysis." *Obesity Reviews* 10, no. 3 (2009): 313–323.

[84] Trapp, E. Gail, Donald J. Chisholm, Judith Freund, and Stephen H. Boutcher. "The effects of high-intensity intermittent exercise training on fat loss and fasting insulin levels of young women." *International Journal of Obesity* 32, no. 4 (2008): 684.

[85] Brand, Serge, Edith Holsboer-Trachsler, José Raúl Naranjo, and Stefan Schmidt. "Influence of mindfulness practice on cortisol and sleep in long-term and short-term meditators." *Neuropsychobiology* 65, no. 3 (2012): 109–118.

[86] Ibid; Tang, Yi-Yuan, Britta K. Hölzel, and Michael I. Posner. "The neuroscience of mindfulness meditation." *Nature Reviews Neuroscience* 16, no. 4 (2015): 213–225; Gotink, Rinske A., Rozanna Meijboom, Meike W. Vernooij, Marion Smits, and MG Myriam Hunink. "8-week mindfulness based stress reduction induces brain changes similar to traditional long-term meditation practice—a systematic review." *Brain and Cognition* 108 (2016): 32–41.

[87] Peterson, Linda Gay, and Lori Pbert. "Effectiveness of a meditation-based stress reduction program in the treatment of anxiety disorders." *American Journal of Psychiatry* 149, no. 7 (1992): 936–943; Goyal, Madhav, Sonal Singh, Erica MS Sibinga, Neda F. Gould, Anastasia Rowland-Seymour, Ritu Sharma, Zackary Berger et al. "Meditation programs for psychological stress and well-being: a systematic review and meta-analysis." *JAMA Internal Medicine* 174, no. 3 (2014): 357–368; Kabat-Zinn, Jon, Elizabeth Wheeler, Timothy Light, Anne Skillings, Mark J. Scharf, Thomas G. Cropley, David Hosmer, and Jeffrey D. Bernhard. "Influence of a mindfulness meditation-based stress reduction intervention on rates of skin clearing in patients with moderate to severe psoriasis undergoing photo therapy (UVB) and photochemotherapy (PUVA)." *Psychosomatic Medicine* 60, no. 5 (1998): 625–632.

[88] Kaplan, Stephen. (1992). "The restorative environment: Nature and human experience." *Role of Horticulture in Human Well-Being and Social Development: A National Symposium*. Arlington, Virginia: Timber Press, 134–142; Bowler, Diana E., Lisette M. Buyung-Ali, Teri M. Knight, and Andrew S. Pullin. "A systematic review of evidence for the added benefits to health of exposure to natural environments." *BMC Public Health* 10, no. 1 (2010): 456; Shanahan, Danielle F., Robert Bush, Kevin J. Gaston, Brenda B. Lin, Julie Dean, Elizabeth Barber, and Richard A. Fuller. "Health benefits from nature experiences depend on dose." *Scientific Reports* 6, no. 28551 (2016): 1–10.

[89] Ulrich, Roger S., Robert F. Simons, Barbara D. Losito, Evelyn Fiorito, Mark A. Miles, and Michael Zelson. "Stress recovery during exposure to natural and urban environments." *Journal of Environmental Psychology* 11, no. 3 (1991): 201–230.

Chapter 14

[1] Iacovides, Stella, Ingrid Avidon, and Fiona C. Baker. "What we know about primary dysmenorrhea today: a critical review." *Human Reproduction Update* 21, no. 6 (2015): 762–778.

[2] Ju, Hong, Mark Jones, and Gita Mishra. "The prevalence and risk factors of dysmenorrhea." *Epidemiologic Reviews* (2013): 104–113.

[3] Lefebvre, Guylaine, Odette Pinsonneault, Viola Antao, Amanda Black, Margaret Burnett, Kymm Feldman, Robert Lea, and Magali Robert. "Primary dysmenorrhea consensus guideline." *Journal of Obstetrics and Gynaecology Canada* 27, no. 12 (2005): 1117–1146; Iacovides, Stella, Ingrid Avidon, and Fiona C. Baker. "What we know about primary dysmenorrhea today: a critical review." *Human Reproduction Update* 21, no. 6 (2015): 763.

[4] Iacovides, Stella, Ingrid Avidon, and Fiona C. Baker. "What we know about primary dysmenorrhea today: a critical review." *Human Reproduction Update* 21, no. 6 (2015): 763; Ju, Hong, Mark Jones, and Gita Mishra. "The prevalence and risk factors of dysmenorrhea." *Epidemiologic Reviews* (2013): 104.

[5] Lefebvre, Guylaine, Odette Pinsonneault, Viola Antao, Amanda Black, Margaret Burnett, Kymm Feldman, Robert Lea, and Magali Robert. "Primary dysmenorrhea consensus guideline." *Journal of Obstetrics and Gynaecology Canada* 27, no. 12 (2005): 1120.

[6] Iacovides, Stella, Ingrid Avidon, and Fiona C. Baker. "What we know about primary dysmenorrhea today: a critical review." *Human Reproduction Update* 21, no. 6 (2015): 763; Ju, Hong, Mark Jones, and Gita Mishra. "The prevalence and risk factors of dysmenorrhea." *Epidemiologic Reviews* (2013): 104.

[7] Iacovides, Stella, Ingrid Avidon, and Fiona C. Baker. "What we know about primary dysmenorrhea today: a critical review." *Human Reproduction Update* 21, no. 6 (2015): 762–778.

[8] Ricciotti, Emanuela, and Garret A. FitzGerald. "Prostaglandins and inflammation." *Arteriosclerosis, Thrombosis, and Vascular Biology* 31, no. 5 (2011): 986–1000.

[9] Jabbour, Henry N., Kurt J. Sales, Rob D. Catalano, and Jane E. Norman. "Inflammatory pathways in female reproductive health and disease." *Reproduction* 138, no. 6 (2009): 909.

[10] Ibid, 903–919.

[11] Ibid, 986; You & Your Hormones | Hormones | Prostaglandins. "You & Your Hormones." Accessed January 12, 2017. www.yourhormones.info/hormones/prostaglandins.aspx

[12] Lundström, V., and K. Green. "Endogenous levels of prostaglandin F 2α and its main metabolites in plasma and endometrium of normal and dysmenorrheic women." *American Journal of Obstetrics and Gynecology* 130, no. 6 (1978): 640–646.

[13] "Nonsteroidal anti-inflammatory drug." Accessed September 28, 2017. en.wikipedia.org/wiki/Nonsteroidal_anti-inflammatory_drug

[14] Iacovides, Stella, Ingrid Avidon, and Fiona C. Baker. "What we know about primary dysmenorrhea today: a critical review." *Human Reproduction Update* 21, no. 6 (2015): 762–778; Gislason, Gunnar H. "NSAIDs and cardiovascular risk." *American Family Physician* 80, no. 12 (2009): 1366–1366; Tamblyn, Robyn, Laeora Berkson, W. Dale Dauphinee, David Gayton, Roland Grad, Allen Huang, Lisa Isaac, Peter McLeod, and Linda Snell. "Unnecessary prescribing of NSAIDs and the management of NSAID-related gastropathy in medical practice." *Annals of Internal Medicine* 127, no. 6 (1997): 429–438; Hörl, Walter H. "Nonsteroidal anti-inflammatory drugs and the kidney." *Pharmaceuticals* 3, no. 7 (2010): 2291–2321.

[15] Rubi-Klein, Katharina, Elisabeth Kucera-Sliutz, Helmut Nissel, Michaela Bijak, Daniela Stockenhuber, Matthias Fink, and Evemarie Wolkenstein. "Is acupuncture in addition to conventional medicine effective as pain treatment for endometriosis? A randomised controlled cross-over trial." *European Journal of Obstetrics & Gynecology and Reproductive Biology* 153, no. 1 (2010): 90–93.

[16] Prasad, A.S. "Zinc is an antioxidant and anti-inflammatory agent: its role in human health." *Frontiers in Nutrition* 1 (2014): 1–10; Kelly, R.W., and M.H. Abel. "Copper and zinc inhibit the metabolism of prostaglandin by the human uterus." *Biology of Reproduction* 28, no. 4 (1983): 883–889; Eby, George A. "Zinc treatment prevents dysmenorrhea." *Medical Hypotheses* 69, no. 2 (2007): 297–301.

[17] Kashefi, Farzaneh, Marjan Khajehei, Mahbubeh Tabatabaeichehr, Mohammad Alavinia, and Javad Asili. "Comparison of the effect of ginger and zinc sulfate on primary dysmenorrhea: a placebo-controlled randomized trial." *Pain Management Nursing* 15, no. 4 (2014): 826–833; Sundari, Luh Putu Ratna, Nyoman Adiputra, I Putu Gede Adiatmika, and I Made Krisna Dinata. "Oral administration of zinc capsule for 4 days before menstrual period decreases prostaglandin (PGF2α) level and pain intensity in women with primary dysmenorrhea." *International Journal of Science and Research* 6, no. 3 (2017): 1081–1084; Sangestani, Gita, Mahnaz Khatiban, Roberto Marci, and Isabella Piva. "The positive effects of zinc supplements on the improvement of primary dysmenorrhea and premenstrual symptoms: a double-blind, randomized, controlled trial." *Journal of Midwifery and Reproductive Health* 3, no. 3 (2015): 378–384.

[18] Malpuech-Brugère, Corinne, Wojciech Nowacki, Maryvonne Daveau, Elyett Gueux, Christine Linard, Edmond Rock, Jean-Pierre Lebreton, Andrzej Mazur, and Yves Rayssiguier. "Inflammatory response following acute magnesium deficiency in the rat." *Biochimica et Biophysica Acta (BBA)–Molecular Basis of Disease* 1501, no. 2 (2000): 91–98; Volpe, Stella Lucia. "Magnesium in disease prevention and overall health." *Advances in Nutrition: An International Review Journal* 4, no. 3 (2013): 378S–383S; Alaimo, Katherine, Margaret A. McDowell, R.R. Briefel, A.M. Bischof, C.R. Caughman, C.M. Loria, and C.L. Johnson. "Dietary intake of vitamins, minerals, and fiber of persons ages 2 months and over in the United States: third national health and nutrition examination survey, phase 1, 1988–91." *Advance Data* 258 (1994): 1–28; Marier, J.R. "Magnesium content of the food supply in the modern-day world." *Magnesium* 5, no. 1 (1985): 1–8.

[19] Chhabra, S. "Primary dysmenorrhea and serum magnesium in young girls: a pilot study." Nessa Publishers: *Journal of Gynecology* 1, no. 3 (2017).

[20] Seifert, B., P. Wagler, S. Dartsch, U. Schmidt, and J. Nieder. "Magnesium — a new therapeutic alternative in primary dysmenorrhea." *Zentralblatt für Gynäkologie* 111, no. 11 (1989): 755–760.

[21] Murray, Michael T., and Joseph E. Pizzorno. (2012). *The Encyclopedia of Natural Medicine,* 3rd edition. London: Simon & Schuster, 896–897.

[22] Calder, Philip C. "Marine omega-3 fatty acids and inflammatory processes: effects, mechanisms and clinical relevance." *Biochimica et Biophysica Acta (BBA)–Molecular and Cell Biology of Lipids* 1851, no. 4 (2015): 469–484.

[23] Deutch, Bente, Eva Bonefeld Jørgensen, and Jens C. Hansen. "Menstrual discomfort in Danish women reduced by dietary supplements of omega-3 PUFA and B12 (fish oil or seal oil capsules)." *Nutrition Research* 20, no. 5 (2000): 621–631; Moghadamnia, A.A., N. Mirhosseini, M.H. Abadi, A. Omranirad, and S. Omidvar. "Effect of Clupeonella grimmi (anchovy/kilka) fish oil on dysmenorrhoea." *Eastern Mediterranean Health Journal* 16, no. 4 (2010): 408–413.

[24] Zafari, M., and F. Behmanesh. "Comparison of the effect of fish oil and ibuprofen on treatment of severe pain in primary dysmenorrhea." *Caspian Journal of Internal Medicine* 2, no. 3 (2011): 279–282.

[25] Wayne, Peter M., Catherine E. Kerr, Rosa N. Schnyer, Anna T.R. Legedza, Jacqueline Savetsky-German, Monica H. Shields, Julie E. Buring et al. "Japanese-style acupuncture for endometriosis-related pelvic pain in adolescents and young women: results of a randomized sham-controlled trial." *Journal of Pediatric and Adolescent Gynecology* 21, no. 5 (2008): 247–257; Rubi-Klein, Katharina, Elisabeth Kucera-Sliutz, Helmut Nissel, Michaela Bijak, Daniela Stockenhuber, Matthias Fink, and Evemarie Wolkenstein. "Is acupuncture in addition to conventional medicine effective as pain treatment for endometriosis? A randomised controlled cross-over trial." *European Journal of Obstetrics & Gynecology and Reproductive Biology* 153, no. 1 (2010): 90–93; Lund, Iréne, and Thomas Lundeberg. "Is acupuncture effective in the treatment of pain in endometriosis?" *Journal of Pain Research* 9 (2016): 157–165.

[26] Viganò, Paola, Fabio Parazzini, Edgardo Somigliana, and Paolo Vercellini. "Endometriosis: epidemiology and aetiological factors." *Best Practice & Research: Clinical Obstetrics & Gynaecology* 18, no. 2 (2004): 177–200; Wu, Meng-Hsing, Yutaka Shoji, Pei-Chin Chuang, and Shaw-Jenq Tsai. "Endometriosis: disease pathophysiology and the role of prostaglandins." *Expert Reviews in Molecular Medicine* 9, no. 2 (2007): 1–20; Farquhar, Cynthia. "Endometriosis." *The BMJ* 334 (2007): 249–253.

[27] Witt, Claudia M., Thomas Reinhold, Benno Brinkhaus, Stephanie Roll, Susanne Jena, and Stefan N. Willich. "Acupuncture in patients with dysmenorrhea: a randomized study on clinical effectiveness and cost-effectiveness in usual care." *American Journal of Obstetrics and Gynecology* 198, no. 2 (2008): 166-e1–166-e8; Lin, Jaung-Geng, and Wei-Liang Chen. "Acupuncture analgesia: a review of its mechanisms of actions." *The American Journal of Chinese Medicine* 36, no. 04 (2008): 635–645; Cho, Z.H., S.C. Hwang, E.K. Wong, Y.D. Son, C.K. Kang, T.S. Park, S.J. Bai et al. "Neural substrates, experimental evidences and functional hypothesis of acupuncture mechanisms." *Acta Neurologica Scandinavica* 113, no. 6 (2006): 370–377; Lin, Li-Li, Cun-Zhi Liu, and Bi-Yu Huang. "Clinical observation on treatment of primary dysmenorrhea with acupuncture and massage." *Chinese Journal of Integrated Traditional and Western Medicine* 28, no. 5 (2008): 418–420; Sriprasert, Intira, Suparerk Suerungruang, Porntip Athilarp, Anuchart Matanasarawoot, and Supanimit Teekachunhatean. "Efficacy of acupuncture versus combined oral contraceptive pill in treatment of moderate-to-severe dysmenorrhea: a randomized controlled trial." *Evidence-Based Complementary and Alternative Medicine* (2015): 1–10.

[28] Grady, H. "Immunomodulation through castor oil packs." *Journal of Naturopathic Medicine* 7 (1997): 84–89; Bhakta, Sonali, and Shonkor Kumar Das. "In praise of the medicinal plant Ricinus communis L: a review." *Global Journal of Research on Medicinal Plants & Indigenous Medicine* 4, no. 5 (2015): 95; Rana, Manpreet, Hitesh Dhamija, Bharat Prashar, and Shivani Sharma. "Ricinus communis L—a review." *International Journal of PharmTech Research* 4, no. 4 (2012): 1706–1711.

[29] McGarey, William A. (1993). *The Oil That Heals: A Physician's Success with Castor Oil Treatments.* Virginia Beach, VA: ARE Press.

[30] FFP 018 | Arvigo Abdominal Therapy | Vaginal Steaming | Traditional Maya Healing for Fertility and Menstrual Cycle Irregularities | Dr. Rosita Arvigo." *Fertility Friday Podcast.* Podcast Audio, April 15, 2015. fertilityfriday.com/rositaarvigo

[31] Definition and History | The Arvigo Techniques of Maya Abdominal Therapy. "Definition and History." Accessed May 11, 2017. arvigotherapy.com/content/definition-and-history

[32] Hendrickson-Jack, Lisa. "FFP 030 | Alignment and Movement for Fertility | Merciér Therapy | Marie Wittman." *Fertility Friday Podcast.* Podcast Audio, June 26, 2015. fertilityfriday.com/30; Hendrickson-Jack, Lisa. "FFP 071 | Connecting with the Wisdom of Your Menstrual Cycle | Fertility Massage Therapy | Clare Blake." *Fertility Friday Podcast.* Podcast Audio, April 1, 2016. fertilityfriday.com/71

[33] "FFP 050 | Journeys in Healing | Arvigo® Therapy for Fertility and Pregnancy | Donna Zubrod & Diane MacDonald." *Fertility Friday Podcast.* Podcast Audio, November 6, 2015. fertilityfriday.com/50

[34] Green, Monica H., ed. (2013). *The Trotula: A Medieval Compendium of Women's Medicine.* Philadelphia, PA: University of Pennsylvania Press.

[35] FFP 018 | Arvigo Abdominal Therapy | Vaginal Steaming | Traditional Maya Healing for Fertility and Menstrual Cycle Irregularities | Dr. Rosita Arvigo." *Fertility Friday Podcast.* Podcast Audio, April 15, 2015. fertilityfriday.com/rositaarvigo

[36] Green, Monica H., ed. (2013). *The Trotula: A Medieval Compendium of Women's Medicine.* Philadelphia, PA: University of Pennsylvania Press.

[37] Hendrickson-Jack, Lisa. "FFP 202 | Vaginal Steaming for Period Problems | Steamy Chick | Keli Garza." *Fertility Friday Podcast.* Podcast Audio, May 25, 2018. fertilityfriday.com/202

Chapter 15

[1] Dueñas, José Luis, Iñaki Lete, Rafael Bermejo, Agnès Arbat, Ezequiel Pérez-Campos, Javier Martínez-Salmeán, Isabel Serrano, José Luis Doval, and Carme Coll. "Prevalence of premenstrual syndrome and premenstrual dysphoric disorder in a representative cohort of Spanish women of fertile age." *European Journal of Obstetrics & Gynecology and Reproductive Biology* 156, no. 1 (2011): 72–77; Takeda, T., K. Tasaka, M. Sakata, and Y. Murata. "Prevalence of premenstrual syndrome and premenstrual dysphoric disorder in Japanese women." *Archives of Women's Mental Health* 9, no. 4 (2006): 209–212.

[1] Tschudin, Sibil, Paola Coda Bertea, and Elisabeth Zemp. "Prevalence and predictors of premenstrual syndrome and premenstrual dysphoric disorder in a population-based sample." *Archives of Women's Mental Health* 13, no. 6 (2010): 485–494; Dueñas, José Luis, Iñaki Lete, Rafael Bermejo, Agnès Arbat, Ezequiel Pérez-Campos, Javier Martínez-Salmeán, Isabel Serrano, José Luis Doval, and Carme Coll. "Prevalence of premenstrual syndrome and premenstrual dysphoric disorder in a representative cohort of Spanish women of fertile age." *European Journal of Obstetrics & Gynecology and Reproductive Biology* 156, no. 1 (2011): 72–77; Takeda, T., K. Tasaka, M. Sakata, and Y. Murata. "Prevalence of premenstrual syndrome and premenstrual dysphoric disorder in Japanese women." *Archives of Women's Mental Health* 9, no. 4 (2006): 209–212; ACOG committee opinion. Premenstrual syndrome. Number 155–April 1995 (replaces no. 66, January 1999). Committee on Gynecologic Practice. American College of Obstetricians and Gynecologists. *International Journal of Gynecology & Obstetrics* 50 (1995): 80–84.

[2] Prior, Jerilynn C., Chiaki Konishi, Christine L. Hitchcock, Elaine Kingwell, Patti Janssen, Anthony P. Cheung, Nichole Fairbrother, and Azita Goshtasebi. "Does molimina indicate ovulation? Prospective data in a hormonally documented single-cycle in spontaneously menstruating women." *International Journal of Environmental Research and Public Health* 15, no. 5 (2018): 1016.

[3] Magyar, David M., Stephen P. Boyers, John R. Marshall, and Guy E. Abraham. "Regular menstrual cycles and premenstrual molimina as indicators of ovulation." *Obstetrics & Gynecology* 53, no. 4 (1979): 411–414; Harvey, Anne T., Christine L. Hitchcock, and Jerilynn C. Prior. "Ovulation disturbances and mood across the menstrual cycles of healthy women." *Journal of Psychosomatic Obstetrics & Gynecology* 30, no. 4 (2009): 207–214.

[4] Owen, Lara. (2008). *Her Blood Is Gold: Awakening to the Wisdom of Menstruation*. Wimborne, UK: Archive Publishing, 60.

[5] Scommegna, Antonio, and W. Paul Dmowski. "Dysfunctional uterine bleeding." *Clinical Obstetrics and Gynecology* 16, no. 3 (1973): 221–254.

[6] Lovick, Thelma A., Vinicius G. Guapo, Janete A. Anselmo-Franci, Camila M. Loureiro, Maria Clara M. Faleiros, Cristina M. Del Ben, and Marcus L. Brandão. "A specific profile of luteal phase progesterone is associated with the development of premenstrual symptoms." *Psychoneuroendocrinology* 75 (2017): 83–90; Munday, M.R., M.G. Brush, and R.W. Taylor. "Correlations between progesterone, oestradiol and aldosterone levels in the premenstrual syndrome." *Clinical Endocrinology* 14, no. 1 (1981): 1–9; Wide, Leif, Ragnar So, and Hans Carstensen. "FSH, LH, TeBG-capacity, estrogen and progesterone in women with premenstrual tension during the luteal phase." *Journal of Steroid Biochemistry* 7, no. 6–7 (1976): 473–476.

[7] Stewart, W.F., C. Wood, M.L. Reed, J. Roy, and R.B. Lipton. "Cumulative lifetime migraine incidence in women and men." *Cephalalgia* 28, no. 11 (2008): 1170–1178; Pizzorno, Joseph E., and Michael T. Murray. (2013). *Textbook of Natural Medicine*, 4th edition. St. Louis, MO: Elsevier/Churchill Livingstone, 1468.

[8] Pavlović, Jelena M., Walter F. Stewart, Christa A. Bruce, Jennifer A. Gorman, Haiyan Sun, Dawn C. Buse, and Richard B. Lipton. "Burden of migraine related to menses: results from the AMPP study." *The Journal of Headache and Pain* 1, no. 16 (2015): 1–11; Granella, Franco, Grazia Sances, Carla Zanferrari, Alfredo Costa, Emilia Martignoni, and Gian Camillo Manzoni. "Migraine without aura and reproductive life events: a clinical epidemiological study in 1300 women." *Headache: The Journal of Head and Face Pain* 33, no. 7 (1993): 385–389; Warnock, Julia K., Lawrence J. Cohen, Harvey Blumenthal, and Jordan E. Hammond. "Hormone-related migraine headaches and mood disorders: treatment with estrogen stabilization." *Pharmacotherapy: The Journal of Human Pharmacology and Drug Therapy* (2016): 120–128; Sacco, Simona, Silvia Ricci, Diana Degan, and Antonio Carolei. "Migraine in women: the role of hormones and their impact on vascular diseases." *The Journal of Headache and Pain* 13, no. 3 (2012): 177–189; MacGregor, E.A., A. Frith, J. Ellis, L. Aspinall, and A. Hackshaw. "Incidence of migraine relative to menstrual cycle phases of rising and falling estrogen." *Neurology* 67, no. 12 (2006): 2154–2158.

[9] MacGregor, E. Anne, and Allan Hackshaw. "Prevalence of migraine on each day of the natural menstrual cycle." *Neurology* 63, no. 2 (2004): 351–353; Warnock, Julia K., Lawrence J. Cohen, Harvey Blumenthal, and Jordan E. Hammond. "Hormone-related migraine headaches and mood disorders: treatment with estrogen stabilization." *Pharmacotherapy: The Journal of Human Pharmacology and Drug Therapy* (2016): 120–128.

[10] Abraham, G.E. "Nutritional factors in the etiology of the premenstrual tension syndromes." *The Journal of Reproductive Medicine* 28, no. 7 (1983): 446–464.

[11] Abraham, G.E., and R.E. Rumley. "Role of nutrition in managing the premenstrual tension syndromes." *The Journal of Reproductive Medicine* 32, no. 6 (1987): 405–422.

[12] Ibid.

[13] Bäckström, T., and B. Mattsson. "Correlation of symptoms in pre-menstrual tension to oestrogen and progesterone concentrations in blood plasma." *Neuropsychobiology* 1, no. 2 (1975): 80–86.

[14] Abraham, G.E., and R.E. Rumley. "Role of nutrition in managing the premenstrual tension syndromes." *The Journal of Reproductive Medicine* 32, no. 6 (1987): 405–422.

[15] Head, Kathleen A. "Premenstrual syndrome: nutritional and alternative approaches." *Alternative Medicine Review* 2, no. 1 (1997): 12–25; White, Colin P., Christine L. Hitchcock, Yvette M. Vigna, and Jerilynn C. Prior. "Fluid retention over the menstrual cycle: 1-year data from the prospective ovulation cohort." *Obstetrics and Gynecology International* 2011 (2011): 1–7.

[16] Abraham, G.E. "Nutritional factors in the etiology of the premenstrual tension syndromes." *The Journal of Reproductive Medicine* 28, no. 7 (1983): 446–464; Schrier, Robert W. "Water and sodium retention in edematous disorders: role of vasopressin and aldosterone." *The American Journal of Medicine* 119, no. 7 (2006): S47–S53.

[17] Abraham, G.E., and R.E. Rumley. "Role of nutrition in managing the premenstrual tension syndromes." *The Journal of Reproductive Medicine* 32, no. 6 (1987): 405–422; Dean, Carolyn, Susan K. Steinberg, and William H. Sylvester. "Medical Management of Premenstrual Syndrome." *Canadian Family Physician* 32 (1986): 841–852.

[18] Abraham, G.E., and R.E. Rumley. "Role of nutrition in managing the premenstrual tension syndromes." *The Journal of Reproductive Medicine* 32, no. 6 (1987): 405–422.

[19] Halbreich, Uriel, Jeff Borenstein, Terry Pearlstein, and Linda S. Kahn. "The prevalence, impairment, impact, and burden of premenstrual dysphoric disorder (PMS/PMDD)." *Psychoneuroendocrinology* 28 (2003): 1–23.

[20] Chocano-Bedoya, P.O., J.E. Manson, S.E. Hankinson, W.C. Willett, S.R. Johnson, L. Chasan-Taber, A.G. Ronnenberg, C. Bigelow, and E.R. Bertone-Johnson. "Dietary B vitamin intake and incident premenstrual syndrome." *The American Journal of Clinical Nutrition* 93, no. 5 (2011): 1080–1086; Abraham, G.E., and R.E. Rumley. "Role of nutrition in managing the premenstrual tension syndromes." *The Journal of Reproductive Medicine* 32, no. 6 (1987): 405–422.

[21] Dexter, James D., John Roberts, and John A. Byer. "The five hour glucose tolerance test and effect of low sucrose diet in migraine." *Headache: The Journal of Head and Face Pain* 18, no. 2 (1978): 91–94.

[22] Kim, S.-Y., H.-J. Park, H. Lee, and H. Lee. "Acupuncture for premenstrual syndrome: a systematic review and meta-analysis of randomised controlled trials." *BJOG: An International Journal of Obstetrics & Gynaecology* 118, no. 8 (2011): 899–915; Taguchi, Reina, Shigeki Matsubara, Sazu Yoshimoto, Kenji Imai, Akihide Ohkuchi, and Hiroshi Kitakoji. "Acupuncture for premenstrual dysphoric disorder." *Archives of Gynecology and Obstetrics* 280, no. 6 (2009): 877–881; Habek, Dubravko, Jasna Čerkez Habek, and Ante Barbir. "Using acupuncture to treat premenstrual syndrome." *Archives of Gynecology and Obstetrics* 267, no. 1 (2002): 23–26.

[23] Appleton, Sarah M. "Premenstrual syndrome: evidence-based evaluation and treatment." *Clinical Obstetrics and Gynecology* 61, no. 1 (2018): 52–61.

[24] Walker, Ann F., Miriam C. De Souza, Michael F. Vickers, Savitri Abeyasekera, Marilyn L. Collins, and Luzia A. Trinca. "Magnesium supplementation alleviates premenstrual symptoms of fluid retention." *Journal of Women's Health* 7, no. 9 (1998): 1157–1165; Abraham, G.E., and R.E. Rumley. "Role of nutrition in managing the premenstrual tension syndromes." *The Journal of Reproductive Medicine* 32, no. 6 (1987): 405–422; Mauskop, Alexander, and Jasmine Varughese. "Why all migraine patients should be treated with magnesium." *Journal of Neural Transmission* 119, no. 5 (2012): 575–579; Mauskop, Alexander, Bella T. Altura, Roger Q. Cracco, and Burton M. Altura. "Intravenous magnesium sulphate relieves migraine attacks in patients with low serum ionized magnesium levels: a pilot study." *Clinical Science* 89, no. 6 (1995): 633–636; Köseoglu, Emel, Abdullah Talaslioglu, Ali Saffet Gönül, and Mustafa Kula. "The effects of magnesium prophylaxis in migraine without aura." *Magnesium Research* 21, no. 2 (2008): 101–108; Facchinetti, Fabio, Grazia Sances, Paola Borella, Andrea R. Genazzani, and Giuseppe Nappi. "Magnesium prophylaxis of menstrual migraine: effects on intracellular magnesium." *Headache: The Journal of Head and Face Pain* 31, no. 5 (1991): 298–301; Mauskop, Alexander, Bella T. Altura, Roger Q. Cracco, and Burton M. Altura. "Intravenous magnesium sulfate rapidly alleviates headaches of various types." *Headache: The Journal of Head and Face Pain* 36, no. 3 (1996): 154–160; Mauskop, Alexander, Bella T. Altura, and Burton M. Altura. "Serum ionized magnesium levels and serum ionized calcium/ionized magnesium ratios in women with menstrual migraine." *Headache: The Journal of Head and Face Pain* 42, no. 4 (2002): 242–248; Sarchielli, Paola, Giuliana Coata, Caterina Firenze, Piero Morucci, Giuseppe Abbritti, and Virgilio Gallai. "Serum and salivary magnesium levels in migraine and tension-type headache: results in a group of adult patients." *Cephalalgia* 12, no. 1 (1992): 21–27.

[25] Chocano-Bedoya, Patricia O., JoAnn E. Manson, Susan E. Hankinson, Walter C. Willett, Susan R. Johnson, Lisa Chasan-Taber, Alayne G. Ronnenberg, Carol Bigelow, and Elizabeth R. Bertone-Johnson. "Dietary B vitamin intake and incident premenstrual syndrome." *The American Journal of Clinical Nutrition* 93, no. 5 (2011): 1080–1086; Abraham, G.E., and R.E. Rumley. "Role of nutrition in managing the premenstrual tension syndromes." *The Journal of Reproductive Medicine* 32, no. 6 (1987): 405–422; Kashanian, M., R. Mazinani, and S. Jalalmanesh. "Pyridoxine (vitamin B_6) therapy for premenstrual syndrome." *International Journal of Gynecology & Obstetrics* 96, no. 1 (2007): 43–44; Wyatt, Katrina M., Paul W. Dimmock, Peter W. Jones, and P.M. Shaughn O'Brien. "Efficacy of vitamin B_6 in the treatment of premenstrual syndrome: systematic review." *The BMJ* 318, no. 7195 (1999): 1375–1381; Doll, Helen, Susan Brown, Amanda Thurston, and Martin Vessey. "Pyridoxine (vitamin B_6) and the premenstrual syndrome: a randomized crossover trial." *The Journal of the Royal College of General Practitioners* 39, no. 326 (1989): 364–368.

[26] Schoenfield, Pam. "Vitamin B_6, the under-appreciated vitamin." The Weston A. Price Foundation. Accessed May 2, 2017. https://www.westonaprice.org/health-topics/abcs-of-nutrition/vitamin-b6-the-under-appreciated-vitamin/.

[27] Kia, Afsaneh Saeedian, Reza Amani, and Bahman Cheraghian. "The association between the risk of premenstrual syndrome and vitamin D, calcium, and magnesium status among university students: a case control study." *Health Promotion Perspectives* 5, no. 3 (2015): 225–230; Penland, James G., and Phyllis E. Johnson. "Dietary calcium and manganese effects on menstrual cycle symptoms." *American Journal of Obstetrics and Gynecology* 168, no. 5 (1993): 1417–1423; Thys-Jacobs, Susan, Paul Starkey, Debra Bernstein, Jason Tian, and Premenstrual Syndrome Study Group. "Calcium carbonate and the premenstrual syndrome: effects on premenstrual and menstrual symptoms." *American Journal of Obstetrics and Gynecology* 179, no. 2 (1998): 444–452; Ghanbari, Zinat, Fedieh Haghollahi, Mamak Shariat, Abbas Rahimi Foroshani, and Maryam Ashrafi. "Effects of calcium supplement therapy in women with premenstrual syndrome." *Taiwanese Journal of Obstetrics and Gynecology* 48, no. 2 (2009): 124–129; Shobeiri, Fatemeh, Fahimeh Ezzati Araste, Reihaneh Ebrahimi, Ensiyeh Jenabi, and Mansour Nazari. "Effect of calcium on premenstrual syndrome: a double-blind randomized clinical trial." *Obstetrics & Gynecology Science* 60, no. 1 (2017): 100–105; Takashima-Uebelhoer, B.B., and E.R. Bertone-Johnson. (2014). "Calcium intake and premenstrual syndrome." *Handbook of Diet and Nutrition in the Menstrual Cycle, Periconception and Fertility*. Wageningen, Netherlands: Wageningen Academic Publishers, 51–65.

[28] Thys-Jacobs, Susan, Don McMahon, and John P. Bilezikian. "Cyclical changes in calcium metabolism across the menstrual cycle in women with premenstrual dysphoric disorder." *The Journal of Clinical Endocrinology & Metabolism* 92, no. 8 (2007): 2952–2959; Lehtovirta, P., D. Apter, and U.-H.. Stenman. "Serum CA-125 levels during the menstrual cycle." *Obstetrical & Gynecological Survey* 46, no. 4 (1991): 245–246; Puskulian, Louiza. "Salivary electrolyte changes during the normal menstrual cycle." *Journal of Dental Research* 51, no. 5 (1972): 1212–1216.

29 Thys-Jacobs, Susan, Paul Starkey, Debra Bernstein, Jason Tian, and Premenstrual Syndrome Study Group. "Calcium carbonate and the premenstrual syndrome: effects on premenstrual and menstrual symptoms." *American Journal of Obstetrics and Gynecology* 179, no. 2 (1998): 444–452; Penland, James G., and Phyllis E. Johnson. "Dietary calcium and manganese effects on menstrual cycle symptoms." *American Journal of Obstetrics and Gynecology* 168, no. 5 (1993): 1417–1423; Ghanbari, Zinat, Fedieh Haghollahi, Mamak Shariat, Abbas Rahimi Foroshani, and Maryam Ashrafi. "Effects of calcium supplement therapy in women with premenstrual syndrome." *Taiwanese Journal of Obstetrics and Gynecology* 48, no. 2 (2009): 124–129; Shobeiri, Fatemeh, Fahimeh Ezzati Araste, Reihaneh Ebrahimi, Ensiyeh Jenabi, and Mansour Nazari. "Effect of calcium on premenstrual syndrome: a double-blind randomized clinical trial." *Obstetrics & Gynecology Science* 60, no. 1 (2017): 100–105.

30 Thys-Jacobs, Susan, Paul Starkey, Debra Bernstein, Jason Tian, and Premenstrual Syndrome Study Group. "Calcium carbonate and the premenstrual syndrome: effects on premenstrual and menstrual symptoms." *American Journal of Obstetrics and Gynecology* 179, no. 2 (1998): 444–452.

31 Michaëlsson, Karl, Håkan Melhus, Eva Warensjö Lemming, Alicja Wolk, and Liisa Byberg. "Long term calcium intake and rates of all cause and cardiovascular mortality: community based prospective longitudinal cohort study." *The BMJ* 346 (2013): f228.

32 Ibid.

33 Douglass II, William Campbell. (2007). *The Raw Truth About Milk: How Science Is Destroying Nature's Nearly Perfect Food and Why Animal Protein and Animal Fat in Your Diet Can Save Your Life*. Republic of Panama: Rhino Publishing, 17; Magee, Hugh Edward, and Douglas Harvey. "Studies on the effect of heat on milk: some physico-chemical changes induced in milk by heat." *Biochemical Journal* 20, no. 4 (1926): 873–884; Vasbinder, Astrid Jolanda. "Casein-whey protein interactions in heated milk." PhD dissertation, 2003. Accessed May 7, 2017. dspace.library.uu.nl/bitstream/handle/1874/765/full.pdf.

34 Thys-Jacobs, Susan. "Micronutrients and the premenstrual syndrome: the case for calcium." *Journal of the American College of Nutrition* 19, no. 2 (2000): 220–227; Saeedian Kia A., R. Amani, and B. Cheraghian. "The association between the risk of premenstrual syndrome and vitamin D, calcium, and magnesium status among university students: a case control study." *Health Promotion Perspectives* 5, no. 3 (2015): 225–230.

35 Schmid, Alexandra, and Barbara Walther. "Natural vitamin D content in animal products." *Advances in Nutrition: An International Review Journal* 4, no. 4 (2013): 453–462; Ovesen, Lars, Rikke Andersen, and Jette Jakobsen. "Geographical differences in vitamin D status, with particular reference to European countries." *Proceedings of the Nutrition Society* 62, no. 04 (2003): 813–821.

36 Nair, Rathish, and Arun Maseeh. "Vitamin D: the 'sunshine' vitamin." *Journal of Pharmacology and Pharmacotherapeutics* 3, no. 2 (2012): 118–126.

37 Mead, M. Nathaniel. "Benefits of sunlight: a bright spot for human health." *Environmental Health Perspectives* 116, no. 4 (2008): A160–167.

38 Bodnar, Lisa M., Hyagriv N. Simhan, Robert W. Powers, Michael P. Frank, Emily Cooperstein, and James M. Roberts. "High prevalence of vitamin D insufficiency in black and white pregnant women residing in the northern United States and their neonates." *The Journal of Nutrition* 137, no. 2 (2007): 447–452; Richard, Aline, Sabine Rohrmann, and Katharina C. Quack Lötscher. "Prevalence of Vitamin D deficiency and its associations with skin color in pregnant women in the first trimester in a sample from Switzerland." *Nutrients* 9, no. 3 (2017): 260–271.

39 Nair, Rathish, and Arun Maseeh. "Vitamin D: the 'sunshine' vitamin." *Journal of Pharmacology & Pharmacotherapeutics* 3, no. 2 (2012): 1–18; Libon, Florence, Justine Courtois, Caroline Le Goff, Pierre Lukas, Neus Fabregat-Cabello, Laurence Seidel, Etienne Cavalier, and Arjen F. Nikkels. "Sunscreens block cutaneous vitamin D production with only a minimal effect on circulating 25-hydroxyvitamin D." *Archives of Osteoporosis* 12, no. 1 (2017): 66; Matsuoka, L.Y., L. Ide, J. Wortsman, J.A. MacLaughlin, and M.F. Holick. "Sunscreens suppress cutaneous vitamin D3 synthesis." *The Journal of Clinical Endocrinology and Metabolism* 64, no. 6 (1987): 1165–1168; Sambandan, Divya R., and Desiree Ratner. "Sunscreens: an overview and update." *Journal of the American Academy of Dermatology* 64, no. 4 (2011): 748–758; Kullavanijaya, Prisana, and Henry W. Lim. "Photoprotection." *Journal of the American Academy of Dermatology* 52, no. 6 (2005): 937–958; Faurschou, A., D.M. Beyer, Anne Schmedes, M.K. Bogh, P.A. Philipsen, and H.C. Wulf. "The relation between sunscreen layer thickness and vitamin D production after ultraviolet B exposure: a randomized clinical trial." *British Journal of Dermatology* 167, no. 2 (2012): 391–395; Norval, M., and Hans Chr Wulf. "Does chronic sunscreen use reduce vitamin D production to insufficient levels?" *British Journal of Dermatology* 161, no. 4 (2009): 732–736.

40 Schmid, Alexandra, and Barbara Walther. "Natural vitamin D content in animal products." *Advances in Nutrition: An International Review Journal* 4, no. 4 (2013): 453–462.

41 McKenna, M.J., and R. Freaney. "Secondary hyperparathyroidism in the elderly: means to defining hypovitaminosis D." *Osteoporosis International* 8, no. 8 (1998): S003–S006; Gómez-Alonso, Carlos, Manuel L. Naves-Díaz, Jose L. Fernández-Martín, Jose B. Díaz-López, Maria T. Fernández-Coto, and Jorge B. Cannata-Andía. "Vitamin D status and secondary hyperparathyroidism: the importance of 25-hydroxyvitamin D cut-off levels." *Kidney International* 63 (2003): S44–S48; Holick, Michael F. "Vitamin D deficiency." *New England Journal of Medicine* 357, no. 3 (2007): 266–281; Souberbielle, Jean-Claude, Jean-Jacques Body, Joan M. Lappe, Mario Plebani, Yehuda Shoenfeld, Thomas J. Wang, Heike A. Bischoff-Ferrari et al. "Vitamin D and musculoskeletal health, cardiovascular disease, autoimmunity and cancer: recommendations for clinical practice." *Autoimmunity Reviews* 9, no. 11 (2010): 709–715; Vieth, Reinhold. "Why the optimal requirement for Vitamin D3 is probably much higher than what is officially recommended for adults." *The Journal of Steroid Biochemistry and Molecular Biology* 89 (2004): 575–579.

42 Daniele, C., J. Thompson Coon, M.H. Pittler, and E. Ernst. "Vitex agnus castus: a systematic review of adverse events, 2005." *Drug Safety* 28, no. 4: 319–332.

[43] Ibid; Milewicz, A., E. Gejdel, H. Sworen, K. Sienkiewicz, J. Jedrzejak, T. Teucher, and H. Schmitz. "Vitex agnus castus extract in the treatment of luteal phase defects due to latent hyperprolactinaemia. I. Results of a randomized placebo-controlled double blind study." *Arzneimittel Forschung* 43 (1993): G-752.

[44] Jang, Su Hee, Dong Il Kim, and Min-Sun Choi. "Effects and treatment methods of acupuncture and herbal medicine for premenstrual syndrome/premenstrual dysphoric disorder: systematic review." *BMC Complementary and Alternative Medicine* 14, no. 1 (2014): 1–13; Cerqueira, Raphael O., Benicio N. Frey, Emilie Leclerc, and Elisa Brietzke. "Vitex agnus castus for premenstrual syndrome and premenstrual dysphoric disorder: a systematic review." *Archives of Women's Mental Health* 20, no. 6 (2017): 713–719; van Die, M. Diana, Henry G. Burger, Helena J. Teede, and Kerry M. Bone. "Vitex agnus-castus extracts for female reproductive disorders: a systematic review of clinical trials." *Planta Medica* 79, no. 07 (2013): 562–575; Dante, Giulia, and Fabio Facchinetti. "Herbal treatments for alleviating premenstrual symptoms: a systematic review." *Journal of Psychosomatic Obstetrics & Gynecology* 32, no. 1 (2011): 42–51; Schellenberg, Rftsg. "Treatment for the premenstrual syndrome with agnus castus fruit extract: prospective, randomised, placebo controlled study." *The BMJ* 322, no. 7279 (2001): 134–137.

Chapter 16

[1] Niwattisaiwong, Soamsiri, Kenneth D. Burman, and Melissa Li-Ng. "Iodine deficiency: clinical implications." *Cleveland Clinic Journal of Medicine* 84, no. 3 (2017): 236–244; Dillon, J.C., and J. Milliez. "Reproductive failure in women living in iodine deficient areas of West Africa." *BJOG: An International Journal of Obstetrics & Gynaecology* 107, no. 5 (2000): 631–636; Delange, F. "Iodine deficiency as a cause of brain damage." *Postgraduate Medical Journal* 77, no. 906 (2001): 217–220; Das, S.C., A.Z. Mohammed, S. Al-Hassan, A.A. Otokwula, and U.P. Isichei. "Effect of environmental iodine deficiency (EID) on foetal growth in Nigeria." *Indian Journal of Medical Research* 124, no. 5 (2006): 535–544; Cobra, Claudine, Kusnandi Rusmil, Diet Rustama, Susi S. Suwardi, Dewi Permaesih, Sri Martuti, and Richard D. Semba. "Infant survival is improved by oral iodine supplementation." *The Journal of Nutrition* 127, no. 4 (1997): 574–578; Pharoah, P.O.D., I.H. Buttfield, and B.S. Hetzel. "Neurological damage to the fetus resulting from severe iodine deficiency during pregnancy." *International Journal of Epidemiology* 41, no. 3 (2012): 589–592; Zimmermann, Michael B. "Iodine deficiency." *Endocrine Reviews* 30, no. 4 (2009): 376–408; Caldwell, Kathleen L., Yi Pan, Mary E. Mortensen, Amir Makhmudov, Lori Merrill, and John Moye. "Iodine status in pregnant women in the National Children's Study and in US women (15–44 years), National Health and Nutrition Examination Survey 2005–2010." *Thyroid* 23, no. 8 (2013): 927–937.

[2] Pharoah, P.O.D., I.H. Buttfield, and B.S. Hetzel. "Neurological damage to the fetus resulting from severe iodine deficiency during pregnancy." *International Journal of Epidemiology* 41, no. 3 (2012): 589–592; Pharoah, P.O.D., and K. J. Connolly. "A Controlled Trial of Iodinated Oil for the Prevention of Endemic Cretinism: A Long-Term Follow-Up." *International Journal of Epidemiology* 16, no. 1 (1987): 68–73; Zimmermann, Michael B., Pieter L. Jooste, and Chandrakant S. Pandav. "Iodine-deficiency disorders." *The Lancet* 372, no. 9645 (2008): 1251–1262; Halpern, Jean-Pierre, Steven C. Boyages, Glenden F. Maberly, John K. Collins, Creswell J. Eastman, and John GL Morris. "The neurology of endemic cretinism: a study of two endemias." *Brain* 114, no. 2 (1991): 825–841; Caldwell, Kathleen L., Yi Pan, Mary E. Mortensen, Amir Makhmudov, Lori Merrill, and John Moye. "Iodine status in pregnant women in the National Children's Study and in US women (15–44 years), National Health and Nutrition Examination Survey 2005–2010." *Thyroid* 23, no. 8 (2013): 927–937.

[3] Caldwell, Kathleen L., Yi Pan, Mary E. Mortensen, Amir Makhmudov, Lori Merrill, and John Moye. "Iodine status in pregnant women in the National Children's Study and in US women (15–44 years), National Health and Nutrition Examination Survey 2005–2010." *Thyroid* 23, no. 8 (2013): 927–937.

[4] Abraham, Guy E., Jorge D. Flechas, and J. C. Hakala. "Orthoiodosupplementation: iodine sufficiency of the whole human body." *The Original Internist* 9, no. 4 (2002): 30–41; Abraham, Guy E., Roxane C. Handal, and J.C. Hakala. "A simplified procedure for the measurement of urine iodide levels by the ion-selective electrode assay in a clinical setting." *The Original Internist* 1 (2006): 125–135.

[5] Aaseth, Jan, Harald Frey, Eystein Glattre, Gunnar Norheim, Jetmund Ringstad, and Yngvar Thomassen. "Selenium concentrations in the human thyroid gland." *Biological Trace Element Research* 24, no. 2–3 (1990): 147–152; Schomburg, Lutz, and Josef Köhrle. "On the importance of selenium and iodine metabolism for thyroid hormone biosynthesis and human health." *Molecular Nutrition & Food Research* 52, no. 11 (2008): 1235–1246; Brownstein, David. (2008). *Iodine: Why You Need It, Why You Can't Live Without It.* Arden, NC: Medical Alternatives Press.

[6] Arthur, John R., Fergus Nicol, and Geoffery J. Beckett. "Selenium deficiency, thyroid hormone metabolism, and thyroid hormone deiodinases." *The American Journal of Clinical Nutrition* 57, no. 2 (1993): 236S–239S; Drutel, Anne, Françoise Archambeaud, and Philippe Caron. "Selenium and the thyroid gland: more good news for clinicians." *Clinical Endocrinology* 78, no. 2 (2013): 155–164; Kohrle, J., F. Jakob, Bernard Contempre, and Jacques Emile Dumont. "Selenium, the thyroid, and the endocrine system." *Endocrine Reviews* 26, no. 7 (2005): 944–984.

[7] Cooper, Glinda S., and Berrit C. Stroehla. "The epidemiology of autoimmune diseases." *Autoimmunity Reviews* 2, no. 3 (2003): 119–125.

[8] Fröhlich, Eleonore, and Richard Wahl. "Thyroid autoimmunity: role of anti-thyroid antibodies in thyroid and extra-thyroidal diseases." *Frontiers in Immunology* 8 (2017) 521: 1–16.

[9] Turker, Omer, Kamil Kumanlioglu, Inanc Karapolat, and Ismail Dogan. "Selenium treatment in autoimmune thyroiditis: 9-month follow-up with variable doses." *Journal of Endocrinology* 190, no. 1 (2006): 151–156; Gärtner, Roland, Barbara C.H. Gasnier, Johannes W. Dietrich, Bjarne Krebs, and Matthias W.A. Angstwurm. "Selenium supplementation in patients with autoimmune thyroiditis decreases thyroid peroxidase antibodies concentrations." *The Journal of Clinical Endocrinology & Metabolism* 87, no. 4 (2002): 1687–1691; Fan, Yaofu, Shuhang Xu, Huifeng Zhang, Wen Cao, Kun Wang, Guofang Chen, Hongjie Di, Meng Cao, and Chao Liu. "Selenium supplementation for autoimmune thyroiditis: a systematic review and meta-analysis." *International Journal of Endocrinology* 2014 (2014): 1–8; Xu, Jian, Xue-Feng Yang,

Huai-Lan Guo, Xiao-Hui Hou, Lie-Gang Liu, and Xiu-Fa Sun. "Selenium supplement alleviated the toxic effects of excessive iodine in mice." *Biological Trace Element Research* 111, no. 1–3 (2006): 229–238; Drutel, Anne, Françoise Archambeaud, and Philippe Caron. "Selenium and the thyroid gland: more good news for clinicians." *Clinical Endocrinology* 78, no. 2 (2013): 155–164.

[10] Mahmoodianfard, Salma, Mohammadreza Vafa, Fatemeh Golgiri, Mohsen Khoshniat, Mahmoodreza Gohari, Zahra Solati, and Mahmood Djalali. "Effects of zinc and selenium supplementation on thyroid function in overweight and obese hypothyroid female patients: a randomized double-blind controlled trial." *Journal of the American College of Nutrition* 34, no. 5 (2015): 391–399.

[11] Nishiyama, Soroku, Yoshiko Futagoishi-Suginohara, Makoto Matsukura, Toshiro Nakamura, Akimasa Higashi, Makoto Shinohara, and Ichiro Matsuda. "Zinc supplementation alters thyroid hormone metabolism in disabled patients with zinc deficiency." *Journal of the American College of Nutrition* 13, no. 1 (1994): 62–67; Ruz, Manuel, Juana Codoceo, Jose Galgani, Luis Muñoz, Nuri Gras, Santiago Muzzo, Laura Leiva, and Cleofina Bosco. "Single and multiple selenium-zinc-iodine deficiencies affect rat thyroid metabolism and ultrastructure." *The Journal of Nutrition* 129, no. 1 (1999): 174–180.

[12] Maxwell, Christy, and Stella Lucia Volpe. "Effect of zinc supplementation on thyroid hormone function." *Annals of Nutrition and Metabolism* 51, no. 2 (2007): 188–194.

[13] Fallah, Soudabeh, Fatemeh Valinejad Sani, and Mohsen Firoozrai. "Effect of contraceptive pill on the selenium and zinc status of healthy subjects." *Contraception* 80, no. 1 (2009): 40–43; Hunt, Janet R. "Bioavailability of iron, zinc, and other trace minerals from vegetarian diets." *The American Journal of Clinical Nutrition* 78, no. 3 (2003): 633S–639S.

[14] Gupta, C.P. "Role of iron (Fe) in body." *IOSR Journal of Applied Chemistry (IOSR-JAC)* 7 (2014): 38–46.

[15] Takamatsu, J., M. Majima, K. Miki, K. Kuma, and T. Mozai. "Serum ferritin as a marker of thyroid hormone action on peripheral tissues." *The Journal of Clinical Endocrinology and Metabolism* 61, no. 4 (1985): 672–676.

[16] Sachdeva, Ashuma, Veena Singh, Isha Malik, Prasanta Saha Roy, Himanshu Madaan, and Rajesh Nair. "Association between serum ferritin and thyroid hormone profile in hypothyroidism." *International Journal of Medical Science and Public Health* 4, no. 6 (2015): 863–865; Kubota, K., J. Tamura, H. Kurabayashi, T. Shirakura, and I. Kobayashi. "Evaluation of increased serum ferritin levels in patients with hyperthyroidism." *The Clinical Investigator* 72, no. 1 (1993): 26–29.

[17] Hess, Sonja Y., Michael B. Zimmermann, Myrtha Arnold, Wolfgang Langhans, and Richard F. Hurrell. "Iron deficiency anemia reduces thyroid peroxidase activity in rats." *The Journal of Nutrition* 132, no. 7 (2002): 1951–1955; Zimmermann, Michael B. "The influence of iron status on iodine utilization and thyroid function." *Annual Review of Nutrition* 26 (2006): 367–389.

[18] Martinez-Torres, C., L. Cubeddu, E. Dillmann, G.L. Brengelmann, I. Leets, M. Layrisse, D.G. Johnson, and C. Finch. "Effect of exposure to low temperature on normal and iron-deficient subjects." *The American Journal of Physiology* 246, no. 3 (1984): R380–R383; Beard, John L, M.J. Borel, and Janice Derr. "Impaired thermoregulation and thyroid function in iron-deficiency anemia." *The American Journal of Clinical Nutrition* 52, no. 5 (1990): 813–819.

[19] Beard, John L, M.J. Borel, and Janice Derr. "Impaired thermoregulation and thyroid function in iron-deficiency anemia." *The American Journal of Clinical Nutrition* 52, no. 5 (1990): 813–819.

[20] Gröber, Uwe, Joachim Schmidt, and Klaus Kisters. "Magnesium in prevention and therapy." *Nutrients* 7, no. 9 (2015): 8199–8226.

[21] Mazur, Andrzej, Jeanette A.M. Maier, Edmond Rock, Elyett Gueux, Wojciech Nowacki, and Yves Rayssiguier. "Magnesium and the inflammatory response: potential physiopathological implications." *Archives of Biochemistry and Biophysics* 458, no. 1 (2007): 48–56; Abbas, Amr M., and Hussein F. Sakr. "Effect of magnesium sulfate and thyroxine on inflammatory markers in a rat model of hypothyroidism." *Canadian Journal of Physiology and Pharmacology* 94, no. 4 (2015): 426–432; Moncayo, Roy, and Helga Moncayo. "The WOMED model of benign thyroid disease: acquired magnesium deficiency due to physical and psychological stressors relates to dysfunction of oxidative phosphorylation." *BBA Clinical* 3 (2015): 44–64.

[22] Moncayo, Roy, and Helga Moncayo. "Proof of concept of the WOMED model of benign thyroid disease: restitution of thyroid morphology after correction of physical and psychological stressors and magnesium supplementation." *BBA Clinical* 3 (2015): 113–122; Moncayo, Roy, and Helga Moncayo. "The WOMED model of benign thyroid disease: acquired magnesium deficiency due to physical and psychological stressors relates to dysfunction of oxidative phosphorylation." *BBA Clinical* 3 (2015): 44–64; Baldini, Marina, Daniela Castagnone, Roberto Rivolta, Laura Meroni, Marco Pappalettera, and Luigi Cantalamessa. "Thyroid vascularization by color doppler ultrasonography in Graves' disease. Changes related to different phases and to the long-term outcome of the disease." *Thyroid* 7, no. 6 (1997): 823–828.

[23] Moncayo, Roy, and Helga Moncayo. "The WOMED model of benign thyroid disease: acquired magnesium deficiency due to physical and psychological stressors relates to dysfunction of oxidative phosphorylation." *BBA Clinical* 3 (2015): 44–64; Moncayo, Roy, and Helga Moncayo. "Proof of concept of the WOMED model of benign thyroid disease: restitution of thyroid morphology after correction of physical and psychological stressors and magnesium supplementation." *BBA Clinical* 3 (2015): 113–122.

[24] Hess, Sonja Y. "The impact of common micronutrient deficiencies on iodine and thyroid metabolism: the evidence from human studies." *Best Practice & Research Clinical Endocrinology & Metabolism* 24, no. 1 (2010): 117–132; Oba, Kiyoshi, and Shuichi Kimura. "Effects of vitamin A deficiency on thyroid function and serum thyroxine levels in the rat." *Journal of Nutritional Science and Vitaminology* 26, no. 4 (1980): 327–334; Zimmermann, M.B. "Interactions of vitamin A and iodine deficiencies: effects on the pituitary-thyroid axis." *International Journal for Vitamin and Nutrition Research* 77, no. 3 (2007): 236–240; Farhangi, Mahdieh Abbasalizad, Seyyed Ali Keshavarz, Mohammadreza Eshraghian, Alireza Ostadrahimi, and Ali Akbar Saboor-Yaraghi. "The effect of vitamin A supplementation on thyroid function in premenopausal women." *Journal of the American College of Nutrition* 31, no. 4 (2012): 268–274.

25 Sarandöl, Emre, Sibel Taş, Melahat Dirican, and Zehra Serdar. "Oxidative stress and serum paraoxonase activity in experimental hypothyroidism: effect of vitamin E supplementation." Cell Biochemistry and Function 23, no. 1 (2005): 1–8; Padayatty, Sebastian J., Arie Katz, Yaohui Wang, Peter Eck, Oran Kwon, Je-Hyuk Lee, Shenglin Chen et al. "Vitamin C as an antioxidant: evaluation of its role in disease prevention." Journal of the American College of Nutrition 22, no. 1 (2003): 18–35.

26 Kivity, Shaye, Nancy Agmon-Levin, Michael Zisappl, Yinon Shapira, Endre V. Nagy, Katalin Dankó, Zoltan Szekanecz, Pnina Langevitz, and Yehuda Shoenfeld. "Vitamin D and autoimmune thyroid diseases." Cellular & Molecular Immunology 8, no. 3 (2011): 243; Yasuda, Tetsuyuki, Yasuyuki Okamoto, Noboru Hamada, Kazuyuki Miyashita, Mitsuyoshi Takahara, Fumie Sakamoto, Takeshi Miyatsuka et al. "Serum vitamin D levels are decreased and associated with thyroid volume in female patients with newly onset Graves' disease." Endocrine 42, no. 3 (2012): 739–741.

27 Wang, Yi-Ping, Hung-Pin Lin, Hsin-Ming Chen, Ying-Shiung Kuo, Ming-Jane Lang, and Andy Sun. "Hemoglobin, iron, and vitamin B12 deficiencies and high blood homocysteine levels in patients with anti-thyroid autoantibodies." Journal of the Formosan Medical Association 113, no. 3 (2014): 155–160; Ness-Abramof, Rosane, Dan A. Nabriski, Menachem S. Shapiro, Louis Shenkman, Lotan Shilo, Eliahu Weiss, Tamar Reshef, and Lewis E. Braverman. "Prevalence and evaluation of B12 deficiency in patients with autoimmune thyroid disease." The American Journal of the Medical Sciences 332, no. 3 (2006): 119–122.

28 Jabbar, Abdul, Aasma Yawar, Sabiha Waseem, Najmul Islam, Naeem Ul Haque, Lubna Zuberi, Ataullah Khan, and Jaweed Akhter. "Vitamin B12 deficiency common in primary hypothyroidism." Journal of the Pakistan Medical Association 58, no. 5 (2008): 258.

29 Dakshinamurti, K., C.S. Paulose, J.A. Thliveris, and J. Vriend. "Thyroid function in pyridoxine-deficient young rats." Journal of Endocrinology 104, no. 3 (1985): 339–344.

30 Chandrasekhar, K., Jyoti Kapoor, and Sridhar Anishetty. "A prospective, randomized double-blind, placebo-controlled study of safety and efficacy of a high-concentration full-spectrum extract of ashwagandha root in reducing stress and anxiety in adults." Indian Journal of Psychological Medicine 34, no. 3 (2012): 255–262.

31 Sharma, Ashok Kumar, Indraneel Basu, and Siddarth Singh. "Efficacy and safety of ashwagandha root extract in subclinical hypothyroid patients: a double-blind, randomized placebo-controlled trial." The Journal of Alternative and Complementary Medicine 24, no. 3 (2018): 243–248.

32 Clements Jr., Rex S., and Betty Darnell. "Myo-inositol content of common foods: development of a high-myo-inositol diet." The American Journal of Clinical Nutrition 33, no. 9 (1980): 1954–1967; Williams, Peter. "The missing vitamin alphabet." Nutrition & Dietetics 73, no. 2 (2016): 205–214.

33 Ferrari, S.M., P. Fallahi, F. Di Bari, R. Vita, S. Benvenga, and A. Antonelli. "Myo-inositol and selenium reduce the risk of developing overt hypothyroidism in patients with autoimmune thyroiditis." European Review for Medical and Pharmacological Sciences 21, no. 2 supplement (2017): 36–42; Nordio, Maurizio, and Raffaella Pajalich. "Combined treatment with myo-inositol and selenium ensures euthyroidism in subclinical hypothyroidism patients with autoimmune thyroiditis." Journal of Thyroid Research (2013): 1–5; Nordio, M., and S. Basciani. "Myo-inositol plus selenium supplementation restores euthyroid state in Hashimoto's patients with subclinical hypothyroidism." European Review for Medical and Pharmacological Sciences 21, no. 2 Suppl (2017): 51–59.

34 Nestler, John E., Daniela J. Jakubowicz, William S. Evans, and Renato Pasquali. "Effects of metformin on spontaneous and clomiphene-induced ovulation in the polycystic ovary syndrome." New England Journal of Medicine 338, no. 26 (1998): 1876–1880.

35 Siavash, Mansour, Majid Tabbakhian, Ali Mohammad Sabzghabaee, and Niloufar Razavi. "Severity of gastrointestinal side effects of metformin tablet compared to metformin capsule in type 2 diabetes mellitus patients." Journal of Research in Pharmacy Practice 6, no. 2 (2017): 73–76.

36 Gower, Barbara A., Paula C. Chandler-Laney, Fernando Ovalle, Laura Lee Goree, Ricardo Azziz, Renee A. Desmond, Wesley M. Granger, Amy M. Goss, and G. Wright Bates. "Favourable metabolic effects of a eucaloric lower-carbohydrate diet in women with PCOS." Clinical Endocrinology 79, no. 4 (2013): 550–557.

37 Nichols, Lily. (2018). Real Food for Pregnancy: The Science and Wisdom of Optimal Prenatal Nutrition. Lily Nichols, 141.

38 Westman, Eric C., William S. Yancy Jr., Mark D. Haub, and Jeff S. Volek. "Insulin resistance from a low carbohydrate, high fat diet perspective." Metabolic Syndrome and Related Disorders 3, no. 1 (2005): 14–18.

39 Atkinson, Fiona S., Kaye Foster-Powell, and Jennie C. Brand-Miller. "International tables of glycemic index and glycemic load values: 2008." Diabetes Care 31, no. 12 (2008): 2281–2283.

40 Gower, Barbara A., and Amy M. Goss. "A lower-carbohydrate, higher-fat diet reduces abdominal and intermuscular fat and increases insulin sensitivity in adults at risk of type 2 diabetes." The Journal of Nutrition 145, no. 1 (2014): 177S–183S; McGrice, Melanie, and Judi Porter. "The effect of low carbohydrate diets on fertility hormones and outcomes in overweight and obese women: a systematic review." Nutrients 9, no. 3 (2017): 1–11.

41 Mavropoulos, John C., William S. Yancy, Juanita Hepburn, and Eric C. Westman. "The effects of a low-carbohydrate, ketogenic diet on the polycystic ovary syndrome: a pilot study." Nutrition & Metabolism 2, no. 1 (2005): 1–5.

42 Gower, Barbara A., Paula C. Chandler-Laney, Fernando Ovalle, Laura Lee Goree, Ricardo Azziz, Renee A. Desmond, Wesley M. Granger, Amy M. Goss, and G. Wright Bates. "Favourable metabolic effects of a eucaloric lower-carbohydrate diet in women with PCOS." Clinical Endocrinology 79, no. 4 (2013): 550–557.

43 Thomson, Rebecca L., Simon Spedding, and Jonathan D. Buckley. "Vitamin D in the aetiology and management of polycystic ovary syndrome." Clinical Endocrinology 77, no. 3 (2012): 343–350; Vieth, Reinhold. "Why the optimal requirement for Vitamin D3 is probably much higher than what is officially recommended for adults." The Journal of Steroid Biochemistry and Molecular Biology 89 (2004): 575–579; Holick, Michael F. "Vitamin D deficiency." New England Journal of Medicine 357, no. 3 (2007): 266–281; Souberbielle, Jean-Claude, Jean-Jacques Body, Joan M. Lappe, Mario Plebani, Yehuda Shoenfeld, Thomas J. Wang, Heike A. Bischoff-Ferrari et al. "Vitamin D and musculoskeletal health,

cardiovascular disease, autoimmunity and cancer: recommendations for clinical practice." *Autoimmunity Reviews* 9, no. 11 (2010): 709–715.

44 Teegarden, Dorothy, and Shawn S. Donkin. "Vitamin D: emerging new roles in insulin sensitivity." *Nutrition Research Reviews* 22, no. 1 (2009): 82–92; Kotsa, Kalliopi, Maria P. Yavropoulou, Olympia Anastasiou, and John G. Yovos. "Role of vitamin D treatment in glucose metabolism in polycystic ovary syndrome." *Fertility and Sterility* 92, no. 3 (2009): 1053–1058.

45 Pal, Lubna, Heping Zhang, Joanne Williams, Nanette F. Santoro, Michael P. Diamond, William D. Schlaff, Christos Coutifaris et al. "Vitamin D status relates to reproductive outcome in women with polycystic ovary syndrome: secondary analysis of a multicenter randomized controlled trial." *The Journal of Clinical Endocrinology & Metabolism* 101, no. 8 (2016): 3027–3035.

46 Muneyyirci-Delale, O., V.L. Nacharaju, M. Dalloul, S. Jalou, M. Rahman, B.M. Altura, and B.T. Altura. "Divalent cations in women with PCOS: implications for cardiovascular disease." *Gynecological Endocrinology* 15, no. 3 (2001): 198–201; von Ehrlich, B., M. Barbagallo, H.G. Classen, F. Guerrero-Romero, F.C. Mooren, M. Rodriguez-Moran, W. Vierling, J. Vormann, and K. Kisters. "Significance of magnesium in insulin resistance, metabolic syndrome, and diabetes recommendations of the Association of Magnesium Research e.V." *Trace Elements and Electrolytes* 34, no. 3 (2017): 124–129; Barbagallo, Mario, and Ligia J. Dominguez. "Magnesium and type 2 diabetes." *World Journal of Diabetes* 6, no. 10 (2015): 1152–1157; Dibaba, Daniel T., Pengcheng Xun, and Ka He. "Dietary magnesium intake is inversely associated with serum C-reactive protein levels: meta-analysis and systematic review." *European Journal of Clinical Nutrition* 68, no. 4 (2014): 510–516.

47 Guerrero-Romero, F., H.E. Tamez-Perez, G. González-González, A.M. Salinas-Martinez, J. Montes-Villarreal, J.H. Trevino-Ortiz, and M. Rodriguez-Moran. "Oral magnesium supplementation improves insulin sensitivity in non-diabetic subjects with insulin resistance. a double-blind placebo-controlled randomized trial." *Diabetes and Metabolism* 30, no. 3 (2004): 253–258; Simental-Mendía, Luis E., Martha Rodríguez-Morán, and Fernando Guerrero-Romero. "Oral magnesium supplementation decreases C-reactive protein levels in subjects with prediabetes and hypomagnesemia: a clinical randomized double-blind placebo-controlled trial." *Archives of Medical Research* 45, no. 4 (2014): 325–330.

48 Kanafchian, Maryam, Soleiman Mahjoub, Sedigheh Esmaeilzadeh, Maryam Rahsepar, and Abbas Mosapour. "Status of serum selenium and zinc in patients with the polycystic ovary syndrome with and without insulin resistance." *Middle East Fertility Society Journal* (2017): 1–5; Guler, Ismail, Ozdemir Himmetoglu, Ahmet Turp, Ahmet Erdem, Mehmet Erdem, M. Anil Onan, Cagatay Taskiran, Mine Yavuz Taslipinar, and Haldun Guner. "Zinc and homocysteine levels in polycystic ovarian syndrome patients with insulin resistance." *Biological Trace Element Research* 158, no. 3 (2014): 297–304.

49 Foroozanfard, F., M. Jamilian, Z. Jafari, A. Khassaf, A. Hosseini, H. Khorammian, and Z. Asemi. "Effects of zinc supplementation on markers of insulin resistance and lipid profiles in women with polycystic ovary syndrome: a randomized, double-blind, placebo-controlled trial." *Experimental and Clinical Endocrinology and Diabetes* 123, no. 04 (2015): 215–220; Ostadrahimi, Alireza. "Effect of zinc supplementation on cardiometabolic risk factors in women with polycystic ovary syndrome." *Journal of Cardiovascular and Thoracic Research* 2, no. 2 (2010): 11–20.

50 Jamilian, Mehri, Fatemeh Foroozanfard, Fereshteh Bahmani, Rezvan Talaee, Mahshid Monavari, and Zatollah Asemi. "Effects of zinc supplementation on endocrine outcomes in women with polycystic ovary syndrome: a randomized, double-blind, placebo-controlled trial." *Biological Trace Element Research* 170, no. 2 (2016): 271–278.

51 Wall, Rebecca, R. Paul Ross, Gerald F. Fitzgerald, and Catherine Stanton. "Fatty acids from fish: the anti-inflammatory potential of long-chain omega-3 fatty acids." *Nutrition Reviews* 68, no. 5 (2010): 280–289.

52 McEwen, Bradley J. "Can omega-3 polyunsaturated fatty acids improve metabolic profile in polycystic ovary syndrome (PCOS)?" *Advances in Integrative Medicine* 4, no. 2 (2017): 82–83; Khani, Behnaz, Farahnaz Mardanian, and Sajadeh Jafari Fesharaki. "Omega-3 supplementation effects on polycystic ovary syndrome symptoms and metabolic syndrome." *Journal of Research in Medical Sciences* 22 (2017); Forouhi, Neda, Sakineh Shab-Bidar, and Kurosh Djafarian. "Effect of omega-3 fatty acids supplementation on testosterone levels in women with polycystic ovary syndrome: Meta-analysis of randomized controlled trials." *Journal of Nutritional Sciences and Dietetics* 1, no. 3 (2015): 165–170.

53 Ghent, W.R., B.A. Eskin, D.A. Low, and L.P. Hill. Iodine replacement in fibrocystic disease of the breast. *Canadian Journal of Surgery* 36, no. 5 (1993): 453–460; Naehrlich, Lutz, Helmuth-Günther Dörr, Azadeh Bagheri-Behrouzi, and Manfred Rauh. "Iodine deficiency and subclinical hypothyroidism are common in cystic fibrosis patients." *Journal of Trace Elements in Medicine and Biology* 27, no. 2 (2013): 122–125.

54 Gerli, S., M. Mignosa, and G.C. Di Renzo. "Effects of inositol on ovarian function and metabolic factors in women with PCOS: a randomized double blind placebo-controlled trial." *European Review for Medical and Pharmacological Sciences* 7 (2003): 151–160; Iuorno, MD, Maria J., Daniela J. Jakubowicz, MD, Jean-Patrice Baillargeon, MD, Pamela Dillon, BS, Ronald D. Gunn, MS, Geoffrey Allan, PhD, and John E. Nestler, MD. "Effects of D-chiro-inositol in lean women with polycystic ovary syndrome." *Endocrine Practice* 8, no. 6 (2002): 417–423.

55 Raffone, Emanuela, Pietro Rizzo, and Vincenzo Benedetto. "Insulin sensitiser agents alone and in co-treatment with r-FSH for ovulation induction in PCOS women." *Gynecological Endocrinology* 26, no. 4 (2010): 275–280.

56 Dinicola, Simona, Tony T.Y. Chiu, Vittorio Unfer, Gianfranco Carlomagno, and Mariano Bizzarri. "The rationale of the myo-inositol and D-chiro-inositol combined treatment for polycystic ovary syndrome." *The Journal of Clinical Pharmacology* 54, no. 10 (2014): 1079–1092; Unfer, Vittorio, and Giuseppina Porcaro. "Updates on the myo-inositol plus D-chiro-inositol combined therapy in polycystic ovary syndrome." *Expert Review of Clinical Pharmacology* 7, no. 5 (2014): 623–631; Monastra, Giovanni, Vittorio Unfer, Abdel Halim Harrath, and Mariano Bizzarri. "Combining treatment with myo-inositol and D-chiro-inositol (40: 1) is effective in restoring ovary function and metabolic balance in PCOS patients." *Gynecological Endocrinology* 33, no. 1 (2017): 1–9.

57 Millea, Paul J. "N-acetylcysteine: multiple clinical applications." *American Family Physician* 80, no. 3 (2009): 265–269.

58 Salehpour, Saghar, Azadeh Akbari Sene, Nasrin Saharkhiz, Mohammad Reza Sohrabi, and Fatemeh Moghimian. "N-acetylcysteine as an adjuvant to clomiphene citrate for successful induction of ovulation in infertile patients with polycystic ovary syndrome." *Journal of Obstetrics and Gynaecology Research* 38, no. 9 (2012): 1182–1186.

59 Javanmanesh, Forough, Maryam Kashanian, Maryam Rahimi, and Narges Sheikhansari. "A comparison between the effects of metformin and N-acetylcysteine (NAC) on some metabolic and endocrine characteristics of women with polycystic ovary syndrome." *Gynecological Endocrinology* 32, no. 4 (2016): 285–289; Dasgupta, M., T.K. Roy, P.S. Mitra, S. Adhikari, and T. Bag. "Is N-acetylcysteine a better insulin sensitizer than metformin in polycystic ovarian syndrome?" *Andrology & Gynecology: Current Research* 3, no. 3. (2015): 1–5; Ali, Hina, Gita Radhakrishnan, and Alpana Singh. "Comparison of metformin and N-acetylcysteine on metabolic parameters in women with polycystic ovarian syndrome." *International Journal of Reproduction, Contraception, Obstetrics and Gynecology* 6, no. 7 (2017): 3076–3084; Cheraghi, Ebrahim, Malek Soleimani Mehranjani, Mohammad Ali Shariatzadeh, Mohammad Hossein Nasr Esfahani, and Zahra Ebrahimi. "N-acetylcysteine improves oocyte and embryo quality in polycystic ovary syndrome patients undergoing intracytoplasmic sperm injection: an alternative to metformin." *Reproduction, Fertility and Development* 28, no. 6 (2016): 723–731.

60 Wei, Wei, Hongmin Zhao, Aili Wang, Ming Sui, Kun Liang, Haiyun Deng, Yukun Ma, Yajuan Zhang, Hongxiu Zhang, and Yuanyuan Guan. "A clinical study on the short-term effect of berberine in comparison to metformin on the metabolic characteristics of women with polycystic ovary syndrome." *European Journal of Endocrinology* 166, no. 1 (2012): 99–105.

61 Li, Lin, Chengyan Li, Ping Pan, Xiaoli Chen, Xiaoke Wu, Ernest Hung Yu Ng, and Dongzi Yang. "A single arm pilot study of effects of berberine on the menstrual pattern, ovulation rate, hormonal and metabolic profiles in anovulatory Chinese women with polycystic ovary syndrome." *PLOS One* 10, no. 12 (2015): e0144072; Orio, Francesco, Giovanna Muscogiuri, Stefano Palomba, Silvia Savastano, Alessio Volpe, Marcello Orio, Giorgio Colarieti et al. "Berberine improves reproductive features in obese Caucasian women with polycystic ovary syndrome independently of changes of insulin sensitivity." *e-SPEN Journal* 8, no. 5 (2013): e200–e204.

62 Hajimonfarednejad, Mahdie, Majid Nimrouzi, Mojtaba Heydari, Mohammad Mehdi Zarshenas, Mohammad Javad Raee, and Bahia Namavar Jahromi. "Insulin resistance improvement by cinnamon powder in polycystic ovary syndrome: a randomized double-blind placebo controlled clinical trial." *Phytotherapy Research* 32, no. 2 (2018): 276–283; Wang, Jeff G., Richard A. Anderson, George M. Graham, Micheline C. Chu, Mark V. Sauer, Michael M. Guarnaccia, and Rogerio A. Lobo. "The effect of cinnamon extract on insulin resistance parameters in polycystic ovary syndrome: a pilot study." *Fertility and Sterility* 88, no. 1 (2007): 240–243.

63 Kort, Daniel H., and Roger A. Lobo. "Preliminary evidence that cinnamon improves menstrual cyclicity in women with polycystic ovary syndrome: a randomized controlled trial." *American Journal of Obstetrics and Gynecology* 211, no. 5 (2014): 1–21.

64 Cialdella-Kam, Lynn, Charlotte P. Guebels, Gianni F. Maddalozzo, and Melinda M. Manore. "Dietary intervention restored menses in female athletes with exercise-associated menstrual dysfunction with limited impact on bone and muscle health." *Nutrients* 6, no. 8 (2014): 3018–3039.

65 Reichman, Marsha E., Joseph T. Judd, Philip R. Taylor, Paomanabhan P. Nair, D.Y. Jones, and William S. Campbell. "Effect of dietary fat on length of the follicular phase of the menstrual cycle in a controlled diet setting." *The Journal of Clinical Endocrinology & Metabolism* 74, no. 5 (1992): 1171–1175.

66 Hendrickson-Jack, Lisa. "FFP 141 | Surviving Hypothalamic Amenorrhea | Getting Your Period Back Without Fertility Drugs | Nicola Rinaldi." *Fertility Friday Podcast*. Podcast Audio, June 9, 2017. fertilityfriday.com/141

Chapter 17

1 Price, Weston A. (2016). *Nutrition and Physical Degeneration*, 8th edition. Lemon Grove, CA: Price-Pottenger Nutrition Foundation, 124–125.

2 Clagett-Dame, Margaret, and Danielle Knutson. "Vitamin A in reproduction and development." *Nutrients* 3, no. 4 (2011): 385–428; Emmett, Susan D., and Keith P. West Jr. "Gestational vitamin A deficiency and sensorineural hearing loss in the developing world?" *Medical Hypotheses* 82, no. 1 (2014): 6–10; Strobel, Manuela, Jana Tinz, and Hans-Konrad Biesalski. "The importance of β-carotene as a source of vitamin A with special regard to pregnant and breastfeeding women." *European Journal of Nutrition* 46, no. 9 (2007): 1–20.

3 Strobel, Manuela, Jana Tinz, and Hans-Konrad Biesalski. "The importance of β-carotene as a source of vitamin A with special regard to pregnant and breastfeeding women." *European Journal of Nutrition* 46, no. 9 (2007): 1–20.

4 Breymann, Christian. "Iron deficiency anemia in pregnancy." *Seminars in Hematology* 52, no. 4 (2015): 339–347; McArdle, Harry J., Lorraine Gambling, and Christine Kennedy. "Iron deficiency during pregnancy: the consequences for placental function and fetal outcome." *Proceedings of the Nutrition Society* 73, no. 1 (2014): 9–15.

5 Alwan, Nisreen A., Janet E. Cade, Harry J. McArdle, Darren C. Greenwood, Helen E. Hayes, and Nigel A.B. Simpson. "Maternal iron status in early pregnancy and birth outcomes: insights from the baby's vascular health and iron in pregnancy study." *British Journal of Nutrition* 113, no. 12 (2015): 1985–1992.

6 Zeisel, Steven H. "Nutrition in pregnancy: the argument for including a source of choline." *International Journal of Women's Health* 5 (2013): 193–199; Shaw, Gary M., Suzan L. Carmichael, Wei Yang, Steve Selvin, and Donna M. Schaffer. "Periconceptional dietary intake of choline and betaine and neural tube defects in offspring." *American Journal of Epidemiology* 160, no. 2 (2004): 102–109; Meck, Warren H., Rebecca A. Smith, and Christina L. Williams. "Pre- and postnatal choline supplementation produces long-term facilitation of spatial memory." *Developmental Psychobiology* 21, no. 4 (1988): 339–353; Gaskins, Audrey J., Sunni L. Mumford, Jorge E. Chavarro, Cuilin Zhang, Anna Z. Pollack, Jean Wactawski-Wende, Neil J. Perkins, and Enrique F. Schisterman. "The impact of dietary folate intake on reproductive function in premenopausal women: a prospective cohort study." *PLOS One* 7, no. 9 (2012): e46276; Zeisel, Steven H.

"The fetal origins of memory: the role of dietary choline in optimal brain development." *The Journal of Pediatrics* 149, no. 5 (2006): S131–S136; Zeisel, Steven H. "Choline: needed for normal development of memory." *Journal of the American College of Nutrition* 19, no. sup5 (2000): 528S–531S; Bibbins-Domingo, Kirsten, David C. Grossman, Susan J. Curry, Karina W. Davidson, John W. Epling, Francisco A.R. García, Alex R. Kemper et al. "Folic acid supplementation for the prevention of neural tube defects: US Preventive Services Task Force recommendation statement." *JAMA* 317, no. 2 (2017): 183–189.

7 Lee, Joyce M., Jessica R. Smith, Barbara L. Philipp, Tai C. Chen, Jeffrey Mathieu, and Michael F. Holick. "Vitamin D deficiency in a healthy group of mothers and newborn infants." *Clinical Pediatrics* 46, no. 1 (2007): 42–44.

8 Mahon, Pamela, Nicholas Harvey, Sarah Crozier, Hazel Inskip, Sian Robinson, Nigel Arden, Rama Swaminathan, Cyrus Cooper, and Keith Godfrey. "Low maternal vitamin D status and fetal bone development: cohort study." *Journal of Bone and Mineral Research* 25, no. 1 (2010): 14–19; Wei, S.Q., F. Audibert, N. Hidiroglou, K. Sarafin, P. Julien, Y. Wu, Z.C. Luo, and W.D. Fraser. "Longitudinal vitamin D status in pregnancy and the risk of pre-eclampsia." *BJOG: An International Journal of Obstetrics & Gynaecology* 119, no. 7 (2012): 832–839; Mulligan, Megan L, Shaili K. Felton, Amy E. Riek, and Carlos Bernal-Mizrachi. "Implications of vitamin D deficiency in pregnancy and lactation." *American Journal of Obstetrics and Gynecology* 202, no. 5 (2010): 429-e1–429-e9.

9 Mumford, Sunni L, Rebecca A. Garbose, Keewan Kim, Kerri Kissell, Daniel L. Kuhr, Ukpebo R. Omosigho, Neil J. Perkins et al. "Association of preconception serum 25-hydroxyvitamin D concentrations with live birth and pregnancy loss: a prospective cohort study." *The Lancet Diabetes & Endocrinology* (2018): 1–8; Ota, Kuniaki, Svetlana Dambaeva, Ae-Ra Han, Kenneth Beaman, Alice Gilman-Sachs, and Joanne Kwak-Kim. "Vitamin D deficiency may be a risk factor for recurrent pregnancy losses by increasing cellular immunity and autoimmunity." *Human Reproduction* 29, no. 2 (2013): 208–219.

10 Yu, C.K.H., L. Sykes, M. Sethi, T.G. Teoh, and S. Robinson. "Vitamin D deficiency and supplementation during pregnancy." *Clinical Endocrinology* 70, no. 5 (2009): 685–690.

11 Innis, Sheila M. "Dietary omega 3 fatty acids and the developing brain." *Brain Research* 1237 (2008): 35–43; Coletta, Jaclyn M., Stacey J. Bell, and Ashley S. Roman. "Omega-3 fatty acids and pregnancy." *Reviews in Obstetrics & Gynecology* 3, no. 4 (2010): 163–171; Helland, Ingrid B., Lars Smith, Kristin Saarem, Ola D. Saugstad, and Christian A. Drevon. "Maternal supplementation with very-long-chain n-3 fatty acids during pregnancy and lactation augments children's IQ at 4 years of age." *Pediatrics* 111, no. 1 (2003): e39–e44; Greenberg, James A., Stacey J. Bell, and Wendy Van Ausdal. "Omega-3 fatty acid supplementation during pregnancy." *Reviews in Obstetrics & Gynecology* 1, no. 4 (2008): 162–169.

12 Dillon, J.C., and J. Milliez. "Reproductive failure in women living in iodine deficient areas of West Africa." *BJOG: An International Journal of Obstetrics & Gynaecology* 107, no. 5 (2000): 631–636.

13 Mills, J.L., G.M. Buck Louis, K. Kannan, J. Weck, Y. Wan, J. Maisog, A. Giannakou, Q. Wu, and R. Sundaram. "Delayed conception in women with low-urinary iodine concentrations: a population-based prospective cohort study." *Human Reproduction* (2018): 426–433.

14 Delange, François. "Iodine requirements during pregnancy, lactation and the neonatal period and indicators of optimal iodine nutrition." *Public Health Nutrition* 10, no. 12A (2007): 1571–1580; Niwattisaiwong, Soamsiri, Kenneth D. Burman, and Melissa Li-Ng. "Iodine deficiency: clinical implications." *Cleveland Clinic Journal of Medicine* 84, no. 3 (2017): 236–244.

15 Vermiglio, F., V. P. Lo Presti, M. Moleti, M. Sidoti, G. Tortorella, G. Scaffidi, M.G. Castagna et al. "Attention deficit and hyperactivity disorders in the offspring of mothers exposed to mild-moderate iodine deficiency: a possible novel iodine deficiency disorder in developed countries." *The Journal of Clinical Endocrinology & Metabolism* 89, no. 12 (2004): 6054–6060; Halpern, Jean-Pierre, Steven C. Boyages, Glenden F. Maberly, John K. Collins, Creswell J. Eastman, and John G.L. Morris. "The neurology of endemic cretinism: a study of two endemias." *Brain* 114, no. 2 (1991): 825–841; Pharoah, P.O.D., I.H. Buttfield, and B.S. Hetzel. "Neurological damage to the fetus resulting from severe iodine deficiency during pregnancy." *International Journal of Epidemiology* 41, no. 3 (2012): 589–592; Hynes, Kristen L, Petr Otahal, Ian Hay, and John R. Burgess. "Mild iodine deficiency during pregnancy is associated with reduced educational outcomes in the offspring: 9-year follow-up of the gestational iodine cohort." *The Journal of Clinical Endocrinology & Metabolism* 98, no. 5 (2013): 1954–1962; Delange, F. "Iodine deficiency as a cause of brain damage." *Postgraduate Medical Journal* 77, no. 906 (2001): 217–220.

16 Marco, Maria L., Dustin Heeney, Sylvie Binda, Christopher J. Cifelli, Paul D. Cotter, Benoit Foligné, Michael Gänzle et al. "Health benefits of fermented foods: microbiota and beyond." *Current Opinion in Biotechnology* 44 (2017): 94–102.

17 Mueller, Noel T., Elizabeth Bakacs, Joan Combellick, Zoya Grigoryan, and Maria G. Dominguez-Bello. "The infant microbiome development: mom matters." *Trends in Molecular Medicine* 21, no. 2 (2015): 109–117; Dunlop, Anne L, Jennifer G. Mulle, Erin P. Ferranti, Sara Edwards, Alexis B. Dunn, and Elizabeth J. Corwin. "The maternal microbiome and pregnancy outcomes that impact infant health: a review." *Advances in Neonatal Care* 15, no. 6 (2015): 377–385.

18 Mueller, Noel T., Elizabeth Bakacs, Joan Combellick, Zoya Grigoryan, and Maria G. Dominguez-Bello. "The infant microbiome development: mom matters." *Trends in Molecular Medicine* 21, no. 2 (2015): 109–117; Vuillermin, Peter J., Laurence Macia, Ralph Nanan, Mimi L.K. Tang, Fiona Collier, and Susanne Brix. "The maternal microbiome during pregnancy and allergic disease in the offspring." *Seminars in Immunopathology* 39 (2017): 669–675; Roduit, Caroline, Salome Scholtens, Johan C. de Jongste, Alet H. Wijga, Jorrit Gerritsen, Dirkje S. Postma, Bert Brunekreef, Maarten O. Hoekstra, Rob Aalberse, and Henriette A. Smit. "Asthma at 8 years of age in children born by cesarean section." *Thorax* 64, (2009): 107–113; Blustein, Jan, Teresa Attina, Mengling Liu, Andrew M. Ryan, Laura M. Cox, Martin J. Blaser, and Leonardo Trasande. "Association of caesarean delivery with child adiposity from age 6 weeks to 15 years." *International Journal of Obesity* 37, no. 7 (2013): 900–906; Algert, C.S., A. McElduff, J.M. Morris, and C.L. Roberts. "Perinatal risk factors for early onset of type 1 diabetes in a 2000–2005 birth cohort." *Diabetic Medicine* 26, no. 12 (2009): 1193–1197; Mårild, Karl, Olof Stephansson, Scott Montgomery, Joseph A. Murray, and Jonas F. Ludvigsson. "Pregnancy outcome and risk of celiac disease in offspring: a nationwide case-control study." *Gastroenterology* 142, no. 1 (2012): 39–45.

19 Rautava, Samuli. "Probiotic intervention through the pregnant and breastfeeding mother to reduce disease risk in the child." *Breastfeeding Medicine* 13, no. S1 (2018): S-14–S-15; Parvez, S., Karim A. Malik, S. Ah Kang, and H.-Y. Kim. "Probiotics and their fermented food products are beneficial for health." *Journal of Applied Microbiology* 100, no. 6 (2006): 1171–1185; Gray, Lawrence E.K., Martin O'Hely, Sarath Ranganathan, Peter David Sly, and Peter Vuillermin. "The maternal diet, gut bacteria, and bacterial metabolites during pregnancy influence offspring asthma." *Frontiers in Immunology* 8 (2017): 365; Derrien, Muriel, and Johan E.T. van Hylckama Vlieg. "Fate, activity, and impact of ingested bacteria within the human gut microbiota." *Trends in Microbiology* 23, no. 6 (2015): 354–366; Kim, J.Y., E.Y. Choi, Y.H. Hong, Y.O. Song, J.S. Han, S.S. Lee, E.S. Han, T.W. Kim, I.S. Choi, and K.K. Cho. "Changes in Korean adult females intestinal microbiota resulting from kimchi intake." *Journal of Nutrition and Food Sciences* 6, no 2 (2016): 1–9; Pelucchi, Claudio, Liliane Chatenoud, Federica Turati, Carlotta Galeone, Lorenzo Moja, Jean-François Bach, and Carlo La Vecchia. "Probiotics supplementation during pregnancy or infancy for the prevention of atopic dermatitis: a meta-analysis." *Epidemiology* (2012): 402–414; Doege, Katja, Donata Grajecki, Birgit-Christiane Zyriax, Elena Detinkina, Christine zu Eulenburg, and Kai J. Buhling. "Impact of maternal supplementation with probiotics during pregnancy on atopic eczema in childhood — a meta-analysis." *British Journal of Nutrition* 107, no. 1 (2012): 1–6; Garcia-Larsen, V., D. Ierodiakonou, K. Jarrold, S. Cunha, J. Chivinge, Z. Robinson, N. Geoghegan, A. Ruparelia, P. Devani, M. Trivella, and J. Leonardi-Bee. "Diet during pregnancy and infancy and risk of allergic or autoimmune disease: a systematic review and meta-analysis." *PLOS Medicine* 15, no. 2 (2018): e1002507.

20 Blomhoff, Rune, Ulla Beckman-Sundh, Christine Brot, C. Solvoll, Laufey Steingrimsdóttir, and Monica Hauger Carlsen. "Health risks related to high intake of preformed retinol (vitamin A) in the Nordic countries." *Nordic Council of Ministers* (2003).

21 Rodahl, K., and T. Moore. "The vitamin A content and toxicity of bear and seal liver." *Biochemical Journal* 37, no. 2 (1943): 166–168; Williams, Peter. "Nutritional composition of red meat." *Nutrition & Dietetics* 64, no. s4 (2007): s113–s119; "Beef, variety meats and by-products, liver, cooked, braised: nutrition facts & calories." Accessed March 1, 2018. nutritiondata.self.com/facts/beef-products/3469/2

22 Russell, Robert M. "The vitamin A spectrum: from deficiency to toxicity." *The American Journal of Clinical Nutrition* 71, no. 4 (2000): 878–884.

23 Rosa, Franz W., Ann L. Wilk, and Frances O. Kelsey. "Vitamin A congeners." *Teratology* 33, no. 3 (1986): 355–364; Lammer, Edward J., Diane T. Chen, Richard M. Hoar, Narsingh D. Agnish, Paul J. Benke, John T. Braun, Cynthia J. Curry et al. "Retinoic acid embryopathy." *New England Journal of Medicine* 313, no. 14 (1985): 837–841.

24 Buss, N.E., E.A. Tembe, B.D. Prendergast, A.G. Renwick, and C.F. George. "The teratogenic metabolites of vitamin A in women following supplements and liver." *Human & Experimental Toxicology* 13, no. 1 (1994): 33–43.

25 Pizzarello, Louis D. "Refractive changes in pregnancy." *Graefe's Archive for Clinical and Experimental Ophthalmology* 241, no. 6 (2003): 484–488; Dinn, Robert B., Alon Harris, and Peter S. Marcus. "Ocular changes in pregnancy." *Obstetrical & Gynecological Survey* 58, no. 2 (2003): 137–144; Naderan, Mohammad. "Ocular changes during pregnancy." *Journal of Current Ophthalmology* (2018): 1–9.

26 Christian, Parul, Keith P. West Jr, Subarna K. Khatry, Elizabeth Kimbrough-Pradhan, Steven C. LeClerq, Joanne Katz, Sharada Ram Shrestha, Sanu M. Dali, and Alfred Sommer. "Night blindness during pregnancy and subsequent mortality among women in Nepal: effects of vitamin A and β-carotene supplementation." *American Journal of Epidemiology* 152, no. 6 (2000): 542–547; Wilson, James G., Carolyn B. Roth, and Josef Warkany. "An analysis of the syndrome of malformations induced by maternal vitamin A deficiency. Effects of restoration of vitamin A at various times during gestation." *American Journal of Anatomy* 92, no. 2 (1953): 189–217; Warkany, Josef, and Elizabeth Schraffenberger. "Congenital malformations induced in rats by maternal vitamin A deficiency: I. Defects of the eye." *Archives of Ophthalmology* 35, no. 2 (1946): 150–169.

27 Ribeiro Neves, Paulo Augusto, Andrea Ramalho, Patricia de Carvalho Padilha, and Cláudia Saunders. "The role of prenatal nutrition assistance on the prevalence of night blindness in pregnant adults." *Nutrición Hospitalaria* 29, no. 5 (2014): 1132–1140; West, Keith P. "Extent of vitamin A deficiency among preschool children and women of reproductive age." *The Journal of Nutrition* 132, no. 9 (2002): 2857S–2866S; Akhtar, Saeed, Anwaar Ahmed, Muhammad Atif Randhawa, Sunethra Atukorala, Nimmathota Arlappa, Tariq Ismail, and Zulfiqar Ali. "Prevalence of vitamin A deficiency in South Asia: causes, outcomes, and possible remedies." *Journal of Health, Population and Nutrition* 31, no. 4 (2013): 413–423; West Jr., Keith P. "Vitamin A deficiency disorders in children and women." *Food and Nutrition Bulletin* 24, no. 4 suppl2 (2003): S78–S90; Saunders, Cláudia, Maria do Carmo Leal, Paulo Augusto Ribeiro Neves, Patricia de Carvalho Padilha, Letícia Barbosa Gabriel da Silva, and Arthur Orlando Corrêa Schilithz. "Determinants of gestational night blindness in pregnant women from Rio de Janeiro, Brazil." *Public Health Nutrition* 19, no. 5 (2016): 851–860.

28 van Stuijvenberg, Martha E., Serina E. Schoeman, Carl J. Lombard, and Muhammad A. Dhansay. "Serum retinol in 1–6-year-old children from a low socio-economic South African community with a high intake of liver: implications for blanket vitamin A supplementation." *Public Health Nutrition* 15, no. 4 (2012): 716–724; Strobel, Manuela, Jana Tinz, and Hans-Konrad Biesalski. "The importance of β-carotene as a source of vitamin A with special regard to pregnant and breastfeeding women." *European Journal of Nutrition* 46, no. 9 (2007): 1.

29 Strobel, Manuela, Jana Tinz, and Hans-Konrad Biesalski. "The importance of β-carotene as a source of vitamin A with special regard to pregnant and breastfeeding women." *European Journal of Nutrition* 46, no. 9 (2007): 2–3.

30 Mozaffarian, Dariush, and Eric B. Rimm. "Fish intake, contaminants, and human health: evaluating the risks and the benefits." *JAMA* 296, no. 15 (2006): 1885–1899.

31 Hibbeln, Joseph R., John M. Davis, Colin Steer, Pauline Emmett, Imogen Rogers, Cathy Williams, and Jean Golding. "Maternal seafood consumption in pregnancy and neurodevelopmental outcomes in childhood (ALSPAC study): an observational cohort study." *The Lancet* 369, no. 9561 (2007): 578–585.

[32] Davidson, Philip W., Gary J. Myers, Christopher Cox, Catherine Axtell, Conrad Shamlaye, Jean Sloane-Reeves, Elsa Cernichiari et al. "Effects of prenatal and postnatal methylmercury exposure from fish consumption on neurodevelopment: outcomes at 66 months of age in the Seychelles Child Development Study." JAMA 280, no. 8 (1998): 701–707.

[33] Ralston, Nicholas V.C., Carla R. Ralston, J. Lloyd Blackwell, and Laura J. Raymond. "Dietary and tissue selenium in relation to methylmercury toxicity." Neurotoxicology 29, no. 5 (2008): 802–811.

[34] Mozaffarian, Dariush, and Eric B. Rimm. "Fish intake, contaminants, and human health: evaluating the risks and the benefits." JAMA 296, no. 15 (2006): 1885–1899.

[35] Scholl, Theresa O., and William G. Johnson. "Folic acid: influence on the outcome of pregnancy." The American Journal of Clinical Nutrition 71, no. 5 (2000): 1295S–1303S; Gernand, Alison D., Kerry J. Schulze, Christine P. Stewart, Keith P. West Jr., and Parul Christian. "Micronutrient deficiencies in pregnancy worldwide: health effects and prevention." Nature Reviews Endocrinology 12, no. 5 (2016): 274–289. Black, Maureen M. "Effects of vitamin B_{12} and folate deficiency on brain development in children." Food and Nutrition Bulletin 29, no. 2 (supplement) (2008): S126–S131.

[36] Mills, Tracey A., and Tina Lavender. "Advanced maternal age." Obstetrics, Gynaecology & Reproductive Medicine 21, no. 4 (2011): 107–111.

[37] Forabosco, Antonino, and Chiarella Sforza. "Establishment of ovarian reserve: a quantitative morphometric study of the developing human ovary." Fertility and Sterility 88, no. 3 (2007): 675–683; Block, Erik. "A quantitative morphological investigation of the follicular system in newborn female infants." Cells Tissues Organs 17, no. 3 (1953): 201–206.

[38] Wallace, W. Hamish B., and Thomas W. Kelsey. "Human ovarian reserve from conception to the menopause." PLOS One 5, no. 1 (2010): e8772; Wilkosz, Pawel, Gareth D. Greggains, Tom G. Tanbo, and Peter Fedorcsak. "Female reproductive decline is determined by remaining ovarian reserve and age." PLOS One 9, no. 10 (2014): e108343; Hansen, Karl R., Nicholas S. Knowlton, Angela C. Thyer, Jay S. Charleston, Michael R. Soules, and Nancy A. Klein. "A new model of reproductive aging: the decline in ovarian non-growing follicle number from birth to menopause." Human Reproduction 23, no. 3 (2008): 699–708.

[39] Lim, Alvin S.T., and Maurine F.H. Tsakok. "Age-related decline in fertility: a link to degenerative oocytes?" Fertility and Sterility 68, no. 2 (1997): 265–271; Sher, Geoffrey, Levent Keskintepe, Meral Keskintepe, Mike Ginsburg, Ghanima Maassarani, Tahsin Yakut, Volkan Baltaci, Dirk Kotze, and Evrim Unsal. "Oocyte karyotyping by comparative genomic hybridization provides a highly reliable method for selecting 'competent' embryos, markedly improving in vitro fertilization outcome: a multiphase study." Fertility and Sterility 87, no. 5 (2007): 1033–1040.

[40] Lim, Alvin S.T., and Maurine F.H. Tsakok. "Age-related decline in fertility: a link to degenerative oocytes?" Fertility and Sterility 68, no. 2 (1997): 265–271; Broekmans, F.J., M.R. Soules, and B.C. Fauser. "Ovarian aging: mechanisms and clinical consequences." Endocrine Reviews 30, no. 5 (2009): 465–493; Hook, Ernest B. "Rates of chromosome abnormalities at different maternal ages." Obstetrics and Gynecology 58, no. 3 (1981): 282–285; Franasiak, Jason M., Eric J. Forman, Kathleen H. Hong, Marie D. Werner, Kathleen M. Upham, Nathan R. Treff, and Richard T. Scott Jr. "The nature of aneuploidy with increasing age of the female partner: a review of 15,169 consecutive trophectoderm biopsies evaluated with comprehensive chromosomal screening." Fertility and Sterility 101, no. 3 (2014): 656–663; Bartmann, Ana Karina, Gustavo Salata Romao, Ester da Silveira Ramos, and Rui Alberto Ferriani. "Why do older women have poor implantation rates? A possible role of the mitochondria." Journal of Assisted Reproduction and Genetics 21, no. 3 (2004): 79–83; Babayev, Elnur, and Emre Seli. "Oocyte mitochondrial function and reproduction." Current Opinion in Obstetrics & Gynecology 27, no. 3 (2015): 175; Tilly, Jonathan L., and David A. Sinclair. "Germline energetics, aging, and female infertility." Cell Metabolism 17, no. 6 (2013): 838–850; Bentov, Yaakov, Tetyana Yavorska, Navid Esfandiari, Andrea Jurisicova, and Robert F. Casper. "The contribution of mitochondrial function to reproductive aging." Journal of Assisted Reproduction and Genetics 28, no. 9 (2011): 773–783.

[41] Jacobsson, Bo, Lars Ladfors, and Ian Milsom. "Advanced maternal age and adverse perinatal outcome." Obstetrics & Gynecology 104, no. 4 (2004): 727–733; Heffner, Linda J. "Advanced maternal age — how old is too old?" New England Journal of Medicine 351, no. 19 (2004): 1927–1929; Barclay, Kieron, and Mikko Myrskylä. "Advanced maternal age and offspring outcomes: reproductive aging and counterbalancing period trends." Population and Development Review 42, no. 1 (2016): 69–94; Dulitzki, Mordechai, David Soriano, Eyal Schiff, Angela Chetrit, Shlomo Mashiach, and Daniel S. Seidman. "Effect of very advanced maternal age on pregnancy outcome and rate of cesarean delivery." Obstetrics & Gynecology 92, no. 6 (1998): 935–939.

[42] Andersen, Anne-Marie Nybo, Jan Wohlfahrt, Peter Christens, Jørn Olsen, and Mads Melbye. "Maternal age and fetal loss: population based register linkage study." The BMJ 320, no. 7251 (2000): 1708–1712.

[43] Linnane, Anthony W., Chunfang Zhang, Natalia Yarovaya, George Kopsidas, Sergey Kovalenko, Penny Papakostopoulos, Hayden Eastwood, Stephen Graves, and Martin Richardson. "Human aging and global function of coenzyme Q10." Annals of the New York Academy of Sciences 959, no. 1 (2002): 396–411.

[44] Ben-Meir, Assaf, Eliezer Burstein, Aluet Borrego-Alvarez, Jasmine Chong, Ellen Wong, Tetyana Yavorska, Taline Naranian et al. "Coenzyme Q10 restores oocyte mitochondrial function and fertility during reproductive aging." Aging Cell 14, no. 5 (2015): 887–895; Özcan, Pınar, Cem Fıçıcıoğlu, Ozge Kizilkale, Mert Yesiladali, Olgu Enis Tok, Ferda Ozkan, and Mukaddes Esrefoglu. "Can coenzyme Q10 supplementation protect the ovarian reserve against oxidative damage?" Journal of Assisted Reproduction and Genetics 33, no. 9 (2016): 1223–1230; Bentov, Yaakov, Navid Esfandiari, Eliezer Burstein, and Robert F. Casper. "The use of mitochondrial nutrients to improve the outcome of infertility treatment in older patients." Fertility and Sterility 93, no. 1 (2010): 272–275; Bentov, Yaakov, and Robert F. Casper. "The aging oocyte — can mitochondrial function be improved?" Fertility and Sterility 99, no. 1 (2013): 18–22.

[45] Xu, Yangying, Victoria Nisenblat, Cuiling Lu, Rong Li, Jie Qiao, Xiumei Zhen, and Shuyu Wang. "Pretreatment with coenzyme Q10 improves ovarian response and embryo quality in low-prognosis young women with decreased ovarian reserve: a randomized controlled trial." Reproductive Biology and Endocrinology 16, no. 1 (2018): 29; Teran,

Enrique, Isabel Hernandez, Belen Nieto, Rosio Tavara, Juan Emilio Ocampo, and Andres Calle. "Coenzyme Q10 supplementation during pregnancy reduces the risk of pre-eclampsia." *International Journal of Gynecology & Obstetrics* 105, no. 1 (2009): 43–45.

46 Purchas, R.W., S.M. Rutherfurd, P.D. Pearce, R. Vather, and B.H.P. Wilkinson. "Concentrations in beef and lamb of taurine, carnosine, coenzyme Q10, and creatine." *Meat Science* 66, no. 3 (2004): 629–637.

47 Hammiche, Fatima, Marijana Vujkovic, Willeke Wijburg, Jeanne H.M. de Vries, Nick S. Macklon, Joop S.E. Laven, and Régine P.M. Steegers-Theunissen. "Increased preconception omega-3 polyunsaturated fatty acid intake improves embryo morphology." *Fertility and Sterility* 95, no. 5 (2011): 1820–1823; Chiu, Y.H., A.E. Karmon, A.J. Gaskins, M. Arvizu, P.L. Williams, I. Souter, B.R. Rueda, R. Hauser, J.E. Chavarro, and EARTH Study Team. "Serum omega-3 fatty acids and treatment outcomes among women undergoing assisted reproduction." *Human Reproduction* 33, no. 1 (2017): 156–165; Nehra, Deepika, Hau D. Le, Erica M. Fallon, Sarah J. Carlson, Dori Woods, Yvonne A. White, Amy H. Pan et al. "Prolonging the female reproductive lifespan and improving egg quality with dietary omega-3 fatty acids." *Aging Cell* 11, no. 6 (2012): 1046–1054; Skaznik-Wikiel, M.E., D.C. Swindle, T.K. Soderborg, J.E. Friedman, and A.J. Polotsky. "Increased tissue omega-3 to omega-6 fatty acid ratio results in improved markers of ovarian reserve and altered systemic cytokines." *Fertility and Sterility* 106, no. 3 (2016): e121; Bauer, J.L., K. Kuhn, Z. Al-Safi, M.A. Harris, R.H. Eckel, A.P. Bradford, C.Y. Robledo, A. Malkhasyan, N. Gee, and A.J. Polotsky. "Omega-3 fatty acid supplementation significantly lowers FSH in young normal weight women." *Fertility and Sterility* 108, no. 3 (2017): e257–e258; Price, Weston A. (2016). *Nutrition and Physical Degeneration*, 8th edition. Lemon Grove, CA: Price-Pottenger Nutrition Foundation, 362.

48 Griswold, Michael D., Cathryn A. Hogarth, Josephine Bowles, and Peter Koopman. "Initiating meiosis: the case for retinoic acid." *Biology of Reproduction* 86, no. 2 (2012): 35.

49 Irani, Mohamad, and Zaher Merhi. "Role of vitamin D in ovarian physiology and its implication in reproduction: a systematic review." *Fertility and Sterility* 102, no. 2 (2014): 460–468.

50 Ozkan, Sebiha, Sangita Jindal, Keri Greenseid, Jun Shu, Gohar Zeitlian, Cheryl Hickmon, and Lubna Pal. "Replete vitamin D stores predict reproductive success following in vitro fertilization." *Fertility and Sterility* 94, no. 4 (2010): 1314–1319; Zhao, Jing, Xi Huang, Bin Xu, Yi Yan, Qiong Zhang, and Yanping Li. "Whether vitamin D was associated with clinical outcome after IVF/ICSI: a systematic review and meta-analysis." *Reproductive Biology and Endocrinology* 16, no. 1 (2018):13, 1–7; Lata, Indu, Swasti Tiwari, Amrit Gupta, Subhash Yadav, and Shashi Yadav. "To study the vitamin D levels in infertile females and correlation of Vitamin D deficiency with AMH levels in comparison to fertile females." *Journal of Human Reproductive Sciences* 10, no. 2 (2017): 86–90.

51 Jiménez Tuñón, Juan Manuel, Paloma Piqueras Trilles, Miguel Gallardo Molina, María Hebles Duvison, Beatriz Migueles Pastor, Pascual Sánchez Martín, Fernando Sánchez Martín, and Rafael Sánchez-Borrego. "A double-blind, randomized prospective study to evaluate the efficacy of previous therapy with melatonin, myo-inositol, folic acid, and selenium in improving the results of an assisted reproductive treatment." *Clinical Medicine Insights: Therapeutics* 9 (2017): 1179559X17742902; Cheraghi, Ebrahim, Malek Soleimani Mehranjani, Mohammad Ali Shariatzadeh, Mohammad Hossein Nasr Esfahani, and Zahra Ebrahimi. "N-acetylcysteine improves oocyte and embryo quality in polycystic ovary syndrome patients undergoing intracytoplasmic sperm injection: an alternative to metformin." *Reproduction, Fertility and Development* 28, no. 6 (2016): 723–731.

52 Tsui, Kuan-Hao, Peng-Hui Wang, Li-Te Lin, and Chia-Jung Li. "DHEA protects mitochondria against dual modes of apoptosis and necroptosis in human granulosa HO23 cells." *Reproduction* 154, no. 2 (2017): 101–110; Hyman, Jordana H., Ehud J. Margalioth, Ron Rabinowitz, Avi Tsafrir, Michael Gal, Sarah Alerhand, Nurit Algur, and Talia Eldar-Geva. "DHEA supplementation may improve IVF outcome in poor responders: a proposed mechanism." *European Journal of Obstetrics and Gynecology and Reproductive Biology* 168, no. 1 (2013): 49–53.

53 Showell, Marian G., Julie Brown, Jane Clarke, and Roger J. Hart. "Antioxidants for female subfertility." *The Cochrane Library* (2013): 1–154.

54 Pasupuleti, Visweswara Rao, Lakhsmi Sammugam, Nagesvari Ramesh, and Siew Hua Gan. "Honey, propolis, and royal jelly: a comprehensive review of their biological actions and health benefits." *Oxidative Medicine and Cellular Longevity* 2017: 1–21.

55 Hampton, Kerry D., Danielle Mazza, and Jennifer M. Newton. "Fertility-awareness knowledge, attitudes, and practices of women seeking fertility assistance." *Journal of Advanced Nursing* 69, no. 5 (2013): 1076–1084.

56 Hendrickson-Jack, Lisa. "FFP 070 | Healing, Illness, Fertility & Pregnancy | Getting to the Root Cause | Dr. Thomas Cowan." *Fertility Friday Podcast.* Podcast Audio, March 25, 2016. fertilityfriday.com/70

57 Kumar, Naina, and Amit Kant Singh. "Trends of male factor infertility, an important cause of infertility: a review of literature." *Journal of Human Reproductive Sciences* 8, no. 4 (2015): 191–196.

58 Stukenborg, Jan-Bernd, Kristín Rós Kjartansdóttir, Ahmed Reda, Eugenia Colon, Jan Philipp Albersmeier, and Olle Söder. "Male germ cell development in humans." *Hormone Research in Paediatrics* 81, no. 1 (2014): 2–12.

59 Hendrickson-Jack, Lisa. "FFP 134 | Optimizing Sperm Health | Motility, Morphology & Sperm Count | Why He Needs to Get Tested ASAP | Marc Sklar." *Fertility Friday Podcast.* Podcast Audio, April 28, 2017. fertilityfriday.com/134

60 Guzick, David S., James W. Overstreet, Pam Factor-Litvak, Charlene K. Brazil, Steven T. Nakajima, Christos Coutifaris, Sandra Ann Carson et al. "Sperm morphology, motility, and concentration in fertile and infertile men." *New England Journal of Medicine* 345, no. 19 (2001): 1388–1393.

61 World Health Organization. "WHO laboratory manual for the examination and processing of human semen." (2010).

62 Gardner, David K., Ariel Weissman, Colin M. Howles, and Zeev Shoham. *Textbook of Assisted Reproductive Techniques: Laboratory and Clinical Perspectives.* Informa Healthcare, 2009: 39–50; Lishko, Polina V., and Nadja Mannowetz. "CatSper: a unique calcium channel of the sperm flagellum." *Current Opinion in Physiology* 2 (2018): 109–113; Sing, Akhand P., and Singh Rajender. "CatSper channel, sperm function and male fertility." *Reproductive BioMedicine Online* 30, no. 1 (2015):

28–38; Aitken, R. John, Fiona S.M. Best, Pamela Warner, and Alan Templeton. "A prospective study of the relationship between semen quality and fertility in cases of unexplained infertility." *Journal of Andrology* 5, no. 4 (1984): 297–303.

63 Menkveld, Roelof. "Clinical significance of the low normal sperm morphology value as proposed in the fifth edition of the WHO Laboratory Manual for the Examination and Processing of Human Semen." *Asian Journal of Andrology* 12, no. 1 (2010): 47–58.

64 Durairajanayagam, Damayanthi, Ashok Agarwal, and Chloe Ong. "Causes, effects and molecular mechanisms of testicular heat stress." *Reproductive Biomedicine Online* 30, no. 1 (2015): 14–27.

65 Zhang, M.-H., L.-P. Zhai, Z.-Y. Fang, A.-N. Li, Y. Qiu, and Y.-X. Liu. "Impact of a mild scrotal heating on sperm chromosomal abnormality, acrosin activity and seminal alpha-glucosidase in human fertile males." *Andrologia* 50, no. 4 (2018): e12985.

66 Mieusset, R., and L. Bujan. "Testicular heating and its possible contributions to male infertility: a review." *International Journal of Andrology* 18, no. 4 (1995): 169–184.

67 Künzle, Robert, Michael D. Mueller, Willy Hänggi, Martin H. Birkhäuser, Heinz Drescher, and Nick A. Bersinger. "Semen quality of male smokers and nonsmokers in infertile couples." *Fertility and Sterility* 79, no. 2 (2003): 287–291.

68 Gundersen, Tina Djernis, Niels Jørgensen, Anna-Maria Andersson, Anne Kirstine Bang, Loa Nordkap, Niels E. Skakkebæk, Lærke Priskorn, Anders Juul, and Tina Kold Jensen. "Association between use of marijuana and male reproductive hormones and semen quality: a study among 1,215 healthy young men." *American Journal of Epidemiology* 182, no. 6 (2015): 473–481.

69 Muthusami, K.R., and P. Chinnaswamy. "Effect of chronic alcoholism on male fertility hormones and semen quality." *Fertility and Sterility* 84, no. 4 (2005): 919–924.

70 Agarwal, Ashok, Fnu Deepinder, Rakesh K. Sharma, Geetha Ranga, and Jianbo Li. "Effect of cell phone usage on semen analysis in men attending infertility clinic: an observational study." *Fertility and Sterility* 89, no. 1 (2008): 124–128.

71 Rubio, C., I. Campos-Galindo, R. Rivera Egea, N. Garrido, C. Simon, and F. Dominguez. "Effect of environmental endocrine disruptor's exposure on sperm quality and aneuploidy rates in fertile sperm donors." *Fertility and Sterility* 106, no. 3 (2016): e28–e29.

72 Rahman, Md Saidur, Woo-Sung Kwon, June-Sub Lee, Sung-Jae Yoon, Buom-Yong Ryu, and Myung-Geol Pang. "Bisphenol-A affects male fertility via fertility-related proteins in spermatozoa." *Scientific Reports* 5 (2015): 9169.

73 Wise, Lauren A., Daniel W. Cramer, Mark D. Hornstein, Rachel K. Ashby, and Stacey A. Missmer. "Physical activity and semen quality among men attending an infertility clinic." *Fertility and Sterility* 95, no. 3 (2011): 1025–1030; Safarinejad, Mohammad Reza, Kamran Azma, and Ali Asgar Kolahi. "The effects of intensive, long-term treadmill running on reproductive hormones, hypothalamus–pituitary–testis axis, and semen quality: a randomized controlled study." *Journal of Endocrinology* 200, no. 3 (2009): 259–271.

74 Busada, Jonathan T., and Christopher B. Geyer. "The role of retinoic acid (RA) in spermatogonial differentiation." *Biology of Reproduction* 94, no. 1 (2016): 10-1; Chung, S.S.W., and D.J. Wolgemuth. "Role of retinoid signaling in the regulation of spermatogenesis." *Cytogenetic and Genome Research* 105, no. 2–4 (2004): 189–202.

75 Fallah, Ali, Azadeh Mohammad-Hasani, and Abasalt Hosseinzadeh Colagar. "Zinc is an essential element for male fertility: a review of Zn roles in men's health, germination, sperm quality, and fertilization." *Journal of Reproduction & Infertility* 19, no. 2 (2018): 69–81; Colagar, Abasalt Hosseinzadeh, Eisa Tahmasbpour Marzony, and Mohammad Javad Chaichi. "Zinc levels in seminal plasma are associated with sperm quality in fertile and infertile men." *Nutrition Research* 29, no. 2 (2009): 82–88; Wallock, Lynn M., Tsunenobu Tamura, Craig A. Mayr, Kelley E. Johnston, Bruce N. Ames, and Robert A. Jacob. "Low seminal plasma folate concentrations are associated with low sperm density and count in male smokers and nonsmokers." *Fertility and Sterility* 75, no. 2 (2001): 252–259; Chia, S.-E., C.N. Ong, L.-H. Chua, L.-M. Ho, and S.-K. Tay. "Comparison of zinc concentrations in blood and seminal plasma and the various sperm parameters between fertile and infertile men." *Journal of Andrology* 21, no. 1 (2000): 53–57.

76 Wong, Wai Yee, Hans M.W.M. Merkus, Chris M.G. Thomas, Roelof Menkveld, Gerhard A. Zielhuis, and Régine P.M. Steegers-Theunissen. "Effects of folic acid and zinc sulfate on male factor subfertility: a double-blind, randomized, placebo-controlled trial." *Fertility and Sterility* 77, no. 3 (2002): 491–498.

77 Karimian, Mohammad, and Abasalt Hosseinzadeh Colagar. "Association of C677T transition of the human methylenetetrahydrofolate reductase (MTHFR) gene with male infertility." *Reproduction, Fertility and Development* 28, no. 6 (2016): 785–794.

78 Balercia, Giancarlo, Fabrizio Mosca, Franco Mantero, Marco Boscaro, Antonio Mancini, Giuseppe Ricciardo-Lamonica, and GianPaolo Littarru. "Coenzyme Q10 supplementation in infertile men with idiopathic asthenozoospermia: an open, uncontrolled pilot study." *Fertility and Sterility* 81, no. 1 (2004): 93–98.

79 Lafuente, Rafael, Mireia González-Comadrán, Ivan Solà, Gemma López, Mario Brassesco, Ramón Carreras, and Miguel A. Checa. "Coenzyme Q10 and male infertility: a meta-analysis." *Journal of Assisted Reproduction and Genetics* 30, no. 9 (2013): 1147–1156; Safarinejad, Mohammad Reza. "Efficacy of coenzyme Q10 on semen parameters, sperm function and reproductive hormones in infertile men." *The Journal of Urology* 182, no. 1 (2009): 237–248.

80 Safarinejad, Mohammad Reza. "The effect of coenzyme Q10 supplementation on partner pregnancy rate in infertile men with idiopathic oligoasthenoteratozoospermia: an open-label prospective study." *International Urology and Nephrology* 44, no. 3 (2012): 689–700.

81 Cyrus, Ali, Ali Kabir, Davood Goodarzi, and Mehrdad Moghimi. "The effect of adjuvant vitamin C after varicocele surgery on sperm quality and quantity in infertile men: a double blind placebo controlled clinical trial." *International Brazilian Journal of Urology* 41, no. 2 (2015): 230–238; Akmal, Mohammed, J. Q. Qadri, Noori S. Al-Waili, Shahiya Thangal, Afrozul Haq, and Khelod Y. Saloom. "Improvement in human semen quality after oral supplementation of vitamin C." *Journal of Medicinal Food* 9, no. 3 (2006): 440–442.

82 Keskes-Ammar, L., N. Feki-Chakroun, T. Rebai, Z. Sahnoun, H. Ghozzi, S. Hammami, K. Zghal, H. Fki, J. Damak, and A. Bahloul. "Sperm oxidative stress and the effect of an oral vitamin E and selenium supplement on semen quality in infertile men." *Archives of Andrology* 49, no. 2 (2003): 83–94.

83 Safarinejad, M.R. "Effect of omega-3 polyunsaturated fatty acid supplementation on semen profile and enzymatic anti-oxidant capacity of seminal plasma in infertile men with idiopathic oligoasthenoteratospermia: a double-blind, placebo-controlled, randomised study." *Andrologia* 43, no. 1 (2011): 38–47; Hosseini, Banafshe, Mahdieh Nourmohamadi, Shima Hajipour, Mohsen Taghizadeh, Zatollah Asemi, Seyed Ali Keshavarz, and Sadegh Jafarnejad. "The effect of omega-3 fatty acids, EPA, and/or DHA on male infertility: a systematic review and meta-analysis." *Journal of Dietary Supplements* (2018): 1–12.

84 Lerchbaum, Elisabeth, and Barbara Obermayer-Pietsch. "Mechanisms in endocrinology: vitamin D and fertility: a systematic review." *European Journal of Endocrinology* 166, no. 5 (2012): 765–778; Blomberg Jensen, Martin, Poul J. Bjerrum, Torben E. Jessen, John E. Nielsen, Ulla N. Joensen, Inge A. Olesen, Jørgen H. Petersen, Anders Juul, Steen Dissing, and Niels Jørgensen. "Vitamin D is positively associated with sperm motility and increases intracellular calcium in human spermatozoa." *Human Reproduction* 26, no. 6 (2011): 1307–1317.

85 Safarinejad, Mohammad Reza, and Shiva Safarinejad. "Efficacy of selenium and/or N-acetyl-cysteine for improving semen parameters in infertile men: a double-blind, placebo controlled, randomized study." *The Journal of Urology* 181, no. 2 (2009): 741–751; Lenzi, Andrea, Paolo Sgro, Pietro Salacone, Donatella Paoli, Barbara Gilio, Francesco Lombardo, Maria Santulli, Ashok Agarwal, and Loredana Gandini. "A placebo-controlled double-blind randomized trial of the use of combined l-carnitine and l-acetyl-carnitine treatment in men with asthenozoospermia." *Fertility and Sterility* 81, no. 6 (2004): 1578–1584.

86 Bretherick, Karla L, Nichole Fairbrother, Luana Avila, Sara H.A. Harbord, and Wendy P. Robinson. "Fertility and aging: do reproductive-aged Canadian women know what they need to know?" *Fertility and Sterility* 93, no. 7 (2010): 2162–2168.

87 Hendrickson-Jack, Lisa. "FFP 109 | The Reality of Aging & Fertility | IVF & Assisted Reproductive Technology | The Future of Fertility Treatments | Dr. Marjorie Dixon." *Fertility Friday Podcast.* Podcast Audio, November 25, 2016. fertilityfriday.com/109

88 Allen, N.C., C.M. Herbert, W.S. Maxson, B. Jane Rogers, Michael Peter Diamond, and A. Colston Wentz. "Intrauterine insemination: a critical review." *Fertility and Sterility* 44, no. 5 (1985): 569–580.

89 Ibid; Kumar, Naina, and Amit Kant Singh. "Trends of male factor infertility, an important cause of infertility: A review of literature." *Journal of Human Reproductive Sciences* 8, no. 4 (2015): 191–196.

90 Schorsch, M., R. Gomez, T. Hahn, J. Hoelscher-Obermaier, R. Seufert, and C. Skala. "Success rate of inseminations dependent on maternal age? An analysis of 4246 insemination cycles." *Geburtshilfe und Frauenheilkunde* 73, no. 8 (2013): 808–811.

91 Ibid.

92 Al-Fozan, Haya, Maha Al-Khadouri, Seang Lin Tan, and Togas Tulandi. "A randomized trial of letrozole versus clomiphene citrate in women undergoing superovulation." *Fertility and Sterility* 82, no. 6 (2004): 1561–1563; Mitwally, Mohamed F.M., and Robert F. Casper. "Use of an aromatase inhibitor for induction of ovulation in patients with an inadequate response to clomiphene citrate." *Fertility and Sterility* 75, no. 2 (2001): 305–309.

93 Fouda, Usama M., and Ahmed M. Sayed. "Extended letrozole regimen versus clomiphene citrate for superovulation in patients with unexplained infertility undergoing intrauterine insemination: a randomized controlled trial." *Reproductive Biology and Endocrinology* 9, no. 1 (2011): 84.

94 Hilgers, T.W., K.D. Daly, A.M. Prebil, and S.K. Hilgers. "Cumulative pregnancy rates in patients with apparently normal fertility and fertility-focused intercourse." *The Journal of Reproductive Medicine* 37, no. 10 (1992): 864–866.

95 Stanford, Joseph B., George L. White Jr., and Harry Hatasaka. "Timing intercourse to achieve pregnancy: current evidence." *Obstetrics & Gynecology* 100, no. 6 (2002): 1333–1341; Gnoth, C, D. Godehardt, E. Godehardt, P. Frank-Herrmann, and G. Freundl. "Time to pregnancy: results of the German prospective study and impact on the management of infertility." *Human Reproduction* 18, no. 9 (2003): 1959–1966.

96 Whitelaw, W. James. "The cervical cap self-applied in the treatment of severe oligospermia." *Fertility and Sterility* 31, no. 1 (1979): 86–87.

97 Flierman, Paul A., Hendrikus V. Hogerzeil, and Douwe J. Hemrika. "A prospective, randomized, cross-over comparison of two methods of artificial insemination by donor on the incidence of conception: intracervical insemination by straw versus cervical cap." *Human Reproduction* 12, no. 9 (1997): 1945–1948; Nachtigall, Robert D., Nacia. Faure, and Robert H. Glass. "Artificial insemination of husband's sperm." *Fertility and Sterility* 32, no. 2 (1982): 404–410; Coulson, C., E.A. McLaughlin, S. Harris, W.C.L. Ford, and M.G.R. Hull. "Randomized controlled trial of cervical cap with intracervical reservoir versus standard intracervical injection to inseminate cryopreserved donor semen." *Human Reproduction* 11, no. 1 (1996): 84–87.

98 Diamond, Michael P., Cathy Christianson, James F. Daniell, and Anne Colston Wentz. "Pregnancy following use of the cervical cup for home artificial insemination utilizing homologous semen." *Fertility and Sterility* 39, no. 4 (1983): 480–484.

99 Corson, S.L., F.R. Batzer, C. Otis, and D. Fee. "The cervical cap for home artificial insemination." *The Journal of Reproductive Medicine* 31, no. 5 (1986): 349–352.

100 Centers for Disease Control and Prevention, American Society for Reproductive Medicine, Society for Assisted Reproductive Technology. 2015 Assisted Reproductive Technology National Summary Report. Atlanta (GA): US Dept of Health and Human Services; 2017.

101 Ibid.

102 Klipstein, Sigal, Meredith Regan, David A. Ryley, Marlene B. Goldman, Michael M. Alper, and Richard H. Reindollar. "One last chance for pregnancy: a review of 2,705 in vitro fertilization cycles initiated in women age 40 years and above." *Fertility and Sterility* 84, no. 2 (2005): 435–445.

103 Cohen, Matthew A., Steven R. Lindheim, and Mark V. Sauer. "Donor age is paramount to success in oocyte donation." *Human Reproduction* 14, no. 11 (1999): 2755–2758.

104 Kim, Chung-Hoon, and Gyun-Ho Jeon. "Fertility preservation in female cancer patients." *ISRN Obstetrics and Gynecology* (2012): 1–6.

105 Hendrickson-Jack, Lisa. "FFP 225 | Egg Freezing and Cryopreservation | Fertility Preservation | Valerie Landis." *Fertility Friday Podcast.* Podcast Audio, October 12, 2018. fertilityfriday.com/225

106 Pierce, Nicole, and Edgar Mocanu. "Female age and assisted reproductive technology." *Global Reproductive Health* 3, no. 2 (2018): e9.

Chapter 18

1 Hendrickson-Jack, Lisa. "FFP 104 | Birth Control Pills From Your Doctor's Perspective | Why Your Physician Isn't Looking at the Root Cause | Alternative Medicine for Women | Dr. Miranda Naylor." *Fertility Friday Podcast.* Podcast Audio, November 4, 2016. fertilityfriday.com/104

2 Hendrickson-Jack, Lisa. "FFP 194 | How Effective Are Fertility Awareness-Based Methods … Really? | Dr. Marguerite Duane, MD." *Fertility Friday Podcast.* Podcast Audio, April 13, 2018. fertilityfriday.com/194

3 World Health Organization Department of Reproductive Health and Research (WHO/RHR) and Johns Hopkins Bloomberg School of Public Health/Center for Communication Programs (CCP), Knowledge for Health Project. *Family Planning: A Global Handbook for Providers (2018 update).* Baltimore and Geneva: CCP and WHO, 2018: 325–326.

4 Sussman, Steve, Thomas W. Valente, Louise A. Rohrbach, Silvana Skara, and Mary Ann Pentz. "Translation in the health professions: converting science into action." *Evaluation & the Health Professions* 29, no. 1 (2006): 7–32.

Appendix

1 Malpuech-Brugère, Corinne, Wojciech Nowacki, Maryvonne Daveau, Elyett Gueux, Christine Linard, Edmond Rock, Jean-Pierre Lebreton, Andrzej Mazur, and Yves Rayssiguier. "Inflammatory response following acute magnesium deficiency in the rat." *Biochimica et Biophysica Acta (BBA)–Molecular Basis of Disease* 1501, no. 2 (2000): 91–98; Volpe, Stella Lucia. "Magnesium in disease prevention and overall health." *Advances in Nutrition: An International Review Journal* 4, no. 3 (2013): 378S–383S; Alaimo, Katherine, Margaret A. McDowell, R.R. Briefel, A.M. Bischof, C.R. Caughman, C.M. Loria, and C.L. Johnson. "Dietary intake of vitamins, minerals, and fiber of persons ages 2 months and over in the United States: third national health and nutrition examination survey, phase 1, 1988–91." *Advance Data* 258 (1994): 1–28; Marier, J.R. "Magnesium content of the food supply in the modern-day world." *Magnesium* 5, no. 1 (1985): 1–8.

2 Walker, Ann F., Georgios Marakis, Samantha Christie, and Martyn Byng. "Mg citrate found more bioavailable than other Mg preparations in a randomised, double-blind study." *Magnesium Research* 16, no. 3 (2003): 183–191; Murray, Michael T., and Joseph E. Pizzorno. (2012). *The Encyclopedia of Natural Medicine,* 3rd edition. London: Simon & Schuster, 896–897.

3 Chandrasekaran, Navin Chandrakanth, Christopher Weir, Sumaya Alfraji, Jeff Grice, Michael S. Roberts, and Ross T. Barnard. "Effects of magnesium deficiency – more than skin deep." *Experimental Biology and Medicine* 239, no. 10 (2014): 1280–1291.

4 Watkins, K., and P.D. Josling. "A pilot study to determine the impact of transdermal magnesium treatment on serum levels and whole body CaMg ratios." *The Nutrition Practitioner* (2010); Wells, Katie, "How to make magnesium oil | Wellness Mama." Wellness Mama®. Accessed May 9, 2017. wellnessmama.com/5804/make-your-own-magnesium-oil

Index

Gratitude

To my husband, John Jack, your love and unwavering support made this book possible. I can't even begin to thank you. To my incredible boys, Wynton and Malcolm, Mommy loves you more than words could say. And of course, to Mom and Dad, Veona and Vincent Hendrickson, thank you for always supporting and believing in me.

A special thank you to Mary Ann Blair and Geraldine Matus for helping me to bring my manuscript to life. To say your contributions were invaluable would be a significant understatement. Thank you to Dana Nichols, Emily Wong, Lily Nichols, Mary Wong, Jerilynn Prior, Rose Yewchuk, Toni Weschler, Lara Briden, Nicola Rinaldi, Adrianne Williams, Katelin Parkinson, Chloe Skerlak, and to all of my early reviewers for your thoughtful feedback and encouragement along the way.

To the fertility awareness educators around the world who have been fighting to get this knowledge into women's hands for decades — without you this book would not exist.

To my clients and the entire Fertility Friday community, thank you for supporting me in my quest to share fertility awareness with women everywhere.

About the Author

Lisa Hendrickson-Jack talks about vaginas *a lot*. She's a certified Fertility Awareness Educator and Holistic Reproductive Health Practitioner who teaches women to chart their menstrual cycles for natural birth control, conception, and monitoring overall health. Drawing heavily from the current scientific literature, Lisa presents an evidence-based approach to fertility awareness and menstrual cycle optimization. She hosts the *Fertility Friday Podcast*, a weekly radio show devoted to helping women connect to their fifth vital sign by uncovering the connection between menstrual cycle health, fertility, and overall health. With well over a million downloads, *Fertility Friday* is the #1 source for information about fertility awareness and menstrual cycle health, connecting women around the world with their cycles and their fertility — something our education systems have consistently failed to do. When she's not researching, writing, and interviewing health professionals, you'll find her spending time with her husband and her two sons. To learn more, visit fertilityfriday.com.

Fertility Friday Publishing Inc.
lisa@fertilityfriday.com
fertilityfriday.com
thefifthvitalsignbook.com

CPSIA information can be obtained
at www.ICGtesting.com
Printed in the USA
LVHW082238260719
625577LV00010B/140/P